MENTAL CONDITION DEFENCES
IN THE CRIMINAL LAW

Mental Condition Defences in the Criminal Law

R.D. MACKAY

CLARENDON PRESS · OXFORD
1995

Oxford University Press, Walton Street, Oxford OX2 6DP
Oxford New York
Athens Auckland Bangkok Bombay
Calcutta Cape Town Dar es Salaam Delhi
Florence Hong Kong Istanbul Karachi
Kuala Lumpur Madras Madrid Melbourne
Mexico City Nairobi Paris Singapore
Taipei Tokyo Toronto
and associated companies in
Berlin Ibadan

Oxford is a trade mark of Oxford University Press

Published in the United States
by Oxford University Press Inc., New York

© Ronald D. Mackay 1995

British Library Cataloguing in Publication Data
Data available

Library of Congress Cataloging in Publication Data
Mackay, R.D.
Mental condition defences in the criminal law / R.D. Mackay.
p. cm. — (Oxford monographs on criminal law and justice)
Includes bibliographical references and index.
1. Insanity—Jurisprudence—Great Britain. 2. Criminal liability—
Great Britain. I. Title. II. Series : Oxford monographs on
criminal law and criminal justice.
KD7897.M33 1995
345.41'04—dc20
[344.1054] 95–632
ISBN 0–19–825995–6

1 3 5 7 9 10 8 6 4 2

Typeset by Graphicraft Typesetters Ltd., Hong Kong

Printed in Great Britain
on acid-free paper by
Biddles Ltd., Guildford and King's Lynn

*For Sally, Roweena
and Alastair × 2*

General Editor's Introduction

Defences based on the mental condition of the accused are widely accepted as grounds of excuse for criminal liability. Insanity has long been so regarded, and has been the subject of various historical and theoretical enquiries. Automatism is a more recently established ground of exculpation, and the doctrine of diminished responsibility has also come to play a significant role in the law of homicide. Professor Mackay's study contains a detailed examination of the state of English law on the 'mental condition' defences, and also on the cognate doctrine of unfitness to plead. It breaks new ground by integrating into the legal analysis the fruits of extensive empirical work carried out by Professor Mackay into the practical operation of the various defences and doctrines. Taking in some comparisons the other jurisdictions, the result is a text which raises a whole raft of issues about the future shape of English law on this subject, and which also demonstrates the value of empirical research in criminal law scholarship. This is a welcome contribution to the series.

Preface

This book offers a critical analysis of a range of defences within the criminal law which I have referred to as 'mental condition defences'. In essence, it deals with those defences where the accused relies on some form of abnormal mental conditon as a source of exculpation. Chapter 1 deals with automatism and the notion of involuntary action to which the defence is inextricably linked. Chapter 2 contains an analysis of the defence of insanity and draws on a range of comparative sources, particularly from the United States of America, as well as empirical research. Chapter 3 discusses the issue of self-induced incapacity and the doctrine of fault with particular reference to mental disorder while Chapter 4 covers both diminished responsibility and infanticide as a means of avoiding a murder conviction. The fifth and final Chapter deals with unfitness to plead which, although not a defence, has been included owing to its symbolic importance and its significant relationship to mental disorder within the criminal process.

The completion of this work has taken longer than I had expected. One of the reasons for this has been my involvement in empirical research, particularly in relation to unfitness to plead and the defence of insanity. The results of this research advocated the need for change in the current legal framework relating to a small group of mentally abnormal offenders whose automatic detention in hospital was triggered by an offence of which none had been convicted. In this connection, some progress has been made with the enactment of the Criminal Procedure (Insanity and Unfitness to Plead) Act 1991. It is hoped that the inclusion of this research will help to give an extra dimension to the discussion of these topics. This view is shared by Andrew Ashworth who not only read all the chapters in draft and commented upon them but was also a continual source of encouragement to me during the writing of this book. Without his support this book might never have been completed and I should like to record my sincere thanks to him as well as to Oxford University Press. Finally, I wish to acknowledge the debt I owe to my wife and family which is impossible to repay. The dedication is for them.

The law is stated as at the end of 1994. However, I have included brief reference to the Law Commission's final reports on Legislating the Criminal Code: Intoxication and Criminal Liability (Law Com No 229, 1995) and on Mental Incapacity (Law Com No 231, 1995).

R. D. M.

Glaston,
Rutland
31 December 1994

Contents

Table of Cases

UNITED STATES

Table of Statutory Material

1

The Defence of Automatism

This Chapter contains a critical examination of the problems which spring from the insistence of common law jurisdictions 'on the requirement of a *voluntary* act as the foundation for criminal responsibility'.[1] This 'voluntary act' requirement has long been accepted by the courts with little comment or criticism as to its philosophical origins or scientific basis. Accordingly, the first Part of this Chapter will contain a discussion of some of the more important philosophical and neuroscientific accounts of the distinction between voluntary and involuntary action. This will be followed in Parts Two and Three by a legal analysis of the involuntary act defence, known to criminal lawyers as automatism.

PART ONE INVOLUNTARY ACTION — A THEORETICAL DISCUSSION

It is proposed in this Part to discuss some of the theoretical arguments surrounding the nature of human action. This will be followed by an examination of the attitude of the criminal law to such ideas.

GENERAL THEORETICAL CONSIDERATIONS

The philosophy of human action is a complex subject on which a great wealth of material exists.[2] At the very centre of philosophical dispute in this area is the problem of volition or the will. What is the difference between an act, such as my writing this sentence, and mere bodily movement, such as the blinking of an eye? The answer traditionally, and perhaps most frequently, given is that 'the act' is the result of an antecedent

---

[1] *DPP* v. *Majewski* [1976] 2 All ER 142, 165.
[2] The following are useful sources: M. Brand (ed.), *The Nature of Human Action* (Scott, Foresman and Company, Glenview, Ilinois, 1970); A.R. White (ed.), *The Philosophy of Action* (Oxford, 1968); Herbert Morris (ed.), *Freedom and Responsibility* (Stanford University Press, Stanford, 1961) chs. 2 and 3; Glenn Langford, *Human Action* (Anchor Books, New York, 1971) which has a thorough bibliography; G.N.A. Vesey, *The Embodied Mind* (George Allen and Unwin, London, 1964) which gives a brief account of many of the more important theories of action; N.S. Care and C. Landesman (eds.), *Readings in the Theory of Action* (Indiana University Press, Indiana 1968); M. Brand, *Intending and Acting* (Bradford Books, Cambridge, Mass, 1984).

conscious mental process called 'volition' which being the product of 'the will' ought to be regarded as a dual process. One of the most famous exponents of this 'dual' approach to action was Descartes who gave his name to the school of thought known as Cartesian dualism. Descartes' main thesis was concerned with the separation of the material body from the non-material mind and his theory of action was based on the existence of a small gland situated near the centre of the brain known as the pineal gland. Of this Descartes wrote: 'and finally, when we want to walk or to move our body in some other way, this volition makes the gland drive the spirits to the muscles which serve to bring about this effect.'[3]

However, nowhere does Descartes successfully explain how the volition in the non-material mind causes the pineal gland to 'drive the spirits to the muscles'.[4] Despite this, dualism has had a profound influence on philosophical thought and, although it can safely be said that few, if any, would now accept Descartes' reasoning in full,[5] the idea of volition is still a prevalent one and, as will be noted later, has found its way into legal theory. A more recent exponent of dualism is H.A. Pritchard who in his essay 'Acting, Willing, Desiring' stated:

When, e.g., we think of ourselves as having moved our hand, we are thinking of ourselves as having performed an activity of a certain kind, and, it almost goes without saying, a *mental* activity of a cerain kind, an activity of whose nature we were dimly aware in doing the action and of which we can become more clearly aware by reflecting on it. And that we are aware of its special nature is shown by our unhesitatingly distinguishing it from other special mental activities such as thinking, wondering, and imagining. If we ask 'What is the word used for this special kind of activity?' the answer, it seems, has to be 'willing'.[6]

Pritchard's account of action raises many difficult problems which it would seem cannot be adequately answered. Firstly, if one accepts that volition is a distinct antecedent process resulting in an act, then surely this process of 'willing' can be further described and analysed. However, at this stage Pritchard is forced to admit 'that while we know the general character of that to which we refer when we use the word "willing", this

---

[3] 'The Passions of the Soul', in *The Philosophical Writings of Descartes*, trans by J. Cottingham et al. (Cambridge University Press, Cambridge, 1985) Art 43, 346. See also Art 41. For a brief discussion, see Colin Blakemore, 'A Mechanistic Approach to Perception and the Human Mind' in K.A. Mohyeldin Said et al. (eds.), *Modelling the Mind* (Clarendon Press, Oxford, 1990), especially 124–5.

[4] See D.C. Dennett, *Consciousness Explained* (Penguin Books, Harmondsworth, 1991), 34: 'How, precisely, does the information get transmitted from pineal gland to mind? Since we don't have the faintest idea (yet) what properties mind stuff has, we can't even guess (yet) how it might be effected by physical processes emanating somehow from the brain'.

[5] Ibid. 33–42.

[6] H.A. Pritchard, 'Acting, Willing, Desiring' in White (ed.), *The Philosophy of Action*, 61 (essay originally printed in H.A. Pritchard, *Moral Obligation* (1949)) (emphasis in original).

character is *sui generis* and so incapable of being defined'.[7] Of this 'last resort' approach, Melden has said 'the appeal to indefinables is a desperate defence that purchases immunity from further attack only at the expense of unintelligibility'.[8] Secondly, if the concept of the will is accepted as being indefinable, why is it that the process should stop there? Where does the will to move the muscles spring from? It cannot just happen and is thus subject to the argument that 'one must will the willing of the muscle movement, and so on *ad infinitum*'.[9] Pritchard is able to counter this particular objection by concluding that volition involves a desire to will and, although it is possible to desire to desire, there is no such thing 'as willing to will'.[10] But this conclusion itself is open to an objection to which Pritchard himself admits he can see no answer. It is simply that a desire to will must be accompanied by some idea of what the willing is likely to produce. If this is so, then it follows that it would be impossible ever to will something for the first time, for we can have no idea that a particular act of volition will result in a particular movement until we have already performed the movement in question.[11]

The doctrine of the will has not been without its critics, the foremost of which was Gilbert Ryle who in *The Concept of Mind* launched a famous attack on what he called the 'artificial concept' of volition.[12] In Ryle's opinion such an idea should be rejected as 'just an inevitable extension of the myth of the ghost in the machine'.[13] One of the specific objections which he raises is that no one in common parlance ever uses the idea of the will to describe his everyday actions despite the fact that 'according to theory, [volitions] should be encountered vastly more frequently than headaches, or feelings of boredom'.[14] It is interesting to note the following example used by Ryle to support this argument: 'an accused person may admit or deny that he did something, or that he did it on purpose, but he never admits or denies having willed. Nor do the judge and jury require to be satisfied by evidence, which in the nature of the case could never be adduced, that a volition preceded the pulling of the trigger'.[15]

Despite Ryle's assurance that such evidence can never be adduced, the criminal law does claim to achieve just that within the context of the automatism defence[16], and finds continued support for its adherence to the doctrine of volition from many modern sources. One recent exponent is Carl Ginet who in his book *On Action* defends volition on the following basis:

---

[7] Pritchard, 'Acting, Willing, Desiring', 61. (emphasis in original).
[8] A.I. Melden, *Free Action* (Routledge and Kegan Paul, New York, 1964), 47.
[9] Ibid. 45 (emphasis in original).
[10] Pritchard, 'Acting Willing, Desiring', 68.   [11] Cf. Melden, *Free Action*, 51.
[12] G. Ryle, *The Concept of Mind* (Hutchinson's University Library, London, 1949), 62.
[13] Ibid. 63.   [14] Ibid. 65.   [15] Ibid. 64.   [16] See below.

Volition does not precede the experience of voluntarily exerting but is a part of it. It is the part whose presence is what makes exertion seem voluntary and whose subtraction would make the exertion seem *in*voluntary, would make it seem that one's own body exerts 'on its own' without the benefit of one's voluntary control . . . volition is essential not only to an exertion *seeming* voluntary but also to its *being* voluntary . . . . The mental act of volition is *simple*: It does not contain within itself the structure of a mental act causing another mental occurrence.[17]

However, when it comes to the fundamental issue of causation, Ginet, whilst admitting that some special 'sort of brain process occurs when and only when volition occurs',[18] leaves open the crucial question of whether or not the volition causes this brain process. As a result we cannot be sure if he is or is not a supporter of dualism.

Anthony Kenny on the other hand is quite clear on this matter in his recent examination of Ryle's *The Concept of Mind*. In a chapter entitled 'The Will' Kenny asks whether volitions are voluntary or involuntary motions of the mind: 'If the latter, then how can the actions that issue from them be voluntary? If the former, then in accordance with the theory they must themselves proceed from prior volitions, and from other volitions, and so on *ad infinitum*'.[19] Kenny concludes that 'if an action is to be voluntary at all, then it must be in some sense done because it is wanted'. This idea of 'want' Kenny considers

is the very minimum that is necessary if an action is to be voluntary: the kind of wanting that we may call 'consent'. Something is wanted in this minimal sense if it is something that the agent chooses neither as a means nor as an end, but which would not take place were it not for the agent's pursuit of one of his purposes. I cross a neighbour's field in order to take a swim in the river; as I walk on my way I do a certain amount of damage to the grass and squash a certain number of minute organisms. Doing so is neither a purpose of mine nor a means to my ends; but I do consent to these things; I prefer to do them than to give up my purposes and the means I have chosen.[20]

Kenny further concludes that, in order to give up one of his chosen purposes it must be 'in the agent's power to act in a manner other than that which amounts to a fulfilment of the want.' Thus Kenny finally accepts that 'conscious actions are voluntary to the extent that they are under our control', but is able to support this line of reasoning without resort to Cartesianism.[21]

At the same time, Kenny does admit a debt to the works of Wittgenstein who likewise rejected dualism and the notion of the will as some magical

[17] Carl Ginet, *On Action* (Cambridge University Press, Cambridge, 1990), 29 (emphasis in original).   [18] Ibid. 31.
[19] A. Kenny, *The Metaphysics of Mind* (Oxford University Press, Oxford, 1989), 32 (emphasis in original).   [20] Ibid. 45, 47.
[21] Ibid.

operator of the lever of voluntary action. Thus, in his *Philosophical Investigations*, Wittgenstein remarks:

When I raise my arm 'voluntarily' I do not use any instrument to bring the movement about. My wish is not such an instrument either.
'Willing, if it is not to be a sort of wishing, must be the action itself. It cannot be allowed to stop anywhere short of the action'. . . .
When I raise my arm, I have *not* wished it might go up. The voluntary action excludes this wish.[22]

It is clear from this that Wittgenstein did not accept the will as some special kind of entity which is causally responsible for all forms of voluntary action. Rather, he concludes that 'voluntary movement is marked by the absence of surprise',[23] an interesting way of once again expressing the notion that voluntary actions are under our control so that there is no element of surprise involved in their performance; contrast the epileptic subject to a seizure and the sleepwalker who when they regain consciousness will doubtless be 'surprised' when informed about their involuntary behaviour.

It is quite clear that the Cartesian notion of volition has come in for its fair share of criticism. But if it is to be regarded as philosophically unacceptable, with what can it be replaced? An interesting alternative account of action, especially for the lawyer, was one originally put forward by H. L. A. Hart.[24] It is as follows. Firstly, that to say that someone did something is not to describe anything that happened but is in fact to 'ascribe' responsibility for the act. Secondly, that the concept of action is a 'defeasible' one to be defined through exceptions and not by a set of necessary and sufficient conditions whether physical or psychological. To support his argument, Hart uses the criminal law which contains certain 'defences or exceptions with which different criminal charges may be met with differing effect'. In his opinion the idea of *mens rea* can only be understood by considering such defences, and not by attempting 'to impose a spurious unity' upon them thus 'suggesting that they are admitted as merely evidence of the absence' of some basic formula. One of the basic formulas which Hart discusses consists of the two elements 'foresight' and 'voluntariness'. He considers it all too 'easy to succumb' to the illusion that an accurate and satisfying 'definition' can be formulated with the aid of notions like 'voluntariness'; the logical character of words like 'voluntary' is, he argues, anomalous and 'ill understood'.[25]

[22] L. Wittgenstein, *Philosophical Investigations*, trans G.E.M. Anscombe (Blackwell, Oxford, 1968) paras 614–16 (emphasis in original).   [23] Ibid. para. 628.
[24] H.L.A. Hart 'The Ascription of Responsibility and Rights', *Proceedings of the Aristotelian Society* XLIX (1949), 171–94, part reprinted in Morris, *Freedom and Responsibility*, 143–8. In his collection of essays, *Punishment and Responsibility* (Clarendon Press, Oxford, 1968), the author excluded this article because 'its main contentions no longer seem to me defensible' (Preface).   [25] Ibid. 145.

Hart then is attempting to combat the problems surrounding volition by concluding that a sentence such as 'A hit B' is essentially ascriptive, and not descriptive. All it does is attribute responsibility for this act to A. There is thus no need to resort to a description of some inner mental process which took place in A's mind at the time he hit B, as the sentence is not descriptive.

Since its publication, Hart's work has been the subject of much dialogue and criticism,[26] some of which merits discussion. Firstly, the word 'responsibility' is notoriously ambiguous.[27] However, Hart seems to have had in mind the notion of legal or moral responsibility, as can be demonstrated from the following statement: 'the sentences "I did it", "you did it", "he did it" are, I suggest, primarily utterances with which we "confess" or "admit" liability, make accusations, or "ascribe" responsibility'.[28] Because of this Hart has been criticised by Geach as contradicting 'the natural view that to ascribe an act to an agent is a causal description of the act', and is accused of 'desperately denying . . . that voluntariness is a causal concept'.[29] The bones of this criticism are that there must be a distinction between a sentence such as 'A hit B' and 'A is responsible for hitting B', for in order to hold A responsible for the hitting we have to know that A performed the act in question. Thus A has to be causally responsible in the first place before he can be found to be legally or morally responsible. It would seem that Hart may have gone too far in denying that a sentence such as the former can be descriptive. There seems to be no doubt that in certain cases a sentence claiming that A performed an act may simply be used to inform us as to what happened.[30] For example, the sentence 'A hit B' may likewise be used simply as a means to inform us of who hit B. Once this is established, the same sentence may then be used to explain why A is being chastised or prosecuted, etc.

Another related criticism directed at Hart is that he 'does not distinguish between the action we take and the deed we do'.[31] In other words, we ascribe responsibility only for A's deed of hitting B, and this should be kept quite distinct from the description of the act (i.e. the delivery of the blow) which led to A's being held responsible. One is forced then to

---

[26] See particularly P.T. Geach, 'Ascriptivism', *Philosophical Review* Vol. 69 (1960), 221; and G.W. Pitcher, 'Hart on Action and Responsibility' ibid. 226. It is these criticisms which Hart considered 'justified'. Cf. J. Feinberg, 'Action and Responsibility' in M. Black (ed.), *Philosophy in America* (Allen & Unwin, London, 1965), 136–60, reprinted in White, *The Philosophy of Action*, 95–119; and M. Moore, 'Responsibility and the Unconscious' (1980) 53 *Southern California Law Review*, 1563, 1569.

[27] Hart himself distinguishes four senses of responsibility in *Punishment and Responsibility*, ch. 9, and it can easily be taken to mean 'causally' responsible.

[28] Hart, 'The Ascription of Responsibility and Rights', 187.

[29] Geach, 'Ascriptivism', 224–5.

[30] Langford, *Human Action*, 50; Feinberg, 'Action and Responsibility', 108.

[31] See White's introduction to *The Philosophy of Action*, 4.

modify Hart's thesis in that a distinction must be drawn between performing an act and being responsible for its performance. But then it may be
argued that when a person performs a normal everyday act no question of
ascribing responsibility for it arises.[32] For example, to say that 'A wrote a
letter' is simply to describe what A did. Similarly, would it not be absurd
to say that 'A is responsible for scratching his head'? To counter this
argument it must be stressed that Hart's discussion was of a legal nature,
not because he wished to ignore everyday behaviour, but simply by reason
of the fact that the legal examples which he gave best suited his purpose
within the context of his discussion. Now it may seem odd to speak of
ascribing responsibility for our everyday acts but, in defence of Hart, it is
argued by David Rayfield that 'this is not because of something "improper"
about speaking of being responsible for one's actions . . . . It certainly does
not mean that we are not responsible for such mundane things as tying
shoes. My responsibility for tying my shoes or sitting down at table is
generally assumed; it is only rarely that an issue could reasonably, properly, be made of it.'[33]

In conclusion, it may be said of Hart's ascriptive theory of action that
it does not rely on the idea of volition and, although it has been subjected
to considerable criticism, it is nonetheless extremely illuminating especially
in relation to the criminal law where the courts are of course involved in
the day-to-day business of ascribing responsibility. Further, in many ways
the remark made by Rayfield rings true when it comes to criminal proceedings in the sense that it is indeed only rarely that the courts will be
interested in whether or not a particular defendant's actions were involuntary; it is generally presumed that his acts were voluntary or, as Dickson
J remarked in *R. v. Rabey*, 'the circumstances are normally such as to
permit a presumption of volition and mental capacity'.[34] However, the
crucial question in cases where automatism is a live issue will be to discover what stance the courts are adopting when they discuss involuntary
action—an issue which will be further considered in Parts Two and Three
of this Chapter.

ACTION THEORY AND THE CRIMINAL LAW[35]

After an outline of some of the problems surrounding philosophical theories of action, it is now time to examine critically the attitude which the

---

[32] Pitcher, 'Hart on Action and Responsibility', 226.

[33] D. Rayfield, *Action: An Analysis of the Concept* (Nijhoff, The Hague, 1972) 44. See also
Feinberg, 'Action and Responsibility', 104–9.

[34] *R. v. Rabey* (1980) 15 CR (3d) 225, 255.

[35] See generally: H.L.A. Hart, *Punishment and Responsibility*, ch. 4, entitled 'Acts of Will
and Responsibility'; M. Moore, *Act and Crime: The Philosophy of Action and its Implications for Criminal Law* (Clarendon Press, Oxford, 1993); R.A. Duff, *Intention, Agency and*

law has adopted within this area. A starting point is the fundamental principle accepted by most common law jurisdictions that, if a person is to be convicted of any criminal offence, his act or omission must have been a voluntary one. If the action is found to be involuntary, then, generally speaking, the agent in question cannot be held criminally responsible.

In order to explain the distinction between a voluntary and an involuntary act, the law has adopted the philosophy of the will. Famous exponents of this doctrine within the framework of the law have been Sir James Stephen and John Austin. In his *General View of the Criminal Law of England*, Stephen considered that 'the sensations which accompany every action and distinguish it from a mere occurrence are intention and will'. The process of 'willing' was, according to Stephen, an essential part of the theory of action and was described by him as 'that inward state which, as experience informs us, is always succeeded by motion, whilst the body is in its normal condition'.[36]

Austin, in his *Lectures on Jurisprudence*, reached a similar conclusion when he examined the idea of the will. The relevant part of Austin's work is to be discussed below. However, at this stage it is worth quoting certain passages from Austin, and I can do no better than to use those selected by Hart himself:

'Certain movements of our bodies follow invariably and *immediately* our wishes or desires for those *same* movements: Provided, that is, that the bodily organ be sane, and the desired movements be not prevented by any outward obstacle . . . These antecedent wishes and these consequent movements, are human *volitions* and *acts* strictly and properly so called . . . And as these are the only *volitions*; so are the bodily movements, by which they are immediately followed, the only *acts* or *actions* (properly so called). It will be admitted on the mere statement, that the only objects which can be called acts, are consequences of volitions. A voluntary movement of my body, or a movement which follows a volition, is an *act*. The *involuntary* movements which are the consequence of certain diseases, are *not* acts. But as the bodily movements which immediately follows volition, are the only *ends* of volition, it follows that those bodily movements are the only objects to which the

Criminal Liability: Philosophy of Action and the Criminal Law (Blackwell, Oxford, 1990); A.R. White, *Grounds of Liability: An Introduction to the Philosophy of Law* (Clarendon Press, Oxford, 1985) ch. 3; P.J. Fitzgerald, 'Voluntary and Involuntary Acts' in White (ed.), *Philosophy of Action*, 120–43; D. O'Connor, 'The Voluntary Act' (1975) 15 *Medicine, Science and the Law* 31–6; J.L. Mackie, 'The Grounds of Responsibility' in P.M.S. Hacker and J. Raz (eds.), *Morality and Society: Essays in Honour of H.L.A. Hart* (Clarendon Press, Oxford, 1977), 175–88; D. Rayfield, *Action* 75–84; G. Williams, *Criminal Law: the General Part* (2nd edn., Stevens, London, 1961), 1–27; J. Austin, *Lectures on Jurisprudence* (Murray, London, 1885) Lecture XVIII; K.W. Saunders, 'Voluntary Acts and the Criminal Law: Justifying Culpability Based on the Existence of Volition' (1988) 49 *University of Pittsburgh Law Review* 443; and M. Corrado, 'Automatism and the Theory of Action' (1990) 39 *Emory Law Journal* 1191.

[36] Sir J. Stephen, *General View of the Criminal Law of England* (MacMillan and Co, London, 1863), 76.

term 'acts' can be applied with perfect precision and propriety ... Most of the names which seem to be names of acts, are names of acts, *coupled with certain of their consequences*. For example, if I kill you with a gun or pistol I *shoot* you: and the long train of incidents which are denoted by that brief expression, are considered (or spoken of) as if they constituted an *act* perpetrated by me. In truth, the only parts of the train which are my act or acts are the muscular motions by which I raise the weapon; point it at your head of body, and pull the trigger. These I *will*. The contact of the flint and steel; the ignition of the powder, the flight of the ball towards your body, the wound and subsequent death, with the numberless incidents included in these, are *consequences* of the act which I *will*, I *will* not those consequences, though I may *intend* them.'[37]

The idea of an act being the product of a person's will has been accepted by the common law courts not only uncritically but almost without comment.[38] A notable exception is Australia where a good deal of complex theoretical discussion has taken place. For example, in *Ryan* v. *R.*[39] the High Court of Australia was called upon to consider the distinction between voluntary and involuntary action. In his judgment Barwick CJ stated: 'the deed which was not the result of the accused's will to act cannot, in my opinion, be made the source of criminal responsibility in him'.[40] And a little later: 'it is of course the absence of the will to act or, perhaps, more precisely of its exercise rather than lack of knowledge or consciousness which, in my respectful opinion, decides criminal liability'.[41] This type of statement can be found in the assumptions underlying judgments throughout the common law world. The judgment of Windeyer J, however, is interesting for its recognition of the problems inherent in the acceptance of the theory of volition when he says:

That an act is only punishable as a crime when it is the voluntary act of the accused is a statement satisfying in its simplicity. But what does it mean? What is a voluntary act? The answer is far from simple, partly because of ambiguities in the word 'voluntary' and its supposed synonyms, partly because of imprecise, but inveterate, distinctions which have long dominated men's ideas concerning the working of the human mind. These distinctions, between will and intellect, between voluntary and involuntary action, may be unscientific and too simple for philosophy and psychology today.[42]

---

[37] Passages from Austin, *Lectures on Jurisprudence* Lecture XVIII, 411, 412, 414 and 415, as cited by Hart, *Punishment and Responsibility*, 98 (emphasis in original).

[38] See for example *R. v. Burr* [1969] NZLR 763, 748 where McArthy J says, 'In their basic approach to the question whether an act is a voluntary one or not, the Courts of the United Kingdom and this country have adopted the Austinian concept of intention, demanding its two essentials of volition in relation to the muscular movement, and foresight of consequences. Some people consider this concept inadequate in the light of modern medical knowledge but it still dominates our law relating to intention'. For more recent similar comment see *Lynch* v. *DPP* [1975] 1 All ER 913, 934 per Lord Simon.

[39] *Ryan* v. *R.* (1966–7) 121 CLR 205.   [40] Ibid. 213.   [41] Ibid. 214.

[42] Ibid. 244.

Similarly in *Timbu Kolian* v. *R*,[43] Windeyer J states: 'one of the difficulties comes from the need to relate will to acts, and to define precisely the distinction, commonly accepted by lawyers, between intention and volition. These words are used glibly; and often with little definition of the sense in which they are used.'[44] In his Lordship's opinion a willed act is to be regarded 'as merely a bodily reaction to a mental stimulus'.[45]

Granted that the concept of the will is the subject of considerable criticism, is it capable of being replaced, or indeed should it be replaced? Before this question is considered, the problems surrounding the words 'voluntary' and 'involuntary' deserve attention. Once again Windeyer J has been quick to point to the 'imprecise and varied senses' in which these words 'are used by lawyers'.[46]

THE VOLUNTARY/INVOLUNTARY ANTITHESIS

The use of the words 'voluntary' and 'involuntary' causes difficulty not only to lawyers but also to philosophers. It has already been shown that as far as traditional theory is concerned the word 'voluntary', when used in conjunction with the word 'act', means 'willed'. The word 'involuntary' is thus often regarded as meaning the opposite of 'voluntary', so that the phrase 'involuntary act' is capable of including all acts which are non-voluntary. It is submitted that this type of reasoning causes confusion since the two words are not opposites.[47] The word 'involuntary', certainly within the area of the law, deserves a limited application, and is not to be confused with words like 'non-voluntary' and 'compulsory'. That these words have different meanings has long been recognised,[48] and Ryle in distinguishing 'voluntary' and 'involuntary' adopts an ascriptive stance when he says: 'we discuss whether someone's action was voluntary or not only when the action seems to have been his fault'.[49] He goes on to note that philosophers 'tend to describe as voluntary not only reprehensible but also meritorious actions' and in his opinion this 'stretched use' of the word has led to 'the tangle of largely spurious problems, known as the problem of the Freedom of the Will'.[50] In ascribing responsibility, therefore, one should judge an action 'with reference to the capacities and opportunities of the agent'.[51] In this way, 'the whole question of involuntariness' can be

---

[43] (1968) 119 CLR 47.   [44] Ibid. 62.   [45] Ibid. 64.

[46] Ibid. 62. relying on Hart, 'The Ascription of Responsibility and Rights' at p. 145.

[47] Cf. J.L. Austin, 'A Plea for Excuses' in White (ed.), *The Philosophy of Action*, 32–3.

[48] For example, Aristotle distinguishes four kinds of human behaviour, namely voluntary, involuntary, non-voluntary, and compulsory action. See Aristotle, *Ethics* trans. by J.A.K. Thompson (Penguin, Harmondsworth, 1982) 111–15. Cf. Rayfield, *Action* ch. 6, 71–5.

[49] Ryle, *The Concept of Mind*, 69.

[50] Ibid. 71.

[51] Ibid. 72. This statement shows a marked resemblance to Hart's test of responsibility in *Punishment and Responsibility*, 152.

decided without the agent 'being asked to report any deliverances of consciousness or introspection about the execution or non-execution of any volitions'.[52]

Because the words 'voluntary' and 'involuntary' may be given divergent meanings, it is important that when they are used in a legal context a precise meaning should be adopted. This, however, does not appear to have occurred within the criminal law, for there are at least two senses which the word 'involuntary' is commonly given. These are: a wide sense, which includes conduct resulting from duress, accident, and mistake; and a narrower sense, which is restricted to the more fundamental type of case listed by Hart in 'Acts of Will and Responsibility'.[53] The wide sense is often used to include duress.[54] But although it may be possible to regard an act performed under threats as 'non-voluntary',[55] it cannot be regarded as involuntary in the sense of being 'unwilled'. It may be that the agent has no 'free' will when he performs the act in question,[56] but he certainly has a conscious choice, albeit perhaps an extremely limited one.

A similar problem has arisen in relation to the defences of accident and mistake. This can be well illustrated by a further examination of the Australian cases already cited. In *Ryan* the defence was that the accused's act was involuntary in the sense of being a reflex action. The facts were that the accused entered a garage in order to rob. He threatened the attendant with a shot-gun and was given the money from the till. The accused then decided to tie up the attendant, and while he was trying to remove a piece of cord from his pocket the gun went off and the attendant was killed. The accused maintained that a sudden movement made by the attendant had caused him to discharge the gun so that his action was purely reflex and not voluntary in the sense required by the criminal law. In his judgment Barwick CJ sought to distinguish between the following views of the discharge of the gun: (1) 'that being startled, he voluntarily but in a panic, pressed the trigger but with no specific intent either to do the deceased any harm or to frighten him'; and (2) 'that being startled so as to move slightly off his balance, the trigger was pressed in a reflex or convulsive, unwilled movement of his hand or its muscles'.[57] But surely, as is pointed out by I.D. Elliot in his valuable discussion of the case,[58] there is no real need for such a distinction. For not only was *Ryan* fully conscious when he discharged the rifle but also 'his reaction was like the sudden

---

[52] Ryle, *The Concept of Mind*, 95–6.   [53] Ibid. 95–6.
[54] See e.g. S. Prevezer 'Automatism and Voluntary Conduct' [1958] Crim LR 361, 365; Fitzgerald, 'Voluntary and Involuntary Acts', 131.
[55] See M. Wasik, 'Duress and Criminal Responsibility' [1977] Crim LR 453, 454.
[56] Stephen, 'A History of the Criminal Law of England' vol II, 102.
[57] *Ryan* v. R. (1966–7) 121 CLR 205, 209.
[58] I.D. Elliot 'Responsibility for Involuntary Acts: Ryan v the Queen' (1968) 41 *Australian Law Journal* 497.

movement of a tennis player retrieving a difficult shot; not accompanied by conscious planning, but certainly not involuntary'.[59] To attempt to maintain this distinction 'between a voluntary panicky movement and an involuntary reflex movement'[60] seems bound lead to confusion. In marked contrast, Windeyer J considered that the phrase 'reflex action' was inappropriate in Ryan's case, for, he asked, 'is an act to be called involuntary merely because the mind worked quickly and impulsively?'[61] The case of *Ryan* is a valuable one because it highlights the difficulties and dangers which can be caused by attaching a wide meaning to the word 'involuntary'.[62] A reflex action ought not to be regarded merely as an accidental, unplanned or impulsive movement.

Similar problems arose for discussion in *Timbu Kolian* v. R.[63] where the High Court of Australia was called upon to deal with section 23(1) of the Queensland Criminal Code,[64] which states that subject to other provisions in the Code 'a person is not criminally responsible for an act or omission which occurs independently of the exercise of his will, or for an event which occurs by accident'. The facts were that the accused picked up a stick to beat his wife. It was dark and so he did not realise that she was carrying their baby in her arms. He aimed a blow in the direction of his wife but it struck and killed the child. The Court decided unanimously that the accused was not guilty of manslaughter because of section 23(1). But the reasoning used by their Lordships was not identical, there being some dispute as to the proper meaning of the word 'act'. Two of their Lordships considered that the word must be taken to include 'the external elements' i.e. the consequences of the act.[65] The accused could therefore be acquitted under the first limb of section 23(1). In contrast, three of their Lordships considered that the word 'act' should be restricted to mean a willed muscular contraction apart from its consequences,[66] basing their decision on the second limb of the section. Finally, Windeyer J considered that the accused was exculpated under each limb of section 23(1), but preferred the wider meaning of 'act'.

It is clear that the first limb of section 23(1) includes the principle of voluntariness. What is by no means clear is how far beyond that principle it extends.[67] The real difficulty seems to stem from the phrase 'independently of the exercise of his will'. If this means 'involuntary' then the word

---

[59] Elliot 'Responsibility for Involuntary Acts', 500. But cf. J.C. Smith and B. Hogan, *Criminal Law* (7th edn., Butterworths, London, 1992) 41.

[60] Elliot, ibid. 500.   [61] *Ryan* v. R. (1966–7) 121 CLR 205, 244–5.

[62] Although Ryan's conviction for murder was unanimously upheld, Barwick CJ did consider there was evidence that the gun was discharged involuntarily: ibid. 209 and 219.

[63] *Timbu Kolian* v. R. (1968) 119 CLR 47.

[64] Identical in Western Australia and adopted by Papua New Guinea.

[65] Barwick CJJ and McTiernan J.   [66] Kitto, Menzies, and Owen JJ.

[67] Elliot, 'Responsibility for Involuntary Acts', 506–8.

'act' ought to be used in its narrow sense, since it is only when the accused's physical movement, as opposed to its consequences, cannot be properly attributed to him that any question of involuntariness comes into play. To hold otherwise would be to include many other types of conduct within this principle, notably accident and mistake. A person, therefore, like Timbu Kolian, who causes something to happen by accident, cannot maintain that his act was involuntary. Instead, he may simply contend that the result was unintended. It may be of course that the phrase in section 23(1) has this latter meaning, in which case the wide interpretation of 'act' is justified. This has been an area of considerable doubt within the Australian Criminal Codes,[68] and the relevant cases are valuable for their extensive discussions on the meaning of 'act'.

As already mentioned, a narrow interpretation of the word 'act' is to be preferred when it is preceded by the word 'involuntary'. Both words ought to be given a narrow meaning. This is not to deny that the word 'act' may often usefully be taken to include its consequences. All that is being maintained at present is that there is no reason to give the word 'act' a wider meaning where one is trying to discover whether the movement in question was involuntary, for what is being denied in calling an act 'involuntary' is so fundamental that all one's attention should be directed towards the movement in question. If this narrow interpretation is accepted, then the one feature which appears to distinguish the voluntary from the involuntary act is the lack of 'will'. Should this also be accepted, then we have, as Hart put it, 'an agreeably simple answer to our question,' the element of will being nothing more than 'the minimum indispensable link between mind and body required for responsibility'.[69] But the crucial question is whether such a 'simple answer' is acceptable. Hart thinks not, and subjects the doctrine of volition to a full-blooded attack. His major objection is that the idea of the will is 'nothing more than an outdated fiction—a piece of eighteenth-century psychology which has no real application to human conduct', the reason being that 'a desire to contract our muscles is a very rare occurrence' which does nothing to explain ordinary action.[70] Hart gives various illustrations to outline his objections, concluding that 'we do not have to launch our muscles into action by desiring that they contract as the Austinian terminology of 'acts' caused by 'volitions' suggests'.[71] In

---

[68] Cf. I.D. Elliot, 'Mistakes, Accidents and the Will: The Australian Criminal Codes' (1972) 46 *Australian Law Journal* 255, 328.

[69] Hart, *Punishment and Responsibility*, 98–9.   [70] Ibid. 101.

[71] Ibid. 103. It seems clear that this is what Austin meant for he talks of one's 'muscular motions' being willed (quoted by Hart, ibid. 98) Also, as Hart points out (ibid. 99), although more recent exponents of the doctrine do not actually mention the desire for muscular contractions when dealing with volition, 'it seems clear that substantially the same doctrine is intended'. For example, O.W. Holmes, *The Common Law* (Harvard University Press, Boston, 1881), 91 states that, 'An act is always a voluntary muscular contraction and nothing

the author's opinion it is time to abandon the idea of the 'will' and replace it with an account 'which involves no fictions; which is better fitted to the facts of ordinary experience; and which could be used by the courts in order to identify a range of cases where the requirement of a minimum mental element for responsibility is not satisfied'.[72]

The solution proposed by Hart is to describe involuntary acts as: 'movements of the body which occurred although they were not appropriate, i.e. required for any act . . . which the agent believed himself to be doing . . . they do not occur as part of anything the agent takes himself to be doing'.[73] This formula has not been without its critics,[74] and as a result Hart altered his account because of 'the obscurity of the expressions "not required for an action", "not appropriate to an action" and "not forming part of an action" '.[75] He would now substitute 'a reference to the agent's *reasons*. The fundamental defective cases would then be those where the bodily movements occurred though the agent had no reason for moving his body in that way'.[76] Hart recognises that his amended version may be vulnerable to the very same criticism which he had made against Austin, namely that 'it assumes unrealistically that the agent is normally aware of the muscular contractions involved in action and desires them before acting'.[77] However, he considers that a 'bodily movement' is different from a 'muscular contraction' and that it is realistic for a person to give a reason for moving his body in a particular way rather than to claim that 'he had or felt a desire for the bodily movement before acting'.[78]

But this amended version has also been the subject of criticism. In his essay entitled 'The Grounds of Responsibility',[79] J.L. Mackie points out that a person may have a reason for making an involuntary movement, but that this fact alone would not make such a movement voluntary. 'If a doctor is testing my knee-jerk reaction I may have a reason for kicking up my leg—perhaps I want him to report that I am in sound health—but the movement may still be involuntary. What would make it voluntary is not my having a reason but my moving it for that reason, and this leads us back to the rejected theory of movements caused by desires.'[80]

Before this criticism is examined it should be noted that Hart did recognise it existed. In the notes to the relevant essay he says:

I appreciate that, against this amended version . . . it may be said that it assumes, and does not explain, the distinction between a bodily movement occurring and a

---

else', and Williams, *Criminal Law*, 12 refers to this definition as 'following Austin'; so also does Fitzgerald, '*Voluntary and Involuntary Acts*', 124. But cf. Moore, *Act and Crime*, 80–2 who points out that bodily movements and muscular contractions are not the same things.

[72] Hart, Ibid. 104.   [73] Ibid. 105.

[74] As Hart acknowledges (ibid. 255). See also Saunders *Voluntary Acts and the Criminal Law*, 456.   [75] Hart, ibid. 255.

[76] Ibid., emphasis in original.   [77] Ibid. 256.   [78] Ibid.

[79] Mackie, 'The Grounds of Responsibility'.   [80] Ibid. 177.

man making a movement of his body for some reason. It is, however, to be observed that the criterion is not offered as a philosophical analysis of this distinction, but as a means of identifying (without importing any fictional elements) and specifying in a terminology which is in ordinary use the common element in those cases where the law exempts a man from responsibility on the grounds that the minimum mental element required is not present.[81]

This could be regarded as an answer to the above criticism. However, if one considers the knee-jerk more closely, it is nothing more than a reflex muscular contraction caused by an external stimulus. But if the agent has a valid reason for performing such a movement and is in fact successful, then what factor makes the movement involuntary? It is surely the link between the agent's capacity to control his performance of the movement in question and his reason for its performance which is broken. Normally when an agent has a reason for moving his body the required movement takes place because he has the capacity to perform it. In the knee-jerk example, even if the agent has a reason for performing this movement, it still cannot be regarded as being appropriate for any action which the agent believes or takes himself to be doing. The knee-jerk is not a movement which is 'subordinated to the agent's conscious plans of action'.[82] He cannot take himself to be performing a knee-jerk since he has no capacity to control such a movement. Indeed if the notion of 'having a reason' is replaced by Kenny's minimal sense of 'want',[83] then the knee jerk cannot be regarded as 'wanted' as the agent has no power to refrain from doing it. Thus, if the agent was unfortunate enough to knock something off his doctor's table with his foot while being tested for his knee-jerk reaction, the reason why we would not seek to ascribe responsibility to him for such a reflex action would be because he lacked any power to control such a movement.

In his essay Mackie openly admits that 'it is difficult to formulate any stable alternative account'[84] and thus reverts to the much-criticised 'Brown-Austin theory'.[85] In doing this he adopts what Hart described as a toned-down version of this theory: namely, 'that when we act we desire to do some action which *involves* muscular contractions.'[86] Such a theory was regarded by Hart as being 'broadly acceptable, if not very informative'.[87] In Mackie's opinion, this toned-down version is the key to distinguishing voluntary from involuntary acts. Thus, an action will be voluntary if it 'incorporates some movement which is appropriate for the fulfilment of a desire that causally brings it about.' That this closely resembles Hart's

---

[81] Hart, *Punishment and Responsibility*, 256.   [82] Ibid. 105.
[83] Kenny, *The Metaphysics of Mind*, 32.
[84] Mackie, 'The Grounds of Responsibility', 177.
[85] Mackie uses this phrase at ibid. 179. It refers to the fact that Austin admits to having derived his theory of volition from Dr. T. Brown's *Enquiry into the Relation of Cause and Effect* (1818) Part 1. See Hart, *Punishment and Responsibility*, 97.
[86] Hart, ibid. 103. Emphasis in original.   [87] Ibid.

original formula, Mackie clearly admits. In his opinion, however, 'there is the vital difference that in my account what the movements are to be appropriate to is the fulfilment of a desire that causes them, not just something that the agent believes he is doing, and the appropriateness can be explained by a more complex relation to that desire. Voluntariness is constituted by certain patterns in which desires play a leading role.'[88]

The essential feature of this toned-down version is that there should be a desire present in voluntary action but that it is not the muscular contractions which are desired. That this is a possible alternative formula has, as already mentioned, been admitted by Hart. He comments that 'it presupposes the ordinary man's ordinary description of what he does and desires to do in terms, not of muscular contractions, but of such things as kicking a ball, hitting a man, or writing a letter'.[89] Is either formula to be preferred? What is most notable is that Hart alone has attempted to give an alternative account in broad common sense terms. Mackie retreats into the obscurity of the Brown–Austin formula and in doing so he resurrects, albeit in a milder form, the concept of volition. Hart's formula makes no such compromise, and is an important attempt to get away from outdated ideas.

One further problem deserves to be mentioned. How, it may be asked, does each formula deal with the habitual action?

Mackie answers this as follows: 'positive acts and actions can also be voluntary in this weaker sense: a habitual, semi-automatic action may be causally ascribable not to any desire which it fulfils or to which it is appropriate, being a learned means to its fulfilment, but merely to the lack of any sufficiently strong desire. My aimless walking along the road is voluntary in that I would stop if I either wanted to stop or wanted to do something else'.[90]

However, to attribute this type of habitual action to a lack of any sufficiently strong desire to do something else seems to stretch common parlance to its utmost. But Hart's formula appears to fare no better. For how can the agent 'believe himself' or 'take himself to be doing' something of which he is not aware? Hart himself makes no mention of the absent-minded or habitual action and thus fails to come to terms with this problem. It may be that Hart thought such acts were not worthy of serious consideration being for the most part trivial and insignificant. As Melden has commented: 'if, for example, I rub my nose, this is not something I need do because I have any intention of doing it, or a desire to do so; nor need I decide or choose to do so. I simply do it—period. Hence with respect to this action, the answer to the question "voluntary or involuntary?" is correctly given by saying "Neither, don't be absurd!"'[91]

[88] Mackie, 'The Grounds of Responsibility', 179.
[89] Hart, *Punishment and Responsibility*, 104.
[90] Mackie, ibid. 180.   [91] Melden, *Free Action*, 218.

On the other hand, some habitual or absent-minded acts can lead to serious consequences,[92] in which case the same question 'voluntary or involuntary?' ceases to be absurd. Although it is difficult to fit this type of act into either Hart's or Mackie's formula, it seems obvious from a common sense point of view that it ought to be classed as voluntary. Certainly such acts cannot qualify as being involuntary, since, although the agent may not be fully aware of them at the time of their performance, they nevertheless form part of a series of bodily movements over which he has full control. That is to say, there is no suggestion of incapacity on the part of the agent sufficient to render his act involuntary.[93] The habitual or absent-minded act is in reality a normal and everyday type of behaviour, in that we all perform certain types of activity which because of long practice no longer demand our full attention.[94]

THE IDEA OF BASIC ACTS

In a more recent criticism of the Austin–Mackie theory of action, Michael Moore states that 'no independent characterisation is given of the kind of causal relation that will do here, except by saying, 'the kind of causation involved in *acting*''. As a result, he concludes that this type of account of human action 'does not say very much. It is about as helpful as Aristotle's idea that an action is where the moving principle is inside a person.'[95] Moore's solution to this difficulty is to focus attention on the distinction between basic acts and complex acts:

What a person can do as a basic act is limited by what that person *knows* he can do as a basic act. For example, the complicated muscle flexings necessary to raise

[92] See J. Reason, 'How Did I Come to Do That?', *New Behaviour* (24 April 1975), 10, where pilot error is identified with absent-minded behaviour. Cf. *R*. v. *Ingram* [1975] Crim LR 457 where the accused's conviction for shoplifting was quashed because of doubt about *mens rea*, the lack of which was alleged to have resulted from absent-mindedness. See also J. Reason and D. Lucas, 'Absent mindedness in Shops: its Incidence, Correlates and Consequences (1984) 23 *British Journal of Clinical Psychology* 121–31.

[93] *The Model Penal Code* in the United States of America attempts to deal with the habitual act but only in the context of volition. See American Law Institute, Proposed Official Draft (1962) section 2.02(2)(d) which states that the following is not a voluntary act: 'a bodily movement that otherwise is not a product of effort or determination of the actor, either conscious or habitual.'

[94] See Dennett *Consiousness Explained*, 137: 'You have probably experienced the phenomenon of driving for miles while engrossed in conversation (or in silent soliloquy) and then discovering that you have no memory of the road, the traffic, your car-driving activities. It is as if someone else had been driving . . . . But were you *really* unconscious of all those passing cars, stop lights, bends in the road at the time? . . . The unconscious driving phenomenon is better seen as a case of rolling consciousness with swift memory loss.' For further discussion of the process involved, see G. Underwood, 'Attention and Awareness in Cognitive and Motor Skills' in G. Underwood (ed.), *Aspects of Consciousness, Volume 3* (Academic Press, London, 1982) ch. 5.

[95] M. Moore, *Law and Psychiatry* (Cambridge University Press, Cambridge, 1985), 72 (emphasis in original).

one's arm are not basic actions because the actor does not know how to move them in just the way that will raise his arm. The act of raising one's arm is a basic act, however, because the actor knows he can raise his arm and he knows when he is exercising that power.

An actor's bodily movement is a basic action only if he knows that he can perform that movement as an action and that he is doing so on that particular occasion.[96]

This notion of 'basic action' is fully developed in the work of Arthur Danto who comments:

Behaviour becomes more uniform and less culturally differentiated as the force of beliefs approaches zero, and hence as responses verge on reflexes. Thus men spontaneously, and without reference to their beliefs, withdraw their hands abruptly from hot irons. What keeps this a basic action and not a pure response is that it is capable of inhibition by a sufficiently determined person, concerned to show self-control or demonstrate innocence at a witch trial, whereas no such options are available with the pre-patellar reflex.[97]

Once again therefore we seem to have returned to the idea of capacity as being the fundamental feature which distinguishes a basic action from a mere bodily movement such as the knee-jerk reflex. However, the concept of 'basic action' is useful insofar as it enables us to trace all forms of complex human behaviour back to a 'basic action', in the sense 'of an act not done by the performance of some further act'.[98] In a sense, therefore, a 'basic act' is the irreducible minimum which is to be found in all cases of human action and requires us to focus attention on initial outward manifestation of all forms of complex human behaviour. This in turn lends support to the argument put forward earlier: namely, that the search for the distinction between a voluntary and involuntary act should be restricted to an enquiry into the bodily movement itself rather than its consequences, if we are to ascertain whether the movement in question should qualify as a basic action or an involuntary movement.[99]

Another important aspect of basic action concerns its relationship to volition. In his recent book entitled *Act and Crime*,[100] Moore has clearly changed direction from having been openly critical of volition,[101] to a clear

---

[96] Moore, *Law and Psychiatry*, 73 (emphasis in original).
[97] A.C. Danto, *Analytical Philosophy of Action* (Cambridge University Press, Cambridge, 1973), 115.   [98] M. Moore, 'Responsibility and the Unconscious', 1574.
[99] Such an enquiry will not of itself answer this question for, as Duff has pointed out, 'a claim that basic actions are bodily movements does not tell us how to distinguish voluntary from involuntary movements . . . we cannot avoid going further, to locate the essence of agency in something lying behind such movements'. See R.A. Duff, 'Acting, Trying and Criminal Liability' in S. Shute, J. Gardiner and J. Horder (eds.), *Action and Value in the Criminal Law* (Clarendon Press, Oxford, 1993), 83.
[100] Moore, *Act and Crime*: The Philosophy of Action and its Implications for Criminal Law (Clarendon Press, Oxford, 1993).
[101] See Moore, 'Responsibility and the Unconscious', 1570–1.

acceptance of the doctrine. In his support for volitional theory, Moore draws on the notion that mental states are functional states:

A functional state is a state whose essential nature is specified by the functional roles such a state plays in causing, and being caused by, other states and events. 'Pain', on this view, names a state specified by its role in causing certain behaviour, being caused by certain stimuli, and entering into a variety of relationships to other mental states such as beliefs and intentions . . . In general terms, volitions are specified by the role they play in proximately causing bodily motions and in being the effects of both more general intentions and the belief–desire sets the latter execute. Volitions are mediating states, and what they mediate between are our motivations and our intentions, on the one hand, and our actions, on the other.[102]

In answer to one of Ryle's fundamental objections to volitions, namely that 'in some way which must forever remain a mystery, mental thrusts [volitions], which are not movements of matter in space, can cause muscles to contract',[103] Moore responds:

One of the beauties of a functionalist interpretation of volitions is that it avoids the horrors of interactionist dualism that Ryle so persuasively depicted. On the functionalist interpretation, volitions are not 'things that exist in time but not in space, having no mass and no energy'. True, the essential nature of volitions is given by their functional role and not by their physical structure; true causal laws about them may well be formulable in terms of concepts using such functional (not structural) criteria; but there is nothing in the functional view that commits one to thinking that such functional states exist in some non-physical realm, or that there is a 'functional substance' different from any physical substance. Rather, a functionalist holds that each particular volition that a person possesses has a structural realisation in the brain of that person. Each such volition thus has a physical nature that may non-anomalously interact with other physical objects [and is] no more problematic or puzzling than is the causal relation between two billiard balls.[104]

Rather than equate volitions with wants of any kind,[105] Moore considers that they have an executory function in that 'they are simply such bare intentions having as their objects the simplest bits of bodily motion that we know how to do'.[106] However, despite his insistence that this 'volitional theory is our current best bet about the nature of action', Moore is nonetheless forced to concede that 'whether volitions exist is . . . very much an open, scientific question'.[107]

In contrast, Danto clearly rejects volition, in the sense of requiring some inner mental event which triggers any basic act. In this context, Danto states: 'I wish first to make clear the sense in which an individual does not

---

[102] Moore, *Act and Crime*, 130–1.   [103] Ryle, *The Concept of Mind*, 63–4.
[104] Moore, *Act and Crime*, 156–7.   [105] Ibid. 120.   [106] Ibid. 121.
[107] Ibid. 165.

cause his basic actions to happen. When an individual M performs a basic action a, there is no event distinct from a that both stands to a as cause to effect *and* is an action performed by M. So when M performs a basic action, he does nothing first that causes it to happen.'[108] In short, Danto's theory reduces a basic act to 'something a person makes happen' without the need to rely on the extra ingredient of volition, and focuses instead on the idea of personal agency and 'the notion of a *person* bringing about some new state of affairs'.[109] This of course is not to deny that the 'essence of human action is the exercise of causal power by a person, principally over his body but also over his thoughts and emotions',[110] but merely refutes the need for a separate volitional trigger every time a person performs a voluntary movement. In essence therefore, normal individuals have the power to perform basic actions without the need for volition in relation to every minor muscular contraction involved.[111] It is even acceptable to refer to this power to perform basic actions as volition, provided it is made clear that when this power is exercised in the form of a basic action such as the raising of an arm, this is what causes the person's muscles to contract rather than the process of some secret mental cue being responsible for the muscular contractions in question. By accepting this approach, we can now focus attention on the question of the agent's capacity to perform basic actions,[112] whenever the issue of whether or not such actions were voluntary becomes a relevant consideration—without the need to resort to the type Cartesianism which has been the subject of so much criticism.

OMISSIONS

The discussion so far has dealt only with 'acts', no mention having been made of 'omissions'. An omission can be regarded simply as inaction or a failure to act. Any test of responsibility must cater for the omission,[113] since although the common law has always been reluctant to impose a

---

[108] A.C. Danto, 'Basic Actions' in White (ed.), *The Philosophy of Action*, 45.

[109] See Moore, *Law and Psychiatry*, 72 (emphasis in original).

[110] M. Moore, 'Causation and the Excuses' (1985) 73 *California Law Review* 1132.

[111] See R. Schopp, *Automatism, Insanity, and the Psychology of Criminal Responsibility* (Cambridge University Press, Cambridge 1991), 90: 'A cough is a basic act–token when done intentionally as a signal to a confederate, but it is not if it occurs reflexively in response to dust. Basic act–tokens are done at will in that they are produced directly by the wants and beliefs of the actor in the ordinary or characteristic way that wants and beliefs cause actions. They are inherently intentional in the sense that it is part of the concept of a basic act that it is caused by the wants of the actor in the manner that intentional acts are caused'.

[112] See Hart, *Punishment and Responsibility*, 181. For recent discussion, see K.J.M. Smith and W. Wilson, 'Impaired Voluntariness and Criminal Responsibility: Reworking Hart's Theory of Excuses—the English Judicial Response' (1993) 13 *Oxford Journal of Legal Studies* 71–98.   [113] Fitzgerald, 'Voluntary and Involuntary Acts', 128.

positive duty to act there are nevertheless many instances of liability being imposed for inactivity.[114] In his essay 'Acts of Will and Responsibility', Hart criticises Austin's doctrine of volition on the ground that it cannot apply to omissions. He comments:

The theory . . . only tells us when a positive intervention is involuntary and gives us no criterion for saying when an omission is involuntary. Moreover we cannot rescue the theory from the difficulty by amending it generously to mean that omissions are voluntary if the *failure* to contract the muscles so as to do the action required was caused by a desire *not* to contract the muscles and involuntary if it was not so caused. This would have very unwelcome consequences for legal responsibility: for the only omissions which would then be culpable would be deliberate omissions. We could then only punish those who failed to stop at traffic lights if they deliberately shot the lights.[115]

It is clear that an accused may be held liable for an omission even though he never applied his mind to the inactivity in question, and this is only right and proper where there has been negligence involved. But what of the case where the unfortunate accused is suddenly paralysed? As Hart again comments, 'in neither case, is there any 'volition' or desire to make (or, in the amended version, to omit) muscular movements'.[116] Now it is obvious that the law must distinguish between these types of case, and Hart considers that if the failure to act resulted from 'inability' on the agent's part, then this inability is the identifying feature which ought to be included in any test of responsibility.[117]

Mackie, who, it will be recalled, relies on a toned-down version of the Brown–Austin theory, answers Hart's criticism in the following manner:

Omissions, like positive acts, can be intended . . . and will then be voluntary. But they can also be voluntary in a weaker, negative sense, that the failure to perform the omitted act was caused by the lack of any sufficiently strong desire. If the agent had some sufficiently strong desire whose fulfilment would have involved the omitted act, or to whose fulfilment that act would have been appropriate, then it would have been performed in execution of that desire; so the omission can be causally ascribed to a lack of desire.[118]

Now it has already been admitted that, in certain limited cases, an omission can be voluntary in the sense that we can deliberately refrain from acting. However, to identify 'the lack of any sufficiently strong desire' as being the feature which indicates that an inadvertent omission is voluntary seems unrealistic. Rather, it is the fact that the accused 'had the opportunity and ability to do the act, was aware that he had the opportunity and

---

[114] For discussion, see A. Ashworth, 'The Scope of Criminal Liability for Omissions' (1989) 105 LQR 424.
[115] Hart, *Punishment and Responsibility*, 100 (emphasis in original).
[116] Ibid. 101.   [117] Ibid. 106.   [118] Mackie, 'The Grounds of Responsibility', 180.

the ability, and the act was reasonably expected of him' which converts a non-doing into a voluntary omission.[119]

It can be seen from this brief discussion that the distinction between voluntary and involuntary omissions raises problems which are similar to the ones previously discussed in relation to the word 'act', and that the notion of capacity in terms of 'inability' seems to be at the root of the concept of involuntariness when applied to omissions. It also seems clear that an agent's inability or incapacity can arise either through lack of control, as in the case of a reflex action, or as a result of what the courts refer to as 'unconsciousness'. Certainly, the notion of 'unconscious invol-untary action' is the definition which the courts have adopted in relation to the automatism defence,[120] and having discussed the concept of the involuntary act in some depth it now seems pertinent to explore likewise the idea of 'unconsciousness'. This can best be done by drawing on the findings of neuroscience and neurophysiology.

SLEEP

The most frequent form of 'unconsciousness' is sleep. As this is a phenom-enon which everyone experiences, some discussion of it may help our understanding of the distinction between voluntary and involuntary action which is at the root of the legal notion of automatism.

Sleep is such a common experience that we tend to take it for granted. However, it is nothing short of remarkable that during each twenty-four hour day the vast majority of the population will spend around one-third of it in a state of 'unconsciousness' during which they are completely unaware of their surroundings. The crucial question is what happens to us when we enter this state of sleep. A good deal of research has been under-taken in this connection and what follows is a brief analysis of some of its more important aspects. Certainly, sleepwalking is not unknown within the context of automatism, and it may be possible therefore to explain some aspects of this phenomenon through the medium of sleep research.

Much of the relevant research has focused on what actually happens in the brain when a subject falls asleep. What is clear is that the brain does not simply cease to function during this time. Instead, it begins to function in a different manner from when we are awake. Thus Blakemore com-ments: 'sleeping is clearly much more than just the temporary loss of this aspect of existence we call consciousness. The *physical* state of the brain totally changes: the activity of the nerve cells in the cerebral cortex be-comes engaged in highly abnormal, rhythmic patterns; the chemistry of the

[119] See G Meade, 'Contractions into Crime: A Theory of Criminal Omissions' (1991) *Oxford Journal of Legal Studies* 147, 148.
[120] See *Bratty* v. *Attorney-General for Northern Ireland* [1963] AC 386, 400.

brain is radically altered; the physical make-up of the brain, as well as the mind, is clearly in a different condition.'[121]

It seems clear from studies of the physiology of sleep that a normal sleep/wake pattern is dependent on a functioning brain stem, or more particularly that part of it which is known as the reticular formation, which controls the sensory pathways to the upper brain and the spinal cord. According to Oswald:

The reticular formation is conceived of as a zone of nervous tissue, the excitement of which periodically undergoes both abrupt and gradual variations. In consequence, the upflow of non-specific impulses, which keep the grey matter pepped up, undergoes continual variations in intensity. It is the presence of an efficiently working cortex which makes possible 'clever' activity, learned activity, the weighing up of past and present evidence, and a rational decision to embark upon, and a power to execute, skilled behaviour. Without the upflow from the reticular formation the cortex cannot serve these purposes.[122]

Accordingly, it has been suggested that when a person suffers from a loss or impairment of consciousness, 'it is because of a failure on the part of the reticular formation to send up a sufficiency of the non-specific or "activating" nerve impulses to the cortex'.[123] However, this does not mean that all brain function ceases during sleep. It is not as if the stream of consciousness is merely like a tap which is somehow turned off by the reticular formation when a person falls asleep. Instead, it seems likely that there are important changes in mental function during sleep in the sense that there is an alteration in the chemical balance of the receptors which transmit nerve impulses to excite or dampen the reticular formation.[124]

A good deal of research has demonstrated by the use of electroencephalograms (EEGs) how the electrical activity of the brain varies during sleep.[125] Not only that, it has also been clearly demonstrated by use of the same technique that there are five stages of sleep which incorporate two distinct kinds of sleep, known as slow wave (NREM) and rapid eye movement (REM) sleep.[126] What is especially significant here is the fact that the physiology of slow-wave and REM sleep is different. Fenwick describes them as follows: 'during slow-wave sleep the cardiac and respiratory rates slow, and muscle tone, although present, decreases. The presence of muscle tone allows the slow-wave sleeper to move, and makes sleepwalking possible.

---

[121] Blakemore, 'A Mechanistic Approach to Perception and the Human Mind', 117 (emphasis in original).

[122] I. Oswald, *Sleep* (Pelican Books, Harmondsworth, 1968), 30.

[123] Ibid. 37–8.   [124] Ibid. 40.

[125] See generally, J.D. Parkes, *Sleep and its Disorders*, (Saunders, London, 1985), ch. 2, 'The Anatomical and Physiological Basis of the Sleep–Wake Cycle'.

[126] Ibid. and see further M. Reite et al., *A Concise Guide to The Evaluation and Management of Sleep Disorders* (American Psychiatric Press, Washington D.C., 1990), ch. 2.

During REM sleep, cardiac and respiratory rates increase and become irregular. The absence of muscle tone is associated with muscular paralysis, so that only small movements are possible during REM sleep.'[127] Oswald further describes these differences: 'we continue breathing throughout sleep, so that not all the muscles of the body are paralysed during paradoxical (REM) sleep. But most are, even to the extent of abolition of the normal reflex twitch of the leg muscles, which in the waking state, and in orthodox (slow-wave) sleep, follows involuntarily upon sudden stimulation of a nerve carrying messages from sense organs to the spinal cord'.[128]

It is clear that REM sleep is associated with dreaming while slow-wave sleep is not. Accordingly, REM sleep mentation, which is typically narrative, is much more easily remembered than slow-wave sleep mentation. It is important here to remember that during REM or dream sleep the subject is virtually paralysed, which means that he is unable to act out his dreams. In this context, it is crucial to note that sleepwalking can only occur during stages three and four of slow-wave sleep, which is usually within two hours of sleep onset. Fenwick describes a typical episode as follows:

the person will sit up, and possibly make small repetitive automatic movements. It is commonplace for the spouse of a sleepwalker to complain that they are kicked, bruised, and sometimes threatened by their sleeping partners: not uncommonly the spouse wakes and finds the partners hands on their body, or even around their neck . . . Sleepwalkers have walked out onto fire escapes, fired guns, driven cars, sometimes with the result of serious self-injury, or injury to others.[129]

It seems clear that for those prone to sleepwalking it is the process of arousal which may spell danger, and for this reason somnambulism has been referred to as an arousal disorder.[130] Again Fenwick remarks that:

During the deepest stage of slow wave sleep . . . if there is an arousal, then in sleepwalkers there may be a physiological dissociation of the wakening process allowing a partial arousal without full awakening. During this dissociated state sleepwalking occurs and complex actions can be carried out . . . There is no memory for these events [as] there is a discrepancy between the act carried out during sleepwalking, and the mentation during the episode (if it can be remembered), and the waking motivation of the individual.[131]

A vital question is why the sleepwalker's behaviour should be regarded as automatism. For example, there is no doubt that we all move to some degree during slow-wave sleep, if only to toss and turn in bed. Thus Parkes states: 'frequent "body movements" occur throughout normal sleep and 8–15 short arousals are normal, even in subjects who sleep well and do

---

[127] P. Fenwick, 'Automatism, Medicine and the Law' (1990) *Psychological Medicine, Monograph Supplement* 17, 13.
[128] Oswald, *Sleep*, 96.   [129] Fenwick, 'Automatism, Medicine and the Law', 14.
[130] See Reite et al., *The Evaluation and Management of Sleep Disorders*, ch. 5.
[131] P. Fenwick, 'Offending While Asleep' (1990) 1 *Journal of Forensic Psychiatry* 274.

not recall these on waking. A shift of posture usually occurs about every 15–20 minutes.'[132] But what makes this different from tossing and turning while trying to fall asleep? The answer of course lies in the fact that, as already mentioned, there is a change in the physiology of the brain during sleep.[133] But this in itself seems ill understood and a great deal more research will be required before the purpose and anatomical basis for sleep can be fully explained.[134] It naturally follows from this that the cause of sleepwalking is likewise unknown and when linked with anti-social behaviour 'it is very difficult to evaluate the evidence that a purposeful criminal act may be performed whilst sleepwalking. Physiological evidence for a true state of sleep has never been presented.'[135]

On the other hand, if such evidence was forthcoming, then it seems to be broadly accepted that no civilised criminal justice system would wish to hold such a person responsible for anything he might have done during such a somnambulistic episode. But why not? If he was able to 'assault' his victim as the accused was in the recent case of *R. v. Burgess*[136], then what makes his behaviour so different from that of a random case of assault? Clearly, he lacks waking awareness in the sense of normal consciousness. But we surely need to know more about the process of consciousness before we can be sure that sleep behaviour is so essentially different from waking behaviour that a person can be excused from criminal responsibility during sleep. So it is to the neuroscientist that one may turn in order to discover more about the physiology of the brain.

One thing is clear: the brain is an immensely complex organ about which comparatively little is understood. For example, although it is well known that neurons, the basic working nerve-cells within the brain, are inextricably linked to consciousness, it is not even known with any degree of certainty how many neurons there are. In volume one of *Mind and Brain*, Ted Honderich discusses contemporary neuroscience and states that 'one estimate is that the nervous system contains 10^{12} neurons ... A single thought has been said to engage many millions of neurons.'[137] Further, in his discussion of the structure of the brain Honderich makes it clear that it is the hindbrain which regulates movement and, in particular, 'the pons, in the brain stem, shares part of the reticular formation. It is important to waking and sleeping, and allows intentional movements to be carried out effectively. It contains neuron tracts that connect the cerebellum and medulla with parts of the upper brain.'[138] Honderich continues:

---

[132] Parkes, *Sleep and its Disorders*, 191.
[133] J.C. Eccles, *The Human Psyche* (Springer International, New York, 1980), 163.
[134] Reite et al., *The Evaluation and Management of Sleep Disorders*, 25–6.
[135] Parkes, *Sleep and its Disorders*, 209.   [136] *R. v. Burgess* [1991] 2 All ER 769.
[137] T. Honderich, *Mind and Brain A Theory of Determinism*, Vol 1 (Cambridge University Press, Cambridge, 1989), 266.
[138] Ibid. 268. See further B. Kolb and I.Q. Wishaw, *Fundamentals of Neuropsychology* (3rd edn. W.H. Freeman, New York, 1990) ch. 11.

The other two principal parts of the motor system—cerebellum and basal ganglia—are as essential to action. The cerebellum provides neural connections between the rest of the cerebral cortex and that part of it which is the motor cortex.
In particular, it plays a fundamental role in passing information from the rest of
the cerebral cortex to the motor cortex. In essence, it is said, its function is one
of feed-forward control . . . it regulates the rate, range and force of movements
. . . the basal ganglia, if less well understood, are as essential to action. They are
like the cerebellum in that they make connections between the rest of the cortex
and the motor cortex. Cells in the basal ganglia are active prior to movement, and
it may be that they are concerned with what can be called the fittingness of a
movement—its suitability to the given environment.[139]

However, although there now seems to be consensus over what parts of
the brain are involved in movement, Honderich is forced to conclude that
little is known about 'any neural counterpart of precisely the episode of
willing or actively intending an action'.[140] In this context it is particularly
interesting to note that Eccles considers that he has at least a partial
answer to the question 'What is happening in my brain when a willed
action is in the process of being carried out?'[141] If this is so then perhaps
it will help to disclose the fundamental difference in terms of brain function between voluntary and involuntary acts. This partial answer would
appear to be based on an analysis of the electrical potential generated in
the cerebral cortex before the performance of a voluntary action. According to Eccles, experiments have demonstrated that in a simple case of the
voluntary flexing of the right index finger a so-called 'readiness potential'
can be observed by means of an EEG which immediately precedes the
movement in question. This has led Eccles to conclude that 'as a consequence, the willing of a movement produces the gradual evolution of
neural responses over a wide area . . . so giving the readiness potential.
Furthermore, the mental act that we call willing must guide or mould this
unimaginably complex neuronal performance of the liaison cortex so that
eventually it "homes in" on to the appropriate modules of the motor
cortex and brings about discharges of their motor pyramidal cells.'[142]

It may be, therefore, that, as with the contrast between wakefulness and
sleep, a difference in neuronal performance can indeed be pointed to which
may help to distinguish between a voluntary and an involuntary act.
However, at this stage it is also important to note that although it is
claimed that this readiness potential,[143] 'is generated by a mental event, an

---

[139] Honderich, *Mind and Brain*, 299–300.   [140] Ibid. 111.
[141] J.C. Eccles, 'Brain and Free Will' in G.G. Globus et al. (eds.), *Consciousness and the
Brain* (Plenum Press, New York, 1976), 115.   [142] Ibid. 117.
[143] Defined as a 'scalp-recorded slow negative shift in electrical potential generated by the
brain' which always precedes voluntary movements and can be monitored by attaching
electrodes to the subject's scalp. See B. Libet, 'Unconscious Cerebral Initiative and the Role
of Conscious Will in Voluntary Action' (1985) 8 *Behavioral and Brain Science* 529.

act of will . . . it is not proposed that the whole readiness potential is generated by an act of will'.[144] Rather Eccles claims that this potential 'builds up during 0.8 s before the onset of a simple movement and that presumably is generated by immensely complex patterns of modular operation'.[145]

It would seem, therefore, that although neuroscience may help to explain some of the mechanics of voluntary action, this in itself will do little to assist us in our quest for a satisfactory legal analysis of automatism. There are two obvious problems. The first is theoretical and concerns the fundamental difficulty that, although neuroscience may be able to produce an adequate physiological account of a particular movement, this is not the same as providing 'an explanation of that movement *as an action*'.[146] As Noble points out, philosophers—and lawyers—'need to make a distinction between movement and action and . . . only if the movements concerned occurred within the framework of necessary conditions for ascribing an *act* to a *subject* could it be said that a particular action occurred'.[147] There seems good reason to argue therefore that a neurophysiological account of the difference between movement and action, while useful in terms of giving some explanation of the mechanics involved, cannot hope in itself to account fully for what converts a bodily movement into an act.[148] Indeed, Eccles himself freely admits this by emphasising that the readiness potential only occurs when the subject is *'consciously willing the movements* that give the muscle responses', thus denying the only alternative account which is 'to maintain that the subjects are illuded in their belief that they voluntarily initiate the movements, whereas the movements are *being entirely generated by the neuronal machinery*'.[149] Such a materialistic conclusion is unacceptable to Eccles, who is a devout supporter of the dualist–interaction theory which is premised on the fundamental principle that mind and brain are independent entities.

However, more recent research casts considerable doubt on Eccles' view and instead supports the notion that the brain starts or initiates movement prior to any conscious awareness relating to it on the part of the subject.[150]

---

[144] J.C. Eccles, *The Human Psyche*, 105.   [145] Ibid. 46.

[146] D. Noble, 'Biological Explanation and Intentional Behaviour' in K.A. Mohyeldin Said et al. (eds.), *Modelling the Mind* (Clarendon Press, Oxford, 1990), 98 (emphasis in original).

[147] Ibid. 99 (emphasis in original).

[148] This is well illustrated by the debate over whether the behaviour of a sleepwalker should be classed as an example 'not just of action, but of purposive action', an opinion strongly put forward by Bernard Williams in 'The Actus Reus of Dr. Caligari' (1994) 142 University of Pennsylvania Law Review 1661–73, but disputed by Moore, *Act and Crime*, 253–9 and 'Reply—More on *Act and Crime*' (1994) 142 *University of Pennsylvania Law Review* 1804–11.

[149] Eccles, *The Human Psyche*, 106 (emphasis in original).

[150] This research, carried out by Benjamin Libet, is well described by A.E. Lelling 'Eliminative Materialism, Neuroscience and the Criminal Law' (1993) 141 *University of Pennsylvania*

Accordingly, it has been suggested that 'Libet himself appears to view volitions as epiphenomena: They themselves do no "causing" of bodily movements, but because of the unconscious nature of the initiating cerebral processes, they let you think that they did'.[151]

Does this mean then that we are not responsible for our actions as we have no conscious control over them? Libet's findings support no such conclusion as his research indicates that the time-lag between unconscious initiation of action and the actual action itself leaves us with an opportunity to veto or stop the action proceeding.[152] Although Libet's work has been the subject of considerable criticism,[153] it is significant insofar as it casts doubt on the traditional nature of volition as a cause of voluntary action.

Further, an additional but important point within the neurophysiological debate has been made by Pribram:

It is not the muscle or its contraction, it is the act, the use to which the muscle is put, the predicted end that needs to be achieved, that is reflected in the activity of the cortical cells.

The fact that actions, not just movements or muscles, are represented in the motor cortex has far reaching consequences. It means that I can with my left hand write Constantinople with muscles that have never been engaged in such a performance or anything like it.[154]

Now if it is indeed the actions themselves which are reflected in cortical activity, this might help to overcome some of the earlier criticisms which have been directed towards volition since, if this notion is tied in with the idea of 'readiness potential', whether conscious or unconscious, what now seems to be available is a mechanistic model of voluntary action which could be taken to support the concept of 'basic action' discussed earlier, in the sense that it is the 'basic act' itself rather than the use to which the muscles are put which is reflected in cortical activity. This in turn seems to lead back to the fundamental proposition that the agent's basic acts can be attributed to him because he has the capacity to perform, or to refrain from performing, them.

Law Review 1471, 1520–6. At ibid. 1522, he remarks: 'In plain English, Libet found that the brain initiates action "before there is any . . . subjective awareness that such a decision has taken place" [quoting 'Libet Unconscious Cerebral Initiative', 536]. It begins movement long before you are aware of desiring movement . . . Libet's straightforward finding has stopped us in our legal tracks, as we are left passively watching the actions our unconscious neurophysiological processes decide to take.'

[151] Lelling, ibid. 1523.

[152] A time-lag of up to 500 milliseconds: Libet, 'Unconscious Cerebral Initiative', 537.

[153] See e.g. Dennett *Consciousness Explained*, 153–168, who at 164 states 'The subjects *were* conscious of their intentions at an earlier moment, but this consciousness was wiped out of memory (or just revised) before they had a chance to recall it' (emphasis in original).

[154] K.H. Pribram 'Problems Concerning the Structure of Consciousness' in G.G. Globus et al. (eds.) *Consciousness and the Brain*, (New York, 1976).

The second problem in developing a satisfactory legal analysis of antomatism is of a practical nature but in a sense follows on from the first. It is the perennial problem of trying to decide what the state of a person's mind was at the time he performed the 'act' in question. As with the question of mens rea, we can never know exactly what an individual's mental state was at any given time. Instead we draw inferences from our own experiences despite the fact that 'we have no objective evidence . . . that mental states determine physical action . . . over and above the impression of a causal relationship given to us by our conscious experiences themselves!'[155] However, this identification of other people's actions with our own conscious experiences is of fundamental importance as far as the law is concerned. The reason for this can be traced to the pragmatic approach of the law over the question of proof. The criminal law, for example, is quite content to allow a jury to attribute mental states to defendants on the basis of its collective common sense experience. Indeed, the law positively encourages this approach by closely monitoring the admissibility of expert evidence which should be available to a jury when it is called upon to deal with a retrospective enquiry into how a defendant's mind was operating at the time of the alleged offence.[156] In short, it is only in cases where there is some suggestion that the defendant's mind was operating in an abnormal manner that such expert evidence will be admitted. Automatism is often given as a prime example of this, although it would be interesting to know how the courts would react to conscious automatism in this connection, such as a case of a reflex action.

The criminal law, then, will accept that expert evidence, such as that offered by psychiatry and neurophysiology, is helpful but not determinative of the issue of criminal responsibility. In essence, therefore, the law accepts that the evidence of experts concerning the notion of unconscious involuntary action should be available to assist a jury because such conditions are outside the realm of ordinary experience.[157] However, a state of automatism is inextricably linked to the concept of involuntary action to which the law is clearly wedded. Accordingly, in much the same way as neuroscience cannot point to the fundamental difference between a mere movement and an act, so the criminal law will not permit expert medical testimony to determine this difference. Instead, as was noted earlier, the law falls back on the traditional notion of volition, and it is now time to discuss how the criminal law has developed this concept within the framework of the automatism defence.

---

[155] Blakemore, 'A Mechanistic Approach to Perception and the Human Mind', 119.
[156] See R.D. Mackay and A. Colman, 'Excluding Expert Evidence: a Tale of Ordinary Folk and Common Experience' [1991] Crim LR 800.
[157] *R. v. Smith* [1979] 3 All ER 605, 611.

PART TWO THE DEVELOPMENT OF THE DEFENCE

INTRODUCTION

As already noted in Part One, where the *actus reus* of a crime requires an act, it seems to have been accepted as a fundamental principle of the criminal law in common law jurisdictions that the accused must be proved to have performed the act in question voluntarily.[158] Older examples of involuntary action tend to take the form of physical compulsion by another, as where A seizes B's hand and with it strikes C.[159] Here the assault can not be said to have resulted from B's act, as he has merely been used as an innocent but physically coerced agent through which A has been able to commit the offence. Cases of this nature seem easy to solve and there seems little need for the concept of automatism to deal with them. However, other factual situations such as spasms and reflex actions raise the question of 'conscious' automatism which will be dealt with later in this Chapter.

The fact that a person's act may be involuntary without any physical compulsion has not figured much historically,[160] and the plea known as automatism, which usually consists of a plea of unconscious involuntary action, is of comparatively recent origin. Although the origin of the word 'automatism' as applied to the criminal law is difficult to trace, its sudden appearance in the 1950s seems to have reflected the courts' increasing awareness of the practical need for a voluntary act before an accused could be convicted. The word itself has been described judicially as 'a modern catchphrase which the courts have not accepted as connoting any wider or looser concept than involuntary movement of the body or limbs of a person'.[161] The use of the term and connected concepts such as 'unconsciousness' and 'involuntary' have been criticised as being 'plainly inaccurate', such terms being used as 'mere code words to trigger a desired legal outcome'.[162] This may well be so, but as long as the desired legal outcome is forthcoming, which again is questionable, then there may be no real need for a change of terminology. At any rate, the courts certainly continue to use these words and to regard the plea of automatism as a defence which may in certain circumstances lead to an outright acquittal.

---

[158] There has been a certain amount of dispute concerning the classification of this element. Should voluntariness be regarded as forming part of the *actus reus* or the *mens rea* of an offence? This is a question which could, at least in theory, have important implications, although it has been suggested that the classification 'is a matter of convenience only'. See J.C. Smith and B. Hogan, *Criminal Law* (7th edn. Butterworths, London, 1992), 39.

[159] See M. Hale, 1 Pleas of the Crown (1736) Vol 1, 434.

[160] N. Walker, *Crime and Insanity in England, Vol 1* (Edinburgh University Press, Edinburgh, 1968), 165–73, gives a brief historical survey.

[161] *Watmore* v. *Jenkins* [1962] 2 QB 572, 586 per Winn J.

[162] H. Fingarette, 'Diminished Mental Capacity as a Criminal Law Defence' (1974) 37 MLR 264, 271.

It is this possibility of outright acquittal which has led the courts, for policy reasons, to restrict the application of the plea of automatism, and to introduce a distinction between 'sane' and 'insane' automatism. The development of this distinction will now be considered, following which there will be an analysis of the problems which it has caused.

THE METAMORPHOSIS OF AUTOMATISM

As has frequently been pointed out, a defence based on a phrase such as 'I had a black-out' or 'I was asleep' would at first sight seem to be a formidable obstacle for the prosecution.[163] To resolve this problem the courts have found it necessary to control this type of defence strictly, but in so doing they have encountered difficulties. The most obvious method of control is to reject the existence of any separate defence of automatism which may lead to an outright acquittal. Until recently, this was the position in Scotland, where all forms of automatism were classed as legal insanity.[164] However, in *Ross* v. *HM Advocate*[165] the High Court of Justiciary has now decided to abandon this approach in favour of recognition of a sane automatism plea which can result in an unqualified acquittal.

The first reported case in England to use the word 'automatism' appears to be *R.* v. *Harrison-Owen*[166] which is concerned with the admissibility of evidence. The facts were that the accused, having been charged with burglary, set up a defence of automatism. In order to rebut this defence, the prosecution were allowed to cross-examine the accused regarding his previous convictions. The Court of Criminal Appeal quashed the accused's conviction on the ground that the nature of the defence did not justify such cross-examination.[167] This decision has been heavily criticised,[168] and it must be conceded that it may be inexpedient, for if the prosecution are to have any chance of rebutting a concocted defence of this nature, then surely such cross-examination is of great value.[169]

Shortly after *Harrison-Owen* there appeared the two important decisions of *R.* v. *Charlson*[170] and *R.* v. *Kemp*.[171] In *Charlson* the accused was acquitted of aggravated assault on the ground that he was suffering from a cerebral tumour which made him liable to outbursts of uncontrollable violence. The issue of insanity was not raised by the defence and the

---

[163] G. Williams, *Criminal Law: The General Part* London (2nd edn., 1961), 482.

[164] See R.D. Mackay, 'The Automatism Defence—What Price Rejection?' (1983) 34 *Northern Ireland Legal Quarterly* 81.

[165] 1991 SLT 564.   [166] [1951] 2 All ER 726.

[167] Namely lack of a voluntary act which negatived *actus reus* rather than *mens rea*.

[168] *Bratty* v. *A-G for Northern Ireland* [1963] AC 386, 410 per Lord Denning; R. Cross, 'Reflections on Bratty's Case' (1962), 78 LQR 236, 243.

[169] Williams, *Criminal Law* (2nd edn.), 15.   [170] [1955] 1 All ER 859.

[171] [1957] 1 QB 399.

medical evidence was to the effect that the accused at the time of the assault was not suffering from a disease of the mind. Barry J in his direction to the jury said: 'if he did not know what he was doing, if his actions were purely automatic and his mind had no control over the movement of his limbs, if he was in the same position as a person in an epileptic fit and no responsibility rests on him at all, then the proper verdict is "not guilty".'[172] In *Kemp* the facts were of a similar nature in that the accused struck his wife with a hammer whilst he was suffering from arteriosclerosis. All the medical witnesses agreed that at the time of the assault the accused did not know what he was doing. However, the same witnesses could not agree as to whether the accused's condition constituted a disease of the mind within the M'Naghten Rules.[173] The defence argued that although the accused's conduct was due to a defect of reason, he was not suffering from a disease of the mind, but from a purely organic or physical illness and should therefore be given an unqualified acquittal, as was Charlson. Devlin J rejected this argument and, by emphasising the use of the word 'mind' as opposed to 'brain' in the M'Naghten Rules,[174] concluded that the law 'is not concerned with the origin of the disease or the cause of it but simply with the mental condition which has brought about the act'.[175] The evidence of automatism was therefore regarded as evidence of insanity and the jury were directed to return a special verdict. His Lordship distinguished *Charlson* on the basis that there the doctors were agreed that the accused was not suffering from a disease of the mind, but this was not so in *Kemp*. In truth, however, the two decisions appear to be irreconcilable and modern opinion has definitely come down in favour of the approach adopted in *Kemp*.[176] This decision heralded the creation of the distinction between sane and insane automatism, a dichotomy which has continued to cause considerable problems to the courts.

Two of the most important early cases to establish this dichotomy were *R. v. Cottle*[177] and *Bratty v. Attorney-General for Northern Ireland*.[178] *Cottle*, a decision of the New Zealand Court of Appeal, contains one of the earliest but nonetheless thorough discussions of automatism. Here the accused was convicted of three offences, a defence of epileptic automatism having been raised on his behalf. The two relevant grounds of appeal were: (1) that the trial judge had failed to give an adequate direction as to the nature of the defence of automatism; (2) that in stating that the onus of

---

[172] [1955] 1 All ER 859, 864.

[173] For full discussion of the Rules, see Chapter 2.

[174] For criticism of this approach and discussion of the intriguing notion of 'split-second insanity', see P. Fenwick, 'Brain, Mind and Behaviour—Some Medico-legal Aspects' (1993) 163 *British Journal of Psychiatry* 565.   [175] [1957] 1 QB 399, 407.

[176] See *Bratty v. A-G for Northern Ireland* [1963] AC 386, 412 per Lord Denning; *R. v. Sullivan* [1983] 2 All ER 673, 677 per Lord Diplock.

[177] [1958] NZLR 999.   [178] [1963] AC 368.

proving automatism rested on the accused the judge had made an error in law. In delivering his judgment Gresson P defined 'automatism' as: 'action without conscious volition . . . in short doing something without knowledge of it, and without memory of afterwards of having done it—a temporary eclipse of consciousness that nevertheless leaves the patient so affected able to exercise bodily movements. In such a case, the action is one which the mind in its normal functioning does not control'.[179] The President then went on to explain the distinction between insane and non-insane automatism concluding that, 'what are known as the M'Naghten Rules can have no application unless there is some form of "disease of the mind", which is not necessarily present in all cases of automatism'; and similarly, 'it is important in any case where automatism is put forward as negativing criminal responsibility that it should be determined whether the case is one in which a finding of insanity would be permissible; this can be only if mental disease in some form or other is present'.[180]

In *Bratty* the accused strangled an eighteen-year old girl whom he had given a lift in his car. He then removed the body and left it by the side of the road. On being arrested he openly admitted what he had done, his only explanation being that 'a terrible feeling' came over him.[181] At the accused's trial for murder, his counsel asked the jury to find 'one of three separate and completely independent verdicts'.[182]

The first and proper verdict, it was submitted, was 'not guilty' on the ground of automatism by reason of the fact that Bratty was suffering from psychomotor epilepsy. The second was 'not guilty' of murder but 'guilty' of manslaughter, since even if he was not in a state of automatism, 'his mental condition was so impaired and confused, and he was so deficient in reason' that he was incapable of forming the necessary intent.[183] The final verdict which counsel asked the jury to consider was that of insanity. McVeigh J refused to leave the first two issues to the jury and the accused was convicted of murder. His appeals to the Court of Criminal Appeal and the House of Lords challenging this refusal were both dismissed.

In arriving at its decision the House of Lords elaborated on the distinction between insane and non-insane automatism, the former being where the accused's condition was caused by a 'disease of the mind' within the M'Naghten Rules, the latter where it was not so caused. In *Bratty*, the medical evidence, which was not particularly strong, pointed only towards insanity. It followed, therefore, that the trial judge was under no duty to direct the jury on the issue of non-insane automatism, since it was not possible to treat the same set of facts as constituting insanity and then at one and the same time treat them as supporting non-insane automatism.

---

[179] [1985] NZLR 999, 1007.   [180] Ibid.
[181] [1963] AC 386, 389.   [182] Ibid.   [183] Ibid.

Viscount Kilmuir LC put it emphatically as follows: 'in my opinion . . . where the only cause alleged for the unconsciousness is a defect of reason from disease of the mind, and that cause is rejected by the jury, there can be no room for the alternative defence of automatism'.[184]

This statement of the law was in reply to the argument put forward by counsel for the appellant, that despite the medical evidence, automatism ought still to have been left to the jury. In support of this contention counsel relied heavily[185] on the following statement by North J in *Cottle*: 'in cases like the present one where the form of the plea is that the prisoner acted unconsciously—in a state of automatism—the rejection of the evidence that he was suffering from a disease of the mind does not wholly dispose of the defence for it is still possible, though perhaps unlikely, that the jury may not be completely satisfied that the act was the conscious and intended act of the prisoner'.[186] In response to this Viscount Kilmuir commented: 'if by this passage North J meant to imply that in every case where insanity is raised, automatism must always be left to the jury as a defence, I should, with respect, be unable to accept what he says as a correct statement of the law'.[187]

Now it seems obvious that this is not what North J meant. Instead, in the Lord Chancellor's view, 'the learned judge was only considering the situation where there was positive evidence which would justify a finding by the jury that the accused acted in a state of automatism'.[188] It has been suggested that Viscount Kilmuir's interpretation of *Cottle* 'cannot be sustained'.[189] The main point at issue here is whether it is always proper to exclude automatism from the consideration of the jury when the medical evidence points exclusively to the existence of a disease of the mind. It has been contended that such an approach is incorrect; for whereas the Lord Chancellor considered that before automatism could be left to the jury there must be some evidence of unconsciousness arising from a condition other than a disease of the mind, it is arguable that, if the accused raises the issue of unconsciousness and has laid a proper foundation for it, then the judge must leave automatism to the jury even if all the evidence points towards a disease of the mind.[190] Failure to do this may mean that a jury could convict the accused even though they were not satisfied that he was conscious at the relevant time.[191] However compelling such an argument may be, it does not appear to have found favour with the courts.[192]

---

[184] [1963] AC 386, 403–4.   [185] Ibid. 394–5.   [186] [1958] NZLR 999, 1036.
[187] [1963] AC 386, 404–5.   [188] Ibid. 405.
[189] I.D. Elliot, 'Automatism and Trial by Jury' (1967) 6 *Melbourne University Law Review* 53,71.
[190] Ibid.   [191] Ibid. 65.
[192] An exception could be New Zealand, where in *R. v. Burr* [1969] NZLR 736, 746 Turner J commented: 'whether a defence of automatism can ever in any circumstances be raised by evidence exclusively relating to a disease of the mind is perhaps a difficult question.

It is clear that the distinction between insane and non-insane automatism is not a happy one. It has been described as 'clumsy and complex',[193] and even the terminology appears to be ill-founded in that it tends to confuse two separate issues, namely those of automatism and insanity. For insane automatism must necessarily entail a plea of insanity within the first limb of the M'Naghten Rules,[194] and it seems unnecessary to label this as a type of automatism unless there is some good reason for doing so. One such reason would be to equate the two issues as regards burden of proof, but this did not happen in *Bratty*. As a result, trial judges may be faced with explaining a very delicate distinction to the jury, for *Bratty* in no way precludes the possibility of both insanity and automatism being left to the jury.[195] Where this occurs the result can only be a direction of considerable complexity,[196] which may, and often does, lead to an appeal.[197]

The law, however, must be applied as it stands, and what the courts have been able to achieve in cases like *Kemp* and *Bratty* is a dual means by which to control the defence of automatism which, if left unchecked, could obviously be abused. One such method of control is inextricably linked with the question of burden of proof and is simply achieved by placing an evidential burden upon the accused. What this amounts to is that until a 'proper foundation' is laid by the accused, the defence need not be left to the jury.[198] Rarely, if ever, therefore will it be sufficient for the accused to say 'I had a blackout', for there must be some medical evidence available from which such a condition can be reasonably inferred.[199] This type of controlling factor has been used consistently by the courts in order to distinguish the genuine case from the fraudulent one.

It might at first sight be thought to have been disposed of by "dicta" in the judgments of Lord Kilmuir and of Lord Denning in the House of Lords in *Bratty* v. *A–G for Northern Ireland* [1963] AC 386; [1961] 3 All ER 523. There is some difference in the headnotes in the two reports which I have mentioned, and it seems to me that it may be still the subject of some uncertainty whether in England a plea of automatism will lie, based exclusively on a diagnosis of a disease of the mind of a degree insufficient to lead to a verdict of acquittal on the ground of insanity. To go as far as this in this country appears to me to present some difficulties in principle; but it is unnecessary to decide the point in this case.' But in the same case, North P accepts the distinction made in *Bratty* without any dissent (ibid. 744). Cf. *R.* v. *Roulston* [1976] 2 NZLR 644 where the following statement of North J in *R.* v. *Cottle* [1958] NZLR 999, 1029 was cited with approval: 'I think the trial judge was obliged also to deal with the case on the assumption that the jury might be of opinion that it had not been shown that the prisoner was suffering from a disease of the mind, for this in the final result is within the province of the jury.' As is pointed out by Elliot, 'Automatism and Trial by Jury', 71, when Viscount Kilmuir in *Bratty* quoted the relevant passage of North J's judgment, he omitted this section.

[193] Hart, 'Punishment and Responsibility' 253.
[194] (1843) 10 Cl & F at 210.   [195] [1963] AC 386, 403 and 413.
[196] See e.g. *R.* v. *Pantelic* (1973) 21 *Federal Law Reports* 253.
[197] See e.g *R.* v. *Stripp* (1978) 69 Cr App R 318.
[198] *Bratty* v. *A–G for Northern Ireland* [1963] AC 386, 405.
[199] *Cook* v. *Atchison* [1968] Crim LR 266.

The second method of control was introduced by Devlin J in *Kemp*[200] where, by using a wide definition of what constitutes a 'disease of the mind' within the M'Naghten Rules, his Lordship was able to ensure that the only defence available to the accused was one of insanity, thus avoiding the result reached in *Charlson*, namely an unqualified acquittal. In *Bratty* Lord Denning alone commented on the apparent conflict between *Charlson* and *Kemp* and in doing so he favoured the opinion of Devlin J stating that 'any mental disorder which has manifested itself in violence and is prone to recur is a disease of the mind. At any rate it is the sort of disease for which a person should be detained in hospital rather than be given an unqualified acquittal.'[201] This last sentence adequately sums up the policy reasons for extending the definition of 'disease of the mind' to include diseases which are purely organic or physical in nature, namely the need to protect society from certain types of mentally abnormal offender whilst at the same time recognising that if such a person is found insane then he is irresponsible and cannot be 'punished'—hence the inevitable special verdict of 'not guilty by reason of insanity'.

However, at the same time, a conflicting principle had begun to develop which recognised the need to control the scope of 'disease of the mind' so that certain types of condition might be excluded where it would be 'an affront to common sense' to declare such a person 'insane'.[202] This principle has been instrumental in the development of the 'sane' automatism defence and indeed it is this development, and the unqualified acquittal that it brings, which has regularly caused the judiciary to consider whether particular mental conditions should be classed as 'diseases of the mind'. This in turn has led the courts to create a distinction between internal and external factors which in many respects is indicative of the conflict mentioned above, in that the courts have sought a pragmatic solution to the question of which of these two principles should be permitted to dominate and thereby shape the development of the automatism defence.

PART THREE THE DEFENCE IN OPERATION

THE 'EXTERNAL FACTOR DOCTRINE'

There is no doubt that the major influence on the distinction between insane and non-insane automatism has been the development of what may be conveniently termed the 'external factor doctrine'. The case which, more than any other, was responsible for the creation of this doctrine is that of *R. v. Quick*[203] where the Court of Appeal traced the doctrine's

---

[200] [1957] 1 QB 399.   [201] [1963] AC 386, 412.
[202] *R. v. Quick* [1973] 3 All ER 347, 352 per Lawton LJ.   [203] [1973] 3 All ER 347.

evolution back to the 1950s. In this case Quick, a diabetic male nurse, was prosecuted for assaulting a disabled patient and causing him actual bodily harm. Evidence showed that at the time of the assault the accused was in a confused mental condition which was consistent with his suffering from hypoglycaemia. In addition there was evidence to the effect that, after his routine morning injection of insulin but before the assault, the accused had eaten little food and had drunk a quantity of alcohol. The accused pleaded not guilty, relying on automatism as a defence. The trial judge, however, ruled that the evidence given could only support a plea of insanity, where-upon the accused changed his plea to guilty. On appeal it was held that the wide definition of 'disease of the mind' as laid down by Devlin J in *Kemp* and reiterated by Lord Denning in *Bratty* should be modified since it would be an affront to common sense to send a diabetic, who had simply suffered from a low blood sugar reaction, to be detained in a mental hospital. But, if the wide definition were applied without qualifica-tion, a defendant such as Quick would set up a defence of insanity. In order, therefore, 'that the law should not give the words "defect of reason from a disease of the mind" a meaning which would be regarded with incredulity outside a court',[204] it was decided that, before a defence of insanity could be successful, the accused must show a malfunctioning of mind caused by disease. According to Lawton LJ: 'a malfunctioning of the mind of transitory effect caused by the application to the body of some external factor such as violence, drugs, including anaesthetics, alcohol and hypnotic influences cannot fairly be said to be due to disease'.[205] Quick's alleged condition was attributable not to his diabetes but to the use of insulin and thus it followed that he was entitled to have his defence of automatism left to the jury, since the malfunctioning of his mind had been caused by an external factor.

The decision in *Quick* has met with the criticism that the use of the 'external factor doctrine' was unnecessary and 'creates arbitrary distinc-tions'.[206] Despite this criticism, the doctrine has continued to be influential. It was referred to with approval by Lord Diplock in *R. v. Sullivan*[207] when he made it clear that an acquittal on the basis of non-insane automatism might arise 'in cases where temporary impairment not being self-induced by consuming drink or drugs, results from some external physical factor such as a blow on the head or the administration of an anaesthetic for therapeutic purposes'.[208]

What follows is a discussion of some of the ramifications of the 'external factor doctrine' within the context of two broad categories of condition, namely the organic and the non-organic. A good deal has been written

---

[204] [1973] 3 All ER 347, 353.   [205] Ibid. 356.
[206] G. Williams, *Textbook of Criminal Law* (2nd edn., Stevens, London, 1983), 671.
[207] [1983] 2 All ER 673.   [208] Ibid. at 678.

recently about the medico-legal aspects of automatism.[209] Although it is not proposed to repeat that discussion but merely to comment upon it where appropriate, it may nevertheless be useful to mention some of the major types of condition which have been used to support a defence of automatism. Obvious examples of organic conditions, which have been considered by the courts,[210] include: cerebral concussion,[211] epilepsy,[212] imbalance in blood sugar causing hypoglycaemia,[213] or hyperglycaemia,[214] the effects of alcohol and/or drugs,[215] and the effects of conditions such as a brain tumour,[216] or arteriosclerosis.[217] With regard to non-organic conditions both sleepwalking,[218] and emotional or psychological blow automatism,[219] have troubled the courts.

ORGANIC CONDITIONS

As already mentioned, a great many organic conditions can cause cerebral impairment leading to involuntary action.[220] Some may result from the type of clear external physical factors described above by Lord Diplock in *Sullivan*, while others may be purely internal as in the case of a spontaneous epileptic seizure. But often it is not so straightforward; there may be a number of interrelated factors involved. The criminal law has not only been reluctant to recognise this, but also has failed to develop any clear principles to deal with such problems.[221]

For example, in the epilepsy cases medication may often be a factor which could have influenced the onset of a seizure. Indeed, in one unreported case, an epileptic defendant was acquitted of murdering his mother having put forward an automatism defence; the basis of the defence was medical evidence to the effect that the accused's automatism had been caused by his taking the prescribed drug maprotiline which had triggered off a latent epileptic condition.[222] It is also noteworthy that in the leading

---

[209] See in particular the excellent review by Peter Fenwick, 'Automatism, Medicine and the Law', (1990) *Psychological Medicine, Monograph Supplement* 17 (Cambridge University Press, Cambridge).

[210] See generally D. Blair, 'The Medico-legal Aspects of Automatism' (1977) *Medicine, Science and the Law* 167. For detail, see P. Fairall, 'Automatism' (1981) 5 *Criminal Law Journal* 335.   [211] *R. v. Budd* [1962] Crim LR 49; *R. v. Carter* [1959] VR 105.

[212] *R. v. Sullivan* [1983] 2 All ER 673.   [213] *R. v. Quick* [1973] 3 All ER 347.

[214] *R. v. Hennessy* [1989] 2 All ER 9.   [215] *DPP v. Majewski* [1976] 2 All ER 142.

[216] *R. v. Charlson* [1955] 1 All ER 859.   [217] *R. v. Kemp* [1957] 1 QB 399.

[218] *R. v. Burgess* [1991] 2 All ER 769.   [219] *R. v. Rabey* (1980) 15 CR (3d) 225.

[220] See Blair, 'The Medico-legal Aspects of Automatism'.

[221] See J.C. Smith and B. Hogan, *Criminal Law* (6th edn., Butterworths, London, 1988), 190–1 for one of the only attempts to discuss these problems. This section was omitted from the 7th edn. (1992), 201.

[222] The case is discussed by H. Milne, 'Epileptic Homicide: Drug Induced.' a letter to the editor in (1979) 134 *British Journal of Psychiatry* 543 and in J. Gunn and P.J. Taylor, *Forensic Psychiatry—Clinical, Legal and Ethical Issues* (Butterworth Heinemann, London 1993) 59.

epilepsy case of *Sullivan* there was mention made in the Court of Appeal of the fact that the accused had been given drugs to control his fits and that 'there were medical reasons to believe that he had not been taking the full dosage which had been prescribed for him, but this may have been due to a misunderstanding between him and the hospital'.[223] Despite what on the face of it appears to be an important external factor, the Court of Appeal chose to ignore the influence this may have had on the seizure which precipitated the alleged assault. Further, the House of Lords in confirming that epilepsy must in law be regarded as a disease of the mind failed to make any mention of the issue. The only conclusion which can be drawn from this is that the classification of epileptic automatism as of the insane variety cannot be avoided by an application of the 'external factor doctrine'. Strictly speaking, therefore, all such cases should lead to a special verdict, unless as occurred in *Sullivan* the accused is permitted to plead guilty in order to avoid this. The only alternative would be for a court to ignore completely the obvious impact of *Sullivan*: this apparently happened during the trial of Sandra Mcfarlane who was prosecuted for assaulting a police officer while the police were unsuccessfully searching her flat for stolen goods. The trial judge in what appears to have been open defiance of the House of Lords' ruling in *Sullivan* directed the jury to acquit if it considered that the defendant had so acted during an epileptic seizure, having accepted medical evidence that psychiatrists no longer regarded epilepsy as a disease of the mind.[224] This last point is of course most unconvincing, as the appellate courts have frequently emphasised that the question of disease of the mind is a question of law which is not to be determined solely by psychiatric testimony. However, what the *Mcfarlane* case does unquestionably demonstrate is the dissatisfaction with *Sullivan* felt by at least one member of the judiciary.[225]

Naturally, the fact that a member of the judiciary feels compelled to refuse to follow a House of Lords' ruling which was applicable in the case in question is hardly a cause for satisfaction. Clearly the problem faced by epileptics when pleading automatism stems from the 'external factor doctrine', which on the face of it seems to have been applied more leniently to diabetics. Certainly in *Quick* Lawton LJ was not prepared to send a diabetic to hospital when his hypoglycaemic condition could be rectified by merely pushing a lump of sugar into his mouth. In order to avoid such a result his Lordship concluded that Quick's 'mental condition . . . was not caused by his diabetes but by his use of insulin . . . such malfunctioning of mind as there was, was caused by an external factor and not by a bodily

---

[223] [1983] 1 All ER 577, 579.   [224] *Guardian*, 11 September 1990, 3.
[225] A great deal of dissatisfaction was expressed after the decision in *Sullivan* which is fully discussed in P. Fenwick and R. Fenwick (eds.), *Epilepsy and the Law—a Medical Symposium on the Current Law* (Royal Society of Medicine, London, 1985).

disorder in the nature of a disease which disturbed the working of his mind'.[226] It is difficult to accept this dictum, if only for the reason that the diabetic surely needs to take insulin because of his internal organic condition, namely the diabetes. The two factors clearly interrelate with one another and cannot be separated in the manner suggested. However, it can be argued that in a case like *Quick* the insulin could have been the primary cause of the hypoglycaemia, in the sense that the automatism would not have occurred without an overdose of this drug. Indeed, this line of reasoning has recently led the Court of Appeal in *R. v. Hennessy*[227] to confirm that if the automatism can be traced to the accused's diabetes rather than to a distinct external factor then the condition in question must be classed as a disease of the mind.

The facts of *Hennessy* were that the accused pled guilty to one count of taking a conveyance and another count of driving while disqualified, following a ruling by the trial judge on his defence of automatism. The accused had given evidence that he had been a diabetic for about ten years for which he required two insulin injections daily. At the time of the offences he claimed to be under considerable stress as a result of marital and employment problems. He was upset, had not been eating, and had not taken his insulin. The defendant's doctor gave evidence, describing his patient's condition as hyperglycaemia resulting from high blood sugar levels which could cause drowsiness, loss of consciousness, and eventually coma. This evidence was corroborated by hospital notes from the evening of the offence which showed that the defendant's blood sugar level was more than twice the normal level. In addition, the GP testified that 'the blood sugar level tends to be increased in the ordinary diabetic by any trauma or psychological stress' with the result he 'might not be clear about what he was doing; he might be a bit befuddled'.[228] As a result the defence argued that the defendant was entitled to an acquittal on the basis of automatism. The response of the trial judge was a ruling that the alleged mental condition was caused by disease, namely diabetes, and that the proper defence in law was one of insanity. This was the sole reason for the change of plea to guilty and the reason for the appeal.

In the course of his argument, counsel for the appellant relied upon *Quick*, where, it will be recalled, the Court of Appeal had concluded that a hypoglycaemic episode which was caused by insulin was not to be regarded in law as a disease of the mind since it 'was caused by an external factor and not by a bodily disorder in the nature of a disease', namely his diabetes. Accordingly, it was argued in *Hennessy* 'that the appellant's depression and marital troubles were a sufficiently potent external factor in his condition to override, so to speak, the effect of the diabetic shortage

[226] [1973] 3 All ER 347, 356.   [227] [1989] 2 All ER 9.   [228] Ibid. 11.

of insulin upon him'.[229] The response of the court was to reject this argument by emphasising the need for the requirement stated by Lord Diplock in *Sullivan*, namely 'some external physical factor'. In the judgment of the Court of Appeal, therefore, 'stress, anxiety and depression can no doubt be the result of the operation of external factors, but they are not in themselves separately or together external factors of the kind capable in law of causing or contributing to a state of automatism. They constitute a state of mind which is prone to recur'.[230]

The implications of this judgment are of considerable importance for the defence of automatism. First, it emphasises that what constitutes an external factor sufficient to take a defence of automatism into the sane variety is a question of law primarily governed by policy considerations. In this connection it is interesting to note that Lord Lane CJ considered that: 'the burden of the argument of counsel to us is this. It is that the appellant's depression and marital troubles were a sufficiently potent external factor to override, so to speak, the effect of the diabetic shortage of insulin on him'.[231] The use of the word 'potent' in this context seems especially important in that it suggests that the external factor must be not only novel or accidental but also satisfy some other legal requirement in the sense of strength or robustness. The precise nature of such a requirement and how it is to be judged will be discussed in the next section as it has been the subject of considerable judicial comment within the area of non-organic automatism.

However, to return to diabetes. The distinction between hypoglycaemia and hyperglycaemia was further confirmed by the Court of Appeal in *R. v. Bingham*.[232] The facts of the case were that the defendant, a long-standing diabetic, was convicted of shoplifting after the trial judge had refused to leave his defence of hypoglycaemic automatism to the jury. In allowing the appeal Lord Lane CJ concluded that the arguments put to the trial judge had failed to distinguish between hyperglycaemia and hypoglycaemia. The former might raise difficult problems about the M'Naghten rules, while the latter 'was not caused by the initial disease of diabetes, but by treatment in the form of too much insulin, or by insufficient quality or quantity of food to counter-balance the insulin. Generally speaking, that would not give rise to a verdict of not guilty by reason of insanity'.[233] Accordingly, because in the present case the problem was hypoglycaemia, the defence of non-insane automatism should have been left to the jury.

Two points concerning *Bingham* deserve comment. First, the court seems to accept that the hypoglycaemia leading to a successful plea of non-insane

---

[229] [1989] 2 All ER 9, 14.   [230] Ibid.   [231] Ibid.
[232] [1991] Crim LR 433.   [233] Ibid. 433.

automatism could arise not only from insulin but also from insulin combined with dietary factors. This in itself is nothing new, as Lawton LJ had to consider both the effects of alcohol and failure to eat regularly in *Quick*. However, in both *Bingham* and *Quick* there was clear evidence of the effects of insulin which enabled the courts safely to conclude that the automatism was caused by this external factor rather than primarily attributable to the diabetes, which is obviously internal. Similarly in *R.* v. *Bailey*[234] the basis of the accused's automatism defence was 'hypoglycaemia caused by his failure to take sufficient food following his last dose of insulin'.[235] In all these cases, therefore, the external factor of insulin could be seen to be a relevant causal agent in the ensuing automatism. What this means is that if the diabetic is fortunate enough to have taken insulin, then he may escape a ruling that his condition was a disease of the mind while his diabetic counterpart who fails to take his insulin and does not stick to a proper diet faces the prospect of being found legally insane if he proceeds with an automatism defence.

This conclusion flows from the argument that if a hypoglycaemic episode resulted purely from a failure to eat enough, then the lack of any external factor ought to lead to a ruling in favour of insanity, in much the same way as was achieved in *Hennessy*.[236] Indeed, this possibility is not entirely ruled out by the court in *Bingham* since it will be recalled that Lord Lane's comment about hypoglycaemia not qualifying for a special verdict began with the words 'generally speaking', which might be taken to indicate that exceptionally such a condition might be classified as insane automatism if no external causal factor could be found. However, it is worth noting that these discussions of hypoglycaemia have all been concerned with diabetics. Thus it might legitimately be argued that if a diabetic like *Hennessy* can qualify for an insanity verdict because of his disease, then so ought his hypoglycaemic counterpart should the automatism likewise be caused by the diabetes rather than insulin.

However, in this context, it must be pointed out that hypoglycaemia is not suffered only by diabetics but may occur in otherwise normal people.[237] Indeed, this is exactly what happened in *R.* v. *Toner*[238] where in answer to charges of attempted murder and wounding with intent to cause grievous bodily harm, the accused put forward an automatism defence, the basis of which was hypoglycaemia resulting from the ingestion of carbohydrates after a long period of fasting. There was no suggestion of diabetes but instead expert evidence was given about the effects of starvation upon the human body's metabolism. Unfortunately the judge refused to leave

---

[234] [1983] 2 All ER 503.   [235] Ibid. 506.
[236] See Williams, *Textbook of Criminal Law* (2nd edn.), 671–2.
[237] See Blair, 'The Medico-legal Aspects of Automatism', 179; Williams ibid. 671 n. 5.
[238] (1991) 93 Cr App R 382.

the automatism defence to the jury owing to the fact that he considered the evidential burden had not been satisfied. This meant that the question of deciding whether such a condition should be classed as a disease of the mind did not have to be answered. However, it is by no means clear what the correct answer would be in this type of case; for unless the ingestion of carbohydrates is to be regarded as an external factor, it is difficult to see why the hypoglycaemia should not be regarded as stemming primarily from an internal bodily malfunction of a purely temporary nature. Naturally, it would be the height of absurdity to conclude that an otherwise healthy and normal person should be regarded as legally insane should he be unfortunate enough to suffer from hypoglycaemia after fasting.[239] However, a blind adherence to the 'external factor doctrine' leads one into the danger of producing just such a result. Certainly, in the light of *Hennessy* and *Bingham* it now seems beyond doubt that automatism caused by insulinoma of the pancreas would fall within the insane variety.[240]

Of course the obvious distinction between such an example and the facts of *Toner* is that in the latter case there was no disease present and it can only be hoped that this common sense type of argument would be accepted by the court in much the same way as it was applied by Lawton LJ in *Quick* when he said: 'no mental hospital would admit a diabetic merely because he had a low blood sugar reaction; and common sense is affronted by the prospect of a diabetic being sent to such a hospital when in most cases the disordered mental condition can be rectified quickly by pushing a lump of sugar or a teaspoonful of glucose into the patient's mouth.[241] However, this remark must now be read in the light of *Hennessy* where Lord Lane CJ did not share the same reluctance at the prospect of sending a diabetic with a high blood sugar reaction to hospital.[242] Instead, he considered that the hyperglycaemia was 'caused by an inherent defect' which should have been controlled by regular injections of insulin.[243] However, the emphasis on the presence of a disease would seem to be the obvious distinction between the abnormal mental conditions in *Toner* and

---

[239] Cf. *State v. Stellmacher* 1983 2 SA 181 where D had been on a diet for a number of weeks and on the day of the alleged murder had performed hard physical labour, had nothing to eat, but had consumed alcohol. There was led expert evidence of hypoglycaemia and/or epilepsy which, it was suggested, had been triggered off by a combination of lack of food, alcohol, and the effect of the sun's reflection through an empty bottle. As a result D was acquitted on the basis of sane automatism.

[240] See Fenwick, 'Automatism, Medicine and the Law', 9.

[241] [1973] 3 All ER 347, 352.

[242] Since the enactment of the Criminal Procedure (Insanity and Unfitness to Plead) Act 1991 flexibility of disposal is now available for all those successfully plead insanity, except those whose defence is the result of a murder charge. This means that defendants like Hennessy and Sullivan need no longer be the subject of an order requiring their indefinite hospitalisation. However, the stigma of the term 'insanity' remains. For full discussion of the 1991 Act, see Chapter Two.   [243] [1989] 2 All ER 9, 14.

Hennessy. If this is correct, then it may still be possible to argue that in the case of an otherwise normal person a lack of food bringing on hypoglycaemia ought in principle to be classed as automatism of the non-insane variety despite the fact that there is no external factor present. Of course if a sudden intake of food is the precipitating factor of the hypoglycaemia as seems to have been the case in *Toner*, then it may be possible to argue that the ingestion of carbohydrates constitutes an external physical factor. Whether such an argument could succeed would seem to depend upon two related factors. The first concerns the nature of the external factor itself which, according to the Lord Chief Justice in *Hennessy*, must contain 'the feature of novelty or accident'.[244] Although it is by no means clear what his Lordship meant by this phrase, there is certainly an argument that the ordinary ingestion of food is neither novel nor accidental. Unless of course the word 'novel' is to be interpreted in connection with the abnormal physical condition of the accused which is the result of his fast. However, this in itself leads to the second factor, namely that in a case like *Toner* the accused has, as result of his fast, reacted abnormally or in a novel way to an external factor which can only be described as ordinary, namely the everyday occurrence of eating. Such an external factor can hardly be described as 'a sufficiently potent external factor', especially as the accused would seem to have demonstrated an abnormal reaction or peculiar susceptibility to what is for everyone a common experience. With regard to this particular point the courts have certainly been prepared to rule out ordinary stress as being capable of constituting an external factor, and it may be that the arguments used in that connection could be applied to a case like *Toner*. In order to explore this matter further, it is now time to turn to an examination of the second broad category of automatism, namely the non-organic variety.

Non-Organic Automatism[245]

While there is no doubt that a defendant may be able to secure an acquittal if at the time of the alleged offence his actions were unconscious and involuntary as a result of the type of organic condition discussed above, the question of whether such a defence may also be open to defendants whose conditions can only be traced to a purely hysterical or emotional cause has only recently begun to trouble the courts. In this connection the problem of what may be conveniently referred to as non-organic automatism is of special interest in that it starkly demonstrates some of the major tensions surrounding the recognition of new forms of automatism.

---

[244] [1989] 2 All ER 9, 14.
[245] See R.D. Mackay, 'Non-Organic Automatism—Some Recent Developments' [1980] Crim LR 350.

The term most commonly used by the medical profession to cover disturbances of consciousness from non-organic causes is 'dissociation'. This term is defined in the Glossary of Mental Disorders as follows: 'The most prominent feature is a narrowing of the field of consciousness that seems to serve an unconscious purpose; it is commonly accompanied or followed by selective amnesia. There may be dramatic but essentially superficial changes of personality sometimes taking the form of a fugue. Behaviour may mimic psychosis, or rather the patient's idea of psychosis.'[245] The most important condition linked with dissociation is hysterical neurosis, which when of the dissociative type may take various forms including somnambulism, fugues, twilight states, fits, and amnesia, each of which may give rise to a state of altered consciousness.

Sleepwalking[246]

If a defendant raises the issue of non-organic automatism, is it to be regarded in law as being of the sane or insane variety? With regard to somnambulism this question has recently been addressed by the Court of Appeal in the important case of *R. v. Burgess*,[247] where once again heavy reliance was placed upon the external factor doctrine. Although prior to *Burgess* no English appellate case had directly answered this question, Lord Lane CJ conceded that 'there had been several occasions during judgments in the Court of Appeal and the House of Lords when observations had been made, obiter, about the criminal responsibility of sleepwalkers, where sleepwalking had been used as a self-evident illustration of non-insane automatism'.[248] Further, it should not be forgotten that this 'self-evident' approach had in the past resulted in a number of jury acquittals, the most famous of which was probably the case of *R. v. Boshears*.[249]

However, it seems clear that the medical evidence in the present case was influential in persuading the trial judge to rule in favour of the prosecution's contention that sleepwalking was a form of insane automatism with the result that the accused was found 'not guilty by reason of insanity' and sent to a hospital as originally provided for by the Criminal Procedure (Insanity) Act 1964. The sole ground of appeal was that the trial judge's ruling was wrong.

In arriving at a decision in *Burgess*, the Court of Appeal emphasised that the fundamental question was whether the accused was suffering from a disease of the mind within the M'Naghten Rules 'rather than a defect or

---

[245] World Health Organisation, *Glossary of Mental Disorders* (Geneva 1978), 35.
[246] Aspects of sleep were discussed in Part One during the theoretical discussion of involuntary action.
[247] [1991] 2 All ER 769.   [248] Ibid. 774.
[249] *The Times*, 17 and 18 February 1961. See also the other cases described by Fenwick in 'Automatism, Medicine and the Law', 15–16.

failure of the mind not due to disease', and that this was 'a distinction, by no means always easy to draw, on which the case depends, as others have depended in the past'.[250]

The Lord Chief Justice relied on a number of important principles in upholding the trial judge's ruling in favour of insane automatism. The first was to underline the importance of the point made by Devlin J in *Kemp*[251] that the M'Naghten Rules refer to 'disease of the mind' and not 'disease of the brain'. In the context of Burgess' sleepwalking, this seems a significant fact in that the medical evidence revealed no history of head injury, epilepsy or other form of brain damage. The second principle concerned the court's attempt to distinguish between sane and insane automatism which it was decided must rest upon 'the distinction between internal and external factors'. According to his Lordship, 'the field of enquiry could be narrowed further by eliminating what were sometimes called the external factors, such as concussion caused by a blow on the head'.[252] On this basis the Court of Appeal was clearly of the opinion that there were no external factors present saying; 'Whatever the cause might have been, it was an internal cause'.[253]

Naturally, it is difficult to accept that sleepwalking does not have an internal cause. But does this mean that external factors have no role to play in the onset of such episodes? On this issue the facts surrounding the offence become important as the appellant had seriously assaulted a female friend after they had fallen asleep while watching a horror video. There was evidence that he was emotionally attached to her but that she did not feel the same way. Consequently, he was under emotional stress at the time of the assault. In dealing with this point Lord Lane said: 'the possible disappointment or frustration caused by unrequited love was not to be equated with something such as concussion'.[254] In arriving at this conclusion, Lord Lane must surely have had in mind his earlier remarks in *Hennessy*[255] concerning stress, anxiety, and depression being regarded as incapable in law of causing or contributing to a state of automatism. Accordingly, the argument which prevailed in *Burgess* was that although sleepwalking can no doubt be triggered by external factors such as stress, such factors are merely to be regarded as external triggers of a condition the primary source of which is internal to the accused.[256] At this stage then it seems to be accepted that the external factor doctrine can have no meaningful role to play as far as sleepwalking cases are concerned,

---

[250] [1991] 2 All ER 769, 773. [251] [1957] 1 QB 399, 407.
[252] [1991] 2 All ER 769, 773. [253] Ibid. [254] Ibid.
[255] [1989] 2 All ER 9, 14.
[256] Peter Fenwick, who gave expert evidence in *Burgess*, describes the position in 'Automatism, Medicine and the Law', 16–17 as follows: 'Trigger factors are important. Drugs, alcohol, excessive fatigue and stress can all precipitate a sleep automatism.'

although whether this should be true of other types of non-organic automatism is an important question which will be addressed in the next section.

However, the next point to be considered is whether, having accepted the medical evidence that sleep-associated automatism must be regarded as due to an internal factor, the court had no alternative but to conclude that Burgess was suffering from a disease of the mind. In this connection particular attention should be paid to the decision of the Ontario Court of Appeal in *R. v. Parks*[257] which was referred to by Lord Lane in *Burgess* as a case where, after full consideration of detailed medical evidence, the accused's acquittal on the basis of automatism through sleepwalking was upheld on the ground that sleep is not an abnormal condition. The only comment Lord Lane chose to make on this crucial point was as follows: 'we accept of course that sleep is a normal condition, but the evidence in the instant case indicates that sleepwalking, and particularly violence in sleep, is not normal'.[258]

What his Lordship did not do, however, was to make any assessment of the reasoning used by the Ontario Court of Appeal in arriving at its decision, which seems unfortunate in view of the fact this is the only other appellate decision, which considers sleepwalking in depth. Not only that, the novel approach adopted by the Canadian court surely deserves comment if only because it is in marked contrast to that used in *Burgess*.

In *Parks* the accused was acquitted of murder and attempted murder after the trial judge had ruled that his defence of sleepwalking was in law one of non-insane automatism. The Crown's appeal was unanimously dismissed for the following reasons. Firstly, Galligan JA, with whom the other members the court concurred, emphatically refused to classify the accused's condition as a disease of the mind despite the fact that it was 'clear on the evidence that the respondent's sleepwalking episode was not the result of some cause external to himself'.[259] Further, he concluded that:

using the meaning of the word 'mind' found in *Sullivan*, I think that a disease of the mind would exist in this case if it were shown that at the relevant time there was an illness, disorder or abnormal condition which caused impairment of the functioning of the respondent's faculties of reason, memory and understanding . . . If a disorder of sleep or the abnormal condition were the cause of the impairment . . . then the defence of insanity would have had to have been left to the jury.[260]

However, having accepted that sleep 'is a perfectly normal condition' Galligan JA then proceeded to ask whether the abnormal condition, namely

---

[257] (1990) 78 CR (3d) 1. Unanimously upheld by the Supreme Court of Canada at (1992) 95 DLR (4th) 27.   [258] [1991] 2 All ER 769, 775.
[259] (1990) 78 CR (3d) 1, 15.   [260] Ibid. 18–19.

the sleepwalking, was the *cause* of the impairment and concluded in the negative, saying:

it seems that for some reason a sleepwalker can perform very complex and to all outward appearances deliberate acts while the faculties of reason memory and understanding are not functioning. However, the condition or state of sleepwalking does not itself cause the cessation of those faculties . . . The cessation of functioning lasts throughout the sleepwalking episode. However, while the lack of function of those faculties of reason, memory and understanding coincides with the sleepwalking episode, it is not caused by it. Therefore, the disorder of sleep or the abnormal condition are not the cause of the impairment.[261]

In arriving at this conclusion Galligan JA gave full consideration to the decision in *Sullivan* and concluded that the words of Lord Diplock, namely ' "if the effect of a disease is to impair these faculties" (of reason memory and understanding)' supported the fact that 'the disease itself must be the cause of the impairment of those faculties'.[262] What is notable here is that while Lord Lane CJ quoted this very passage from *Sullivan* during the course of his judgment in *Burgess*[263] he did not see fit to comment upon its interpretation by Galligan JA. And yet the point is one of considerable importance as the M'Naghten Rules clearly require a causal connection between the 'disease of the mind' and the 'defect of reason', the result of which must be a relevant impairment of faculties of reason, memory, and understanding.

Indeed, this causal connection is at the whole root of the distinction between sane and insane automatism, in the sense that if the involuntary action in question can be traced to a cause other than a 'disease of the mind' then the accused will receive an ordinary acquittal even if he is suffering from a mental illness at the relevant time. This much was made clear as long ago as 1960 when in *Bratty* Viscount Kilmuir LC said: 'what I have said does not mean that, if a defence of insanity is raised unsuccessfully, there can never, in any conceivable circumstances, be room for an alternative defence based on automatism. For example, it may be alleged that the accused had a blow on the head, after which he acted without being conscious of what he was doing.'[264] Similarly, in *Revelle v. R.*[265] Martin JA remarked:

We do not wish to be taken, however, as holding that, where an accused is suffering from a disease of the mind, the defence of non-insane automatism can never arise. By way of example only, a person suffering from a disease of the mind might as a result of a blow on the head resulting in concussion go into an automatic state. If the jury were left in a state of doubt whether the blow on the head,

---

[261] (1990) 78 CR (3d) 1, 19–20.   [262] Ibid. 21.   [263] [1991] 2 All ER 769, 773.
[264] [1963] AC at 403.   [265] (1981) 21 CR (3d) 161,166.

as distinct from the disease of the mind, resulted in the automatism, the jury would be entitled to return a verdict of acquittal based on non-insane automatism.

Of course the example given above by Viscount Kilmuir LC and Martin JA is one where the automatism can be traced to a clear external factor which could be independent of the accused's disease of the mind, as where, for instance, a schizophrenic patient is concussed by a blow to his head inflicted by another patient. But even if his schizophrenia caused him to bang his head against the wall, the fact that the disease of the mind was causally related to the automatism does not necessarily mean that it should be removed from the non-insane category; for the primary cause of the automatism surely remains the external factor.[266]

What these illustrations further demonstrate is the need for a causal relationship between a defect of reason and a disease of the mind. Once this fundamental qualification is accepted, the reasoning of Galligan JA in *Parks* seems difficult to refute; for, unlike other conditions which result in episodes of automatism, sleepwalking is different in that the state of unconsciousness, namely sleep, precedes the automatism itself, namely somnambulism. Further, it seems beyond argument that it is sleep itself, and not sleepwalking, that is the cause of the automatism. It follows that although somnambulism necessarily occurs together with sleep, just as hyperglycaemia (as in *Hennessy*) necessarily occurs together with diabetes, the essential difference is that the hyperglycaemia itself was the major cause of the defect of reason in that case, whereas sleepwalking is an abnormal behavioural manifestation which can only occur during sleep. In short, the defect of reason can only be traced to sleep, a condition which itself, as Lord Lane expressly admitted, in *Burgess*, is 'a normal condition'.[267]

However, his Lordship then added the crucial remark: 'but the evidence in the instant case indicates that sleepwalking and particularly violence during sleep, is not normal'. This runs counter to the findings in *Parks*[268], but, even if it is accepted that violence during sleep is abnormal, it does nothing to explain how the sleepwalking, which is what Lord Lane CJ accepted here as a disease of the mind, caused a defect of reason; it might be regarded merely as an abnormal condition which coincided with sleep but did not itself cause the impairment of mental faculties, an essential prerequisite, surely, of any insanity defence. Further, while violence during sleep may not be normal, neither can violent behaviour during concussion or after an anaesthetic be regarded as normal. It is surely the *cause* of the violence which is crucial rather than the violence itself, otherwise there

---

[266] Smith and Hogan discuss the point (*Criminal Law*, 6th edn., 190–1) and are ambivalent about the correct analysis.   [267] [1991] 2 All ER 769, 775.
[268] See in particular the judgment of Brooke JA at (1990) 78 CR (3d) 1, 5–6.

would be no room for a defence of non-insane automatism after any violent automatic episode. In short, although sleepwalking may be described as abnormal, it cannot be regarded as any more abnormal than similar behaviour during concussion; which in this context may be described as 'concussion walking' in contrast to sleepwalking. And yet, in adopting Lord Denning's definition of disease of the mind from *Bratty*, namely 'any mental disorder which has manifested itself in violence', the Court of Appeal in *Burgess*[269] accepted the need for an abnormality factor but sidestepped the issue of the causal relationship between the abnormality in question and the impairment of the defendant's faculties. Instead, Lord Lane seems to have been heavily influenced by the medical evidence, commenting that 'Dr. d'Orban . . . stated it as his view that the condition would be regarded as pathological. Pathology is the science of diseases. It seems therefore that in this respect at least there is some similarity between the law and medicine'.[270] But even if one accepts that sleepwalking can properly be described as pathological, there is still the problem that the *cause* of the impairment was sleep rather than the sleepwalking itself. Nor do all pathological conditions doom the accused to an insane automatism plea: for example, the diabetic who suffered from a hypoglycaemic episode caused by too much insulin (the recent case of *Bingham* referred to earlier).[271]

So once again we are driven back to the 'external factor doctrine' upon which the decision in *Burgess* may be seen to depend. Discounting the stress involved there is no doubt that the accused's condition was 'internal' in the sense of being the result of a sleep disorder. This has led Professor Smith, in his commentary on *Burgess*, to describe the decision as 'right in principle'.[272] However, unless the requirement of a causal link between disease of the mind and defect of reason within the M'Naghten rules is to be disregarded in the case of sleepwalkers, it seems difficult to accept that a sleepwalker who is otherwise mentally normal should be classed as legally insane. Indeed, if this were so, then a person prone to sleepwalking who reacted violently during his recovery from an anaesthetic ought not in principle to fall within the category of the non-insane automaton; for the violence could only be traced to the accused's internal sleep disorder, although the sleep itself was precipitated by a clear external factor. Further, the fact that sleepwalking is not well suited to an application of the 'external factor doctrine' was fully recognised in the Supreme Court of Canada's decision in *Parks* when La Forest J remarked:

The poor fit arises because certain factors can legitimately be characterised as either internal or external sources of automatistic behaviour. For example the

---

[269] [1991] 2 All ER 769, 774.   [270] Ibid. 776.
[271] [1991] Crim LR 433.   [272] [1991] Crim LR 549.

Crown in this case argues that the causes of the respondent's violent sleepwalking were entirely internal, a combination of genetic susceptibility and the ordinary stresses of everyday life . . . However, the factors that for a waking individual are mere ordinary stresses can be differently characterised for a person who is asleep, unable to counter with his conscious mind the onslaught of the admittedly ordinary strains of life. One could argue that the particular amalgam of stress, excessive exercise, sleep deprivation and sudden noises in the night that causes an incident of som-nambulism, is for the sleeping person, analogous to the effect of concussion upon the waking person . . . In the end, the dichotomy between internal and external causes becomes blurred in this context, and is not helpful in resolving the enquiry.[273]

It is also interesting to note that the Supreme Court of Canada considered that *Burgess* could be distinguished from *Parks* on the ground that the expert evidence in each case 'was completely different',[274] in that in *Parks* 'the expert witnesses unanimously stated that at the time of the incidents the respondent was not suffering from any mental illness and that, medically speaking, sleep-walking is not regarded as an illness, whether physical, mental or neurological'.[275] This was not to say 'that sleep-walking could never be a disease of the mind, in another case on different evidence',[276] but rather that, if it were to be so, there must be evidence 'tending to show that sleep-walking was the cause of the respondent's state of mind'.[277] Thus, although the Supreme Court of Canada did not completely rule out the possibility of a finding of insanity in a different sleepwalking case, that seems unlikely for, as already mentioned, it makes little or no sense to refer to the sleepwalking as the cause of the accused's impaired mental condition.

'Psychological Blow' Automatism

Another form of non-organic automatism which has recently attracted the attention of the courts has been that of 'emotional' or 'psychological blow' automatism precipitated by shock. Recent cases show a marked inconsistency when the question of legal classification of non-organic automatism arises. As far as English law is concerned, there is little direct appellate authority. For example, in *R. v. Issitt*[278], where psychiatric testimony supported a defence based on hysterical fugue, the issue of insanity was not raised as there was no evidence to suggest that the defendant's condition was one of automatism. In short, the defendant seemed to have sufficient awareness of what he was doing to mean that an automatism defence was out of the question. However, in the more recent first instance case of *R.*

---

[273] (1992) 95 DLR (4th) 27, 48.   [274] Ibid. 38.   [275] Ibid. 35.
[276] Ibid. 40.   [277] Ibid. 39.   [278] [1978] RTR 211.

v. *T*[279], a defence of psychological blow automatism was recognised by the trial judge and left to the jury. The basis of the defence was that, as a result of being raped some three days prior to the alleged offences of robbery and assault, the accused had suffered from post-traumatic stress disorder. This had caused her to enter a dissociative state which meant that the offences were committed during a psychogenic fugue.

The trial judge in *R. v. T*, who was asked to rule on the question of whether this condition constituted a disease of the mind, pointed out that there was no authority on the question of whether rape could be regarded as an external factor. However, in deciding that this was so, Southan J stated that 'such an incident could have an appalling effect on any young woman, however well-balanced normally',[280] and that a condition of post-traumatic stress should not be regarded as a disease of the mind, even if there is a delay before the dissociative state occurs.

In arriving at this conclusion, Southan J considered the important Canadian case of *R. v. Rabey* which he felt able to distinguish.[281] In *Rabey* the defendant put forward a defence of non-insane automatism in answer to an assault charge. The facts were that Rabey (D), a university student, was infatuated by the victim (V). The day before the offence D had discovered a letter in V's handwriting stating that she found other men more exciting, and describing D as a nothing. On the day of the offence D stated that he had picked up a rock from the geology laboratory, met V by chance, and began to feel 'strange'. During the course of the conversation which followed he struck V and began to choke her. A witness described D at this time as being very pale, sweating, glassy-eyed, and having a frightened expression. D claimed he could not remember striking V. The medical witnesses disagreed as to the proper classification of D's condition. The defence psychiatrist considered that D was in a dissociative state caused by a psychological blow. This condition was not a disease of the mind and was unlikely to recur owing to the fact that D 'was a young man of average health, with no predisposition to dissociate'.[282] A psychiatrist for the prosecution, however, classified D's condition as a disease of the mind, namely a subdivision of hysterical neurosis a mental illness for which he would require treatment but on an out-patient basis.[283]

In deciding, by a bare majority, that D's condition must in law be classified as a disease of the mind, the Supreme Court of Canada adopted the reasoning of the Ontario Court of Appeal, which had reached a similar conclusion.[284] The crucial aspect of that decision concerns the 'external factor doctrine'. In the words of Martin JA speaking for the Ontario Court of Appeal:

[279] [1990] Crim LR 256.   [280] Ibid.
[281] (1980) 15 CR (3d) 225 (Supreme Court of Canada).
[282] Ibid. 241.   [283] Ibid. 242.   [284] (1978) 79 DLR (3d) 414.

the ordinary stresses and disappointments of life which are the common lot of mankind do not constitute an external cause constituting an explanation for a malfunctioning of the mind which takes it out of the category of a 'disease of the mind'. To hold otherwise would deprive the concept of an external factor of any real meaning . . . In my view . . . the dissociative state must be considered as having its source primarily in the respondent's psychological or emotional make-up. I conclude, therefore, that in the circumstances of this case, the dissociative state in which the respondent was said to be constituted a 'disease of the mind'. I leave aside, until it becomes necessary to decide them, cases where a dissociative state has resulted from emotional shock without physical injury, resulting from such causes, for example, as being involved in a serious accident although no physical injury has resulted . . . Such extraordinary events might reasonably be presumed to affect the average normal person without reference to the subjective make-up of a person exposed to such experience.[285]

The majority of the Supreme Court of Canada upheld the conclusion that D's dissociative state was a disease of the mind by pointing out that the accused's 'infatuation with this young woman had created an abnormal condition in his mind, under the influence of which he acted unnaturally and violently to an imagined slight to which a normal person would not have reacted in the same manner'.[286]

It is clear that the judgment of the majority in *Rabey* was heavily influenced by policy considerations, hence the objective requirement relating to the 'average normal person'. However, to classify an accused who is susceptible to an emotional blow as suffering from a disease of the mind while at the same time concluding that his robust counterpart who dissociates as a result of severe shock is not to be so classified seems both extreme and illogical. So much so that this reasoning led to a powerful dissent in *Rabey* based upon the unacceptability of the proposition 'that whether an automatic state is an insane reaction or a sane reaction may depend upon the intensity of the shock',[287] together with the argument that 'where the condition is transient rather than persistent, unlikely to recur, not in need of treatment and not the result of self-induced intoxication, the policy objectives served in finding such a person insane are not served'.[288] However, it has been pointed out that there is an important distinction between those who are susceptible to psychological as opposed to physical

---

[285] This passage is quoted from (1980) 15 CR (3d) 225, 233–4 where the Sepreme Court adopted Martin JA's words.
[286] Ibid. 234.   [287] Ibid. 259 per Dickson J.
[288] Ibid. 256. But cf. F. McAuley, *Insanity, Psychiatry and Criminal Responsibility* (Round Hill Press, Dublin, 1993), 77 n. 48 who argues 'the fact is that defendants who are abnormally susceptible to shock or stress are dangerous in a way that the normally susceptible defendant is not, and seem naturally to attract the insanity defence for that reason'. However, the logic of this argument must surely lead to the conclusion that a diabetic like defendant in *Quick* who is abnormally susceptible to an imbalance in blood sugar levels should likewise attract the insanity defence rather than be acquitted on the basis of sane automatism.

blows in that 'the fact of the physical blow is externally demonstrable [while] a psychological blow is an abstraction'.[289] While there is certainly some substance to this point, it brings with it the danger of undue reliance on the physical nature of the external factor, a point considered further below.

Despite these difficulties the objective requirement espoused in *Rabey* may be finding a foothold in English law.[290] Thus, in *R. v. T* it will be recalled that Southan J felt able to distinguish *Rabey* on the ground that the rape could have had an appalling effect on any well-balanced young woman. It is likely, therefore, that rape would be regarded as falling within Martin JA's 'extraordinary external events', but, even if this were not so, it is the type of incident which qualifies as an external 'physical' factor in the sense referred to by Lord Diplock in *Sullivan*. For the rape in *T* was different from the type of extreme psychological blow discussed in *Rabey*, in that T the victim was the subject of a serious sexual assault which played a causative role in the resulting dissociative state. Had T, for example, witnessed the rape of her mother or sister rather than been the subject of the rape, then the court would have been directly called upon to consider the 'extreme psychological blow' point raised in *Rabey*.

As it is, however, the English Court of Appeal in *Hennessy* and *Burgess* seems to have ruled out ordinary stress and disappointment as being legally capable of constituting an external factor. For it will be recalled that in *Hennessy* Lord Lane CJ did not regard the defendant's stress and anxiety as a 'sufficiently potent external factor', while in *Burgess* his Lordship went further when he approved of Martin JA's reasoning in *Rabey* saying 'the possible disappointment or frustration caused by unrequited love is not to be equated with something such as concussion'.[291] The reluctance of the Court of Appeal to allow this type of emotional factor to qualify as an 'external' factor for the purposes of sane automatism clearly stems from the susceptibility of the accused or, as Martin JA opined in *Rabey*, the fact that an extraordinary reaction to ordinary stress can be traced to the accused's 'psychological or emotional make-up'. From this, it can be argued that the cause must be primarily 'internal'.

The Court of Appeal in *Burgess*, therefore, seems to be using two interrelated lines of reasoning to deprive sleepwalkers of a sane automatism defence. The first is to restrict external factors to those of a physical nature, thus ensuring that stress and depression can be distinguished from

---

[289] M. Goode, 'On Subjectivity and Objectivity in Denial of Criminal Responsibility' (1987) 11 *Criminal Law Journal* 131, 143.

[290] It is approved by Smith and Hogan (*Criminal Law* (7th edn., 1992) 199–200) on the ground that a person who dissociates under ordinary stress is 'a highly dangerous person' while his robust counterpart 'has done nothing to show that he is any more dangerous to others than anyone else.'   [291] [1991] 2 All ER 769, 773.

concussion. The second is to exclude from sane automatism those defendants who are peculiarly susceptible to external factors, on the ground that
such susceptibility is to be viewed as having its source primarily in a
weakness internal to the accused.

But neither of these points, if taken on its own, will stand scrutiny. The
first would rule out psychological blow automatism irrespective of the
extraordinary nature of the shock; while Lord Lane CJ did not expressly
approve Martin JA's statement about extraordinary external events, there
is nothing to suggest that his Lordship would wish to deny that such
events might in appropriate circumstances be regarded as external factors.
To hold otherwise would be to elevate the word 'physical' in Lord Diplock's
dictum to a position of undue prominence, understanding it to refer to
something with 'tactile' physical force, that is, being raped as opposed to
watching another being raped.

The second line of reasoning about the susceptible defendant is objectionable in the sense that it only seems to apply to those who are the
subject of psychological or emotional factors. For example, the diabetic is
abnormally susceptible to variations in blood sugar levels, but this does
not prevent his insulin-based hypoglycaemic episode being regarded as
non-insane automatism. In his commentary on *R. v. T*, Professor Smith
approves the distinction formulated in *Rabey* between the ordinary stresses
of life and an extraordinary event such as rape.[292] However, it must not
be forgotten that the accused in *T* did not dissociate until three days after
the rape. Although the court was prepared to ignore this delay, it does
raise problems in the sense that it is the traumatic event, namely the rape,
which causes the post-traumatic stress disorder. The dissociative state is
then the result of some later triggering event, which in *T* appears to have
been of an undefined but minor nature. Strictly, therefore, it is not the rape
but some other emotional trigger which caused the automatism. Further,
many post-traumatic stress sufferers will continue to experience such dissociative episodes months and even years after the original traumatic
event.[293] Surely there comes a time when the court would regard such a
condition as primarily 'internal'.[294] But at what stage in the development
of post-traumatic stress disorder will this transformation be regarded as
having taken place? It is also interesting to note that the diagnostic criteria

[292] [1990] Crim LR 258.
[293] The American Psychiatric Association's *Diagnostic and Statistical Manual of Mental
Disorders* (1994) known as DSM-IV classifies post-traumatic stress disorder (PTSD) into two
types, acute and chronic. Acute PTSD lasts no longer than six months, while the chronic
sufferers may continue to experience symptoms long after this period.
[294] See L.F. Sparr and R.M. Atkinson 'Posttraumatic Stress Disorder as an Insanity Defense:
Medicolegal Quicksand' (1986) 143 *American Journal of Psychiatry* 608–13; P.S. Applebaum
et al., 'Use of Posttraumatic Stress Disorder to Support an Insanity Defense' (1993) 150
American Journal of Psychiatry 229.

for post-traumatic stress disorder contained in the American Psychiatric Association's *Diagnostic and Statistical Manual of Mental Disorders* (revised third edition), known as DSM-III(R), included a triggering event described as 'a recognisable stressor that would evoke significant symptoms of distress in almost everyone',[295] but that this has now been dropped in DSM-IV which merely requires that 'the stressor be of an extreme (i.e. life-threatening) nature'.[296] By way of contrast, DSM-IV has a separate category of conditions known as the 'adjustment disorders' which result from common stress-producing events such as illness, financial difficulties, bereavement and marital conflicts.[297] However, both forms of disorder fall within a broad category in DSM-IV known as 'reactive disorders' which encompass all forms of unusual or bizarre behaviour exhibited under stress-producing conditions.

What is immediately apparent about the DSM-III and DSM-IV approaches is the similarity with the distinction they make between extreme and everyday stressors, and the approach of the courts towards psychological blow automatism and external factors. To make matters more complex it should be noted that DSM-IV has a separate diagnostic category known as 'dissociative disorders' which cater for the type of condition which is said to result in psychological blow automatism.[298] However, there seems to be an interrelationship between these two categories insofar as stress is said to be an important triggering factor in both, although their precise aetiology is far from clear.

The difficulties with the DSM-III and DSM-IV approaches become readily apparent if the medical evidence in the cases of *T* and *Rabey* is compared. In the former case, there was a diagnosis of post-traumatic stress disorder, which was triggered off by an extraordinary or extreme stressor but followed three days later by a dissociative state itself caused by an everyday stressor. In the latter case, there was a dissociative state triggered

---

[295] DSM-III(-R) (1987), code 309.81. See G. Mendelson, 'The Concept of Posttraumatic Stress Disorder—A Review' (1987) 10 *International Journal of Law and Psychiatry* 45. See also *International Statistical Classification of Diseases and Related Health Problems Class of Mental and Behavioural Disorders—Diagnostic Criteria for Research*, published by the World Health Organisation (Geneva, 1993), 99 which describes the triggering event required for PTSD as involving a 'stressful event or situation (either short- or long-lasting) of an exceptionally threatening or catastrophic nature, which would be likely to cause pervasive stress in almost everyone'.

[296] DSM-IV code 309.81. See D.A. Tomb, 'The Phenomenology of Post-traumatic Stress Disorder in *Post-traumatic Stress Disorder, The Psychiatric Clinics of North America* (ed. D.A. Tomb) (Pennsylvania, W.B. Saunders Company, 1994 Vol 17), 237 who states at 238: 'in short, DSM-IV has shifted from a primary emphasis on the severity of the stressor to a mixture of (1) exposure to a traumatic stressor coupled with (2) a patient's reaction (and implied vulnerability) to it'.

[297] DSM-IV, code 309.81, 427: 'in adjustment disorder the stressor can be of any severity'.

[298] DSM-IV 477, see particularly code 300.15 which deals with 'Dissociative Disorders Not Otherwise Specified'.

by an everyday stressor. Unlike Rabey, T was found to be suffering from a major reactive disorder and yet her later reaction, which to all intents and purposes was identical to that of Rabey, was classed as automatism of the sane variety while Rabey was categorised as an insane automaton. And yet both dissociative states seem to have been precipitated by common stressors.

All these points further demonstrate the complexities within this area of the automatism defence. The solution proposed by Dickson J in his dissenting judgment in *Rabey* is as follows: 'I agree with the requirement that there be a shock precipitating the state of automatism. Dissociation caused by a low stress threshold and surrender to anxiety cannot fairly be said to result from a psychological blow'.[299] By emphasising the need for a psychological blow in the form of a shock Dickson J is seeking to exclude those who dissociate as a result of a gradual build-up of ordinary stress or anxiety from automatism of the non-insane variety. This approach would seem to accord with that adopted by Lord Lane CJ in *Hennessy* and *Burgess* in the sense that in neither of these cases did the stress or anxiety seem to fall within the notion of a shock. In the former case the defendant was encountering marital and employment problems, while in the latter he may have been repressing his true feelings towards the victim. In short, there was little or no evidence of a stressor in the form of a psychological blow. However, it may not always be easy to apply the type of distinction made by Dickson J; the division between a psychological blow and ordinary stress is far from clear cut, and when applied could easily lead to the conclusion drawn in *R. v. Falconer* that 'it may be difficult for an accused who raises automatism to show that psychological trauma has not acted upon some underlying infirmity of mind to produce the automatism'.[300] It is of considerable interest to note that in the recent decision in *Falconer* the High Court of Australia has not only refused to permit this difficulty to work against the accused, but also has rejected the 'external factor doctrine'.

Rejecting the external factor doctrine

The above discussion has shown the unsatisfactory nature of an 'internal/external' test when seeking to distinguish insane and non-insane automatism. In an attempt to resolve some of these problems, Smith and Hogan build on the notion that the various factors which play a causal role in automatism 'may operate consecutively or concurrently'.[301] They suggest that if insanity causes automatism, then the best policy is a special verdict.

---

[299] (1980) 15 CR (3d) 225, 258.
[300] *R. v. Falconer* (1990) 65 ALJR 20, 30 per Mason CJ.
[301] Smith and Hogan, *Criminal Law*, 6th edn., 190–1.

Accordingly, if a schizophrenic repeatedly bangs his head against the wall causing concussion, then this latter condition might be better classed as insane automatism. By way of contrast, they suggest that if automatism causes insanity, or automatism and insanity occur concurrently, then a verdict of acquittal is appropriate. With regard to the former (automatism causes insanity), Smith and Hogan comment that 'it is difficult to envisage a convincing case'. However, perhaps sleepwalking fits the bill. The sleep and the sleepwalking are consecutive in a temporal sense, but, alternatively, the sleepwalking does not cause the impairment in the sense required by Smith and Hogan, in which case it may better be described as 'concurrent' with sleep.[302] However, whichever class it falls into, the authors suggest an acquittal, which is of course contrary to the approach in *Burgess*.[303] It is extremely doubtful, therefore, whether the consecutive/concurrent distinction can in any sensible way resolve the problems created by the 'external factor doctrine' which one American commentator has succinctly criticised as giving rise to the conundrum that 'in effect, internal disorders are diseases of the mind that ground the insanity defence, except when they are not'.[304] In short, the distinction is an unprincipled reaction to policy considerations.

But could the distinction safely be rejected? In this context it is useful to turn to Australia where the courts have recently gone some way to achieving this result. The forerunner of such a rejection is *R. v. Radford*,[305] a decision of the Supreme Court of South Australia reached in 1985. The facts were that D had spent a year in Vietnam in 1969. In 1981 his wife met the deceased and became very friendly with her. After that the marriage deteriorated and D and his wife separated in 1983 and were divorced in 1984. D believed his wife had formed a lesbian relationship with the deceased and that this had led to the breakdown of his marriage. He eventually went to the deceased's house seeking a reconciliation with his ex-wife. He claimed that the deceased abused him and came at him with a cricket bat, and that under extreme emotional stress he shot her with a rifle he had retrieved from his car. He claimed that he felt the presence of a soldier next to him carrying a rifle. He felt as if he was a mere observer, as if his 'whole body was just a head about two feet above the shoulder—

---

[302] In *Parks* (1990) 78 CR (3d) 1, 19 Galligan JA states: 'But the impairment of his mind and its functioning was not the result of his sleepwalking. The impairment of his faculties of reason, memory and understanding coincided with his sleepwalking, but the sleepwalking did not cause the impairment.'

[303] A decision which Professor Smith has described as 'right in principle': [1991] Crim LR 549.

[304] R.F. Schopp, *Automatism, Insanity, and the Psychology of Criminal Responsibility—a Philosophical Enquiry* (Cambridge University Press, Cambridge, 1991), 81.

[305] (1985) 42 SASR 266. For critical comment see M. Goode, 'On Subjectivity and Objectivity in Denial of Criminal Responsibility: Reflections on Reading Radford' (1987) 11 *Criminal Law Journal* 131.

the right shoulder of the soldier'.[306] He heard the rifle firing, but did not remember seeing the deceased. A psychiatrist for the defence testified that he was in a state of derealization brought about by emotional stress. This was not due to any disease or chronic disorder or disturbance of the mind. There was in his opinion no inherent liability to recurrence. The trial judge ruled that this evidence did not raise the defence of sane automatism since in his opinion the derealization must in law be regarded as a disease of the mind. The jury convicted and D appealed on the ground that the trial judge was under an obligation to leave the issue of sane automatism to them.

In allowing the appeal, the Supreme Court of South Australia made some interesting remarks. First, with regard to disease of the mind, King CJ stated:

The expression 'disease of the mind' is synonymous, in my opinion with mental illness . . . In one sense automatism must always involve some disorder or disturbance of mental faculties, but I do not think that a temporary disorder or disturbance of an otherwise healthy mind caused by external factors can properly be regarded as a 'disease of the mind'.

The essential notion appears to be . . . an underlying pathological infirmity of the mind . . . which can properly be termed mental illness, as distinct from the reaction of a healthy mind to extraordinary external stimuli.[307]

Further, in dealing with external factors, King CJ stated:

There is no reason in principle for making a distinction between disturbances of mental faculties by reason of stress caused by external factors and disturbance of mental faculties caused by the effects of physical trauma or somnambulism. The significant distinction is between the reaction of an unsound mind to its own delusions or to external stimuli on the one hand and the reaction of a sound mind to external stimuli, including stress-producing factors, on the other hand. I appreciate that if it is true that a state of depersonalisation or dissociation is not itself a disease of the mind, although it may result from mental illness, the result may be that certain cases of unwilled acts which would formerly have founded special verdicts will now result in outright acquittals. I do not see any reason to shrink from that consequence . . . If a person is not mentally ill and there is no reason to suppose that the act will be repeated, detention for the protection of others is pointless and an embarrassment to the mental health authorities.[308]

Accordingly, although the court was skeptical as to whether sane automatism would have been accepted on the facts, it decided that such a defence ought to have been left to the jury.

The decision in *Radford* has since been considered by the High Court of Australia in *Falconer*[309] where the accused's conviction for the murder

---

[306] (1985) 42 SASR 266, 268.   [307] Ibid. 274.
[308] Ibid. 276.   [309] (1990) 65 ALJR 20.

of her husband was quashed on the ground that the trial judge had wrongly refused to admit psychiatric evidence as to the possible existence of non-insane automatism. The evidence in question suggested that psychological stress, including *inter alia* a recent discovery that her husband had sexually assaulted two of their daughters and marital conflict, had caused the accused to enter into a dissociative state at the time of the killing.

In a joint judgment, Mason CJ and Brennan and McHugh JJ approved the first passage in *Radford* quoted above, but went further by rejecting the internal/external distinction, stating 'there seems no reason in principle why psychological trauma which produces a transient non-recurrent malfunction of an otherwise healthy mind should be distinguished from a physical trauma which produced like effect'.[310] Similarly, Toohey J in his judgment was openly critical of the distinction, saying 'the application of the "external factor test" is artificial and pays insufficient regard to the subtleties surrounding the notion of mental disease. As well, there is confusion in the idea of an external factor. A physical blow will readily answer that description . . . But, it may be asked, why should not a psychological blow resulting from external events result in non-insane automatism?'[311] In Toohey J's opinion cases like *Sullivan* and *Hennessy* had placed too much emphasis on physical trauma at the expense of recognising that automatism could be the reaction of a sound mind to a psychological or emotional blow.

At the heart of these judgments in *Falconer*, however, lies the central problem of distinguishing between a sound or healthy mind and a diseased mind. On this issue, Mason CJ relied on the need for the mental disturbance to be transient and not prone to recur, but went further by recognising the particular problem which psychological trauma posed, saying:

the difficulty [lies] in choosing between the reciprocal factors—the trauma and the natural susceptibility of the mind to affection by psychological trauma—as the cause of the malfunction. Is one factor or the other the cause or are both to be treated as causes? To answer this problem, the law must postulate a standard of mental strength which, in the face of a given level of psychological trauma, is capable of protecting the mind from malfunction to the extent prescribed in the respective definitions of insanity. That standard must be the standard of the ordinary person: if the mind's strength is below that standard, the mind is infirm; if it is of or above that standard, the mind is sound or sane. This is an objective standard which corresponds with the objective standard imported for the purpose of determining provocation.[312]

This objective standard bears all the hallmarks of that adopted by the Supreme Court of Canada in *Rabey* and is subject to similar criticism, namely that it is difficult to understand why physical susceptibility such as

---

[310] (1990) 65 ALJR 20, 30.   [311] Ibid. 39.   [312] Ibid. 30.

diabetes does not deny the diabetic in a case like *Quick* an outright sane automatism acquittal, so why should sensitivity to a particular form of minor psychological blow which results in automatism not be treated in a similar way? Clearly the answer to this question is entirely policy-based and is bound to continue to influence the development of the law within this area.

However, what the decision in *Falconer* does achieve is the eradication of the internal/external distinction in automatism, with the result that someone like the defendant in *Hennessy* might receive an unqualified acquittal provided he was not found to be suffering from any 'underlying mental infirmity'.[313] In short, the diabetic would be acquitted on the basis of sane automatism irrespective of whether the temporary mental malfunction arose from hypoglycaemia or hyperglycaemia. At the same time, however, it would follow that in appropriate cases external factors alone could qualify for a plea of insane automatism, as for example in *Re Bromage*[314] where mental disorder caused by external poisoning was held to be sufficient to raise the issue of insanity. However, if such a condition was more than merely transitory and was prone to recur, then there seems little doubt that English law would also regard this as falling within the category of disease of the mind irrespective of the fact that the mental abnormality could only be traced to a specific external factor such as a virus which had permanently affected the defendant's brain.[315]

There is no doubt that criticism of the external factor doctrine in *Falconer* is justified and in that respect the decision seems especially welcome. Essentially, what the High Court of Australia has done is to emphasise the need for a 'diseased mind', which in turn requires evidence of some underlying infirmity.[316] If this is not present, in that the defendant's mind remains healthy but has been temporarily disturbed by some stimuli, such as sleep,[317] or metabolic factors, then there is no reason to class such a condition as a 'disease of the mind'. Clearly, this places great emphasis on the word 'disease' within the insanity defence; it acknowledges however

---

[313] (1990) 65 ALJR 20, 27.

[314] (1990) 48 A Crim R 79.

[315] Cf. *Burnskey* v. *Police* (1991–2) 8 CRNZ 582 where the New Zealand High Court decided a brain injury at birth was an external factor which in turn meant that the brain injury which had resulted should not be classed as a 'disease of the mind'. Contrast *Re Bromage* (1990) 48 A Crim R 79, 87 where McPherson J gave 'Traumatic brain injury' as an example of where 'its difficult to deny to [it] the status of "mental disease" . . . even though [it results] from external agents or events'.

[316] See *R.* v. *Milloy* [1993] 1 Qd R 298 where, unlike in *Falconer*, all the medical evidence attributed D's dissociation to mental disease.

[317] Cf. the remarks of La Forest J in *Parks* (1992) 95 DLR (4th), 48 where he finds the dichotomy between internal and external causes unhelpful in resolving the problem of somnambulism. Further in referring to criticisms of the 'internal cause' approach La Forest J states (ibid. 47) 'that the theory is really only meant to be used as an analytical tool, and not as an all-encompassing methodology'.

the 'affront to common sense' argument raised in *Quick* without resorting to the artificialities of the 'external factor doctrine'.

The Question of Reform

The issue of reform of the automatism defence is of course inextricably linked to that of insanity and will be returned to in Chapter Two. However, at this stage there are a number of points which can be raised concerning reform alternatives.

To date, two major reports have considered the need for change in the automatism defence. The first was the Butler Report in 1975 which concentrated upon excluding certain conditions from the definition of mental disorder in order to retain the defence of non-insane automatism. The effect of these proposals would have been to restrict the scope of non-insane automatism 'to transient states not related to other forms of mental disorder and arising solely as a consequence of (a) the administration, maladministration or non-administration of alcohol, drugs or other substances or (b) physical injury'.[318] This approach was supported in part by the Law Commission in its Draft Criminal Code which at clause 34 defines 'mental disorder' to include 'a state of automatism (not resulting only from intoxication) which is a feature of a disorder, whether organic or functional and whether continuing or recurring, that may cause a similar state on another occasion';[319] while at clause 33(1) it is stated that a person will not be convicted:

if he acts in a state of automatism, that is, his act:—
(i) is a reflex, spasm or convulsion; or
(ii) occurs while he is in a condition (whether of sleep, unconsciousness, impaired consciousness or otherwise) depriving him of effective control of the act.[320]

This provision does have the merit of making it clear that unconsciousness should no longer be the sole criterion of automatism, but that the defence must include conditions which give rise to impaired consciousness.[321] This is further recognised by the insertion of the word 'effective' before 'control' which marks a change from the preliminary draft by the Code Team which required deprivation 'of all control of his movements'.[322]

---

[318] *Report of the Committee on Mentally Abnormal Offenders*, Cmnd. 6244 (1975), para 18.23. For criticism of this approach being unduly restrictive, see R.D. Mackay, 'Non-Organic Automatism' [1980] Crim LR 350, 360 and A. Ashworth, 'The Butler Report and Criminal Responsibility' [1975] Crim LR 690.

[319] The Law Commission, *A Criminal Code for England and Wales* (Law Commission No. 177) (1989), Vol 1, 58.   [320] Ibid. 57–8.

[321] For a good example of automatism being equated with a total loss of consciousness, see the civil case of *Roberts v. Ramsbottom* [1980] 1 All ER 7, 15. For critical comment, see R.D. Mackay, 'Automatism in the Civil Law' (1980) 96 LQR 503.

[322] The Law Commission, *Criminal Law: Codification of the Criminal Law—A Report to the Law Commission* (1985), 193 cl 43(1).

In this respect, the shift of emphasis away from the need for a total lack of control before an automatism defence can succeed is surely to be welcomed since, as the Law Commission remarked, the 'governing principle should be that a person is not guilty of an offence if, without relevant fault on his part, he cannot choose to act otherwise than as he does'.[323] Such an approach, as the Law Commission openly recognises, would ensure that the defendant such as the one in *Broome* v. *Perkins*[324] would not be convicted merely because, despite his hypoglycaemic state, he was able to 'drive' erratically for some five miles. Clearly his condition had not deprived him of all control of the motor vehicle which is why the Divisional Court refused to regard the case as one of automatism.[325] However, if this was the true basis of automatism, then the defence would virtually be restricted to spasms, convulsions, and reflex acts which is clearly not the case.

In its attempt to distinguish insane and non-insane automatism, the Law Commission recognises that the former ought to be restricted to 'pathological automatism that is liable to recur',[326] and that this is achieved by clause 34 cited above. At the same time the Commission is well aware of the problem surrounding the scope of this proposal, stating that some may feel that it includes too much. The reason for this is obvious and is well put by the Commission as follows:

The Butler Committee wished, in particular, to protect from a mental disorder verdict a diabetic who causes a harm in a state of confusion after failing to take his insulin. We do not think, however, that there is a satisfactory way of distinguishing between the different conditions that may cause repeated episodes of disorder; nor do we think it necessary to do so. There is not, so far as we can see, a satisfactory basis for distinguishing between (say) a brain tumour or cerebral arteriosclerosis on the one hand and diabetes or epilepsy on the other. If any of these conditions causes a state of automatism in which the sufferer commits what would otherwise be an offence of violence, his acquittal should be 'on evidence of mental disorder'. Whether a diabetic so affected has failed to seek treatment, or forgotten to take his insulin, or decided not to do so, may affect the court's decision whether to order his discharge or to take some other course. What is objectionable in the present law is the offensive label of 'insanity' and the fact that the court is obliged to order the hospitalisation of the acquitted person, in effect as a restricted patient.[327]

---

[323] Law Commission, *A Criminal Code*, Vol 2, 219.

[324] (1987) 85 Cr App R 321.

[325] Support for this harsh approach has now been given in the Court of Appeal's decision in *Attorney General's Reference (No 2 of 1992)* [1993] 4 All ER 693, 689 where Lord Taylor states 'the defence of automatism requires that there was a total destruction of voluntary control on the defendant's part. Impaired, reduced or partial control is not enough'.

[326] Law Commission, *A Criminal Code*, Vol 2, 224.   [327] Ibid. para 11.28.

Since this passage was written, the law has developed very much along the lines proposed by the Commission in the sense that flexibility of disposal has been introduced by the Criminal Procedure (Insanity and Unfitness to Plead) Act 1991, although the stigma of 'insanity' remains. Further, the approach of the Commission towards diabetics is now supported by the Court of Appeal's decisions in *Hennessy* and *Bingham*. However, it is of interest to note that the Commission provides the following example which substantiates the distinction between *Quick* and *Hennessy*: 'There is evidence that D, who suffers from diabetes, had taken insulin on medical advice. This had caused a fall in his blood sugar level which deprived him of control or awareness of his movements. If D is acquitted, a mental disorder verdict is not appropriate. His 'disorder of mind' was caused by the insulin, an 'intoxicant' (see cl. 22(5)(a)). It was therefore a case of 'intoxication' and not of 'mental disorder'.[328] However, the result favoured in this example is difficult to support since it surely cannot be regarded as a pure case of 'intoxication' but seems instead more likely to qualify as a 'combination of mental disorder and intoxication' within clause 36(a) of the Draft Code and as such would attract the newly proposed 'mental disorder' verdict. This result seems to follow once it is accepted that the diabetic who fails to take insulin should be classed as mentally disordered, since the taking of the insulin cannot prevent the accused's diabetic condition from being classed as an underlying 'mental disorder' which manifests itself when combined with the intoxicant (in this case, insulin). Of course if this argument was accepted it would inevitably put an end to cases like *Quick* falling within the non-insane automatism defence. However, in the light of the Draft Code it may be difficult to continue to justify this result not only because it is difficult to argue that the hypoglycaemia results 'only from intoxication' but also because it seems equally difficult to deny that the automatism is anything other than 'a feature of a disorder', namely the diabetes.[329] If 'feature' is given its ordinary dictionary meaning of 'characteristic' or 'peculiarity', then hypoglycaemia as a result of an insulin injection clearly qualifies as a major 'feature' of diabetes which itself is a continuing organic disorder.

Not only that, the same wording causes problems in respect of a case like *Toner*[330] where the hypoglycaemia resulted from an episode of fasting,

---

[328] Law Commission, *A Criminal Code*, Vol 2, 164. See further ibid. 224 n 39 where the Commission cites *Quick*, stating 'a mental disorder verdict is not intended to be available in a case of automatism caused by the taking of drugs for an illness.' Presumably if the drug an epileptic was taking was shown to have sparked off a seizure then a mental disorder verdict would likewise be inappropriate. Cf. *Burns* (1974) 68 Cr App R 364.

[329] Cl 34 cited above. The Law Commission now seems to have conceded the point, see *Legislating the Criminal Code: Intoxication and Criminal Liability* (1995), where it is stated at para 6.49: 'we recommend that automatism caused partly by intoxication and partly by disease of the mind should be dealt with under the existing law of insanity'.

[330] (1991) 93 Cr App R 382.

since it seems possible to argue that the automatism was a 'feature' of a metabolic 'disorder' which, if the accused was to fast again, could easily 'cause a similar state on another occasion'. Such a case is certainly different from that of an episode of automatism due to concussion from an accidental blow to the head which would clearly qualify under the Draft Code for an unqualified acquittal. However, in the fasting episode what the defendant has done is to render himself susceptible to metabolic dysfunction owing to a self-induced change in his body chemistry. Clearly, if such a condition could be regarded as 'recurring' then it would seem difficult to extricate it from the Commission's definition of 'mental disorder'.

What the above discussion demonstrates is the difficulty inherent in attempting to preserve the distinction between insane and non-insane automatism. The question which arises therefore is whether there are any viable alternatives to the continued preservation of this distinction.

Revision Alternatives

A radical solution to the intractable problems discussed above would be to abolish the distinction between insane and non-insane automatism. This could be achieved in two very different ways. The first would be to emphasise the fundamental burden on the prosecution to prove that the defendant's act was voluntary and to argue that if, as a result of an automatism defence, the prosecution fails to achieve this, then the accused cannot be convicted, irrespective of the nature of the condition which gave rise to the automatism. Indeed, this may well be the position in some jurisdictions in the United States,[331] where, interestingly, in a country renowned for its volume and scope of litigation, the problems surrounding the sane/insane automatism dichotomy have rarely arisen. A possible reason for this is that so-called automatism cases are either not prosecuted or they result in outright acquittals. For example, one leading commentator has remarked that 'manifestly the epileptic in a grand mal whose clonic movements strike and injure another commits no crime; but we need no special defence of insanity to reach that result, well-established *actus reus* doctrines suffice'.[332]

Of course what this approach fails to take account of are the policy considerations which have led the English courts to develop the distinction between insane and non-insane automatism. Such considerations are encapsulated by the Law Commission in the following remark: 'it would not, we think, be acceptable to propose that the courts should lose all control over a person acquitted because of what is now termed "insane

---

[331] See R. Schopp, *Automatism, Insanity, and the Psychology of Criminal Responsibility*, 73.

[332] N. Morris, *Madness and the Criminal Law*, (University of Chicago Press, Chicago, 1982), 65.

automatism"'.[333] However, while the social defence factors inherent in such an approach are clearly important it is perhaps worth considering the numerical scope of the problem. Is there really any great cause for concern here? In this respect one thing is clear. There are virtually no special verdicts returned on the basis of insane automatism. For example, research on the insanity defence has shown that during the years 1975 to 1989 there were only four findings of not guilty by reason of insanity on the basis of insane automatism.[334] Naturally, it must be conceded that this in itself gives only a partial picture of the total number of cases in which insane automatism may have been a relevant issue as it is well known that some defendants prefer to plead guilty rather than proceed with such a defence.[335] It is impossible to give any estimate of the annual number of such cases although it is likely to be small. However, even a single case of this nature is too much, for to 'force' criminally irresponsible defendants to plead guilty is surely untenable. Of course it can be argued that the real reason for this unfortunate state of affairs has been the inflexible disposal consequences of a special verdict and that, with the introduction of the Criminal Procedure (Insanity and Unfitness to Plead) Act 1991 bringing with it much needed discretion in the treatment of such cases, this may change. However, while this development will be discussed further in Chapter Two, it is important to realise that the courts seem quite willing to punish in the normal way a defendant who has chosen to plead guilty to avoid a ruling of insane automatism. Thus, in *Hennessy* it is significant that the defendant, after pleading guilty, received *inter alia* a suspended prison sentence. Clearly, therefore, neither the trial judge nor the Court of Appeal considered that he required any treatment for his condition. Accordingly, there was no need for continued control over this defendant, which at the very least demonstrates that not all insane automatism cases fall within the category of those where social defence is a real concern.

Another point which may be raised concerning the development of insane automatism relates to the scope of the M'Naghten Rules. There is an argument that the Rules were never intended to encompass cases of automatism. Indeed, this very argument was accepted by Lawton LJ in the Court of Appeal's decision in *Sullivan*[336] where it was concluded that it was the pre-1800 common law concept of insanity which covered cases of insane automatism. While this argument was briefly disposed of by Lord Diplock in the House of Lords' decision as being quite contrary to the

---

[333] Law Commission, *A Criminal Code*, para 11.28.

[334] Three of these were cases of epileptic automatism while the fourth was the sleepwalking case of *Burgess*. See R.D. Mackay, *The Operation of the Criminal Procedure (Insanity) Act 1964—An Empirical Study of Unfitness to Plead and the Insanity Defence*, (De Montfort University Law Monographs, 1991), 20.

[335] Ibid. 24–5.   [336] [1983] 1 All ER 577, 581.

decision in *Bratty*, it does seem more than likely that the Rules were never conceived as a vehicle for cases of involuntary action. However, with the development of the Rules it is hardly surprising that the courts should have chosen to extend them to include such cases.

The primary problem here is whether it would be acceptable to allow all cases of automatism, irrespective of cause, to qualify for an outright acquittal. The answer seems to be: No! The social defence considerations cannot be swept aside in this way. Inevitably there will be some cases of what is now classed as insane automatism, where the accused is regarded as dangerous and requires treatment. To refuse to give the criminal law any power to deal with such a case is simply unacceptable. It is the price which must be paid for public security. Accordingly, the first radical revision proposal seems impractical.

The second approach to an abolition of the distinction between insane and non-insane automatism would be to move in the opposite direction. Thus, instead of advocating a simple acquittal for all cases of automatism, the scope of the special verdict could be widened to encompass the existing law on automatism.[337] An obvious problem with this approach is that an unqualified acquittal would no longer be possible after a successful automatism plea irrespective of its nature. To many criminal lawyers this might seem like too heavy a price to pay for eradication of the complex distinction between sane and insane automatism. However, once again it must be asked whether the practical implications of such a proposal would as serious as might at first be thought. In particular, it can be argued that through their application of the 'external factor doctrine' the courts have now effectively reduced the scope of non-insane automatism to a defence of very little practical significance. The major reason for this does of course continue to derive from the area of social defence and the continued suspicion with which the courts have generally viewed the non-insane automatism defence.

However, the mere fact that the sane automatism defence has, and continues to be, whittled away by successive appellate decisions does not of itself justify its abolition so as to collapse all such cases into the special verdict, unless this verdict is to be altered to one very different from its present counterpart. This is a matter which will be fully discussed in Chapter Two. However, at this stage it must be pointed out that only the most radical departure from the M'Naghten Rules could be viewed as

---

[337] See E.A. Tollefson and B. Starkman, *Mental Disorder in Criminal Proceedings*, (Carswell, Canada, 1993), who (ibid. 53) refer to the Canadian Psychiatric Association's brief to the Canadian House of Common's Subcommittee on the Reform of the General Part of the Criminal Code, November 9, 1992. This recommended abolition of automatism on the ground that all cases of automatism, whatever the cause, involve a brain malfunction and are therefore mental disorders.

justifying the rejection of non-insane automatism together with the simple acquittal which it presently attracts. Further, in the light of the recent enactment of the Criminal Procedure (Insanity and Unfitness to Plead) Act 1991 any such major legal change now seems unlikely. So is there any compromise approach which might go some way to improving the existing legal position?

Certainly, the approach proposed by the Law Commission in the Draft Criminal Code Bill would be an improvement insofar as it would rid the criminal law of complex terminology such as 'involuntary act', 'disease of the mind' and 'insanity'. However, as already discussed, it would essentially retain the present distinction between those forms of automatism resulting in an acquittal and those attracting a 'mental disorder verdict'. In this connection it is noticeable that the Law Commission has decided to include 'a reflex, spasm or convulsion' within the Draft Code's definition of automatism (clause 33(1)), which means that any epileptic convulsion resulting in damage or injury to another could continue to qualify for the newly proposed mental disorder verdict. While such an approach seems to be modelled upon the existing common law, it may be argued that the automatism defence could be narrowed in the sense of excluding convulsions, muscular spasms, and reflex actions.

Indeed, in *Burgess* Lord Lane CJ seems to have had in mind this distinction when he remarked: 'his mind was to some extent controlling his actions, which were purposive rather than the result simply of a muscular spasm, but without his being consciously aware of what he was doing'.[338] The crucial point here is that for all practical purposes cases of automatism invariably deal with cases where, as Lord Lane CJ went on to remark, the defendant lacked 'conscious motivation' but outwardly his alleged criminal conduct appeared purposeful. It is difficult to think of a single case of automatism which does not fit this picture,[339] the reason being that spasms and reflex actions are much more likely to be viewed as cases of pure accident and are therefore unlikely to attract the interest of the prosecuting authorities.[340] Rather it is those cases where the defendant's mental condition causes him to react in an apparently purposeful but anti-social manner that form the backbone of automatism litigation. In a sense this is why automatism is viewed with so much skepticism by both the judiciary and the prosecution. For how, it may be asked, is it possible for a person who claims to have been in such a state to have been physically

---

[338] [1991] 2 All ER 769, 773.

[339] A case reported in the *Rutland Times* in 1992 deals with a motorist answering a careless driving charge with a defence of automatism based on a sneezing fit. The magistrates appeared unimpressed with the plea and duly convicted.

[340] Law Commission, *A Criminal Code*, Vol 2, para 11.3 refers to 'an act over which the person concerned, although conscious, has no control: the "reflex, spasm or convulsion". Such an act would rarely, if ever, be the subject of a prosecution.'

able to control a motor vehicle or 'assault' the victim. And yet it is well known that this does happen, albeit rarely.

It can be argued, therefore, that Lord Lane CJ has done the law a service by drawing attention to this distinction, although it would have been preferable if he had added the word 'outwardly' or 'apparently' before 'purposeful'. In this way the definition of automatism could be amended so as to exclude muscular spasms, reflex actions, and convulsions, leaving them to be dealt with as cases of accident. This would not be difficult to achieve, since the *Bratty* definition of 'unconscious involuntary action' could easily be supplemented with the words 'performed in an outwardly purposeful manner'.

It is submitted that there is a good deal to be said for ridding the automatism defence of a series of conditions which, to all intents and purposes, have no relevance to its application or development. It would also rid the law of the somewhat anomalous notion of conscious automatism, an anomaly which was recognised by Lord Denning in *Bratty* when, in defining automatism, he made a clear distinction between 'an act which is done by the muscles without any control by the mind, such as a spasm, a reflex action or a convulsion; or an act done by a person who is not conscious of what he is doing'.[341]

The crucial question is whether a definition of automatism should encompass the former. If the answer is in the affirmative, then the implications would seem to be serious for those who suffer from spasms or the like. For example, Hart, in his discussion of conscious but involuntary action, makes a distinction between:

Muscular control impaired by disease. A is afflicted by St. Vitus dance. Harm results from his uncontrolled movements.
Reflex muscular contraction. A while driving a car is attacked by a swarm of bees or hit by a stone and the car is temporarily out of his control.[342]

It seems clear from the earlier discussion of the external factor doctrine that while both of these examples would qualify for a defence of automatism the former would be classed as insane while the latter would be non-insane.

It is of interest to note that a related point was the subject of consideration by the Supreme Court of Zimbabwe in the *State* v. *Evans*[343] where the accused was convicted of culpable homicide after a collision between two trains, one of which he had been driving. The accused claimed to have suffered a blackout at the crucial time. The magistrates rejected this defence because of lack of evidence but also ruled that, if established, it could only result in a special verdict. On this latter point the Supreme Court

[341] [1963] AC 386, 409.   [342] Hart, *Punishment and Responsibility*, 96.
[343] [1985] LRC (Crim) 504.

ruled that the magistrates had 'confused cases of automatism with the instant case of a blackout. On the peculiar facts of the instant case a special verdict . . . would have been wrong.'[344] The basis of this distinction is that 'once the appellant had a blackout, he ceased to drive the locomotive because he was inactive. He could not in that state react to any situation'.[345] In short, the accused was at that time incapable of any movement whatsoever and should not be classed as an automaton. Surely, spasms, convulsions, and reflex actions deserve similar treatment, in the sense that they also are far removed from apparently purposeful conduct.

A more difficult problem in this context would be the case of an epileptic seizure which resulted in muscular spasms causing damage to property or injury to those rendering first aid. Here the distinction already made becomes crucial. If the damage or injury can be traced purely to spasms, in the sense of clonic convulsions, then automatism should not be relevant. But if it is a case of involuntary action in the sense of apparently coordinated acts which have the outward appearance of being purposeful, then the automatism defence becomes a live issue. A great many epileptics will be unfortunate enough to suffer seizures but it is only those whose behaviour during such episodes have the outward appearance of being motivated and purposeful that are proper candidates for an automatism defence and its accompanying enquiry into the question of 'disease of the mind'.

A final compromise solution would be to retain the sane/insane automatism distinction but rather than permit an automatic acquittal in all cases of sane automatism give the courts some degree of power over the accused to be exercised in appropriate cases. This could only be achieved in one of two ways. The first would be to utilise existing common law powers. In this connection it is interesting to note that an attempt at such a compromise is to be found in the judgment of Chief Justice Lamer in *Parks* where he considered that some control, in the form of the common law power to make an order to keep the peace, should be used. Accordingly, he stated that 'in appropriate cases of outright acquittals on grounds of automatism measures that would reinforce sleep hygiene and thereby provide greater safety for others should always be considered'.[346] However, the majority of the Supreme Court of Canada rejected such an approach,[347] but suggested 'that the possibility of supervisory orders in this situation may be a matter which Parliament would wish to consider in the near future'.[348] Statutory intervention is the second and more obvious way in

---

[344] [1985] LRC (Crim) 504, 516.   [345] Ibid.   [346] (1992) 95 DLR (4th) 27, 41–2.
[347] But cf. A. Tomison, 'Case Report: M'Naghten today' (1993) 4 *Journal of Forensic Psychiatry* 369 where it is reported that an accused was acquitted on the grounds of insanity and received a two-year supervision and treatment order under the Criminal Procedure (Insanity and Unfitness to Plead) Act 1991 together with a bind-over for a similar period in the sum of £200 to keep the peace and not to have contact with the victim whom he had seriously assaulted.   [348] 95 DLR (4th) 27, 56 per McLachlin J.

which power could be exerted over the sane automaton and, since the Supreme Court's decision in *Parks*, proposals have been published in Canada which would create a new 'verdict of not criminally responsible on account of automatism' which would result in a disposition hearing before a Review Board. The hearing would require the Board to take 'into consideration the likelihood of recurrence of a state of automatism, the danger to the public if a state of automatism were to recur, the reintegration of the accused into society and the other needs of the accused' before making a disposition which could consist of an absolute or conditional discharge or a hospital order.[349] The proposals also make it clear that if 'a state of automatism was caused by mental disorder', then the correct verdict would be one of 'not criminally responsible on account of mental disorder'.[350] Clearly therefore these proposals retain the distinction between sane and insane automatism and, although it has been suggested that, if implemented, 'there would be less incentive for the prosecution and the court to contort the evidence and the law to find the accused mentally disordered' owing to the new disposal powers,[351] such an approach, even if it did shift the balance of the sane/insane automatism dichotomy, would not entirely rid the law of this complex distinction. However, if this proposal did lead to renewed emphasis on the need for definite proof of mental disorder before a finding of insane automatism could be made, then this in itself would be a desirable development. Nevertheless, such a development would take place at the expense of the unqualified acquittal which a successful plea of sane automatism currently attracts. Whether such a change is either just or desirable is a vexed policy question and it remains to be seen how these Canadian proposals will be applied, should they become law.

Conclusion

The defence of automatism raises a conflict of principle which is extremely difficult to resolve. On the one hand, there is a social defence need to protect society from dangerous automatons whose conditions are likely to recur, while, on the other hand, there is a reluctance to categorize conditions like diabetes as a form of insanity. There seems little doubt that the courts in their consideration of the automatism defence have favoured social defence at the expense of sane automatism with the result that the latter defence has been narrowed to a considerable degree.

This restriction on sane automatism has been primarily achieved through the development of the 'external factor doctrine'. There is no doubt that

---

[349] '*Proposal to Amend the Criminal Code*, a White Paper issued by the Minister of Justice of Canada, 28 June 1983 quoted in Appendix C of Tollefson and Starkman, *Mental Disorder in Criminal Proceedings*, 214.
[350] Ibid.   [351] Tollefson and Starkman, ibid. 59.

this doctrine is arbitrary in its application and 'has no medical significance'.[352] Further, the doctrine has been criticised by Glanville Williams on the ground that 'it adds nothing of value' to the famous rule put forward by Lord Denning in *Bratty*.[353] However, while the danger of recurrence was regarded by Lord Lane in *Burgess* as 'an added reason for categorising the condition as a disease of the mind',[354] his Lordship further remarked that 'the absence of the danger of recurrence is not a reason for saying that it cannot be a disease of the mind'. This remark, together with the reliance of the court in *Burgess* on the 'external factor doctrine', seems to point the way for future developments within this area of the law.

A more sensible approach would be to adopt the reasoning favoured by the High Court of Australia in *Falconer* which supports the notion: 'that in order to constitute insanity in the eyes of the law, the malfunction of mental faculties called "defect of reason" in the M'Naghten Rules must result from an underlying pathological infirmity of the mind, be it of long or short duration and be it permanent or temporary, which can properly be termed mental illness, as distinct from the reaction of a healthy mind to extraordinary external stimuli.'[355] In short, the crucial distinction ought to be between a mind which is healthy or sound and one which is not. It would not be difficult to develop the Law Commission's recommendations along these lines. As it stands, the Draft Criminal Code's approach towards automatism has the merit of defining an act without using the word 'involuntary' which in turn helps to avoid the complexities discussed in Part One of this Chapter. Instead, the Draft Code proceeds on the footing that a person is to be regarded as having 'acted' even if he was in a state of automatism at the time of the alleged offence. However, the definition of automatism could be narrowed by excluding the reference to 'a reflex, spasm or convulsion' in the manner suggested above. Further, the definition of 'mental disorder' in clause 34 could be simplified and improved in sub-clause 3 by changing the phrase 'a feature of a disorder' to 'a feature of an underlying infirmity of the mind'. This would focus on the need for the 'mental disorder' to have its origins in some mental pathology rather than permitting the retention of the 'external factor doctrine', which in turn would go a long way to improving this complex area of the law.

---

[352] G.M. Paul and K.W. Lange, 'Epilepsy and Criminal Law' (1992) 32 *Medicine, Science and the Law* 160, 164.   [353] G. Williams, *Textbook of Criminal Law* (2nd edn.), 671.
[354] [1991] 2 All ER 769, 774.   [355] (1990) 65 ALJR 20, 29.

2

The Insanity Defence

Perhaps more than any other area of the criminal law, the insanity defence generates heated discussion and debate. The literature discussing the insanity plea is immense,[1] and reform proposals are continuously formulated. In short, there is an ongoing debate about whether the law should recognise that some crazy people ought not to be punished for behaviour which would normally be adjudged criminal. This debate, which tends to ebb and flow in the light of notorious cases, is one which deserves to be within the public domain since the underlying question of whether it is appropriate to excuse a mentally abnormal offender is a question with fundamental moral and social implications. Equally, however, it is a question of great legal complexity as it addresses issues which are at the very cutting edge of the criminal justice system.

This Chapter will present a detailed critical analysis of the insanity defence from its historical roots to its current status in Anglo-American jurisprudence, and will open with a discussion of the defence's theoretical basis. Although a recurrent theme of this Chapter will be that the insanity defence, far from being a merciful and therapeutic device to deal with 'crazy criminals', has often been used instead for the purpose of incapacitation, this will be counterbalanced by a consideration of recent empirical research on the operation of the defence in practice. This research together with the reforms contained in the Criminal Procedure (Insanity and Unfitness to Plead) Act 1991 could herald a major shift in restoring the defence to one of practical importance. Finally, the chapter will close with a discussion of some proposals concerning alternative approaches to revising the insanity defence.

---

[1] Much of the literature, most of which is from the United States, will be referred to during this Chapter. For up-to-date and extensive US references, see M.L. Perlin, *The Jurisprudence of the Insanity Defense* (Carolina Academic Press, Durham, North Carolina, 1994). For additional, though less recent, bibliographies, see Donald H.J. Hermann, *The Insanity Defense, Philosophical, Historical and Legal Perspectives* (Charles C. Thomas, Illinois, 1983) and N. Finkel, *Insanity on Trial: Perspectives on Law and Psychology*, (Plenum Press, New York 1988). See also F. McAuley, *Insanity, Psychiatry and Criminal Responsibility* (Round Hill Press, Dublin, 1993) which focuses on Irish law but not to the exclusion of other jurisdictions.

Theoretical Issues

There has been and continues to be ceaseless debate about the status of the insanity defence within contemporary criminal law. While there is no doubt that this debate outstrips the practical significance of the insanity defence, it is nonetheless important to consider why the criminal law exculpates some crazy people and not others.

In the Report of the Committee on Mentally Abnormal Offenders (hereafter referred to as the Butler Report),[2] reference is made to the remarks of the Royal Commission on Capital Punishment,[3] relating to the 'ancient and humane principle that has long formed part of our common law', namely 'that if a person was, at the time of his unlawful act, mentally so disordered that it would be unreasonable to impute guilt to him, he ought not to be held liable to conviction and punishment under the criminal law'.[4] In advocating the need for continued recognition of this fundamental assumption, the Royal Commission had opined that 'we should hardly have thought it necessary to state explicitly if it had not lately been questioned in some quarters'.[5]

In agreeing with this approach the Butler Report merely stated 'we share the [Commission's] view that this is right in principle'.[6] But nowhere does the Report probe the nature of this 'ancient and humane principle', being content instead to accept the Royal Commission's reasoning that it must continue.

There are three fundamental and related theoretical points which deserve consideration. The first concerns the nature of insanity, in the sense of what it is within this legal concept which leads to a recognition by the criminal law that persons so adjudged should be acquitted. The second surrounds the way in which the law seeks to achieve this, in the sense of whether insanity is in the nature of a status or an excuse. The third concerns the question of why punishment is felt to be improper in cases of insanity. Each of these points will now be considered in turn.

The Nature of Insanity

In its discussion of criminal responsibility, the Royal Commission on Capital Punishment points to the difficulties of achieving consensus over the defence of insanity owing to the fact that degrees of mental abnormality and responsibility vary widely. However, in the Commission's opinion the real question is 'whether the offender, as a result of insanity or mental

---

[2] Cmnd 6244 (1975).
[3] *Report of the Royal Commission on Capital Punishment 1949–1953* Cmd 8932 (1953).
[4] Butler Report, para 18.2.   [5] Cmd 8932, para 278.
[6] Butler Report, para 18.10.

abnormality, is so much less responsible than a normal person that it is just to treat him as wholly irresponsible'.[7] But in no way does this tell us what is it about the nature of insanity which leads the law to adjudge a particular individual as criminally irresponsible, and neither the Commission nor the Butler Report makes any further attempt to probe this problem.

However, a number of scholars have grappled with this issue and to a considerable extent they have arrived at similar conclusions. For example, Michael Moore, in his discussion of the legal concept of insanity, concludes that the proper question for a jury is whether the accused's mental illness is severe enough for them to conclude that he was 'so irrational as to be nonresponsible'.[8] Similarly Morse, in his assessment of the moral basis of the insanity defence, states that the crucial issue 'is whether in some cases extreme craziness (involved in the defendant's offensive conduct) so compromises the defendant's rationality or creates such compulsion that it would be unjust to hold the defendant responsible'.[9] The additional reference by Morse to 'compulsion' is clearly designed to cater for the notion of 'uncontrollable impulse', a concept which itself gives rise to a great deal of difficulty and will be referred to further during this chapter. However, at this stage it is the idea of 'irrationality' which merits further analysis as it appears to be central to so many discussions about the exculpatory nature of insanity. One of the most thorough discussions is by Fingarette and Hasse who, in their analysis of the concept of capacity for rational conduct, state that 'it is the absence of this capacity that is central to what we wish to express when we speak of someone as "out of his mind", "out of touch with reality", "mentally incompetent", "crazy", or "mad"'.[10] In the authors' opinion this concept has 'a far deeper and more global significance, than such traditional concepts as "intent", "knowledge", "deliberation", and "voluntariness"'.[11] Instead it is 'rationality' which governs these latter traditional concepts in the sense that they only remain significant if the person in question is rational.

Rationality, therefore, appears to be synonymous with normal mental functioning, in the sense that society expects an individual to share 'at least to a minimal practical extent, in a background of basic concepts, perceptions, values, skills, and attitudes common to members of the community'.[12] If some of this background fails to be reflected in the manner in which an individual conducts himself, then it is at that stage that an inquiry into

---

[7] Cmnd 8932, para 285.

[8] M. Moore, *Law and Psychiatry—Rethinking the Relationship* (Cambridge University Press, Cambridge, 1984), 245.

[9] S.J. Morse, 'Excusing the Crazy: The Insanity Defense Reconsidered' (1985) *Southern California Law Review* 777, 788.

[10] H. Fingarette & A.F. Hasse, *Mental Disabilities and Criminal Responsibility* (University of California Press, Berkeley, 1979), 218.

[11] Ibid. 223.   [12] Ibid.

'rationality' may become necessary. Moore makes much the same point when he states: 'one is a moral agent only if one is a rational agent. Only if we can see another being as one who acts to achieve some rational end in the light of some rational beliefs will we understand him in the same fundamental way that we understand ourselves and our fellow persons in everyday life. We regard as moral agents only those beings we can understand in this way.'[13]

From the above discussion it is clear that the contrasting concepts of 'rationality' and 'irrationality' are often used as triggers to an enquiry into an individual's mental condition at the time when he is engaged in conduct viewed as abnormal. There is no doubt that mental illness can affect sufferers in a myriad of different ways and may alter a person's thought processes in such a manner that it profoundly influences his behaviour. The real problem of course is that if the concept of 'rationality' underpins the notions of normality and responsibility for one's actions, then it is crucial to have a basic understanding of what this term means.

Rationality and Responsibility

The criminal law is premised on free will in the sense that it presumes that individuals are moral agents who are capable of making free choices as to how they behave.[14] Naturally, the fundamental notion of free will has been a source of unending philosophical debate into which it is not proposed to enter fully in the context of this discussion. Suffice to say that even those who argue in favour of determinism tend to concede that the crazy or mad ought to be excused from crimes which can be shown to have been committed whilst they were suffering from the effects of mental illness.[15] In short, it seems to be almost universally accepted, irrespective of whether one takes a free will or determinist stance, that only those who have the capacity to act 'rationally' ought to be held accountable for criminal acts. But what does the word 'rationally' mean in this context? At the root of the concept lies the notion that in order to be held responsible, an agent must be viewed as having acted 'autonomously' in the sense that 'his behaviour is motivated by certain kinds of motivational factors—such as reasons, desires, intentions, motives, attitudes and emotions—that arise critically in his motivational system. Responsibility signifies that the individual's behaviour satisfies a particular societal or legal conception of this critical process.'[16] Another way of looking at this critical process is to

---

[13] Moore, *Law and Psychiatry*, 244–5.

[14] For a strong judicial pronouncement favouring such an approach, see *Lynch* v. *DPP* [1975] 1 All ER 913, 933–4, per Lord Simon.

[15] See in particular Moore, *Law and Psychiatry*, 351–65.

[16] R.J. Lipkin, 'Free Will, Responsibility and the Promise of Forensic Psychiatry' (1990) 13 *International Journal of Law and Psychiatry*, 331–2.

describe it as the exercise of the agent's capacity for practical reasoning,[17] which according to Moore involves:

(1) the ability to form an object we desire to achieve through action,
(2) the ability to form a belief about how certain actions will or will not achieve the objects of our desires, and
(3) the ability to act on our desires and our beliefs so that our actions form the 'conclusion' of a valid practical syllogism.[18]

It is clear that most of the population have the capacity for practical reasoning as described by Moore and that society operates by virtue of the fact that individuals can interact with one another on this basis. However, sometimes an individual's capacity is interfered with as a result of mental illness which may in turn mean that his behaviour can no longer be viewed as 'rational'. The difficulty here is deciding at what stage such a conclusion may be reached. For example, just because a person is suffering from schizophrenia does not mean that everything that he does lacks 'rationality'. To hold otherwise would be to deny such persons any degree of autonomy,[19] which would clearly be unacceptable not only to the mentally ill themselves but also to all those involved in their care and treatment. Instead, it is only when the schizophrenic's actions are viewed as out of the ordinary that any enquiry about 'rationality' will generally ensue. The questions raised by any such enquiry are many, but in the end may be reduced to three. The first is whether the insanity defence should be built upon the notion of capacity for rational choice or whether it ought instead to concern itself with an enquiry into the agent's character. The second question is, if rationality is accepted as the proper approach, what is the boundary between 'rationality' and 'irrationality'. The third and final question is how, in any particular case, is this boundary to be established?

The first question is fundamental in that it questions the 'choice' theory of excuse, which would excuse the mad or crazy person on the basis that he did not have the capacity or opportunity to do otherwise and would seek to replace it with a character theory which focuses on the individual's 'goals, desires, values, emotions, and perceptions of what courses of action are available to him—that motivate his rational choices'.[20] This 'character' conception of responsibility has been referred to by Lacey as 'dispositional responsibility',[21] and would apply to insanity in the following way:

---

[17] R.F. Schopp, *Automatism, Insanity and the Psychology of Criminal Responsibility—a Philosophical Inquiry* (Cambridge University Press, Cambridge, 1991), 188–201.

[18] M. Moore, 'Causation and the Excuses' (1985) *California Law Review*, 1091, 1148.

[19] A problem which seems to beset those who favour the 'status' approach towards insanity, see below.

[20] P. Arenella, 'Character, Choice and Moral Agency: The Relevance of Character to Our Moral Culpability Judgments', in E.F. Paul et al. (eds.), *Crime, Culpability and Remedy*, (Blackwell, Oxford, 1990), 59.

[21] N. Lacey, *State Punishment* (Routledge, London, 1988), 74.

we cannot take it, in the case of insane persons, that their actions do in fact manifest settled dispositions, character traits, in any real sense, or at least anything like the sense we take non-insane persons' actions to do so. The link between disposition and action seems to be severed by insanity, not because it alters the capacities of the insane person, but because it involves disordered thought and behaviour which is not patterned by the structure of thought (both in terms of reason and emotion) by which we normally communicate and interpret each other's actions.[22]

The essence of this 'character-based' approach is that it is only fair to hold people responsible 'for actions in which their settled dispositions are centrally expressed' as opposed to 'actions which are out of character'.[23] For those who wish a wider insanity defence, it also has the effect of broadening the enquiry beyond the narrow limits of a cognitively based insanity plea, such as that contained in the M'Naghten Rules,[24] and instead permits a consideration of the accused's 'attitudes, concerns and values'.[25]

In his robust defence of the 'choice' model of excuse, Moore classes insanity as a status excuse because 'it is the general condition of the agent (his status) that determines whether or not he is excused'.[26] However in doing so he makes it clear that this status category is grounded in the notion of 'disturbed practical reason' as opposed to the character disposition of the individual. This point needs further elaboration and will be returned to in the next section which probes the nature of 'status excuses'. Before doing so, it should be pointed out that the search for a single theory upon which to base criminal culpability may be mistaken, and that instead it may be preferable to look to a mixed theory of choice, capacity, and character.[27]

However, to return to the second question raised above, it is all very well to argue that at the root of the notion of the insanity defence is the concept of 'irrationality'. But in order to support this proposition we must surely be able to recognise or identify 'irrationality' in the particular sense in which it is used as a key term to excuse the mad or crazy. The problem here is that 'irrationality' can have several meanings, only some of which are applicable to the mentally normal. For example, the dictionary definition of 'irrational' includes the terms 'unreasonable' and 'illogical',[28] which

---

[22] Lacey, *State Punishment*, 74.   [23] Ibid. 68.

[24] The Rules focus on whether the accused 'knew' what he was doing and whether he was doing what was legally wrong, and thus only excuse those who in a minimal sense had no choice to do otherwise. For discussion of the Rules in practice, see below.

[25] R.A. Duff, 'Choice, Character and Criminal Liability' (1993) 12 *Law and Philosophy* 345, 361.

[26] M. Moore, 'Choice, Character, and Excuse' in E.F. Paul et al. (eds.), *Crime, Culpability and Remedy*, 31.

[27] Duff, 'Choice, Character and Criminal Liability', 379. See also J. Horder, 'Criminal Culpability: The Possibility of a General Theory' (1993) 12 *Law and Philosophy* 193.

[28] See e.g. the *Concise Oxford Dictionary*, 7th edn.

are terms which commonly apply to the vast majority of the population, in the sense that we all act 'unreasonably' and 'illogically' from time to time. However, this is not what 'irrational' means in the context of the insanity defence, which has led some commentators to adopt alternative terms such as 'non-rational'[29] and 'unreason'.[30] Rather the term 'irrational' in this context must denote a more extreme form of lack of reason which may conveniently be described as 'an aberration of normal mental functioning'. Thus, it is only when an agent's normal mental functioning is interfered with to such an extent that he no longer possesses his normal critical powers of practical reasoning that we should be prepared to consider whether during such an episode he may have been acting 'irrationally'. This then leads to the third question, which is how can 'irrationality' be established in any particular case?

A simplistic answer to this question is that the 'irrationality' required to establish an insanity defence is founded on medical evidence which can describe and explain the agent's aberrant mental condition. In this respect there is no doubt that the medical model of mental illness has been extremely influential in shaping modern attitudes towards the insanity defence and in many respects could be regarded as the major reason why, in England at least, there has been little modern discussion of the theoretical grounds for excusing the insane. Instead, since the 1950s there has been an increasing influence of psychiatric expertise within the broad area of the mentally abnormal offender, which in turn has relegated the issue of criminal responsibility within the framework of the insanity defence to one of little practical importance.

It is not hard to see how this result has been achieved. First, the introduction of diminished responsibility in the Homicide Act 1957 has had the effect of eclipsing the insanity defence in murder prosecutions. Secondly, the introduction of hospital orders in the Mental Health Act 1959 has meant that the vast majority of mentally disordered offenders are convicted, and if needs be sent to hospital, with no attempt being made to consider their criminal responsibility. The policy behind these developments has been to shift the emphasis in criminal proceedings from a consideration of the exculpatory nature of mental disorder to one where the primary role of mental disorder is one relating to the sentencing process.[31]

As evidence of this shift, one only has to examine relevant statistics before and after the passing of the 1957 and 1959 Acts. This exercise has been carried out by Nigel Walker, who concluded that diminished

---

[29] R.A. Duff, 'Mental Disorder and Criminal Responsibility' *Proceedings of 10th Annual Conference of International Association of Legal and Social Philosophy* (1983), 42.

[30] J. Radden, *Madness and Reason* (Allen & Unwin, London, 1985), chs 4 and 5.

[31] H.L.A. Hart, *Punishment and Responsibility* (Oxford University Press, Oxford, 1968), ch. 8.

responsibility had taken 'over the sort of case which previously would have been accepted by the courts as within the M'Naghten Rules'.[32] As far as hospital orders are concerned, Walker traced their upward trend, showing how the provisions of the 1959 Act immediately accounted 'for the overwhelming majority of cases in which the courts officially recognise that an offender is mentally disordered';[33] as a result, 'the traditional procedures which involve consideration of the accused's mental state by the jury before conviction' became numerically insignificant, with the insanity defence accounting for under 0.5% of the total of such cases.[34] Not surprisingly this trend has continued, with the number of insanity defences falling in recent years to an average of three to four per annum.[35] Thus, as will be demonstrated later in this chapter, although the insanity defence has not been completely eradicated by the combination of diminished responsibility and hospital orders, it has certainly become a rare finding, and there can be little doubt that since the late 1950s many defendants have preferred to plead guilty rather than be subject to the original disposal consequences of the special verdict.[36] The obvious problem with such an outcome is one of fairness, for as Ashworth has pointed out 'it is likely that in a completely fair system, some of these [convicted offenders] would not be burdened with a criminal conviction but would be granted a defence of mental disorder instead'.[37]

However, the problem goes much deeper than this. With the introduction of the 1959 Act has come the increasing domination of the medical model, in the sense that mental illness is accepted as a disease which can be treated. Further, it has also been accepted that people who suffer from such diseases are not in any way to blame for their affliction. This is clearly the philosophy behind hospital orders in the sense that no punishment follows conviction.[38] Thus, although the accused is found guilty of the offence in question, his mental disorder has been viewed as a reason for changing his status from prisoner to patient. In short, his illness results in no punishment in the traditional sense, despite the fact that the mental disorder may have had no connection with the offence which resulted in a conviction. Once cured, no matter how quickly, he may be released and cannot be sent to prison to serve any further period of time as the remainder

[32] N. Walker, *Crime and Insanity in England, Vol 1* (Edinburgh University Press, Edinburgh 1968), 158.

[33] Walker, *Crime and Insanity in England, Vol 2* (1993), 78.   [34] Ibid. 78.

[35] See R.D. Mackay, *The Operation of the Criminal Procedure (Insanity) Act 1964—An Empirical Study of Unfitness to Plead and the Insanity Defence* (De Montfort University Law School Monographs, 1991) part 2.

[36] Prior to the Criminal Procedure (Insanity and Unfitness to Plead) Act 1991 this entailed mandatory, indeterminate hospitalisation.

[37] A. Ashworth, *Principles of Criminal Law* (Oxford University Press, Oxford, 1991), 182.

[38] See R.A. Duff, *Trials and Punishments* (Cambridge University Press, Cambridge 1986), 23–8 for a useful discussion of this issue.

of his 'sentence'. The overall effect of this type of approach has been to attract attention away from the ethico-legal issues surrounding the criminal responsibility of the mentally disordered towards a treatment-orientated approach. This has been welcomed by some as a step in the right direction,[39] while for others it has regrettably signalled 'the eclipse of an earlier analysis of madness to which appeal could be made in grounding the moral intuition to excuse'.[40] A further trend towards this eclipse may be detected both in the debate concerning whether insanity ought to operate as a defence or as a status excuse, and in relation to recent English reform proposals.

Is Insanity a Status or an Excuse?

An argument which may have considerable bearing on the exculpatory nature of insanity concerns the question whether it ought to operate as a defence, in the sense of acting as an excuse, or whether it is a more fundamental concept, which ought to be regarded in law as a status that automatically brings with it exemption from punishment. The difference is important, but is rarely discussed by English commentators.[41]

If it acts as an excuse, then the defence of insanity should only become relevant once it has been established that the accused's act was wrongful. Accordingly, as Fletcher has pointed out, if an allegedly insane defendant killed in self-defence, then this latter defence 'should preclude consideration of insanity' since the act of killing would be regarded in law as being justified.[42]

On the other hand, if insanity is in the nature of a status, then the whole notion of defence becomes irrelevant,[43] since instead the fundamental nature of the plea is that the prosecution process and criminal jurisdiction of the court are inappropriate to deal with this class of defendant. In short, insanity would therefore be similar in nature to 'infancy' in that the criminal law refuses to convict very young children of criminal offences irrespective of what proof the prosecution may have against them. The status of being a child under a certain age automatically means that a criminal prosecution cannot be proceeded with. In much the same way, therefore,

---

[39] See B. Wootton, *Social Science and Social Pathology* (Allen & Unwin, London 1958), ch. 8.   [40] Radden, *Madness and Reason*, 1.

[41] For an exception, see C. Wells, 'Whither Insanity?' [1983] Crim LR 787.

[42] G. Fletcher, *Rethinking Criminal Law* (Little Brown, London, 1978), 836.

[43] In her dissenting judgment in *R.* v. *Chaulk* (1990) 2 CR (4th) 1, 81–2, McLachlin J supports this view, stating 'the proper inquiry is . . . not into what the accused *actually* appreciated but, rather, into what the accused's *capacity* was . . . a person without the capacity for choice as defined in s. 16 of the Criminal Code, is not morally culpable. Because of lack of capacity, therefore, the issue of actus reus and mens rea never arises' (emphasis in original).

it is argued that the insane 'like young infants, lack one of the essential attributes of personhood—rationality. For this reason, human beings who are insane are no more the proper subjects of moral evaluation than are young infants, animals or even stones.'[44] This would suggest that the insane are exculpated on the basis of class membership, although as Schopp has pointed out there are other 'plausible interpretations of status defences' including the notion of 'nonexculpatory exemptions from punishment',[45] which would mean that crazy people who commit crimes should not be convicted even if blameworthy. In short, this last approach would represent a policy exemption from punishment which implied that 'the defendant's psychological processes are not a central concern . . . because culpability is not at issue'.[46] In some ways the approach of the criminal law to children who are under ten years of age could be viewed in this light. This, however, is not what Moore means since his notion of craziness clearly betokens a need for irrationality at the time of the alleged offence.

Although the analogy with children seems attractive, it is not without major problems. First and foremost is the difficulty of establishing insanity; for while infancy rests on a status which can be established with certainty[47]—namely a particular age—the same is certainly not true of insanity. It is difficult to understand therefore how such an approach towards insanity could operate in practice, and what procedural device might be used to establish the status. For example, it might be argued that the status approach could be applied to mentally impaired defendants if it could be shown that the accused's IQ was under a certain level,[48] as there is at least some degree of certainty established in relation to IQ testing. But to argue that the status approach could be equally applied to mental illness would seem to be wholly unrealistic, as psychiatrists themselves often disagree over matters of diagnosis. And what would the position be where such a disagreement occurred? Presumably a normal trial would then have to take place in order to establish guilt or innocence. But would an insanity defence as we now know it remain available in such cases? A further problem concerns the continuing nature of the status. This causes no difficulty in respect of children but what of the crazy person who is irrational one day and rational the next? If 'his condition remains presumptively constant',[49] then why should he not be similarly dealt with on the basis of his crazy status for offences committed on both days? Indeed Moore seems

---

[44] Moore, 'Causation and the Excuses', 1137. An obvious objection to this type of approach is that it demeans the mentally ill by attaching to them a quasi-permanent status which on the face of it gives them little or no autonomy.

[45] Schopp, *Automatism, Insanity and the Psychology of Criminal Responsibility*, 211.

[46] Ibid. 16.

[47] See the remark of Lord Simon in *Lynch* v. *DPP* [1975] 1 All ER 913, 933.

[48] Cf. *R.* v. *Masih* [1986] Crim LR 395.

[49] Fletcher, *Rethinking Criminal Law*, 836.

to support this approach when he remarks of both the insane and infants that 'in both cases we excuse because the actors lack the status of moral agents . . . they cannot be blamed because *in general* they lack our rational capacities'.[50]

Of course it can be argued that for practical purposes we have something approaching a status approach in England at present in the sense that it is clearly government policy to divert mentally abnormal offenders from the criminal justice system in order that they may receive care and treatment from the health and social services.[51] However, the crucial factor here is that this diversion occurs outside the formal law and is a matter of structured discretion, in that it has been decided that prosecution is not required in the public interest. This is far removed from the status approach which would take away this discretion from the prosecuting authorities, in much the same way as has happened with children under ten years of age.

Another fundamental point is whether the analogy drawn between children and the insane is an acceptable one. It is often suggested that the rationale behind the criminal law's approach towards both these groups is the same.[52] But is this so?[53] The policy reasons which underscore the removal of children under ten from the criminal process scarcely seem to resemble those which have guided the criminal law's response to the insane. Some have argued that it is the lack of reasoning power in both children and the insane which is evidence of this analogy. But if this is true, then why does the criminal law rely on a definite age in its approach towards young children rather than relying on a test relating to intellectual

---

[50] Moore, 'Causation and the Excuses', 1137 (emphasis in original).

[51] See Home Office Circular 66/90 (1990).

[52] See e.g. Radden, *Madness and Reason*, ch. 10.

[53] Cf. the interesting remarks of Lamer CJC in *R. v. Chaulk* (1990) 2 CR (4th) 1, 16 where he states: 'while the state of insanity and the state of childhood cannot be equated, the connection between these two situations for the purpose of the criminal law is apparent. What these two situations have in common is that they both indicate that the individual in question does not accord with one of the basic assumptions of our criminal law model: that the accused is a rational autonomous being who is capable of appreciating the nature and quality of an act or of knowing right from wrong. With respect to the state of childhood, these basic assumptions are brought into question because of the *immaturity* of the individual—he or she has not yet developed the basic capacity which justice and fairness require be present in a person who is being measured against the standards of the criminal law. With the state of insanity, these basic assumptions are brought into question because the accused is suffering from some disease of the mind . . . This mental condition means that the accused is largely incapable of criminal intent and should not, therefore, generally be subject to criminal liability in the same way that sane people are. (I note here that s. 16 does not exempt *all* people with a disease of the mind from criminal liability. The insanity defence is defined in a particular way, and only if an accused meets those criteria will his or her mental condition preclude a finding of guilt.)' (emphasis in original). It is clear, therefore, that Lamer CJC does not consider that insanity acts as a status excuse but rather as a claim that '[the accused] does not fit within the normal assumptions of our criminal law model because he does not have the capacity for criminal intent' (ibid. 18).

development or IQ?[54] The answer is not just a quest for certainty, but is also inextricably linked to society's attitude towards young children which is one of enthusiastic support and encouragement, in that child care and development are viewed as an essential part of the function of parents with government playing a strongly supportive role. It is difficult to see the same enthusiastic support being directed towards the mentally ill in society. Instead the mentally ill are viewed with suspicion and distrust. Hardly surprising therefore to find a completely different policy toward these two groups when it comes to the question of criminal accountability. Thus, while the blanket approach towards the non-prosecution of children is viewed as entirely proper, with the consequence that children under ten irrespective of how 'guilty' they might be are not to be dealt with in the criminal courts, the mentally ill as a group, although some may receive sympathy for their affliction, are on the whole regarded as deviant and in many cases even dangerous. The result has been the development of a broadly unsympathetic approach towards their plight, leading to a lack of resources which in turn has resulted in a great many mentally disordered offenders being sent to prison.

In short, although the analogy already referred to between these two groups may seem to have some validity, it is unconvincing. Children and the insane may well both lack essential reasoning capacity, but there is much more than this factor at the root of the criminal law's approach towards the under tens. Indeed, it might be argued instead with respect to young children that the 'character' approach towards excuse could be the real reason why the under tens are not prosecuted, in the sense that their immaturity entails a lack of settled dispositions or character traits. As one commentator puts it:

we do not treat young children as full moral agents, despite their capacity for practical reason and their freedom to act on the basis of their reasoned choices. Young children do not qualify as moral agents because they have not yet fully developed this capacity to respond appropriately to moral reason for action. This capacity for *moral responsiveness* presupposes that moral agents appreciate the normative significance of the moral norms governing their behaviour. It also assumes that moral agents can exercise *moral judgment* about how these norms apply in a particular context. Acting on the basis of moral judgment also requires *moral motivation*: the capacity to use the applicable moral norms as the basis for acting.[55]

---

[54] Cf. the approach of majority of the House of Lords in *Gillick* v. *West Norfolk and Wisbech Area Health Authority* [1985] 3 All ER 402 which decided that a child's right to make decisions about medical treatment should be based on a doctor's assessment of whether he or she has reached a sufficient understanding and intelligence to be capable of giving consent. Accordingly, a girl under 16 years of age does not, merely by reason of her age, lack the legal capacity to consent to contraceptive advice and treatment.

[55] Arenella, 'Character, Choice and Moral Agency', 68 (emphasis in original).

If this is the true explanation of a status excuse for young children, then might such an explanation not apply equally to the insane, in the sense that both classes of person lack the status of moral agency? The difficulty with this approach however is not only that it would have important implications in relation to a broad range of excuses,[56] but also that it would include some psychopaths even though they could have acted otherwise had they chosen to do so.[57] This in turn would involve a major shift in emphasis if the law was to accommodate such persons within an insanity status excuse. However, this is not to say that the 'character' model might not have advantages over the traditional 'choice' model, as it would enable a broadening of enquiry into the underlying character traits that motivate and govern our choices. Further, this model could be viewed as a more appropriate vehicle for a 'status excuse' approach to insanity on the ground that the crazy are so clearly non-accountable moral agents that, like children, they are not suitable agents for prosecution, or as Fletcher puts it 'it is implicit in the medical conception of insanity that the actor's true character is distorted by his mental illness'.[58]

An additional matter of importance in this respect, however, is the historical shift from regarding the insane or lunatics as a special class of people who were thought to be possessed 'and treated as generally incapable of evil', towards regarding insanity as a matter for medical experts and not 'as a condition discernible to the untutored eye'.[59] Accordingly, it can be argued that, with the development of the medical model, came a distinct move away from treating the insane as a distinct class of person towards regarding the mentally ill as persons who could be treated but only after diagnosis had taken place. Once medical labelling was introduced and insanity became the province of medical experts, any real prospect of decoupling the insane from the criminal process seems to have disappeared. Lunatics could no longer be regarded as a distinctive group like children who could be easily recognised in the community, but were instead viewed as persons who might or might not be ill depending on expert medical judgment.

A final significant point relating to the status approach concerns the argument that, if adopted, there is then no need to prove any causal connection between the accused's mental illness and the alleged offence if the plea of insanity is to operate. Indeed, Moore is highly critical of the causal theory of excuse, arguing that 'it is not because crazy people are caused

---

[56] Arenella, 'Character, Choice and Moral Agency', 65 states: 'Choice theorists offer different formulations of the cognitive and volitional excuses that negate the individual's fair opportunity to avoid violating the law's dictates. But most accounts of these excuses adopt a narrow time frame that focuses on whether the circumstances immediately preceding the criminal act prevented the defendant from complying with the law's dictates. Very few criminal defendants escape blame by relying on such narrowly drawn cognitive and volitional excuses.'

[57] Ibid. 65–9.   [58] Fletcher, *Rethinking Criminal Law*, 800.   [59] Ibid. 837.

to do what they do that they are excused; rather crazy people are excused because they are crazy . . . Insanity betokens a difference so fundamental that we deny moral agency to those afflicted with it . . . the very status of being crazy precludes responsibility. Seeking some hidden cause of the accused's criminal behaviour is, accordingly, beside the point.'[60] However, Moore is quick to admit that legal doctrine clearly has been influenced by the causal view of insanity in that 'all tests of legal insanity require that the defective mental condition be causally connected to the criminal act it purports to excuse'.[61]

This is certainly true in the sense that the M'Naghten Rules have been interpreted to require a causal relation between the accused's 'defect of reason' and his 'disease of the mind'.[62] Moore's basic criticism of causality here is that the test in the M'Naghten Rules is wrong-headed in so far as it exemplifies the notion that 'insanity excuses because it causes criminal acts'.[63] Although this may be something of an overstatement in the sense that the M'Naghten test does not expressly require proof that the insanity 'caused' the accused to commit the alleged offence, nevertheless Moore is correct when he states: 'rather than trying to determine when a being is enough like us to be considered a moral agent, courts have officially treated insanity as a true excuse rather than a status excuse'.[64] In short, he claims that this undue reliance on the need for a causal link between a person's actions and factors which are outside his control, such as mental illness, has led to the false conclusion 'that it is causation that underlies our established excuses'.[65] Further, in Morse's opinion this tendency to confuse 'causation with excuse [is] a confusion that has constantly bedevilled criminal law theorists. Causation is not an excuse, however, for all behaviour is caused. If causation were an excuse, no one would ever be held responsible for any behaviour, criminal or not . . . Causation is not the issue; nonculpable lack of rationality and compulsion is.'[66]

The difficulty here of course for the 'choice' theorist is that his notion of responsibility depends wholly upon the actor's choices being free, unlike the 'character' theorist who 'can happily admit that responsible choices are caused by character, and that character in turn is caused by factors not themselves chosen by the actor'.[67] Accordingly, provided we do not choose our characters, then individuals can be held responsible for their acts which are 'in character' even in the face of determinism. By way of contrast, the 'choice' theorist faces a difficulty in relation to hard determinism

---

[60] Moore, 'Causation and the Excuses', 1137, 1139.   [61] Ibid. 1093–4.

[62] In *R.* v. *Sullivan* [1983] 2 All ER 673, 677 Lord Diplock states: 'But the meaning of the expression "disease of the mind" as the *cause* of a "defect of reason" remains unchanged for the purposes of the M'Naghten Rules' (emphasis added).

[63] Moore, 'Causation and the Excuses', 1109.   [64] Ibid. 1138.   [65] Ibid. 1091.

[66] Morse, 'Excusing the Crazy', 789.

[67] Moore, 'Choice, Character and Excuse', 50.

which argues that choice and causation are incompatible, since 'the factors that *cause* choice, being themselves unchosen, *preclude* choice'.[68] This in turn means that, if determinism is true, no one is responsible for anything. The way out of this dilemma is to accept that choice and causation are compatible, in the sense that 'his choice was a cause of his behaviour (even if it itself was caused)'.[69] In short, the crux of the problem is whether our choices are caused, for if they are, then this compatibilist approach towards responsibility becomes essential as a means of rescuing the 'choice' theory from the grip of hard determinism, involving the claim that one can be held 'responsible for actions that result from one's choices, even though choices are caused by factors themselves unchosen'.[70] In this context, common sense dictates that choices, although influenced by all sorts of unchosen factors, do cause us to act in certain ways for which we are usually responsible but that mental illness, for example, may interfere with an agent's normal capacity for choice, thus making it impossible or very difficult for him to have acted in any other way.

The causality issue then is one of considerable importance. It clearly influenced the Butler Report in its recommendations concerning a revised special verdict which, it proposed, should be returned in any case where it could be shown that at the time of committing the alleged offence the accused was suffering from severe mental illness or severe subnormality. According to the Butler Report, 'such a person is exempted from responsibility on account of his disordered mental state notwithstanding technical proof of *mens rea*'.[71] This type of provision would certainly accord with Moore's philosophy insofar as it would help to convert the insanity defence from one of excuse into one of status,[72] while at the same time ridding the law of the complex issue of causality by turning 'over the test of criminal responsibility to medical opinion'.[73] As a model for this approach, the Butler Report used the Code Napoleon stating: 'similar provisions are still in force in France and some other countries . . . The essence of the formula is that it simply presumes absence of responsibility when it is established that the accused was suffering from a sufficiently severe degree of mental disorder (*démence*) at the time of his act or omission.'[74]

No further details are given about the French position, and in this context it is interesting to note two points. First, although Article 64 of the French Penal Code exempted a defendant from criminal responsibility if he was in a state of *démence* 'at the time of the offence', it would appear that

---

[68] Moore, 'Choice, Character and Excuse', 35 (emphasis in original).   [69] Ibid.
[70] Moore, 'Causation and the Excuses', 1147.   [71] Butler Report, para 18.17.
[72] The Butler Report also recommended a *mens rea* element which would allow for a special verdict where the accused lacked *mens rea* 'by reason of the evidence of mental disorder' (ibid. 238), thus retaining a degree of causality. See below.
[73] Butler Report, para 18.36.   [74] Ibid. 18.29.

this required not only that the mental disorder be contemporaneous with the offence but also that there be 'a relationship between the mental disorder and the offence committed [so that] if the offence is in no way connected with the mental disorder, the accused is not considered to be exempt from criminal responsibility'.[75] It would seem therefore that the French did not entirely succeed in cutting 'the Gordian Knot',[76] as was suggested by the Butler Report.

Secondly, Article 64 of the French Penal Code was replaced by a new provision in June 1990 which provides: 'the person who, at the moment of his action, was suffering from a psychic or neuro-psychic disorder which had abolished his discernment or his control over his actions, is not penally responsible'.[77] It seems clear from this that although severe forms of mental disorder will continue to exclude penal responsibility in France, there has been a major shift in that country towards an excuse-based insanity defence rather than one of status. Further, some other European countries have adopted a similar approach in respect of reform of the insanity defence,[78] and seem to be returning to a M'Naghten Rule based approach.

It is also important to note that in its recent consideration of the Butler Report's proposals concerning the special verdict, the Law Commission felt it necessary to retain a degree of causality, stating: 'some people take the view that it would be wrong in principle that a person should escape conviction if, although severely mentally ill, he has committed a rational crime which was uninfluenced by his illness and for which he ought to be liable to be punished. They believe that the prosecution should be allowed to persuade the jury (if it can) that the offence was not attributable to the disorder. We agree'.[79] It seems clear therefore that the idea of the insanity defence being regarded as a status excuse is one which has not yet found favour in common law jurisdictions. Indeed, there seems little doubt that the status approach is so far removed from the traditional approach contained in the M'Naghten Rules that it is simply not fully acceptable to policy makers. There is also a strong argument that to hand over part of the test of criminal responsibility to psychiatrists in the way suggested by the Butler Report would be a dangerous step as it would continue the eclipse of the traditional approach towards moral guilt and criminal

---

[75] M.G. Lloyd and M. Benezech, 'Criminal Responsibility and the French Judicial System' (1991) 2 *Journal of Forensic Psychiatry* 281, 285.

[76] Butler Report, para 18.29.

[77] Lloyd and Benezech, 'Criminal Responsibility and the French Judicial System', 291.

[78] A good example of this is to be found in Finland. For a brief discussion, see R.D. Mackay, 'The Insanity Defence and Criminal Responsibility in England' in R. Lahti and K. Nuotio (eds.), *Criminal Law Theory in Transition—Finnish and Comparative Perspectives* (Finnish Lawyers Publishing Company, Helsinki, 1992), 346–7.

[79] The Law Commission, *A Criminal Code for England and Wales* (Law Commission No 177) (1989), Vol 2, para 11.16.

responsibility. Thus, it has been stated 'we do not want to excuse lunatics for their action if it connects in no way with the psychological states, or their effects, which constitute their madness. A person with paranoia has no excuse for burglary if it relates in no way to the beliefs and desires making up his or her delusions.'[80] In response to this type of argument, the Butler Report opined that 'the causative links between the offence and the defendant's mental condition can safely be assumed',[81] indicating that causation was still the fundamental reason why a severely mentally ill person should not be convicted. However, as already noted, the Law Commission found this assumption unacceptable, and perhaps not without good reason. For it can be argued that the law has already been too willing to permit the fundamental issue of criminal responsibility to be bypassed so that many defendants who could perhaps have qualified for acquittal on the basis of an insanity defence have preferred to plead guilty owing to the wide sentencing powers granted to the courts to deal with mentally disordered offenders. However, as will be argued subsequently in this Chapter, to 'force' potential irresponsible offenders to plead guilty is unacceptable. It is surely time to allow such mentally abnormal offenders to test the issue of their moral guilt without fear of the inflexible disposal consequences which have been the hallmark of the insanity defence under the M'Naghten Rules. In this respect, the flexibility of disposal which has recently been introduced by the Criminal Procedure (Insanity and Unfitness to Plead) 1991 Act may do just that.

Another important point concerning the type of status excuse envisaged by the Butler Report is its reliance on psychiatric notions of severe mental illness 'rather than on abstractions (such as "disease of the mind")'.[82] If this new type of insanity defence became law, then Hart's prediction that 'the apparently coarser-grained technique of exempting persons from liability to punishment if they fall into certain recognised categories of mental disorder is likely to be increasingly used')[83] would seem well-founded. However, his optimism about such a technique being 'more likely to lead in practice to satisfactory results' is much more problematical.[84] The essential difficulty surrounds the idea that it is proper to alter the nature of the insanity defence to one which is built on psychiatric categories.[85] The Butler Report's solution was 'to identify the abnormal mental phenomena which occur in the various mental illnesses and which when present would be regarded by common consent as being evidence of severity'.[86]

In the Law Commission's opinion this 'symptomatic mode of definition

---

[80] Radden, *Madness and Reason*, 9.   [81] Butler Report, para 18.36.
[82] Law Commission, *A Criminal Code*, Vol 2, para 11.17.
[83] Hart, *Punishment and Responsibility*, 229.   [84] Ibid.
[85] See e.g. J. Glover, *Responsibility* (Routledge, London, 1970), 139–40.
[86] Butler Report, para 18.34.

has much to commend it. The psychiatric expert will give evidence of strict "factual tests" '.[87] Accordingly, a diagnostic label such as schizophrenia will not be enough. Instead, it is only those schizophrenics whose mental illness is regarded by psychiatrists as 'severe' who will qualify for a special verdict, provided the jury agrees. Like it or not, however, this approach 'turns over the test of criminal responsibility to medical opinion'[88] in relation to severe abnormal mental phenomena which are inevitably part and parcel of a psychiatric diagnosis. Such an approach may accord more with psychiatric practice, but seems to tell us little about the fundamental nature of the insanity defence which as mentioned earlier seems deeply embedded in our notions of lack of rationality.

In the meantime of course it is important to realise that the Criminal Procedure (Insanity and Unfitness to Plead) Act of 1991 in no way alters the legal test of insanity which remains enshrined within the M'Naghten Rules. Accordingly, although the Rules continue to be the subject of unflagging criticism, it is equally important to make some attempt to gauge how, even if infrequently used, they are operating in practice. For it could be that Moore is correct when he remarks that perhaps 'the "unofficial" version of the insanity test . . . restricts the excuse of legal insanity to those who are so clearly lacking in rationality that they are popularly considered crazy.'[89] Certainly, my own empirical study of the insanity defence in this country could be interpreted as lending support to Moore's contention[90], especially as both judges and juries do appear to be approaching the interpretation of the M'Naghten Rules in a liberal manner: the 'wrongness limb' is not only more frequently used than the 'nature and quality limb' but also seems to be applied in cases where the accused believed that what they were doing was morally right. Why is this? Could it be that judges and juries simply consider such mentally ill persons to be 'crazy'?

PUNISHMENT AND THE INSANE[91]

It is abundantly clear that the vast majority of prosecuted mentally disordered offenders in England and Wales are convicted rather than excused. In most cases, therefore, mental disorder does not negate criminal responsibility but instead may lead to treatment in the form of a hospital order or to some other form of supervisory disposal such as a psychiatric probation order. Despite this clear trend of holding mentally abnormal offenders criminally liable, there is a small handful of cases each year where defendants are found not guilty by reason of insanity. But why does the

[87] Law Commission, *A Criminal Code*, para. 11.17.
[88] Butler Report, para. 18.36.   [89] Moore 'Causation and the Excuses', 1139.
[90] R.D. Mackay, *The Operation of the Criminal Procedure (Insanity) Act 1964*, Part Two.
[91] See Moore, *Law and Psychiatry*, 232–45; Finkel, *Insanity on Trial*, ch. 6.

insanity defence continue to attract a finding of 'not guilty'? The answer to this question is inextricably linked to the notion of punishment; for if none of the purposes behind punishment can be legitimately applied to the person who is adjudged insane at the time of the committing the offence, then exculpation ought to follow.

In this connection Western society seems universally to have considered it unjust and immoral to punish those who have been adjudged legally insane as 'the practice of punishment presupposes the very responsibility the legally insane lack'.[92] The practice of punishing the insane is often said to be inconsistent with the utilitarian theory of punishment, in the sense that those who are unaware of what they are doing cannot be deterred by criminal sanctions. However, as Hart points out, this argument is open to the criticism that while it is true 'that the threat of punishment will be ineffective so far as the class of persons who suffer from these conditions is concerned', it is still possible that 'the actual infliction of punishment on those persons, may secure a higher measure of conformity to law on the part of normal persons'.[93] In this respect, as already mentioned, it is clear that as far as English law is concerned, the vast majority of mentally disordered offenders are convicted in the normal way. Of course it must be conceded that many such offenders will not be punished in the traditional sense but will instead be sentenced to hospital. However such hospitalization presupposes responsibility for the offence and brings with it the stigma of guilt. Further, if the hospital order has restrictions attached, then this may be viewed by many as a form of punishment. Indeed, this notion inevitably spills over into the insanity defence, since if mandatory commitment follows a successful defence, then this incarceration is no different from that of the convicted mentally ill defendant who is the subject of a restriction order, except that the latter is labelled guilty while the defendent who is adjudged insane receives a technical special acquittal. However, although this analogy is a compelling one, it has to be conceded that while the sentencing judge could in his discretion have punished the convicted offender in the normal way, he does not have this discretion where the verdict is one of not guilty by reason of insanity. Finally, and very significantly, the new provisions of the Criminal Procedure (Insanity and Unfitness to Plead) Act 1991 now give the judge disposal options when deciding how best to deal with those subject to the special verdict.[94] These options include an absolute discharge. At long last, therefore, the deep-seated punitive history behind the insanity defence may be laid to rest once and for all. However, this is likely to take time, and that history itself deserves some discussion as it goes a long way to explain the demise of the defence of insanity in England.

---

[92] D.H. Hermann, *The Insanity Defence*, 151.
[93] Hart, *Punishment and Responsibility*, 19.   [94] Except in relation to murder charges.

However, before turning to the history, it should be pointed out that it is rather the retributive aspects of punishment which many would find distasteful if the legally insane were to be punished in the normal manner. Clearly this ties in with the personal nature of retribution in that it is related to the view that society is punishing the offender because he deserves to be punished. This in turn rests on the notion that only those who are responsible for their actions deserve to be punished for them. This view is well encapsulated by Morse: 'in sum, the moral basis of the insanity defence is that there is no just punishment without desert and no desert without responsibility. Responsibility is, in turn, based on minimal cognitive and volitional competence. Thus, an actor who lacks such competence is not responsible, does not deserve punishment, and cannot justly be punished'.[95] Naturally, this in turn raises the fundamental problem of what degree of incompetence is required before a mentally disordered person can be adjudged legally irresponsible: a problem which continues to tax all common law jurisdictions and will make up a considerable bulk of the remainder of this Chapter. However, before the current legal position is considered, a brief comment will be made about the history of the insanity defence in England.

HISTORICAL PERSPECTIVES

BEFORE 1800

Although the historical development of the special defence of insanity at common law is shrouded in obscurity, Nigel Walker's scholarly study entitled *Crime and Insanity in England* is both instructive and illuminating. In it, Walker describes how in pre-Roman England, with its adherence to strict liability stemming from a lack of differentiation between crime and tort, there was 'simply a straightforward rule for ensuring that compensation was paid for an insane killer's victim, and that the insane man did not become in turn the victim of the spear'.[96] However, by the eleventh century certain grave wrongs such as murder and arson came to be recognised as being punishable by death or forfeiture of property unless the offender could secure the king's pardon. As a result, it seems that the royal pardon became the appropriate method of dealing with clearly insane offenders,[97] which meant no doubt that the offender's kinsfolk were charged with his care or failing that the offender remained in jail. So far as forfeiture was concerned, 'his goods and lands were also to be seized; but he

---

[95] Morse, 'Excusing the Crazy', 783.
[96] Nigel Walker, *Crime and Insanity in England, Vol 1 The Historical Perspective* (Edinburgh University Press, Edinburgh, 1968), 15–16.   [97] Ibid.

was to be allowed sustenance from then, and the persons charged with their management were not to commit any waste'.[98] Clearly, therefore, this form of forfeiture was not identical to criminal forfeiture, where the felon would lose all rights to his property. Walker then adds: 'The period during which it became the regular practice to acquit the insane accused instead of leaving him to be pardoned by the king cannot be identified with certainty.'[99] However, the earliest case of such an acquittal discovered by Walker is in 1505, where the relevant passage from the Year Books of Henry VII reads: 'it was found at the time of the murder the felon was of unsound mind . . . Wherefore it was decided that he should go free'.[100] As far as the justification for excusing the insane was concerned, although there appears to have been no fixed test, Walker makes it clear that prior to 1800 the insanity defence began to be used much more commonly than has generally been suggested. A particular reason for this phenomenon may well have been the lack of any fixed test, since 'if the jury were trying an ordinary theft or case of violence—not a Jacobite or a terrorist—the important question for them was whether the defendant was really insane'.[101] If that was the case, then on acquittal the prisoner might be discharged, although again there was no fixed practice in this. 'Much depended on whether relatives were willing to take care of the prisoner and guarantee his future behaviour. If no such person could be found, the court could send the discharged lunatic back to jail' until he recovered his senses.[102]

FROM 1800 TO 1843

During this brief period of 43 years, certain crucial developments took place which, more than any others, were to shape the modern law relating to the defence of insanity.

The first of these developments was the trial and acquittal of James Hadfield for the attempted assassination of King George III, which until recently had received little detailed historical analysis. This deficiency has now been rectified by Richard Moran who, during a very full discussion of the Hadfield case,[103] points out that judicial concern over the need to confine the prisoner, should the jury acquit him on the grounds of insanity, led to the court's acceptance of the suggestion:

---

[98] Walker, *Crime and Insanity Vol 1*, 24.   [99] Ibid. 25.   [100] Ibid. 26.

[101] Walker, 'The Insanity Defence Before 1800' (1985) 477 *Annals* 30; Walker, *Crime and Insanity Vol 1*, 70.

[102] J.M. Beattie, *Crime and the Courts in England 1660–1800* (Princeton University Press, New Jersey, 1986), 84. See also Walker, *Crime and Insanity, Vol 1*, 42.

[103] Richard Moran, 'The Origin of Insanity as a Special Verdict: The Trial for Treason of James Hadfield (1800)' (1985) 18 *Law and Society Review* 487.

that if the jury stated the reason for the acquittal, there would be sufficient legal cause to detain Hadfield. The jurors, who were in the jury box during the entire discussion, obliged the court. They returned the following verdict: 'We find the prisoner is not guilty; he being under the influence of insanity at the time the act was committed.' This was probably the first time an Anglo-American jury had ever been asked to attach an explanation to the verdict in an insanity case. It was to have an enormous impact on the disposal of those defendants who would be found, in the soon-to-be-abridged phrase, 'not guilty by reason of insanity'.[104]

Although the Hadfield case is often credited with adding insane delusions to the so-called 'wilde beeste' test as a basis for a finding for insanity,[105] it seems to have little or no importance as a legal precedent. Moran explains that 'this is probably because the verdict can best be explained by the court's acceptance of the physical cause of Hadfield's mental disorder and not by the persuasiveness of the legal or medical arguments'.[106] In short, Hadfield's insanity was freely accepted by everyone, owing to the visible severity of the head wounds he had received during military service. As a result of this lack of controversy, Hadfield's acquittal failed to create any public criticism. By way of contrast, however, it did cause a good deal of judicial concern owing to the fact that there was no clear legal power over him. The direct result of this concern was the enactment of the Criminal Lunatics Act 1800[107], which was retrospectively applied to Hadfield thus legalising his lifelong detention until his death some 41 years later. Furthermore, it is clear from the debate in the House of Commons that the Bill's supporters 'believed that the mentally ill deserved to be punished and that such persons could be deterred by the threat of punishment'.[108]

This view of the insanity defence as a punitive measure is further emphasised by Moran in his study of the trial for treason of Edward Oxford in 1840.[109] In that case the accused was acquitted on the ground of insanity after he had fired two shots at the royal carriage in which Queen Victoria was travelling. The result was that Oxford spent 27 years in confinement before being conditionally discharged. This, despite the fact that when the jury returned its verdict, it stated that it was unsure whether the pistols were even loaded.[110] If this was indeed the case, then at worst

---

[104] Richard Moran, 'The Modern Foundation for the Insanity Defence: The Cases of James Hadfield (1800) and Daniel M'Naghten (1843)' 477 *Annals* 31, 35.

[105] This test was used in the trial of Edward Arnold in 1724 when it was stated that in order to be legally insane the prisoner must 'not know what he is doing, no more than an infant, than a brute or wild beast.' For discussion see Walker, 'The Insanity Defence Before 1800', 28.

[106] Moran, 'The Origin of Insanity as a Special Verdict', 35.

[107] An Act for the Safe Custody of Insane Persons Charged with Offences, 39 & 40 Geo III, c 94 (1800).   [108] Moran, 'The Origin of Insanity as a Special Verdict', 36.

[109] Richard Moran, 'The Punitive Uses of the Insanity Defence: The Trial for Treason of Edward Oxford (1840)' (1986) 9 *International Journal of Law and Psychiatry* 171.

[110] Ibid. 184.

Oxford's crime was merely a misdemeanour. Consequently, Moran concludes that:

Far from representing an enlightened, humanitarian view of criminal responsibility by a judge and jury concerned with the welfare of a mentally ill defendant, the verdict in the Oxford case was the result of limitations in the law of high treason combined with the absence of hard evidence that Oxford actually intended to assassinate the Queen. Once these factors are appreciated, the case exemplifies the ability of the prosecution—not the defence—to manipulate the law to produce a desired outcome. The verdict served the prosecutor's interests of punishment and incapacitation more than it did the alleged interest of the defence.[111]

Finally, continuing the same theme, Moran in his exhaustive study of the infamous case of Daniel M'Naghten,[112] not only seriously questions whether the accused was truly mentally ill at the time he assassinated the Prime Minister's secretary,[113] but also forcefully argues that 'the trial functioned to reinforce the public impression of Daniel M'Naghten as a deranged murderer. It sealed him forever in history—a criminal lunatic whose motives for attempting to assassinate the prime minister of England were not worthy of serious consideration'.[114] In addition to his being completely discredited, M'Naghten's indefinite incapacitation was also ensured by means of his insanity acquittal and he died in Broadmoor some 22 years later.

Of course, it is true that the public furore following M'Naghten's special acquittal gave rise to the formulation of the famous Rules which are named after him and that these Rules narrowed the scope of the insanity defence thus ensuring that subsequent offenders like M'Naghten would be convicted.[115] However, it would be an error to think that M'Naghten's acquittal was motivated in any way by humanitarian concerns. Instead, the historical evidence points clearly to the fact that once again this special verdict was used not only to discredit but also to punish, incapacitate, and serve as an example to others.[116]

From 1800 onwards, the theme of this brief historical analysis has remained consistent. It is best summarised by Moran when he states: 'it might be said that the trial of James Hadfield marked the abolition of the insanity defence, not its origin, since in most jurisdictions a successful defence of insanity now leads to automatic commitment for an indefinite period of time'.[117]

---

[111] Moran, 'The Punitive Uses of the Insanity Defence', 171.

[112] Richard Moran, *Knowing Right from Wrong, The Insanity Defence of Daniel M'Naghten* (Free Press, New York, 1981).

[113] Cf. H.R. Rollin, 'M'Naghten's Madness' in D.J. West and A. Walk (eds.), *Daniel M'Naghten: His Trial and the Aftermath* (Gaskell Books, Ashford, Kent, 1977).

[114] Moran, *Knowing Right from Wrong*, 109.   [115] Ibid. 111.

[116] Ibid.   [117] Moran, 'The Origin of Insanity as a Special Verdict', 517.

This inflexibility of disposal[118] combined with other factors led to the demise of the insanity defence in England. It is now time to consider these additional factors in conjunction with the attitude of the judiciary towards the M'Naghten Rules.

JUDICIAL INTERPRETATION OF THE M'NAGHTEN RULES

Ever since their inception in 1843, the Rules named after Daniel M'Naghten have been shrouded in controversy. Their very existence stems from a decision taken during the House of Lords' debate on the issue, that the judges should be summoned to give their opinion 'as to the law respecting crimes committed by persons afflicted with insane delusions'.[119] As is well known, the Rules resulted from certain questions which the judges were required to answer in consequence of this summons. However, it is not clear who was responsible for drafting the questions, nor what gave the resulting Rules the power of law in England. They have never been adopted by Parliament in any statute and were clearly not the direct product of judicial proceedings. In short, the Rules seem unique as a source of English law. But despite this, they have been applied so often and for so long that they unquestionably form part of the common law of England.

Although it is not even known with any degree of certainty how many of the judges concurred in the formulation of the famous Rules,[120] their essentials have become a standard test of criminal responsibility. The basic test is now so well known that it hardly merits repetition. It is as follows:

that to establish a defence on the ground of insanity, it must be clearly proved that, at the time of the committing of the act, the party accused was labouring under such a defect of reason, from disease of the mind, as not to know the nature and quality of the act he was doing, or, if he did know it, that he did not know he was doing what was wrong.[121]

As far as English law is concerned, this test has remained unchanged despite constant criticism from both the legal and medical professions. The fundamental criticisms are twofold. First, the Rules are much too narrow in scope and if strictly interpreted will excuse almost no mentally abnormal offenders. Second, the Rules are based on outmoded concepts which fail to

---

[118] Disposal options have now been introduced by the Criminal Procedure (Insanity and Unfitness to Plead) Act 1991, see below.

[119] Moran, *Knowing Right From Wrong*, 168.

[120] It has been generally assured that all 15 judges were involved. However, the House of Lords' record speaks only of 11. Apart from Tindal LCJ who delivered the collective ruling and Maule J who dissented, we cannot now be sure who the others were. See Current Topics, 'The Judges Responsible for the Rulings in M'Naghten's Case' (1983) 57 *Australian Law Journal* 315.   [121] (1843) 10 Cl & F 200, 210; [1843–60] All ER Rep 229, 233.

reflect medical reality. Both of these criticisms will now be examined in the light of a brief analysis of the way in which the English courts have set about interpreting the Rules.

With regard to adopting a narrow construction of the Rules, the courts have been consistent in their attitude towards the two 'knowledge' requirements, namely 'nature and quality' and 'wrong'. Thus, as is well known, in *R. v. Codere*[122] the Court of Criminal Appeal refused to draw any distinction between 'nature' and 'quality', holding that the phrase referred only to the physical character of the act and not to its moral quality, whilst in *R. v. Windle*[123] the same court restricted the meaning of the word 'wrong' to legal wrong and refused to extend its meaning to incorporate moral wrong. In short, the court adopted an extremely narrow cognitive approach towards the rules, ensuring that their application would be restricted to fundamental or extreme intellectual defects.

Of course, the threshold requirement for a successful insanity defence under the Rules is that the accused be found to have been 'labouring . . . under a defect of reason from disease of the mind' and here there has been some inconsistency in the scope of judicial interpretation.

'DISEASE OF THE MIND'

The phrase 'disease of the mind' initially seems to have attracted no judicial scrutiny. A possible reason for this could be that the phrase may well have been used 'convertibly with "insanity"',[124] in which case perhaps elaboration was felt to be unnecessary. However, the development of the automatism defence changed this. For suddenly the courts were confronted by the fact that a successful defence based on 'unconscious involuntary action' could result in an unqualified acquittal.[125] For obvious social defence reasons this fact began to worry the courts and in order to restrict the availability of such acquittals the judiciary began to develop a complex body of law built upon the phrase 'disease of the mind'. The result, which was discussed fully in Chapter One, has been the division of automatism into two types: namely, sane and insane.

The approach of the English courts towards this question is best summed up by referring to two well-known House of Lords' decisions, both of which concern epileptic offenders. First, in *Bratty* v. *Attorney-General for Northern Ireland*, Lord Denning made the following influential remark:

---

[122] (1916) 12 Cr App R 21.
[123] [1952] 2 QB 826. For a recent refusal to follow *Windle*, see the decision of the Supreme Court of Canada in *R. v. Chaulk* (1990) 2 CR (4th) 1.
[124] Glanville Williams, *Textbook of Criminal Law* (2nd edn., Stevens, London, 1983), 644.
[125] *Bratty* v. *Attorney-General for Northern Ireland* [1963] AC 386, 401 per Viscount Kilmuir LC.

The major mental diseases which doctors call psychoses, such as schizophrenia, are clearly diseases of the mind. But in Charlson[126], Barry J. seems to have assumed that other diseases such as epilepsy or cerebral tumour are not diseases of the mind, even when they are such as to manifest themselves in violence. I do not agree with this. It seem to me that any mental disorder that manifests itself in violence and is prone to recur is a disease of the mind. At any rate it is the sort of disease for which a person should be detained in hospital rather than be given a unqualified acquittal.[127]

Second, in *R. v. Sullivan*, Lord Diplock speaking for a unanimous House of Lords said:

The nomenclature adopted by the medical profession may change from time to time; Bratty was tried in 1961. But the meaning of the expression 'disease of the mind' as the cause of 'a defect of reason' remains unchanged for the purposes of the application of the M'Naghten Rules. I agree with what Devlin J said in R. v. Kemp[128] that 'mind' in the M'Naghten Rules is used in the ordinary sense of mental faculties of reason, memory and understanding. If the effect of a disease is to impair these faculties so severely as to have either of the consequences referred to in the latter part of the Rules, it matters not whether the aetiology of the impairment is organic, as in epilepsy, or functional, or whether the impairment itself is permanent or is transient and intermittent, provided that it subsisted at the time of the commission of the act. The purpose of the legislation relating to the defence of insanity . . . has been to protect society against recurrence of the dangerous conduct. The duration of a temporary suspension of mental faculties of reason, memory and understanding, particularly if, as in the appellant's case, it is recurrent, cannot on any rational ground be relevant to the application by the courts of the M'Naghten Rules . . . it is natural to feel reluctant to attach the label of insanity to a sufferer from psychomotor epilepsy of the kind to which the appellant was subject, even though the expression in the context of a special verdict of not guilty by reason of insanity is a technical one which includes a purely temporary and intermittent suspension of the mental faculties of reason, memory and understanding resulting from the occurrence of an epileptic fit. But the label is contained in the current statute, it has appeared in this statute's predecessors ever since 1800. It does not lie within the power of the courts to alter it. Only Parliament can do that. It has done so twice; it could do so again.[129]

It is obvious from these dicta that the manner in which the judiciary have interpreted 'disease of the mind' is largely governed by policy considerations, and has little or nothing to do with the practice of psychiatry.[130]

---

[126] *R. v. Charlson* [1955] 1 All ER 859.

[127] [1963] AC 386, 412. More recently in *R. v. Burgess* [1991] 2 All ER 769, 774 the Court of Appeal added the following rider to Lord Denning's definition: 'the absence of the danger of recurrence is not a reason for saying that [the condition] cannot be a disease of the mind'.

[128] [1957] QB 399, 406.　　　　[129] [1983] 2 All ER 673, 677–8.

[130] See e.g. the statement of Martin JA in *R. v. Rabey* (1977) 79 DLR (3d) 414, 426: 'The opinions of medical witnesses as to whether an abnormal mental state does or does not

Instead, as Lord Diplock makes clear, the concept is a wide-ranging one which is capable of encompassing all forms of mental impairment which give rise to a defect of reason. Hence it caters for those who suffer from epilepsy, brain tumours, and arteriosclerosis. Taken at face value, therefore, the scope of 'disease of the mind' seems alarmingly wide and the only thing which stops it swallowing up every conceivable form of temporary mental impairment has been the recognition by the courts that it would be 'an affront to common sense' to equate certain forms of common condition with legal insanity.[131] This concession was expressly made by Lord Diplock in *R. v. Sullivan* when he remarked that despite his ruling on epilepsy, the defence of non-insane automatism should not be excluded 'in cases where temporary impairment . . . results from some external physical factor such as a blow on the head causing concussion or the administration of an anaesthetic for therapeutic purposes'.[132] By implication his Lordship was admitting that such conditions are not proper candidates for 'disease of the mind' classification, provided they are 'temporary' and the result of 'some external physical factor'. However, as was emphasised in Chapter One, this 'external factor' approach to distinguishing between sane and insane automatism has led to the creation of a complex body of law which is neither clear nor satisfactory.

'DEFECT OF REASON'

Although the courts have adopted a wide policy-based approach towards 'disease of the mind', their attitude towards 'defect of reason' has been consistent with their restrictive interpretation of the knowledge requirements referred to earlier. Thus in *R. v. Kemp*, Devlin J said: 'a defect of reason is by itself normally enough to make the act irrational and therefore to deny responsibility in law, but it was not intended by the rule that it should apply to defects of reason which were caused simply by brutish stupidity without rational power'.[133] His Lordship went on to emphasise that in order to qualify for legal insanity, the defect of reason must be clearly attributable to a disease of the mind. However, because of the wide interpretation given to this latter phrase within the Rules, there are bound to be many persons suffering from diseases of the mind who in day to day life may act with 'brutish stupidity'. If such a person commits a criminal offence, then is he to be regarded as legally insane? A clear answer to this question can now be given. For in *R. v. Clarke*[134] the Court of Appeal

constitute a disease of the mind are not . . . determinative, since what is a disease of the mind is a legal question.'

[131] *R. v. Quick* [1973] 3 All ER 347, 352 per Lawton LJ.
[132] [1983] 2 All ER 673, 678.
[133] [1957] 1 QB 399, 406.   [134] [1972] 1 All ER 219.

made it very clear that although a depressed shop-lifter might be regarded as suffering from a 'disease of the mind',[135] her confusion and absent-mindedness at the time of the alleged theft fell far short of a 'defect of reason'. Instead, 'the picture painted by the evidence was wholly consistent with this being a woman who retained her ordinary powers of reason but who was momentarily absent-minded or confused and acted as she did by failing to concentrate properly on what she was doing and by failing adequately to use her mental powers'.[136] Once again, therefore, the court adopted a 'common sense' approach towards its interpretation of this part of the Rules because it would be 'absurd to call anyone in the appellant's condition insane'.[137]

It can be seen from this brief analysis of the approach of the English judiciary towards the M'Naghten Rules that, although an expansionary approach has been adopted towards the scope of 'disease of the mind', this has been counterbalanced by the narrow interpretation given to the other elements of the Rules. The effect of this has been to exclude the vast majority of mentally disordered persons from the realms of the insanity defence, as inevitably in most cases they will know what they are doing and that the offence they are committing is legally wrong. On the other hand, the courts have shown a willingness to include a wide range of malfunctionings of the mind within the scope of 'disease of the mind' in order to ensure that the vast majority of states of automatism do not lead to unqualified acquittals but will instead fall within the special verdict.[138] As will be noted in the next Section, the result of this judicial attitude towards the Rules together with a number of other factors, such as disposal, has led to the demise of the insanity defence in England.

THE OPERATION OF THE INSANITY DEFENCE IN ENGLAND

One of the most frequently voiced criticisms of the M'Naghten Rules has concerned the fact that the insanity defence is so rarely used in England. Thus, according to Dell, 'not more than one or two people a year are acquitted in the courts on the grounds of insanity'.[139] Similarly, Smith and Hogan state 'that in 1986 no person charged with murder was found unfit to plead, only one was acquitted on the ground of insanity, [but] 55 charges of murder were reduced to manslaughter on the ground of diminished responsibility'.[140] It is this latter plea of diminished responsibility which, it is argued, had led to the demise of the insanity defence in murder cases, with the result that some defendants preferred to plead guilty to

---

[135] [1972] 1 All ER 219, 221. [136] Ibid. [137] Ibid.
[138] See Chapter One on automatism.
[139] Susanne Dell, 'Wanted: An Insanity Defence that can be Used' [1983] Crim LR 431.
[140] Smith and Hogan, *Criminal Law* (7th edn., 1992), 215.

manslaughter rather than be subject to the inflexible disposal consequences of a special verdict: namely automatic and indeterminate hospitalization under the Criminal Procedure (Insanity) Act 1964, prior to its amendment by the 1991 Act. The reasons given in support of this argument are well-known and seem to have been accepted without challenge. They are summarized in the Butler Report as follows:

With the introduction, under section 2 of the Homicide Act 1957, of the defence of diminished responsibility in murder cases, which enabled the court to pass any appropriate sentence from life imprisonment to absolute discharge, according to the degree of blame attributable to the offender, another possibility was opened up to defendants which has proved increasingly popular. Then the Mental Health Act 1959 enabled the court to substitute a hospital order for a sentence of imprisonment in all cases where it had a discretion as to sentence. The abolition of capital punishment has gone still further in removing any incentive on the part of the defence to seek a special verdict, and the insanity defence is in fact almost unheard of nowadays.[141]

Certainly, the *Criminal Statistics* for England and Wales reveal that as far as murder was concerned the insanity defence was very rarely used.[142] However, what of other offences? Here the *Criminal Statistics* revealed no information as figures concerning the insanity defence are not published separately for offences other than murder. This in itself is misleading in that the existing statistics inevitably give a distorted picture,[143] as to the paucity of successful insanity defences.[144] However, my recent research about the use of the insanity defence in England, which examined the Home Office documentation in all special verdict cases between 1975 and 1989, a period of 15 years, raises some basic questions about the practical role of the insanity defence as hitherto commonly understood by the majority of English lawyers.[145]

---

[141] Butler Report, para 18.9, pp 218–19.

[142] The *Criminal Statistics* for 1993, Cm 2680, at Table 4.8 reveal no such special verdicts in 1987 or 1988, one in 1989 and in 1990 and two in 1991. The figure of three recorded for 1992 corresponds with the first year of the operation of the Criminal Procedure (Insanity and Unfitness to Plead) Act 1991.

[143] *The Home Office Statistical Bulletin*, Issue 28/88, contains 'Statistics of Mentally Disordered Offenders in England and Wales' in 1985 and 1986. However, nowhere does it give a breakdown of successful insanity defences. See ibid. 11, table 3, which gives totals for unfitness to plead and insanity taken together.

[144] P.J. Taylor in 'Reading about Forensic Psychiatry' (1988) 153 *British Journal of Psychiatry* 271, 272 gives some statistics which comes closest to the truth. However, even these figures supplied by the Home Office are a little misleading in that they are based upon the date of admission to hospital rather than the date of the finding which means that they fail to include the cases where those found 'not guilty by reason of insanity' were never hospitalized.

[145] Kindly supported by a grant from the Nuffield Foundation. Special thanks are owed to C3 division of the Home Office for allowing me access to relevant documentation and for their generous co-operation throughout this research.

THE INSANITY DATA[146]

During the research period of 1975 to 1989 there was a total of 52 successful insanity defences in England and Wales. The greatest number of special verdicts in any single year was six in 1975, 1976, and 1986 respectively, while the smallest number was one in 1982.

When those who made successful insanity defences are analysed as regards criminal records, 25 of the males (61%) compared to only 2 females (18.1%) had previous convictions. In addition, the same number of males, namely 25 (61%), had a history of some form of psychiatric treatment compared to 8 of the females (72.7%).

As can be seen from Table 2.1, the types of charge which predominated were fatal and non-fatal offences against the person, which, if robbery is included within this group, account for an overwhelming 44 cases (84.6%).

With regard to diagnostic groups, schizophrenia dominated with 27 (52%) of the sample falling within this diagnosis: see Table 2.2.

It should be further noted that within the research sample of 52 insanity findings only one individual had been found not guilty by reason of insanity on more than one occasion, once in 1985 and again in 1988, for common assault.

In addition, as far as prior findings of unfitness to plead are concerned, there were only two cases of remission for trial followed by a special verdict. The first was in 1975 where the accused had earlier been found unfit to plead in 1974 for a deception offence and was again found unfit to plead in 1981 for similar offences. In the second, the accused's special verdict in 1977 followed an initial finding of unfitness to plead for a wounding offence.

With regard to the manner in which the M'Naghten Rules were being used to support an insanity defence, despite the fact that the 'wrongness' limb of the rules has been the subject of criticism which has even led to its being abandoned by jurisdictions such as Montana in the United States,[147] it was this particular limb which was most commonly used to secure a special verdict. This therefore seems to run counter to the view of, for example, Glanville Williams who has remarked: 'the only one of the M'Naghten Rules not going to mens rea . . . is question 2, relating to knowledge of wrong. This is held to mean legal wrong. Unless very benevolently interpreted it adds almost nothing to the other questions.'[148] The Butler Report was also critical of the 'wrongness' test, stating at paragraph 18.8: 'Knowledge of the law is hardly an appropriate test on which to base ascription of responsibility to the mentally disordered. It is

---

[146] For more detail, see Mackay, *The Operation of the Criminal (Procedure) Insanity Act 1964*.   [147] See below.
[148] Williams, *Textbook of Criminal Law*, 645.

TABLE 2.1   *Not Guilty by Reason of Insanity Disposals 1975–89—*
Types of Charge

	Frequency	As % of Total Sample
Murder	15	28.9%
Manslaughter	1	1.9%
Non-fatal assaults	25*	48.1%
Arson	4	7.7%
Robbery	3	5.8%
Burglary	2	3.8%
Deception	1	1.9%
Reckless Driving	1	1.9%
TOTAL	52	100.0%

*Note: this figure breaks down further into 5 attempted murders, 9 wounding/
GBH charges (s. 18 Offences against the Person Act 1861), 6 wounding/GBH
charges (s. 20, 1861 Act) and 5 common assaults.

TABLE 2.2   *Not Guilty By Reason of Insanity Disposals 1975–89—*
Diagnostic Groups

	Frequency	As % of Total Sample
Schizophrenia	27	52.0%
Alcohol/drug abuse	5	9.6%
Depression	4	7.7%
Epilepsy	4	7.7%
Personality disorder	3	5.8%
Psychosis (unspecified)	3	5.8%
Hypomania	2	3.8%
Brain damage	2	3.8%
Other	2	3.8%
TOTAL	52	100.0%

a very narrow ground of exemption since even persons who are grossly
disturbed generally know that murder and arson are crimes.'[149]

In the light of these remarks it is interesting to note that an analysis of
the psychiatric reports used in the 52 insanity cases revealed that the
'wrongness' limb was clearly identified as the relevant source of M'Naghten
insanity in 23 cases (44.2%), together with a further 6 cases (11.5%), where
both limbs of the rules were regarded as having been satisfied, making a

[149] Butler Report, para 18.8.

total of 29 cases (55.7%). By way of contrast the 'nature and quality' limb alone was used in only 6 cases (11.5%), three of which were instances of epileptic automatism.

Typical examples of the manner in which the 'wrongness' limb was utilised in psychiatric reports are as follows:

A 22 year old male attempted to kill his parents because he believed that they were to be tortured and that he must kill them in order that they would die in a humane way. Two psychiatrists stated that while he knew the nature and quality of the act of stabbing his parents, he did not know that what he was doing was wrong. One of the psychiatrists gave the following description: 'His mind was plagued with delusional perceptions which confused his rational thinking to the extent that the wrongness of his act would not have been a consideration.'

The defendant believed the devil was in his daughter and killed her by stabbing her over 150 times with a pair of scissors. He then proceeded to gouge out her eyes. One of the examining psychiatrists stated: 'I consider that at the time he killed his daughter he was aware of the nature and quality of his acts but believed that he was right and that therefore it would be appropriate to plead not guilty by reason of insanity.'

In many of these cases there seems to have been little attempt made to distinguish between lack of knowledge of legal wrong, which is what the Rules have been judicially interpreted to require,[150] as opposed to unawareness of moral wrong. Indeed, the general impression gained from reading the documentation in these cases was that the wrongness issue was being treated in a liberal fashion by all concerned, rather than in the strict manner regularly depicted by legal commentators.[151]

As far as the use of the Rules in the rest of the cases was concerned, there were 12 cases (23.8%) where the Rules could be regarded as having been considered by implication in the sense that psychiatric reports concluded, for example, that the accused lacked intent because of mental illness, or was not responsible for his actions because of psychosis.

Of the remaining cases, two (3.8%) were accounted for by lack of any information, while three (5.8%) were cases where there was no medical evidence whatsoever to put before the court and yet insanity verdicts were recorded. (Strangely this occurred in each of the robbery cases.)

A particularly important question is what happens to those found 'not guilty by reason by insanity' (NGRI) after the special verdict is returned. In view of the fact that the Criminal Procedure (Insanity) Act 1964 mandates hospitalization following an insanity acquittal, one would have

---

[150] See *R.* v. *Windle* [1962] 2 QB 826.
[151] See for example Dell, 'Wanted: An Insanity Defence that can be Used', 431 and S.N. Verdun-Jones, 'Sentencing the Partly Mad and the Partly Bad: The Case of The Hospital Order in England and Wales', (1989) 12 *International Journal of Law and Psychiatry* 1, 21.

expected this result in all 52 cases. It was a surprise to find, therefore, that in three of the cases this did not occur. In the first, a case of wounding in 1975 by a 57 year old man suffering from brain damage caused by alcoholism, a psychiatric report stated that D had suffered 'a severe confusional state coincident with abrupt withdrawal from alcohol but no longer suffered from any mental disorder and did not require further treatment or any hospitalization'. This was accepted by the Home Office and, as a result, the warrant was simply allowed to expire without D being hospitalized. In the second case in 1987, D was acquitted of reckless driving on the grounds of insanity, having caused an accident by driving up the wrong side of a motorway. A psychiatric report stated that he was suffering from schizophrenia and could not be held responsible for his actions. The court rather amazingly allowed D to be released as soon as the jury returned the special verdict, with the result that he never came under Home Office control and was never hospitalized. In the third case in 1983, D was found NGRI on two counts of arson. However, the warrant to admit him to hospital was never issued, in view of the fact that his appeal against the special verdict was successful.

As far as the other cases were concerned, 22 (42.3%) were sent to special hospitals while the remaining 27 (52%) were received by local National Health Service hospitals, including Regional Secure Units. With regard to length of detention, it was found that the local hospital patients were detained for much shorter periods: indeed 10 out of 27 were released in under nine months.

The results of this study of 52 insanity acquittals seem to support the following conclusions:

1. The defence of insanity is used a little more often than is commonly thought to be the case. More often than not it is used in cases of offences against the person, usually, but by no means always, of a serious nature.
2. The most common diagnosis used to support an insanity acquittal is that of schizophrenia, which in turn often leads to a use of the 'wrongness' limb under the M'Naghten rules.
3. The majority of those acquitted on the grounds of insanity are sent to local hospitals where in some instances they are released within a mere matter of months.

The second conclusion is especially interesting in the light of the criticisms which have been directed at the 'wrongness' limb of the M'Naghten Rules. In this connection the Butler Report remarked: 'it might seem at first more attractive to have regard to the defendant's appreciation of what is morally wrong, but problems in applying such a test to the mentally disordered would be very great. "Knowledge of wrong" as included in

M'Naghten, is not therefore a satisfactory test of criminal responsibility.'[152] But nowhere does the Butler Report discuss the problems which the introduction of a moral wrongfulness test might cause, even though its authors wished to ensure the acquittal of 'a person who killed someone quite deliberately but under the delusion that he had been ordered by God to do so'.[153] The solution of the Butler Report, which is built on the psychiatric notions of 'severe mental illness' and 'severe mental impairment', will be discussed shortly, but in the meantime it is interesting to note that the strict approach of legal wrongfulness adopted in *Windle*[154] not only seems, according to the empirical research, to be ignored in practice in England, but also has been rejected in both Australia[155] and Canada. Indeed, in the latter jurisdiction, the Supreme Court of Canada in the case of *Chaulk*[156] recently overruled an earlier decision of its own,[157] which had restricted the meaning of wrong to 'legally wrong' and instead concluded that the insanity defence must be extended to cover one who kills 'in the belief that it is in response to a divine order and therefore not morally wrong' even though he knows that it is legally wrong to kill.

It seems clear then that a test encompassing moral wrongfulness is still regarded by many jurisdictions as adding the dimension to the insanity defence which is necessary to ensure that the severely morally-deluded psychotic will be regarded as legally insane even though he knows what he is doing and that it is unlawful.

Further, and most importantly, there seems little doubt that a major reason why the M'Naghten Rules were used so rarely in England was fear of the inflexible disposal consequences. For example, it is well known that defendants like the epileptic in *Sullivan*[158] and the diabetic in *Hennessy*[159] prefer to plead guilty rather than to proceed with an insane automatism defence. Similarly, in cases of diminished responsibility, defendants prefer to plead guilty to manslaughter than be found legally insane. Indeed, Dell reported finding 15 cases where, despite definite evidence of M'Naghten insanity, diminished responsibility manslaughter convictions were recorded.[160]

There was no doubt then that the mandatory disposal consequence of an insanity acquittal was unsatisfactory, and it is gratifying to note that at long last this has been remedied by the Criminal Procedure (Insanity and Unfitness to Plead) Act 1991. As the title of the statute suggests, flexibility of disposal has been introduced in conjunction with unfitness to plead. However, it seems more than likely that a major reason for extending this reform measure to insanity was not merely because it would have been

---

[152] Butler Report, para 18.8.   [153] Ibid. para 18.26.
[154] [1952] 2 QB 826.   [155] See *Stapleton* v. R. (1952) 86 CLR 358.
[156] (1990) 2 CR (4th) 1, 42–3.   [157] See *Schwartz* v. R. (1976) 29 CCC (2d) 1.
[158] [1983] 2 All ER 678.   [159] [1989] 2 All ER 9.
[160] Dell, 'Wanted: An Insanity Defence that can be Used', 432.

incongruous to extend flexibility only to unfitness cases but also because it was felt that not all those who are subject to the special verdict need hospitalization: a point fully supported by the empirical research.

Briefly, the 1991 Act introduces a much more flexible range of disposals for both unfitness to plead and the defence of insanity.[161] In addition to the restriction' order which inevitably resulted from a finding of unfitness or legal insanity under the 1964 Act, the court has been given the discretion to order admission to hospital without restrictions; or to make a guardianship order under the Mental Health Act 1983 or a supervision and treatment order, or an order for the absolute discharge of the accused.

It is important to note that the only restriction on these flexible disposal provisions is in relation to a charge of murder, where the trial judge will continue to be required to impose a restriction order. On this point, the only comment made by the Minister of State, John Patten, during the debate was that this preservation of the mandatory hospital disposal was 'very important for public protection'.[162] It is abundantly clear, therefore, that this decision to retain restriction orders for murder charges is a pure policy decision. This is a cause for concern in that there seems little doubt that its effect will be to continue to 'force' those mentally ill defendants charged with murder to avoid a finding unfitness to plead and insanity by pleading guilty to manslaughter by reason of diminished responsibility. For this group of offenders, therefore, the problems which the Act sought to remedy remain unresolved.

With the exception of murder charges, there is, however, now good reason to suppose that when lawyers, psychiatrists, and other interested parties begin to appreciate the full effect of the 1991 Act, this will lead to an increased use of these new provisions, the availability of which, according to the Law Commission, 'would undoubtedly give the [special verdict] greater practical importance than the insanity defence now has'.[163] In this context it is interesting to note that ongoing research into the 1991 Act reveals for 1992—the first year of the Act's operation—the following data (Table 2.3).

The number of special verdicts in 1992 was six, which is slightly above average. However, what is immediately apparent from Table 2.3 is that none of these cases resulted in a restriction order. Rather, the judiciary made full use of their new, flexible, disposal powers. If this practice continues, then it seems likely that the number of insanity defences will increase as lawyers and psychiatrists become more familiar with the operation of the 1991 Act.

---

[161] For detailed comment, see S. White 'The Criminal Procedure (Insanity and Unfitness to Plead) Act' [1992] Crim LR 4.
[162] *Hansard*, 1 March 1991, Volume 186 No 167 at Column 1275.
[163] Law Commission, '*A Criminal Code*', Volume 2, p 221, para 11.11.

TABLE 2.3.   *Not Guilty by Reason of Insanity Disposals for 1992 under the Criminal Procedure (Insanity and Unfitness to Plead Act) 1991*

Offence	Age	Diagnosis	Sex	Disposal
S.18 Assault	28	Hypomania	M	Hospital Order (without Restrictions)
S.18 Assault	49	Acute psychotic Reaction	M	Supervision and Treatment Order 2 Year
Attempted Murder	37	Somnambulism	M	Supervision and Treatment Order 2 Year
Attempted GBH	42	Post-Ictal state	M	Supervision and Treatment Order 2 Year
Attempted Rape	35	Mental Impairment	M	Absolute Discharge
Actual Bodily Harm	42	Transient psychosis	M	Supervision and Treatment Order 2 Year

The final question which must now be addressed is whether any of the alternative approaches to the insanity defence offered by overseas jurisdictions or law reform bodies might lead to a more satisfactory test than that contained in the M'Naghten Rules.

THE US EXPERIENCE AND EXISTING REVISION PROPOSALS

The overseas jurisdiction which has produced the most discussion about the insanity defence is without doubt the United States of America where the very existence of the defence has recently been the subject of much turbulent debate and change, the nature of which is both important and instructive. Accordingly, having considered how the insanity defence operates in England, it is now proposed to consider the position in the United States where the Rules have been and continue to be extremely influential.

THE TRANSMOGRIFICATION OF THE INSANITY DEFENCE IN THE USA

Prior to 1954, with the notable exception of New Hampshire, the M'Naghten Rules applied in every state, although by that date a number of jurisdictions had added an 'irresistible impulse' limb.[164] With regard to

---

[164] See E. Keedy, 'Irresistible Impulse as a Defense in the Criminal Law' (1952) 100 *University of Pennsylvania Law Review* 956; A. Goldstein, *The Insanity Defense* (Yale University Press, New Haven and London, 1967) ch. 5.

the latter, it is clear that the limitations imposed by the Rules were viewed as a major reason for adding a volitional limb. For example, in *Parsons v. Alabama*[165] one of the leading early cases within this area, the court criticises the Rules as being out of step with 'the discoveries of modern psychological medicine', and concludes that a defendant suffering from a disease of the mind

may nevertheless not be legally responsible if the two following conditions concur: (1) If, by reason of the duress of such mental disease, he had so far lost the power to choose between the right and wrong, and to avoid doing the act in question, as that his free agency was at the time destroyed; (2) and if, at the same time, the alleged crime was so connected with such mental disease, in relation to cure and effect, as to have been the product of it solely.[166]

This decision led the way in the United States for a wide variety of 'irresistible impulse' formulations, all of which emphasised the need to consider volitional or emotional defects in addition to purely cognitive or intellectual defects. However, this development has itself been the subject of considerable criticism on the part of both the legal and psychiatric communities, primarily on the basis that 'special provision for the irresistible impulse is unnecessary since the mind is not functionally compartmentalized but, in keeping with the now universally accepted psychological theory of integration, the will, the intellect and the emotions are interdependent. One function cannot be affected by disease without affecting the others.'[167] It has been suggested that 'the strength of this criticism perhaps accounts for the fact that only twelve states . . . adopted a pure irresistible impulse test for the defence of legal insanity'.[168]

Other developments in the United States were initially concerned with finding acceptable alternatives to the M'Naghten Rules. They took two forms. The first, known as the 'product test', was again built upon criticisms of M'Naghten. This particular test dates from 1869 when, in his opinion in *State of New Hampshire* v. *Pike*, Judge Doe stated: 'the whole difficulty is that the courts have undertaken to declare that to be a matter of law which is a matter of fact, and that if the homicide was the offspring or product of mental disease in the defendant, he was not guilty by reason of insanity'.[169]

Thus, it was made clear that, rather than being a question of law, 'insanity' was a question of fact which must be decided by the jury on the evidence put before it. Although this particular 'test' has remained

---

[165] 2 So 854 (1886)   [166] Ibid. 857.
[167] M.S. Guttmacher, 'Principal Difficulties with the Present Criteria of Responsibility and Possible Alternatives' in The American Law Institute, *Model Penal Code, Tentative Draft No. 4* American Law Institute, Philadelphia (1955), 175–7.
[168] Hermann, *The Insanity Defense*, 42.   [169] 49 NH 399, 442 (1869).

unchanged in New Hampshire since its inception in 1869, the reason why it has operated successfully is apparently 'because the State Hospital has limited its definition of insanity to psychosis and defence counsel . . . has shown a remarkable willingness to go along with whatever the Hospital says'.[170] According to one critic, therefore, the psychiatrists 'had to take upon themselves the task Judge Doe and his successors on the New Hampshire bench should have undertaken; namely, to give a separate, legal definition of mental illness as a legally excusing condition'.[171]

Whilst the working relationship between lawyers and psychiatrists seems to have permitted the 'product test' to operate successfully in New Hampshire, unfortunately the same could not be said of the attempt to introduce this test in 1954 into the District of Columbia in the Court of Appeal's decision in *Durham* v. *US*.[172] At the time, this decision was hailed by many as a major breakthrough since it 'was decided explicitly to facilitate psychiatrists in placing their knowledge before the court'.[173] The new rule was expressed as follows:

It is simply that an accused is not criminally responsible if his unlawful act was the product of mental disease or mental defect.[174]

The primary reason for the adoption of the 'product test' in *Durham* was the profound dissatisfaction which the court felt for both the M'Naghten Rules and the 'irresistible impulse' supplement. This dissatisfaction was well expressed by Judge Bazelon in the following remark:

We find that as an exclusive criterion the right–wrong test is inadequate in that (a) it does not take sufficient account of psychic realities and scientific knowledge, and (b) it is based upon one symptom and so cannot be validly applied in all circumstances. We find that the 'irresistible impulse' test is also inadequate in that it gives no recognition to mental illness characterised by brooding and reflection and so relegates acts caused by such illness to the application of the inadequate right–wrong test. We conclude that a broader test should be adopted.[175]

The 'product test', otherwise known as the Durham Rule, was a spectacular failure, being abandoned by the Court of Appeals for the District of Columbia in 1972 in favour of the American Law Institute's test of legal insanity.[176] The major reasons for this change of approach are best expressed by Judge Bazelon himself when he said: 'in the end, after 18 years, I favoured the abandonment of the Durham rule because in practice it had failed to take the issue of criminal responsibility away from the experts.

---

[170] J.P. Reid, 'The Working of the New Hampshire Doctrine of Criminal Insanity' (1960) 15 *University of Miami Law Review* 14, 19.   [171] Moore, *Law and Psychiatry*, 228.
[172] 214 F 2d 847 (DC Cir 1954).   [173] Moore, *Law and Psychiatry*, 228.
[174] *Durham* v. *US* 214 F 2d 847, 874–5 (DC Cir 1954).
[175] Ibid. For a defence of the 'product test', see Henry Weihofen, *The Urge to Punish* (Victor Gollancz, London, 1957).   [176] *US* v. *Brawner* 471 F 2d 969 (DC Cir 1972).

Psychiatrists continued to testify to the naked conclusion instead of providing information about the accused so that the jury could render the ultimate moral judgment about blameworthiness. Durham had secured little improvement over M'Naghten'.[177]

The American Law Institute's (ALI) test of insanity was first formulated in 1955 and received finalapproval in 1962. The test is as follows:

> A person is not responsible for criminal conduct if at the time of such conduct as a result of mental disease or defect he lacks substantial capacity either to appreciate the criminality (wrongfulness) of his conduct or to conform his conduct to the requirements of law.[178]

Despite criticisms that this test was little better than the Durham Rule,[179] the ALI formulation has had considerable impact in the United States. Thus, until the Hinckley trial and verdict, '[t]his test, or some variant of it, [had] been adopted within the last twenty years by all of the federal courts of appeals and by a substantial number of states'.[180]

However, this trend which favoured a test described by one commentator as 'a modernised and much improved rendition of M'Naghten and the "control" test',[181] was suddenly halted in 1982.

THE POST-HINCKLEY PERIOD[182]

On 21 June 1982, a District of Columbia jury found John Hinckley 'not guilty by reason of insanity' for the attempted assassination of President Reagan. The jury's decision was based upon its consideration of the ALI test, although it is by no means clear which limb they considered Hinckley fell within.[183] What followed, however, must be the most intense onslaught ever directed against the insanity defence within its long and chequered history.

In many ways the jury's acquittal of John Hinckley on the grounds of

---

[177] D.L. Bazelon, 'Psychiatrists and the Adversary Process' *Scientific American* 230 (1974) cited in the Butler Report, 221. For discussion of the failure of the Durham Rule, see Moore, *Law and Psychiatry* 228–33; Goldstein, *The Insanity Defense*, 82–6; Hermann, *The Insanity Defense* 46–50.

[178] The American Law Institute, *Model Penal Code, Proposed Official Draft* (Philadelphia, 1962) s 4.01(1), p 66.   [179] Butler Report, 221.

[180] Moore, *Law and Psychiatry*, 220.   [181] Goldstein, *The Insanity Defense*, 87.

[182] See R.J. Simon and D.E. Aaronson, *The Insanity Defense: a Critical Assessment of Law and Policy in the Post-Hinckley Era* (Praeger, New York, 1988); M.L. Perlin, *The Jurisprudence of the Insanity Defense*.

[183] *US* v. *Hinckley* 672 F 2d 115 (DC Cir 1982). For detailed discussion, see P.W. Low, J.C. Jeffries, and R.J. Bonnie, *The Trial of John W. Hinckley, Jr.: A Case Study in the Insanity Defense* (Foundation Press, New York 1986). See also A.A. Stone, 'The Trial of John Hinckley' ch. 4 of his *Law, Psychiatry, and Morality* (American Psychiatric Press, Washington, 1984); L. Caplan, *The Insanity Defense and the Trial of John W. Hinckley, Jr.* (Dell Publishing Co, New York, 1987).

insanity bears striking similarities to the special verdict returned in the case of Daniel M'Naghten, insofar as they both sparked off massive public debate and consequent changes in the insanity defence. The unprecedented criticism surrounding the Hinckley verdict has led more than half of the states to reconsider the insanity plea.[184] In addition a host of official bodies including Congress, the American Bar Association, the American Medical Association, the American Psychiatric Association, and the National Mental Health Association all produced reports dealing with the rationale, role, and scope of the insanity defence.[185]

The result of all this discussion has been a series of rapid and varied changes consistently aimed at abolishing or restricting the use of the insanity defence. A major reason for these changes was the public's perception that the insanity plea was being abused and manipulated,[186] a view which was powerfully provoked by the *Hinckley* acquittal, but which has been cogently criticised by Michael Perlin on the ground that such changes exemplify the fundamental incoherence of insanity defence jurisprudence in the United States and perpetuate a whole series of social, empirical, and behavioural myths.[187] For example, Perlin presents to his readers the following eight empirical myths which he argues are completely without foundation. The first concerns the use of the insanity defence which research indicates is completely overestimated by the American public when in reality the defence 'is used in only about one percent of all felony cases, and is successful just about one-quarter of the time'.[188] The second is that the insanity defence is used primarily in murder cases when in reality the data reveal that murder accounts for less than one-third of successful insanity pleas. The third myth is that defendants who plead insanity unsuccessfully do not risk heavier punishment than those who do not use the defence. Once again research reveals that this is not the case. Myth four claims that those acquitted on the grounds of insanity are released quickly from hospital, but this is patently not the case; the same is true of myth five which posits that such persons spend less time in custody than those convicted in the ordinary way of identical offences. The reality is that many of those found not guilty by reason of insanity spend around twice the time in hospital that ordinary offenders spend in prison. The sixth

---

[184] See L. Callahan, C. Mayer, and H.J. Steadman, 'Insanity Defense Reform in the United States—Post Hinckley' (1987) 11 *Mental and Physical Disability Law Reporter* 54.

[185] For references see R.D. Mackay, 'Post-Hinckley Insanity in the U.S.A.' [1988] Crim LR 88, 88–9.

[186] All the research demonstrates that this is untrue, with the insanity plea being rarely used and even more rarely successful. See R.A. Pasewark, 'A Review of Research on the Insanity Defense' (1986) 47 *Annals of the American Academy of Political and Social Science* 100. For extensive and detailed discussion, see Perlin, *The Jurisprudence of the Insanity Defense*, chs. 3 and 5.

[187] Perlin, ibid. n 1.   [188] Ibid. 108.

myth is that those who plead insanity are often faking. But once more the empirical research reveals that those who plead insanity are very likely to have a history of serious mental illness and prior hospitalizations. Myth seven claims that insanity defence trials often involve major disagreements amongst expert witnesses. Although this occurred in the *Hinckley* case, such disagreements are rare and many NGRI cases are uncontested. The eighth and final myth is that defence counsel use the insanity defence to 'beat the rap' in order to avoid a deserved conviction. However, the picture painted by research reveals that 'lawyers . . . enter an insanity plea to obtain immediate mental health treatment of their client, as a plea bargaining device to insure that their client receives mandatory mental health care, and to avoid malpractice litigation'.[189] This type of attitude stands in marked contrast to the position in England where the defence of insanity has become virtually redundant.

The states of the United States which have recently made changes in relation to the insanity defence can be conveniently divided into five major groups, each of which will be discussed in turn. They are those states which have (1) opted to change their test of legal insanity; (2) enacted an alternative verdict of 'guilty but mentally ill'; (3) altered the rules of evidence, including the allocation and the *quantum* of the burden of proof; (4) changed the disposal consequences of an insanity acquittal; or (5) opted to abolish a separate insanity defence.

CHANGING THE TEST

A number of jurisdictions in the United States have opted for a change in the substance of the insanity defence itself. To date, this has taken the form of a move away from the volitional tests, especially that originally proposed by the ALI, towards a so-called tightening up of the insanity plea. Ironically, the M'Naghten Test, which was formerly the target of so much criticism in the United States, has re-emerged as influential. Thus, the Federal law, under which the jury acquitted Hinckley in 1982, was altered by the Insanity Defence Reform Act 1984 which enacts a new test that is something of a cross between M'Naghten and the cognitive branch of the ALI test, and provides a defence if the defendant 'as a result of a severe mental disease or defect was unable to appreciate the nature and quality or the wrongfulness of his acts'.[190] Additionally, in California, the ALI test has been abandoned in favour of an apparently 'conjunctive' M'Naghten test which provides that the accused must 'prove by a preponderance of

---

[189] Perlin, *The Jurisprudence of the Insanity Defense*, 114.
[190] Insanity Defense Reform Act 1984 18 USC s 20(a). For discussion, see Comment, 'Recent Changes in Federal Law: The Federal Insanity Defense' (1985) 46 *Louisiana Law Review* 337.

the evidence that he was incapable of knowing or understanding the nature and quality of his act *and* of distinguishing right from wrong at the time of the offence'.[191] Although this test was approved by the electorate after a referendum, the California Supreme Court recently held in *People v. Skinner*[192] that the new test must be read in the disjunctive, as creating two distinct and independent limbs upon which an insanity plea may be based. The reasons for this rather remarkable decision appear to be, first, that the court considered that a new conjunctive test might be so strict as virtually to eliminate insanity as a defence (which would be unconstitutional) and, second, that in any event the word 'and' instead of 'or' was more than likely to have been the result of a draftsman's error.

Finally, Alaska also repealed the ALI test in 1982, and replaced it with a test which is restricted to the first limb of the M'Naghten Rules. The new test provides: 'In a prosecution for a crime, it is an affirmative defense that when the defendant engaged in criminal conduct, the defendant was unable, as a result of mental disease or defect, to appreciate the nature and quality of the conduct.'[193] To date, although this new test has survived constitutional challenge,[194] it has also received a wide interpretation.[195] It would seem, therefore, that although the legislatures in California and Alaska have enacted narrow insanity pleas, the responses of the appellate courts in both these states have been much more moderate than could perhaps have been anticipated.

It is clear that these changes in the wording of the test of legal insanity have been aimed at eliminating the volitional prong; a development which has been advocated by many as both necessary and desirable. A pertinent question, therefore, is whether there was any empirical evidence in the United States that the volitional limb was operating in an undesirable manner. The short answer appears to be in the negative. Instead, the *Hinckley* verdict seemed to focus a great deal of attention upon the theoretical imprecision of a test of legal insanity built upon 'lack of control' or volitional impairment, with criticism coming from both the medical and legal professions. A good summary of the forms which this criticism has taken is given by the Fifth Circuit of the United States Court of Appeals

---

[191] California Penal Code (Supp 1987) s 25(b) (emphasis added).

[192] 39 Cal 3d 765, 217 Cal Rptr 685, 704 P 2d 752 (1985). For discussion, see R.F. Schopp, 'Returning to M'Naghten to Avoid Moral Mistakes: One Step Forward, or Two Steps Backward for the Insanity Defense?' (1988) 30 *Arizona Law Review* 135.

[193] Alaska Statutes s 12.47.010 (Supp 1986).

[194] See *Hart* v. *State* 702 P 2d 651 (1985).

[195] In *Pattenson* v. *State* 708 P 2d 712, 717 (1985), the Court of Appeals of Alaska stated 'we believe that the language that now appears in AS 12.47.010 is to be interpreted broadly rather than restrictively, referring not only to the defendant's bare awareness of the physical acts he or she is performing, but also to his or her appreciation of the nature and quality of that conduct and its consequences'.

when in *US* v. *Lyons* the court unilaterally decided to abandon the ALI test, saying:

[W]e conclude that the volitional prong of the insanity defense—a lack of capacity to conform one's conduct to the requirements of the law—does not comport with current medical and scientific knowledge, which has retreated from its earlier, sanguine expectations. Consequently, we now hold that a person is not responsible for criminal conduct on the grounds of insanity only if at the time of that conduct, as a result of mental disease or defect, he is unable to appreciate the wrongfulness of that conduct.

We do so for several reasons. First, as we have mentioned, a majority of psychiatrists now believe that they do not possess sufficient accurate scientific bases for measuring a person's capacity for self- control or for calibrating the impairment of that capacity.

In addition, the risks of fabrication and 'moral mistakes' in administering the insanity defense are greatest 'when the experts and the jury are asked to speculate whether the defendant had the capacity to "control" himself or whether he could have "resisted" the criminal impulse.' . . . Moreover, psychiatric testimony about volition is more likely to produce confusion for jurors than is psychiatric testimony concerning a defendant's appreciation of the wrongfulness of his act . . . It appears, moreover, that there is considerable overlap between a psychotic person's inability to understand and his ability to control his behaviour. Most psychotic persons who fail a volitional test would also fail a cognitive test, thus rendering the volitional test superfluous for them.[196]

This change of view, particularly on the part of the medical profession, was further emphasised by the American Psychiatric Association (APA) when it opined:

Many psychiatrists . . . believe that psychiatric information relevant to determining whether a defendant understood the nature of his act, and whether he appreciated its wrongfulness, is more reliable and has a stronger scientific basis than, for example, does psychiatric information relevant to whether the defendant was able to control his behaviour. The line between an irresistible impulse and an impulse not resisted is probably no sharper than between twilight and dusk.[197]

Similarly, the American Medical Association (AMA) remarked: 'because free will is an article of faith, rather than a concept that can be explained in medical terms, it is impossible for psychiatrists to determine whether a mental impairment has affected the defendant's capacity for voluntary choice, or caused him to commit the particular act in question'.[198] As

---

[196] 731 F 2d 243, 248 (1984), quoting in final para. R.J. Bonnie, 'The Moral Basis of the Insanity Defense', 69 *American Bar Association Journal*, 194, 196.

[197] APA, 'Statement on the Insanity Defense' (1983) 140 *American Journal of Psychiatry* 681.

[198] AMA, 'The Insanity Defense in Criminal Trials and Limitations of Psychiatric Testimony: Report of the Board of Trustees' (1984) 251 *Journal of the American Medical Association* 2967.

already mentioned, there appear to be no empirical data to support the 'assumption that the cognitive prong has a stronger scientific basis and more reliable measurement than the volitional prong and can be more reliably measured'.[199] Indeed, in an assessment of the few relevant empirical studies which exist, Rogers concludes not only that 'this research flatly contradicts the . . . unsupported assertion regarding the scientific superiority of the cognitive prong' but also that 'psychiatrists were more confident in their decisions regarding the volitional prong' and that there were 'no significant differences between the cognitive and volitional prongs in the frequency of insanity recommendations'.[200]

A further argument put forward by the APA in favour of eliminating the volitional prong is the assertion that it is superfluous, since most volitionally impaired defendants will at the same time be cognitively impaired. Again, no empirical evidence is tendered to support this contention. Instead the relevant research 'indicates that a high proportion of offenders who are unanimously classified by a psychiatric team as acquittable under the volitional prong would not be if the volitional prong were removed and capacity to appreciate became the exclusive test for responsibility'.[201]

Clearly, more empirical research would be desirable to establish the criticisms which have been recently directed against the volitional prong. Although this lack of research has in no way deterred the medical profession from advocating its abandonment, to date comparatively few states have heeded this call with the result that twenty jurisdictions continue to apply the ALI test or a modified version of it.[202] It is certain, therefore, that the volitional prong will continue to be applied in a substantial number of states for the foreseeable future. More importantly, the effect of its abandonment in those jurisdictions which have taken that step seems likely to have been minimal. This is one of the clear findings made by Henry Steadman and his colleagues in their important multi-jurisdiction research into the effects of the post-Hinckley reforms including California's change from an ALI to a M'Naghten test.[203] After detailed examination of the cases of all persons who raised the insanity plea in seven California counties over a six-year period, the three years before and the three years after the reform, their clear conclusion was that 'no significant changes occurred in the rate of insanity acquittal, or the success rate of insanity pleas'.[204] This in turn seems to support the view that this 'reform was nothing more

[199] R. Rogers, 'American Psychological Association Position on the Insanity Defense: Empiricism versus Emotionalism' (1987) 42 *American Psychologist* 840, 841.

[200] Ibid, 842–3.

[201] A.D. Brooks, 'The Merits of Abolishing the Insanity Defense' 477 *Annals of the American Academy of Political and Social Science* 134.

[202] See Callahan, Mayer, and Steadman, 'Insanity Defense Reform in the United States', 56.

[203] H.J. Steadman et al *Before and After Hinckley: Evaluating Insanity Defense Reform* (The Gilford Press, New York, 1993).   [204] Ibid. 142.

than an expression of the public's growing concern about crime and its desire for greater punishment for the perpetrators'.[205] It would be preferable, therefore, if more emphasis was laid on the fact that the rejection of the volitional test was essentially a policy decision based primarily on a perceived need to narrow the scope of the insanity defence rather than the result of alleged difficulties which the assessment of volitional impairment presents to psychiatrists.

STANDARD AND BURDEN OF PROOF

Questions surrounding the proper allocation of the standard and burden of proof for insanity received a great deal of publicity during and immediately after the trial of John Hinckley. The reason for this was that under the federal law as it then stood in the District of Columbia the prosecution was required to prove beyond reasonable doubt that Hinckley was sane at the time that he shot President Reagan before the insanity defence could be rejected and he could be convicted. To many commentators this seemed like an impossible task and was viewed as a major reason why Hinckley was found 'not guilty by reason of insanity'.[206]

At the time of the Hinckley trial a bare majority of states had a similar requirement relating to burden of proof, as that in the District of Columbia and in other federal courts. However, this position has now been reconsidered by many of the states in question and by Congress. As a result, and not surprisingly, around two-thirds of the states which accept the insanity plea currently place the burden of proof on the defendant, usually by a preponderance of the evidence. Moreover, federal law and that of the state of Arizona have recently been changed to require the defendant to prove his insanity 'by clear and convincing evidence'.[207] Both of these provisions have since survived constitutional challenge.[208]

As the American Psychiatric Association pointed out in their statement on the insanity defence, 'it is commonly believed that the likely effect of assigning the burden of proof (burden of persuasion) to defendants rather than to the state in insanity trials will be to decrease the number of such successful defenses. This matter clearly requires empirical study.'[209] Steadman and his colleagues have now undertaken such a study by considering alteration to the burden and standard of proof in two states. In Georgia the

[205] Steadman et al., *Before and After Hinckley*, 62.
[206] W. Winslade and J. Ross, *The Insanity Plea* (Scribner, New York, 1983) remark at p 189 'It is . . . hard to imagine how any prosecutor could prove John Hinckley, or anyone else, for that matter, sane beyond a reasonable doubt.'
[207] See, respectively, 18 USC s 20(b) (1984) Arizona Revised Statutes Annotated s 13–502(b) (1984).
[208] See, respectively, *US* v. *Amos* 803 F 2d 419 (8th Cir 1986); *Arizona* v. *Moorman* 744 P 2d 679 (1987). [209] APA, 'Statement on the Insanity Defense'.

burden of proof was shifted to the defendant on a preponderance of the evidence in 1978, well before the *Hinckley* verdict, while in New York a similar change was made after *Hinckley* in 1984. To assess the impact of these reforms, data were collected before and after the enactment of the changes. Although the results revealed 'a reduction in the use of the insanity defense',[210] at the same time no change was found in the success rate. The explanation for these findings was that, while these reform measures resulted in fewer defendants being prepared to try to prove their insanity, when such an attempt is made 'a diagnosis of schizophrenia, another major psychosis, or a major affective disorder almost becomes a prerequisite for success'.[211] Not surprisingly, the success rate of the plea should remain unaltered as 'those with questionable cases were less likely to plead insanity'.[212]

It seems likely therefore that altering the burden and quantum of proof is a more effective way of reducing the use of the insanity defence than changing the test.

GUILTY BUT MENTALLY ILL

Twelve states have enacted provisions providing for an alternative verdict of 'guilty but mentally ill' (GBMI).[213] The first state to establish this new verdict was Michigan in 1975, again well before the *Hinckley* verdict. The Michigan law, upon which many other GBMI statutes are modelled, is designed to offer a compromise to the jury whenever a defendant pleads insanity.[214] He may be found 'guilty but mentally ill' provided it is proved beyond reasonable doubt 'that the defendant (i) is guilty of the offence charged, (ii) was mentally ill at the time of the commission of the offence and (iii) was not legally insane at the time of the commission of the offence.[215]

A major difficulty surrounding this new verdict concerns its interrelationship with the insanity defence. Although the statutory language varies among the 12 states, the distinction between the insanity plea and the GBMI verdict clearly revolves around which definition of insanity is accepted in

---

[210] Steadman et al. *Before and After Hinckley*, 84.

[211] Ibid. 85.   [212] Ibid. 143.

[213] Those states are Alaska, Delaware, Georgia, Illinois, Indiana, Kentucky, Michigan, New Mexico, Pennsylvania, South Carolina, South Dakota, and Utah.

[214] Michigan Statutes Annotated ss 28–1059 (1985). Most GBMI statutes also allow the accused to plead GBMI, which of course avoids the issue being put to a jury. For the implications behind this procedure, see J. Klofas and R. Weisheit, 'Pleading Guilty but Mentally Ill: Adversarial Justice and Mental Health' (1986) 9 *International Journal of Law and Psychiatry* 491.

[215] Once the GBMI verdict is returned, the court can then sentence the defendant in the same way as if an ordinary conviction had been returned; if psychiatric treatment is required, then this may follow.

any particular state. Thus, for example, in Michigan the insanity defence is based upon the ALI test and provides that a person may be found 'not guilty by reason of insanity' if, as a result of 'mental illness' or 'mental retardation', he 'lacks substantial capacity either to appreciate the wrongfulness of his conduct or to conform his conduct to the requirements of law.' In comparison, the Michigan GBMI provision defines mental illness as 'a substantial disorder of thought or mood which significantly impairs judgment, behaviour, capacity to recognise reality, or ability to cope with the ordinary demands of life'.[216]

By way of contrast, Pennsylvania, which adopted the GBMI verdict in 1983 as a direct response to the *Hinckley* verdict, defines 'mental illness' in precisely the same way as the Michigan ALI-based insanity defence.[217] The reason why such a definition of 'mental illness' is regarded in Pennsylvania as appropriate to trigger off a finding of GBMI is because that state adheres to the M'Naghten Rules as the basis of its insanity defence. However, it is difficult to understand what relevance the ALI test, which is built entirely around the concept of excusing a person from criminal responsibility, can have to the notion of a finding of guilty, unless it is somehow to diminish the individual's criminal responsibility or at the very least mitigate punishment. But there is nothing written into the Pennsylvania GBMI provision to reflect this. Instead, the enactment makes it clear that, once found GBMI, a defendant may receive the same sentence as if convicted in an ordinary manner.

These two examples of GBMI standards will at least give some indication of the differing approaches which have been adopted by the states which have enacted the GBMI verdict. Not unsurprisingly the new verdict has been constantly criticised for a number of reasons including the following:

the overlapping definitions raise questions about whether a jury or an expert witness can understand clearly the distinction between being guilty but mentally ill and not guilty by reason of insanity; juries will misuse the verdict as a compromise device, finding someone guilty but mentally ill when a finding of not guilty by reason of insanity might have been more appropriate; the verdict is a legal hoax or fraud, a political response to public outrage about a particular case, and it gives the illusion that something positive has been done when in reality there has been little if any change in what happens to criminal defendants pleading incapacity[218]

A number of these criticisms do indeed seem to be substantiated by the results of empirical research conducted in Michigan, the state which has

[216] Respectively, Michigan Statutes Annotated 28–1044(1) (1985) and 14.800 (400a) (1985).
[217] Pennsylvania Consolidated Statutes Annotated, tit 18. s 314(c) (1) (Purdon's 1983).
[218] S.J. Brakel, J. Parry, and B.A. Weiner, *The Mentally Disabled and the Law* (American Bar Foundation, Chicago, 1985) 3rd edn., 715.

had the GBMI verdict for the longest period. Amongst the conclusions reached by the authors of the various Michigan empirical studies are, first, that although one of the underlying purposes behind the new verdict was an attempt to reduce the number of persons found not guilty by reason of insanity, this has not happened and instead 'the displacement in disposition is from the guilty to the GBMI population'.[219] Secondly, 'although the verdict was designed for jury trials, over 60 percent of those defendants found GBMI have come through plea bargains and another 20 percent have come from bench trials'.[220] Thirdly, 'as a practical matter, the GBMI prisoner is not more likely to receive mental health treatment than the prisoner with a simple guilty verdict'.[221] Finally, the GBMI verdict does not appear to mitigate punishment but instead may have the reverse effect.[222]

By way of contrast, similar research conducted by the present writer dealing with the first four years of GBMI in Pennsylvania revealed a slightly different picture.[223] Thus, although a GBMI verdict again did not mitigate punishment, the majority of those found GBMI did receive hospital treatment, albeit for relatively brief periods before being returned to prison. Further, unlike in Michigan, the number of insanity acquittals has fallen in Pennsylvania since GBMI was introduced. However, the explanation for this reduction is complex since it has occurred on a purely regional basis; it may be partly attributable to shifting the burden of proving insanity from the prosecution to the defence, a change which was implemented by the Pennsylvania Legislature at the same time as it enacted GBMI. In short, the research reveals that GBMI is not operating in a uniform manner within Pennsylvania. For, while the GBMI verdict appears to be acting as a substitute for insanity acquittals in the Philadelphia area, the same is not true of the Pittsburgh area where GBMI has emerged as an increasingly used verdict in its own right. In this respect, therefore, as far as Pittsburgh is concerned, once again the displacement is from the guilty to the GBMI population.

Until recently, however, none of the GBMI research studies had considered the total population *pleading* insanity as opposed to those actually *acquitted* on that ground, with the result that the conclusions drawn about the impact of GBMI could well be misleading. Such a study has now been

---

[219] L.W. Blunt and H.V. Stock, 'Guilty but Mentally Ill: An Alternative Verdict' (1985) 3 Behavioural Sciences and the Law 49, 63.

[220] G.A. Smith and J.A. Hall, 'Evaluating Michigan's Guilty But Mentally Ill Verdict: An Empirical Study' (1982) 16 *University of Michigan Journal of Law Reform* 77, 104. A bench trial is the term used in the USA for a jury-waived trial where the accused elects to be tried before a judge alone.

[221] Klofas and Weisheit, 'Pleading Guilty but Mentally Ill', 494.

[222] I. Keilitz, 'Researching and Reforming the Insanity Defense' (1987) 39 *Rutgers Law Journal* 289.

[223] R.D. Mackay and J. Kopelman, 'The Operation of the Guilty But Mentally Ill Verdict in Pennsylvania' (1988) 16 *Journal of Psychiatry and Law* 247.

completed by Steadman et al.;[224] it relates to Georgia's 1982 GBMI re-form, which was enacted in response to a series of court rulings that resulted in the release of insanity defendants from hospital. Data were obtained on all persons pleading insanity from 1979 to 1985 in a series of Georgia counties. The results revealed that while there was no alteration in the success rate of insanity pleas overall, 'there was a significant decline in the success rate for violent crimes associated with the reform'.[225] Ac-cordingly, those found GBMI were more likely to be violent offenders and receive longer sentences and periods of confinement than those who pleaded insanity but were convicted. The conclusion reached is that GBMI makes 'an insanity plea a less appealing option for those with serious mental illness'.[226] Further, it is predicted that 'given the harsh reality of what can happen when a mentally ill defendant is not successful in his or her bid for an insanity acquittal, but is instead found GBMI, . . . over time, defense attorneys for mentally ill defendants will be less willing to enter an insanity plea for their clients. GBMI without question changed the odds on a favorable outcome for an insanity plea in Georgia.'[227] One cannot help but agree, therefore, that this type of compromise verdict not only seems con-ceptually confusing but may also be highly misleading and prejudicial to the defendant. It appears to hold out little or no benefit to the defendant since 'it results neither in acquittal nor reduction in the grade of the offence'.[228]

DISPOSAL CONSEQUENCES

The most prevalent type of reform during the post-Hinckley period has been in relation to commitment and release procedures for insanity acquit-tees.[229] Although these procedures vary widely within the United States, the trend has undoubtedly been towards stricter disposition schemes.[230] In this connection, the decision of the United States Supreme Court in *Jones* v. *US*[231], decided a year after the *Hinckley* verdict, has been influential. In that case the defendant had in March 1976 pleaded not guilty by reason of insanity to attempted petty larceny of a jacket, an offence punishable by a maximum prison sentence of one year. The plea was uncontested and as a result Jones was automatically committed to St. Elizabeth's Hospital pursuant to the District of Columbia statutory provision. The issue before

---

[224] Steadman et al. *Before and After Hinckley*, ch. 7.   [225] Ibid. 114.
[226] Ibid. 145.   [227] Ibid. 120.
[228] C. Slobogin, 'The Guilty But Mentally Ill Verdict: An Idea Whose Time Should Not Have Come' (1985), 53 *George Washington Law Review* 494, 518. See further Keilitz, 'Researching and Reforming the Insanity Defense'.
[229] Callahan, Mayer, and Steadman, 'Insanity Defense Reform in the United States', 55.
[230] Steadman et al. *Before and After Hinckley*, 35–6.   [231] 463 US 354 (1983).

the Supreme Court was the constitutionality of committing Jones beyond the maximum term for the offence in question on the basis of his future dangerousness. In upholding the District of Columbia statutory scheme of indefinite commitment, the Supreme Court held that 'the fact that a person has been found beyond a reasonable doubt to have committed a criminal act certainly indicates dangerousness.'[232] This, despite the fact that the act in question was non-violent. Thus the Supreme Court concluded that Jones could be detained without any finding that he remained dangerous and mentally ill. Instead, it was Jones who was required to prove the absence of these factors on a preponderance of the evidence. Therefore, although in theory Jones was less culpable by virtue of his insanity acquittal than a guilty counterpart, the fact of his mental illness which existed at the time of the alleged offence weighed very heavily against him and was sufficient, when added to the presumption of continuing 'dangerousness', to ensure his indefinite detention. The decision in *Jones*, predictably, led a number of states, and the federal law, to provide for automatic and indeterminate hospitalization of those acquitted on the ground of insanity.[233] However, although the *Jones* decision has been heavily criticised,[234] its impact is likely to be reduced by the more recent decision of the United States Supreme Court in *Foucha* v. *Louisiana*.[235] Here it was decided that a person found NGRI could not be detained if he was no longer mentally ill, even though he might still be considered dangerous. In the opinion of the Court delivered by Justice White: '*Jones* established that insanity acquittees may be treated differently in some respects from those persons subject to civil commitment, but Foucha, who is not now thought to be insane, can no longer be so classified . . . Freedom from restraint being a fundamental right, the State must have a particularly convincing reason, which it has not put forward, for such discrimination against insanity acquittees who are no longer mentally ill.'[236] *Jones* had made it clear that the legally insane could only continue to be detained as long as they are both mentally ill and dangerous, but no longer. The importance of the decision in *Foucha*, therefore, is its emphasis on the need for continuing mental illness as a reason for detention. It must be conceded, however, that, without the support of his own doctors which Foucha had, the patient is unlikely to succeed in arguing that he is no longer mentally ill where he is required to prove, as was Jones, that he is mentally well.

　　Until recently no empirical study had addressed the impact which altering the conditions of confinement and release of insanity acquittees might have on the operation of the insanity defence. Once more it is to Steadman

---

[232] 463 US 354, 364 (1983).
[233] See J.Q. La Fond and M.L. Durham, *Back to the Asylum* (Oxford University Press, Oxford, 1992), 79. 　　　　　　　　　　　　[234] La Fond and Durham, ibid. 77–9.
[235] 112 S Ct 1780 (1992). 　　　　[236] Ibid., 1788.

and his colleagues that we must turn for such research.[237] In order to assess the changes in commitment and release procedures contained in New York's Insanity Defense Reform Act of 1980, which was designed to safeguard the public by tightening release procedures, data were collected on all insanity pleas and acquittals from 1978 to 1983. The results showed no real change in the plea rate; however, the success rate for insanity pleas rose, but only in the cases of violent crimes where 'the original criminal courts were assured that they would have nearly total control over the movement of defendants who were acquitted by reason of insanity'. This increase in 'the prospect of preventive detention for insanity acquittees in New York'[238] seems to have resulted in judges and prosecutors being more prepared to accept an insanity plea, which in turn greatly increased the number of such cases resolved by plea bargain. However, the overall effect of these changes was not major, and it was concluded that 'this dispositional reform did have some impact, but its impact was not as large as . . . had been anticipated'.[239]

THE QUESTION OF ABOLITION

In England there has not been any significant support for an abolition of the insanity defence. Instead, as has already been mentioned, both the Royal Commission on Capital Punishment in 1953 and the Butler Report in 1975 emphasised the need to continue to recognise the 'ancient and humane principle that if a person was at the time of his unlawful act mentally so disordered that it would be unreasonable to impute guilt to him, he ought not to be held liable to conviction and punishment under the criminal law'.[240] The retention of an insanity defence was therefore grounded on 'a fundamental assumption, which it should hardly be necessary to state, that this "ancient and humane principle that has long formed part of our common law" should continue'.[241] The result of this approach seems to be an almost unquestioning acceptance of the need to keep some form of 'insanity' defence within the English criminal justice system, and consequently debate concerning abolition has been virtually non-existent. The Butler Report merely concludes that retention 'is right in principle', as if any alternative conclusion is so unthinkable that it is not worth taking seriously.

By way of marked contrast, proposals for abolition of a separate insanity defence have not only been taken seriously in the United States but

---

[237] Steadman et al., *Before and After Hinckley*, ch. 6.
[238] Ibid. 95.   [239] Ibid. 101.   [240] Cmd 8932 (1953), para 278.
[241] Cmnd 6244, para 18.2. Cf. para 18.10. There is a brief discussion of abolitionist proposals at paras. 18.11–12 but this is exclusively related to a two-stage trial approach and fails to address the reasons which prompted proposals for abolition.

have also been adopted in several jurisdictions. Not unsurprisingly, the *Hinckley* verdict has again been important in this connection in that it rekindled the abolitionist debate.

What is Meant By 'Abolition'?

'Abolition' may mean one of two things: 'total' or 'partial' abolition. 'Total' abolition would disallow completely any evidence of an accused's mental abnormality during the guilt phase of the trial, while 'partial' abolition would continue to permit psychiatric testimony to be admissible but only within the traditional framework of *actus reus* and *mens rea*. The distinction is important and must be further explored.

Total abolition proposals have surfaced from time to time in the United States but they have fared badly, mainly for constitutional reasons. For example, early in the twentieth century, statutes preventing defendants from pleading insanity under any conditions were passed in Washington State, Mississippi, and Louisiana. The first court to review such a statute was the Supreme Court of Washington State which, in *State* v. *Strasburg*,[242] declared unconstitutional the following statutory provision: 'It shall be no defense to a person charged with the commission of a crime that at the time of its commission he was unable, by virtue of his insanity, idiocy or imbecility, to comprehend the nature and quality of the act committed, or to understand that it was wrong; or that he was afflicted with a morbid propensity to commit prohibited acts: nor shall any testimony or other proof thereof be admitted in evidence'. The court concluded that this provision violated due process requirements by relieving the government of its fundamental obligation to prove *mens rea*. Similarly, in *Sinclair* v. *State*[243], and in *State* v. *Lange*[244], the Supreme Courts of Mississippi and Louisiana, respectively, reviewed insanity abolition statutes and declared them unconstitutional.

Since those decisions, there had, until comparatively recently, been little or no support for total abolition of the insanity defence. However, during the US Senate hearings on the insanity defence which followed the Hinckley acquittal, a proposal put forward by two Senators recommended eliminating the insanity defence completely and replacing it with a 'guilty but insane' verdict.[245] This provision would also have ensured that no psychiatric evidence would be admissible on the issue of *mens rea*. Once again, the constitutionality of this approach was questioned and the proposal proceeded no further.

---

[242] 110 P 1020 (1910).   [243] 132 So 581 (1931).

[244] 123 So 639 (1929). For discussion of these three cases, see J. Robitcher and A.K. Haynes, 'In Defense of the Insanity Defense' (1982) 31 *Emory Law Journal*, 51.

[245] US Senate, *Hearings before the Committee on the Judiciary*, 97th Cong. 2nd Sess, S 1106.

It would appear, therefore, that total abolition is too extreme a measure, even post-Hinckley, and not without good reason. To refuse to permit psychiatric testimony even on the issue of *mens rea* seems tantamount to penalizing the defendant for the fact that he was mentally disordered at the time of the offence. Thus, if the defendant alleged mere intoxication, most jurisdictions would admit evidence of his drunken or drugged condition to negate, at least, the *mens rea* of a specific intent crime. Total abolition of the insanity defence, however, would ensure that all evidence relating to mental disorder was inadmissible even when it was relevant to *mens rea*. And yet the mentally disordered defendant is generally not to blame for his incapacitated state, unlike his intoxicated counterpart. In short, total abolition is unjust and cannot be supported under any circumstances while the doctrine of *mens rea* continues to be regarded as a fundamental tenet of modern criminal jurisprudence.

'Partial' abolition, on the other hand, is less extreme. For here the *mens rea* doctrine is left intact, and together with *actus reus*, becomes the sole means of exculpation for the mentally abnormal offender. This type of measure has received a good deal of discussion in the United States, and merits careful analysis.

Arguments For and Against 'Partial' Abolition

A leading advocate of 'partial' abolition is Professor Norval Morris, who in a series of influential writings has argued cogently that there should be no special rules of the M'Naghten or any other type and that instead mental illness should 'be admissible on the "mens rea" issue to the same limited extent that deafness, blindness, heart condition, stomach cramps, illiteracy, stupidity, lack of education, "foreignness", drunkenness and drug addiction are admissible. In practice, such cases are rare, and they would remain rare were mental illness added to the list.'[246] Morris therefore supports a restricted exculpatory doctrine where mental illness would remain relevant and admissible, but only on the questions of *actus reus* and *mens rea*. The former remains relevant 'since the criminal law can seek to control only voluntary acts and not those achieved in fugue states. Manifestly, the epileptic in a "grand mal" whose clonic movements strike and injure another commits no crime; but we need no special defence of insanity to reach that result, well established "actus reus" doctrines suffice. [Whilst] in the broad run of cases, certainly in those where the special defense is now pleaded, ordinary "mens rea" principles can well carry the freight.'[247]

[246] N. Morris, 'Psychiatry and the Dangerous Criminal' (1968) 41 *Southern California Law Review* 514, 518–19.

[247] N. Morris, *Madness and the Criminal Law* (University of Chicago Press, Chicago, 1969), 180.

Morris' contentions are not without their supporters. For example, the American Medical Association fully endorsed the partial abolition approach in their report on the insanity defence made after the *Hinckley* verdict, stating: 'meaningful reform can be achieved only if the focus of the inquiry into responsibility is shifted away from the elusive notion of free will, and its relationship to mental disease, and back to the relatively objective standards of "mens rea" '.[248] Both Morris and the AMA recognise that their approach, by eliminating the extra moral dimension contained within traditional insanity defences, will ensure the conviction of a certain type of mentally ill offender who might currently be the subject of a special verdict. 'The assassin acting under "instructions" from God, and the individual who kills in the irrational belief that the victim is demonically possessed and represents a threat to his life' are frequently given as examples of such cases.[249] Although such cases are rare, neither Morris nor the AMA shy away from the proposition that conviction is required in the light of their proposal, with the factor of mental illness remaining relevant to mitigation of penalty and disposal. Thus Morris maintains that 'there would be no greater injustice involved in convicting such [cases] and applying the psychological diagnosis to the decision how to treat the offender than in convicting in any of the other thousands of cases that daily flow through our criminal courts.'[250] For there is no reason to assume 'that the psychotic is more morally innocent than the person gravely sociologically deprived and pressed towards criminality.'[251]

Naturally enough, the partial abolition approach has been the subject of considerable criticism. In particular, Professor Richard Bonnie, whose views have been influential in shaping recent United States insanity defence reforms, argues that:

The fundamental flaw in the mens rea approach is that it is morally underinclusive. Mens rea requirements in the definition of criminal offences refer, for the most part, to conscious states of awareness. They have no qualitative dimension.

In short, [this] approach fails to take adequate account of the morally significant effects of severe mental illness. Specifically, it does not encompass claims of delusional motivation, or the severe impairment of insight or judgment so manifestly evident in cases of gross psychotic deterioration. In order to encompass . . . the range of

---

[248] AMA, 'The Insanity Defense in Criminal Trials', 2978.   [249] Ibid.

[250] N. Morris and G. Hawkins, *The Honest Politician's Guide to Crime Control* (University of Chicago Press, Chicago, 1969), 80.

[251] Morris, 'Psychiatry and the Dangerous Criminal', 521. For criticism of this aspect of Morris' argument, see P.E. Johnson, 'Review of *Madness and the Criminal Law*' (1983) 50 *University of Chicago Law Review* 1534, 1541: 'We do not excuse psychotics because psychosis is highly correlated with crime, but because they are thought to lack the ability to make morally responsible choices.' See also Morse, 'Excusing the Crazy', 787–90; and R. Delgado, ' "Rotten Social Background" Should the Criminal Law Recognize a Defence of Severe Environmental Deprivation?' (1985) 3 *Law and Inequality* 9.

claims which ought to have exculpatory significance in the penal law, there must be some criterion . . . which is extrinsic to the definition of mens rea.[252]

Bonnie makes it clear that the extra dimension which he regards as fundamental to the moral integrity of the criminal law is 'appreciation of wrongfulness' rather than any test relating to volitional impairment. But what exactly does this 'wrongfulness' element add to the existing doctrines of *actus reus* and *mens rea* and does its special significance really justify the retention of a general and separate insanity defence?

Certainly, so far as England is concerned, because the M'Naghten Rules have been interpreted so strictly, commentators have invariably concluded that 'in sum the . . . rules can be read as saying little more than that insanity may negative "mens rea" '.[253] Since the English courts can scarcely be described as having been 'benevolent' in their attitude toward the insanity defence, it might be thought that the abolition of the 'wrongfulness test' would have little or no practical effect. However, recent empirical research on the operation of the M'Naghten Rules in England described earlier might suggest otherwise.

Partial Abolition in Operation

In the United States partial abolition is now a reality in three jurisdictions, namely Montana, Idaho, and Utah. The legislative frameworks providing for partial abolition in these states are broadly similar and are as follows.

The Montana provision was enacted in 1979, well before the public outcry prompted by Hinckley's acquittal, and states: 'evidence that the defendant suffered from a mental disease or defect is admissible whenever it is relevant to prove that the defendant did not have a state of mind which is an element of the offence.'[254] Similarly, the Idaho statute enacted in 1982 provides: 'mental condition shall not be a defense to any charge of criminal conduct—[But] nothing herein is intended to prevent the admission of expert evidence on the issues of mens rea or any state of mind which is an element of the offence'.[255] In both these states the mental condition of a person who is convicted must be considered by the court before sentence. By way of contrast, however, in Montana if he is found 'not guilty by reason of lack of mental state' the court must order a predisposition investigation in order to determine the most appropriate method of disposal, whilst in Idaho there is no specific analogous provision relating

---

[252] R.J. Bonnie, 'Should the Insanity Defense be Abolished? An Introduction to the Debate' (1986–7) 113 *Journal of Law and Health* 113, 123–4.

[253] Williams, *Textbook of Criminal Law*, 645.

[254] Montana Code Annotated s 46–14–102 (1985). See J.M. Bender, 'After Abolition: The Present State of the Insanity Defense in Montana' (1984) 45 *Montana Law Review* 133.

[255] Idaho Code s 18–207 (1986 Supp). See L.E. Thomas, 'Breaking the Stone Tablet: Criminal Law Without the Insanity Defense' (1983) 19 *Idaho Law Review* 239.

to disposition, which strongly suggests that civil commitment is the only available way of compulsorily hospitalizing a mentally ill person acquitted for lack of *mens rea*.

Utah, the third state to abolish the insanity plea, adopts a more complex approach by not only enacting a new verdict of 'guilty and mentally ill',[256] but also by replacing its original plea of 'not guilty by reason of mental illness' with a new verdict 'not guilty by reason of insanity' which only applies where 'the defendant, as a result of mental illness, lacked the mental state required as an element of the offence charged'. As with the Montana statute, such a verdict brings with it an automatic pre-disposition hearing. The effect of the Utah statute is that, in a convoluted and confusing manner, the affirmative defence of insanity has been eliminated, despite the retention of a separate verdict of 'not guilty by reason of insanity'.

Perhaps because the three states in question are not heavily populated, there has been little appellate consideration of their provisions to date. However, in *State of Montana* v. *Korell*[257], the Supreme Court of Montana was called upon to consider the constitutionality of partial abolition. The facts of the case were that the defendant, a Vietnam veteran, who had been receiving treatment for post-traumatic stress disorder, seriously wounded his treatment supervisor. Psychiatric testimony introduced at the trial indicated that Korell felt that he had to kill the victim before the victim killed him. However, three of the four psychiatrists who testified stated that Korell had the required mental state for the offence despite his condition. The jury convicted Korell of attempted murder and aggravated assault. In its judgment upholding the conviction the Supreme Court was required to answer the contention that insanity is a broader concept than *mens rea* in that some individuals who are clearly insane may also be capable of forming the requisite intent to commit a crime. However, whilst recognising that both delusional and volitionally-impaired defendants could now be convicted under the law of Montana when formerly they might have been 'acquitted' on the ground of insanity,[258] the court was quick to point out that 'as a practical matter, the prosecutor who seeks a conviction of a delusional and psychotic defendant will be faced with a heavy burden of proof'. For 'the State retains its traditional burden of proving all elements beyond a reasonable doubt' and in that sense the hurdle which mentally disturbed defendants must clear in order to be exculpated 'may actually be lower than with a traditional insanity defense.' The court also confirmed that: 'the volitional aspect of mental disease or defect has not been eliminated from our criminal law. Consideration of a defendant's ability to conform his conduct to the law has been moved from the jury

---

[256] Utah Code Annotated s 77–35–21 (1986 Supp).   [257] 690 P 2d 992 (1984).
[258] Prior to abolition, Montana adhered to the ALI test of legal insanity.

to the sentencing judge.' In that context, because the trial judge had re-fused to review the defendant's mental condition prior to sentencing, the matter had to be remanded for resentencing. In short, 'the fact that a jury has found the existence of a required mental state does not conclusively establish the defendant's sanity or fitness for penal punishment.'

However, in a powerful dissent, Justice Sheehy was highly critical of Montana's abolition of the insanity plea claiming that it had been 'held up for criticism and disrespect by national authorities and scholars'. The fundamental reasons for his dissent he expressed as follows:

> Sometimes . . . mentally aberrant persons commit a criminal act. If the criminal act is the product of mental aberration, and not of a straight-thinking cognitive direction, it would seem plausible that society should offer treatment, but if not treatment, at least not punishment. The State of Montana is not such a society.
>
> I do not hold with the majority that there is no independent constitutional right to plead insanity. I would hold that he has an independent constitutional right to trial by jury of the fact of his ability to commit a crime by mental aberration.[259]

As yet the abolition provisions have not received the scrutiny of the appellate courts in Utah, although the Supreme Court of Idaho in *State of Idaho v. Beam*[260] concluded that the legislative framework did not mandate the existence of a separate insanity defence but rather reduced the question of mental condition from the status of a formal defence to that of an evidentiary question relating to the existence of *mens rea*.

Clearly, the experiences of the abolitionist states need to be continuously monitored in order to discover whether the critics' fears are well founded. In this connection an empirical study conducted in Montana is of interest:[261] it reveals that while there was no reduction in the volume or rate of insanity pleas, there was a dramatic reduction in the number of successful insanity defences from an average of seven per each six months prior to abolition to a mere five acquittals during the six and a half years after reform. Further, during the same post-reform period the number of defendants found unfit to plead or incompetent to stand trial (IST) rose, which led to the conclusion 'that IST became a surrogate for the insanity defense in the years following the reform'.[262]

It is quite possible, therefore, that partial abolition might merely alter the legal category of those found legally insane to that of unfitness to plead.[263]

---

[259] 690 P 2d 992, 1005 and 1007 (1984).   [260] 710 P 2d 526 (1985).

[261] Steadman et al. *Before and After Hinckley*, ch. 8. See also H. Steadman et al. 'Maintenance of an Insanity Defense Under Montana's "Abolition" of the Insanity Defense' (1989) 146 *American Journal of Psychiatry* 357.

[262] Steadman et al. *Before and After Hinckley*, 130.

[263] Steadman et al. (ibid. 136) comment about the experience in Montana: 'faced with the loss of one avenue, the legal and mental health systems simply found another way to accomplish the same end.'

However, the question of the moral acceptability of abolition remains: Here, in response to the argument that abolition is immoral, it has to be pointed out that the trend in the United States has been to eliminate the volitional test in favour of a return to the M'Naghten framework. In this connection, Morris remarks: 'As a moral matter, not as a prudential matter, surely defects of control capacity should be given the same moral and exculpatory reach as defects of cognitive capacity.'[264] And yet the US reformers are prepared to allow for conviction of the volitionally-impaired offender not because it is somehow more morally acceptable to convict in such cases but merely because 'the dangers of the volitional inquiry are too great because it is so unstructured'.[265] In short, 'morality is sacrificed to expediency.'[266]

THE *HINCKLEY* LEGACY

Never in the history of the insanity defence has there been so much legislative change in such a brief period of time as in the United States since the *Hinckley* verdict. Taken together, these legal developments form an overall pattern which unmistakably comprises grave concern, criticism, and suspicion in relation to the role of the insanity defence in contemporary American society.[267] From an English perspective, this transmogrification is somewhat ironic. For, after the United States embraced and welcomed the idea of volitional impairment together with flexibility of disposal for insanity acquittees, there has suddenly been a complete reversal in public, medical, legal, and legislative opinion. Suddenly, the M'Naghten Rules, maligned for so long, are once again viewed as an appropriate test of legal insanity at the same time as there is a return to less flexible disposal consequences. All these 'reforms' are fundamentally policy changes, their implementation having received virtually no support from any empirical study. Small wonder therefore that the clearest result produced by Steadman and his colleagues in their evaluation of US insanity defence changes should be 'that legislative reforms are likely to have subtle and often unintended consequences'.[268]

The parallels between the *Hinckley* and *M'Naghten* cases are almost uncanny. The United States has moved back toward a more punitive approach in relation to the insanity defence, with the result that many states have become much more closely aligned to the English position as it stood prior to the enactment of the Criminal Procedure (Insanity and Unfitness

---

[264] Morris, 'Psychiatry and the Dangerous Criminal', 133.
[265] Bonnie, 'Should the Insanity Defense be Abolished', 133.
[266] Brooks, 'The Merits of Abolishing the Insanity Defence', 134.
[267] See generally Perlin, *The Jurisprudence of the Insanity Defense*.
[268] Steadman et al., *Before and After Hinckley*, 151.

to Plead) Act of 1991. The irony, of course, is that in England the M'Naghten Rules and their inflexible disposal consequences have had few supporters. Rather, the pressure here has been for change which would be the complete reverse of the current post-Hinckley trend in the United States. Indeed, the reforms contained in the 1991 Act have achieved important changes in respect of disposal. However, the M'Naghten Rules remain unaltered and it is now time to consider what alternatives have been offered by English law reform bodies.

ENGLISH REVISION PROPOSALS

The M'Naghten Rules, unchanged since 1843, have so far weathered constant criticism including three official reports each of which recommended their total abrogation. The first was in 1923 when the Atkin Committee on Insanity and Crime proposed that a defendant should not be held responsible 'when the act is committed under an impulse which the prisoner was by mental disease in substance deprived of any power to resist'.[269] This was followed thirty years later by the Royal Commission on Capital Punishment which suggested that the best course would be to 'leave the jury to determine whether at the time of the act the accused was suffering from disease of the mind (or mental deficiency) to such a degree that he ought not to be held responsible'.[270] It is interesting to note that the American Law Institute (ALI) rejected this test because it considered that 'the legal standard ought to focus on the *consequences* of disease or defect that have a bearing on the justice of conviction and of punishment'.[271] As an alternative, however, the ALI offered the following test:

A person is not responsible for criminal conduct if at the time of such conduct as a result of mental disease or defect his capacity to appreciate the criminality of his conduct or to conform his conduct to the requirements of law is so substantially impaired that he cannot justly be held accountable.[272]

Although this test has been much less influential than the ALI's primary test, it has been adopted by one state where it has remained unchanged since 1979.[273]

The most recent proposals in England for revision of the law relating to automatism and insanity are those contained in the Report of the Committee on Mentally Abnormal Offenders published in 1975, commonly known

---

[269] Cmd 2005 (1923).   [270] Cmd 8932, para 333.
[271] American Law Institute, *Model Penal Code*, 160 (emphasis in original).
[272] Ibid. 27.
[273] See *State of Rhode Island* v. *Johnson*, 399 A 2d 469 (1969). For discussion, see Hermann, *The Insanity Defense*, 54–8.

as the Butler Report.[274] Fresh impetus to these proposals has now been given by the work of the Law Commission in its report on the Codification of English Criminal Law,[275] which contains a detailed reconsideration of the original Butler recommendations.[276] Most English criminal lawyers accepted that there was a desperate need for flexibility of disposal after a successful insanity plea. In that respect, the Butler proposals which recommended such flexibility had been welcomed,[277] and have now been implemented by the Criminal Procedure (Insanity and Unfitness to Plead) Act 1991 which will be considered shortly. However, at this point consensus ends. Inevitably of major concern has been the proper scope of any new insanity defence. In this respect the Butler proposals have been, to say the least, controversial. For in recommending a new verdict of 'not guilty on evidence of mental disorder',[278] the Butler Report proposed that this verdict should be available not only where mental disorder negatives *mens rea* but also in all cases where the defendant is shown to be suffering from severe mental illness or severe subnormality.[279] Both of these proposed limbs deserve comment.

The first concerns cases where the accused's mental disorder negatives the fault element required for the offence in question. Initially the Butler Report recommended a definition of 'mental disorder' which was extremely wide, being identical to that contained in the Mental Health Act 1983.[280] The Commission was concerned that the result of adopting such a wide definition 'might be to subject too many acquitted persons to a possibly stigmatising and distressing verdict and to inappropriate control through the courts' disposal powers'.[281] As an example of this, the Commission referred to the depressed shoplifter in *R. v. Clarke*[282] who it thought should continue 'to enjoy a plain acquittal rather than an acquittal on "evidence of mental disorder"'.[283]

The effect of the Commission's approach towards the definition of mental disorder is, it admits, to limit strictly such cases, with the result that so far as this first limb of the Butler Report's proposal is concerned, it appears to add little to the first limb of the M'Naghten Rules. Accordingly, as was

---

[274] Cmnd 6244 (1975).
[275] The Law Commission, *A Criminal Code for England and Wales* (1989).
[276] Ibid. 102–13.
[277] See E. Griew, 'Let's Implement Butler on Mental Disorder and Crime' [1984] *Current Legal Problems* 47, 49.   [278] Butler Report, para 18.18.
[279] Ibid. paras 18.20–25 and 18.26–36 respectively.
[280] S 1(2) of the Mental Health Act 1983 provides: ' "Mental disorder" means mental illness, arrested or incomplete development of mind, psychopathic disorder and any other disorder or disability of mind'. However, the Law Commission rejected this approach, expressing surprise that a definition 'designed for the very different purposes of the Mental Health Act, should have been thought suitable as the basis of a qualified acquittal' (The Law Commission, *A Criminal Code*, para 11.27).   [281] Law Commission, ibid. para 11.27.
[282] [1972] 1 All ER 219.   [283] Law Commission, ibid. 224 n 38.

made clear in the discussion of 'abolition', the implementation of this measure could be achieved in conjunction with the rejection of a separate insanity defence. Such an approach has undoubted attractions insofar as simplicity is concerned but it was felt by the Butler Report that it did not go far enough.[284] Thus, the second limb, built upon the notions of severe mental illness or severe subnormality, was offered as the necessary extra dimension for a separate insanity plea in lieu of a 'wrongfulness' limb.

As far as severe subnormality is concerned, the definition proposed by the Butler Report equated with that originally enacted in the Mental Health Act of 1959, namely 'a state of arrested or incomplete development of mind which includes subnormality of intelligence and is of such a nature or degree that the patient is incapable of living an independent life or of guarding himself against serious exploitation, or will be so incapable when of an age to do so'.[285]

This term should not be confused with the replacement expression 'severe mental impairment' defined in the Mental Health Act 1983 as 'a state of arrested or incomplete development of mind which includes severe impairment of intelligence and social functioning and is associated with abnormally aggressive or seriously irresponsible conduct on the part of the person concerned'.[286] This new definition was felt by the Law Commission Codification Team in their 1985 Report to be inappropriate in that 'exemption from criminal liability on the ground of severe mental handicap ought not to be limited to cases where the handicap is associated with aggressive or irresponsible conduct'.[287]

Although this point is endorsed by the Law Commission in its 1989 report, the Commission has nevertheless decided to adopt the expression 'severe mental handicap,' adopting the terms of the definition of 'severe mental impairment' up to and including the word 'functioning'.[288] Although the Commission considers that 'this will give effect to the Butler Report's intention', the result of this proposed change is likely to ensure that a narrower range of mentally impaired persons will qualify for the new mental disorder verdict.

With regard to severe mental illness, the Butler Report decided not 'to equate the definition of severe mental illness with the concept of psychosis',[289] but instead proposed the following complex definition:[290]

A mental illness is severe when it has one or more of the following characteristics:-

---

[284] Butler Report, para 18.26.   [285] S 4(2) Mental Health Act 1959.
[286] S 1(2) Mental Health Act 1983.
[287] The Law Commission, *Codification of the Criminal Law—a Report to the Law* Commission (1985), para 12.8.
[288] Law Commission, *A Criminal Code*, Vol 2. para 11.19.
[289] Butler Report, para 18.34.   [290] Ibid. para 18.35.

(a) Lasting impairent of intellectual functions shown by failure of memory, orientation, comprehension and learning capacity.

(b) Lasting alteration of mood of such degree as to give rise to delusional appraisal of the patient's situation, his past or his future, or that of others, or to lack of any appraisal.

(c) Delusional beliefs, persecutory, jealous or grandiose.

(d) Abnormal perceptions associated with delusional misinterpretation of events.

(e) Thinking so disordered as to prevent reasonable appraisal of the patient's situation or reasonable communication with others.

The Butler Report gave further detailed notes on this definition in Appendix 10 of its Report and, while the above definition has been adopted by the Law Commission in clause 34 of the Draft Criminal Code, no mention is made of these notes. Instead, the Law Commission remarks that their own psychiatric advisers were satisfied 'with the proposed criteria of severe mental illness and with the way in which they are expressed'.[291]

Concern has already been expressed about this 'symptomatic mode of definition' and its shift away from a legal concept like 'disease of the mind' to a definition supposedly based on factual tests pertaining to the severity of the mental illness in question. A major reason for this concern is that this 'severe disorder' defence is undoubtedly a radical proposal in that the new verdict would be available even though the crime could not be shown to have been in any way influenced by the defendant's condition. The rationale behind this approach was expressed by the Butler Report in the following terms: 'the essence of the formula is that it simply presumes absence of responsibility when it is established that the accused was suffering from a sufficiently severe degree of mental disorder at the time of his act or omission and thus confines argument to a question of fact which psychiatrists can reasonably be expected to answer'.[292]

The Law Commission Codification Team was clearly ambivalent about this proposal, stating in its Report that their draft bill could easily be amended to reflect the view that there ought to be some connection between the offence and the disorder. But The Codification Team comments: 'some people, however, take the view that it would be wrong in principle that a person should escape conviction if, although severely mentally ill, he has committed a rational crime which was uninfluenced by his illness and for which he ought to be punished. They believe that the prosecution should be allowed to persuade the jury (if it can) that the offence and the disorder were unconnected... There is undoubtedly force in this point of view.'[293] Naturally, the prospect of eradicating the need for any such causal link between the offence and the disorder is extremely attractive

---

[291] Law Commission, *A Criminal Code*, para 11.18.
[292] Butler Report, para 18.29.
[293] Law Commission, *Codification of the Criminal Law*, para 12.6

insofar as it 'certainly simplifies the task of psychiatric witnesses and the court'.[294]

Significantly, however, the Butler Report did acknowledge that 'it is theoretically possible for a person to be suffering from a severe mental disorder which has in a causal sense nothing to do with the act or omission for which he is being tried: but in practice it is very difficult to imagine a case in which one could be sure of the absence of any such connection'.[295] This comment goes to the very heart of the problem. Is it appropriate to acquit someone on the grounds of mental disorder if it can be shown that at the time of the alleged offence the accused was suffering from a severe form of mental illness which may have had no bearing on the commission of the offence in question? In this connection the Butler Report's 'presumption of irresponsibility' has been criticised as 'rather weak' for 'might not a person, though suffering from "severe mental illness", nevertheless commit a rational crime? Might it not be demonstrable that he had done so? If so, should he not be convicted?'[296] The radical nature of this proposal has caused considerable problems in England over the implementation of the Butler Report recommendations with the result that the Law Commission has now accepted the view 'that it would be wrong in principle that a person should escape conviction if, although severely mentally ill, he has committed a rational crime which was uninfluenced by his illness and for which he ought to be liable to be punished'. Accordingly, 'the prosecution should be allowed to persuade the jury (if it can) that the offence was not attributable to the disorder'.[297] This view is now reflected in clause 35(2) of the Draft Criminal Code which provides that a mental disorder verdict shall not be returned 'if the jury is satisfied beyond reasonable doubt that the offence was not attributable to the severe mental illness or severe mental handicap'.[298] The Commission believes that this sub-clause 'must improve the acceptability of the Butler Committee's generally admirable scheme as the basis of legislation'.[299]

There is no doubt that this particular sub-clause is aimed at achieving a compromise. Thus although there would no longer be any specific test such as knowledge of wrong, the question arises as to what must the prosecution prove to show this lack of attribution in respect of a severe disorder. The Law Commission is silent on this point, and indeed the answer is far from clear and must surely bring with it a continuation of the very type of complex and conflicting psychiatric testimony which the Butler Report had hoped to eradicate. It can even be argued that by

---

[294] Law Commission, *Codification of the Criminal Law*, para 12.6.
[295] Butler Report, para 18.29.
[296] Griew, 'Let's Implement Butler', 56. See also A. Kenny, *Freewill and Responsibility* (Routledge, London, 1978), 83.
[297] Law Commission, *A Criminal Code*, Vol 2 para 11.16.
[298] Ibid. 59. [299] Ibid. para 11.16.

compromising in this manner the Law Commission has completely altered the philosophy behind the Butler Report's radical recommendation and has reinstated the need for a causal link while shifting the burden of disproof to the prosecution. And yet this seems very similar to the problem which caused the demise of the Durham Rule in the United States of America, where Justice Bazelon had originally directed the jury as follows: 'unless you believe beyond a reasonable doubt that . . . the act was not a product of a diseased or defective mental condition, you must find the accused not guilty by reason of insanity. Thus your task would not be completed upon finding, if you did find, that the accused suffered from a mental disease or defect. He would still be responsible for his unlawful act if there was no causal connection between such mental abnormality and the act'.[300] Thus, even in the 'product test',[301] there was a clear need for a causal link which it might be possible for the prosecution to disprove. When we turn to the idea of attribution, then, if it is interpreted in the manner suggested by the Law Commission—namely that the offence should be 'uninfluenced' by the severe disorder—it seems so vague that one must wonder whether the prosecution could ever satisfy the burden which clause 35(2) of the draft Code places upon them.

In much the same way as with the 'product test', the jury under the Law Commission's proposal would be instructed to return a mental disorder verdict unless sure that the act was 'not attributable' or was uninfluenced by the severe disorder. To put this matter into perspective, the notorious case of Peter Sutcliffe may be used as an example. In that case four psychiatrists who examined Sutcliffe all agreed that he was suffering from paranoid schizophrenia: a mental illness which seems to fall squarely within the Butler Report's definition of severe mental illness. Whilst it must be conceded that Sutcliffe's plea of diminished responsibility failed, one cannot be sure that this failure resulted from the jury's dissatisfaction with the psychiatrists' diagnosis.[302] If, therefore, the original Butler Report recommendations had been implemented at this time and Sutcliffe had pleaded 'not guilty on evidence of mental disorder', the chances of an acquittal on this basis would have been high, to say the least. This then illustrates the potential scope of the original proposal and is probably why the Law Commission favoured the compromise in respect of attribution. However, while Sutcliffe was required to prove not only an 'abnormality of mind' but also that this condition had 'substantially impaired his mental responsibility',[303] the Law Commission proposal would instead shift the

---

[300] 214 F 2d 847, 862 (DC Cir 1954).

[301] On defining 'product', see *Carter* v. *US* 252 F 2d 608 (DC Cir 1957).

[302] For detailed discussion of the Sutcliffe case, see H. Prins, *Dangerous Behaviour, The Law, and Mental Disorder* (Tavistock, London, 1986), 33–8 and S. Spencer, 'Homicide, Mental Abnormality and Offence' in M. and A. Craft (eds.), *Mentally Abnormal Offenders* (Ballière-Tindall, London, 1984).   [303] See s 2(1) Homicide Act 1957.

burden of proving lack of attribution to the prosecution. Bearing in mind that the defence will already have proved to the jury's satisfaction that the accused was severely disordered when he committed the offence and will be relying on the notion that the disorder must have had some bearing on the offence, this would seem to place the prosecution in an extremely difficult position.

Of course it might be argued that this 'severe disorder' limb is unlikely to be widely used, since it might be restricted in the 'de minimis' fashion suggested by Norval Morris,[304] especially as the term 'severe mental illness' is defined in the hope of excluding 'mild or incipient forms of psychosis'.[305] The same problem applies to distinguishing between 'subnormality' and 'severe subnormality' which again seems to rest entirely on clinical judgment, that is psychiatric testimony concerning the characteristics of the subnormality or mental illness in question. What, therefore, is to prevent most, if not all, forms of schizophrenia from falling into the category of severe mental illness? The answer must again depend upon the clinical judgment of psychiatrists. Certainly, many types of schizophrenia would seem to satisfy some elements of the definition of 'severe mental illness'. In which case, there is a potential for opening up this new special verdict to schizophrenic offenders in general.[306] While it seems clear that this was not the intention behind this proposal, there is certainly room for concern as to how wide-ranging it would become, if implemented. For it has the potential either to be restricted to a very narrow range of cases or to be interpreted much more broadly. Either way, the workings of this second limb of the Butler Report proposal fall to be determined almost exclusively by psychiatrists. It is highly doubtful whether this is an acceptable way to resolve what is essentially an ethico-legal question: namely, whether a defendant should be relieved of criminal responsibility for his acts.

A further problem with the Butler Report and Law Commission proposals concerns the question of stigma. This point does not appear to have worried those jurisdictions in the United States which have opted for change, since almost without exception the term insanity or some other similar label has continued to figure largely in the special verdict or its alternatives.[307] Of course, since the jury's verdict in *Hinckley*, the stigma which

---

[304] *Madness and the Criminal Law*, 68 where Morris states 'The Butler . . . recommendation of a restricted retention of a special defense of insanity is thus almost a de minimis inconsequential recognition of an extremely severely mentally ill or retarded group who need not be brought within the criminal process.'   [305] Butler Report, para 18.36.

[306] Cf. R.D. Mackay and R.E. Wight, 'Schizophrenia and Anti-Social (Criminal) Behaviour' (1984) 24 *Medicine, Science and the Law* 192 who conclude that a significant number of schizophrenics commit minor offences of a bizarre or disruptive nature. Does this mean that all such offenders would now potentially qualify for this new mental disorder verdict?

[307] E.g. the State of Oregon which since *Hinckley* has altered the wording of its special verdict from 'not responsible' to 'guilty except for insanity'. See Oregon Revised Statutes s 161.295 (1983).

a successful insanity pleas brings with it may be regarded in the United States as entirely appropriate.[308] The initial question of course is whether it is morally proper to stigmatize such an acquittee by retaining highly prejudicial and archaic concepts such as 'insanity', 'madness', 'craziness' or the like. Certainly in England it seems to be generally accepted that the sooner we remove the word 'insanity' from our legal vocabulary the better.[309] Such a move would undoubtedly assist in destigmatizing the special verdict. But to replace 'insanity' with the phrase 'mental disorder' retains a degree of stigma which still seems unacceptable. As an illustration of this, the decision in *R. v. Hennessy*[310] is useful. In that case a diabetic who suffered a hyperglycaemic episode preferred to plead guilty than to be found legally insane. And yet there seems little doubt that under the Draft Code provisions Hennessy would qualify for the newly proposed mental disorder verdict. There is a clear danger here that Hennessy, like Sullivan, the epileptic, might prefer to plead guilty rather than be labelled as 'mentally disordered'. Professor Griew counters this problem of stigma by stating: 'what must develop is an appreciation that the expression "mental disorder" in the verdict refers only to an impairment of function at the time of the act, and that the impairment may be of no terrible significance . . . There will be a job of public education to be done in this connection—including the re-education of the legal profession'.[311] However, it must be open to considerable doubt whether any degree of public education can have this destigmatizing effect. It is submitted, therefore, that it becomes imperative that a more neutral term be found so that defendants who are mildly depressed or diabetic or who suffer from isolated epileptic fits should not be reluctant to seek a special verdict because of some psychiatric label attached to it, such as 'mental disorder'.

ALTERNATIVE APPROACHES

An alternative which was rejected by the Butler Report would be to update the M'Naghten Rules.[312] Such an approach was recently adopted in Canada

---

[308] See e.g. *Jones* v. *US* 463 US 354 (1982), where, in the course of delivering the opinion of the Court, Justice Powell remarked at 367, n 16: 'A criminal defendant who successfully raises the insanity defense necessarily is stigmatized by the verdict itself, and thus the commitment causes little additional harm in this respect.'

[309] See e.g. Butler Report, para 18.18: 'the continued use of the words "insanity" and "insane" in the criminal law long after their disappearance from psychiatry and mental health has been a substantial source of difficulty, and we attach importance to the discontinuance of the use of these words in the criminal law'. See also the Law Commission Codification Team Report, '*Codification of the Criminal Law* para 12.14: 'the offensive label of "insanity" will no longer be used. So the verdict should not seem preposterous in the way that its present counterpart does.'   [310] [1989] 2 All ER 9.

[311] Griew, 'Let's Implement Butler', 52.

[312] Extensive discussion has been taking place in Australia over reform of the insanity

where, after extensive consideration, the Canadian Criminal Code was altered in order to introduce flexibility of disposal for those found legally insane. However, unlike the Criminal Procedure (Insanity and Unfitness to Plead) Act 1991 which leaves the M'Naghten Rules intact, the Canadian reforms have altered the test for insanity by replacing the terms 'insanity' and 'disease of the mind'. The result is a reformulated M'Naghten test which reads:

No person is criminally responsible for an act or omission committed while suffering from a mental disorder that rendered the person incapable of appreciating the nature and quality of the act or omission or of knowing that it was wrong.[313]

It is vital to appreciate however that judicial activity on the part of the Supreme Court of Canada has enabled a wide meaning to be given to the words 'appreciate'—which does not appear in the M'Naghten Rules—and 'wrong', thus enabling the insanity defence to operate in a wider range of cases than would be possible in England.[314] The result is that merely to alter the wording of the Rules might just perpetuate the courts' narrow interpretation of the major defect of intellect which must at present be proved before a special verdict can be returned in England.

A simple alternative has recently been proposed by Professor Gunn who suggests that the power given to magistrates under section 37(3) of the Mental Health Act 1983 to make a hospital order without recording a conviction could be extended to the Crown Court, thus allowing the judge to send the 'insane' offender to hospital without a finding of guilt. According to Gunn, 'all that is required is for the power to be extended to the Crown Court and poor old Daniel M'Nghten would be left in peace'.[315]

However, although this solution has the merit of simplicity, it has a number of drawbacks pointed out by Nigel Walker. In particular, section 37(3) is not concerned with the accused's mental state at the time of the offence but at the time of the trial and in that sense it has more in common with unfitness to plead. Further, 'the section merely permits: it does not compel.'[316] Thus to introduce it as it stands would give judges a discretion as to whether or not a hospital order should be made. If the answer was in the negative, then under the section the magistrates could record a conviction in the normal way. To allow this in respect of insanity would

defence. For brief comment, see I.G. Campbell, 'Retention of the Insanity Defence' (1992) 3 *International Bulletin of Law and Mental Health* 15.

[313] S 16 of the Canadian Criminal Code, as amended.

[314] For discussion, see R.D. Mackay, 'Insanity and Fitness to Stand Trial in Canada and England—A Comparative Study of Recent Developments' (1995) 6 *Journal of Forensic Psychiatry* 121.

[315] J. Gunn and K.R. Herbst, *The Mentally Disordered Offender* (Butterworth-Heinemann, London, 1991), 30.

[316] 'Fourteen Years On', ch. 1 of Gunn and Herbst op. cit., p 8.

be to completely undermine the mandatory exculpatory nature of the defence, leaving it to judges as to whether or not to convict the legally insane. Such an approach would be a radical and dangerous departure from the notion, discussed earlier, that it is morally indefensible to punish those who are adjudged insane at the time of the alleged offence.

A major factor in considering any new insanity defence is to decide what influence psychiatric concepts should have in shaping its structure. In this respect it has already been noted that both the Butler Report and the Draft Criminal Code have decided that the proper approach is to rely heavily on psychiatric notions such as 'mental disorder' and 'severe mental illness'. However, while this approach will undoubtedly make the task of psychiatrists easier than it is at present, there is a danger that the type of 'mental disorder' defence proposed in the code will take the real decision-making out of the hands of the jury, in much the same manner as appears to have occurred in findings of unfitness to plead.[317] If, on the other hand, one views the insanity defence not as primarily about whether or not the offender was suffering from some recognisable psychiatric disorder at the time of the offence, but instead as having a bearing on a matter which is fundamentally moral, then there is good reason to argue that the test should be determined by a jury largely uncluttered by psychiatric notions about which they know little or nothing.

With this in mind, a tentative proposal for a revised special verdict could be based upon the following notion: that the accused be found 'not guilty on account of an aberration of normal mental functioning present at the time of the commission of the alleged offence'. This would have the merit of demedicalizing the new verdict as well as spelling out that the 'aberration' was present when the alleged offence was committed. This last point is not unimportant since it would serve as a reminder that the 'aberration' in question may have been an isolated and/or transitory impairment of 'normal mental functioning' which is no longer present at the time of the trial. In short, an express reference in this proposed new special verdict to the point that the court is necessarily concerned with an inquiry into a 'past' mental condition of the defendant may in its own small way assist in the destigmatization process. For without this express reference there may be a continued tendency to assume that the condition in question is both present and operative at the time of the trial; an assumption which must inevitably be fostered by the wording of the special verdict as it presently exists in English law.

Naturally, the precise scope of a defence based upon the notion of 'an aberration of normal mental functioning' would have to be carefully considered and inevitably this raises once again the complex question of the

---

[317] See Chapter 5 on unfitness to plead.

proper ambit of any such plea. In this connection, an important question is whether English law should attempt to incorporate a volitional limb within any new test. Clearly, the practicality of this is not beyond question since English juries and psychiatrists have been judging 'the difficulty or even inability of an accused person to exercise will power to control his physical acts' ever since the Court of Appeal in *R. v. Byrne*[318] decided that volitional impairment could fall within the plea of diminished responsibility. However, for policy reasons it seems very doubtful whether any defect of the volition or will would be accepted in England as being appropriate for an acquittal, albeit a special one. In this context, therefore, the plea of diminished responsibility seems a more appropriate vehicle for a consideration of these questions since it allows for a conviction whilst at the same time giving complete flexibility in sentencing.[319]

Of course, 'the difficult task is to craft a cognitive test for legal insanity that excuses those who are fundamentally irrational without allowing spurious claims to succeed',[320] as well as a test which can be readily understood by a jury. Whilst the term 'aberration of normal mental functioning' could perhaps be adapted in such a way as to encompass the present law or the Butler Report proposals based on the absence of *mens rea*, the following alternative tests are suggested:

(a) A defendant will be found not guilty on account of an aberration of normal mental functioning present at the time of the commission of the offence if, at that time, his normal mental functioning was so aberrant that he failed to appreciate either what he was doing or that it was wrong according to the standards of ordinary, reasonable people and as a result ought to be acquitted; or
(b) A defendant will be found not guilty on account of an aberration of normal mental functioning present at the time of the commission of the alleged offence if, at that time, his normal mental functioning was so aberrant and affected his criminal behaviour to such a substantial degree that he ought to be acquitted.[321]

Although the second test is wider in scope than the first, it is submitted that either would allow for the revised special verdict to be returned only in cases where there was a fundamental lack of, or reduction of, mental functioning at the time of the alleged offence. In addition, it is submitted that either test would be readily comprehensible to a jury. The reasons for this are threefold. First, neither test is clouded by pseudo-psychiatric

---

[318] *R. v. Byrne* [1960] 3 All ER 1, per Parker LCJ.
[319] For a detailed discussion of diminished responsibility, see Chapter 4.
[320] Morse, 'Excusing the Crazy', 811.
[321] It might be possible to include all forms of automatism within a truly destigmatized defence of this nature. For arguments favouring this approach, see R.D. Mackay, 'Craziness and Codification—Revising the Automatism and Insanity Defences' in I.H. Dennis (ed.) *Criminal Law and Justice—Essays from the W.G. Hart Workshop* (Sweet & Maxwell, London, 1986).

concepts. Second, the phrase 'normal mental functioning' is one which a jury could readily identify with and which needs no elaboration or explanation. Third, the word 'aberration' can be explained to a jury by merely using the dictionary definition, which includes the following: 'deviation from normal; mental irregularity; lapse from a sound mental state'.[322] Thereafter the problem, as in all tests governing criminal responsibility, is one of deciding whether the accused falls within the parameters of the relevant test. In some cases this may be an easy decision for the jury to make whilst in others it may be much more difficult. However, both the suggested tests are an attempt at an uncomplicated approach which should give the jury clear guidance as to what is required of them.

CONCLUSION

Debate and argument concerning the insanity defence seem destined to rumble on indefinitely. In a sense there are no 'right' solutions, although inevitably some solutions seem more acceptable than others.

In Anglo-American jurisprudence the M'Naghten Rules still hold sway. This is all the more remarkable given the fact that they have been the subject of scathing criticism ever since their inception. Despite this the Rules have again risen to prominence in the United States where they seem destined to hold their own for the foreseeable future. Chief Justice Tindal and his fellow judges can little have realised what influence their Rules would exert within the common law world.

Clearly, the United States has moved closer to the English approach to the insanity defence by embracing a more punitive model when excusing the mentally aberrant. This same model has succeeded in England in reducing the practical effect of the insanity defence to virtual non-existence. The disincentives to using the defence have been so great that virtually no one was ever advised to proceed with it. To speak of a general defence of insanity in England has been to speak a lie. However, with the passing of the 1991 Act, this may change, although it must be pointed out that, as shown above, in the first year of its operation the number of insanity defences remained very low at only six. It seems clear, therefore, that despite the introduction of flexibility of disposal it may be some time before the number of insanity defences increases.

There is of course no guarantee that this will ever occur while the M'Naghten Rules remain intact. Indeed there is a strong argument that the Rules are so narrow that few defendants will ever satisfy them. Not only

---

[322] The Oxford English Dictionary Vol 1 (Oxford University Press, Oxford, 1970) includes within its definition of aberration: 'an abnormal state of intellectual faculty; deficiency or partial alienation of reason.'

that, with the retention of the mandatory disposal for murder under the 1991 Act there is every chance that defendants will continue to use diminished responsibility rather than plead insanity. Accordingly, there is unlikely to be any real shift in the relative use of these pleas when murder is the charge.

The crucial question is whether an annual rate of six or so insanity defences per annum is acceptable. To some this might seem nothing short of disgraceful, in the sense that it can in no way reflect the number of 'crazy' defendants who might have been able to take advantage of a wider insanity defence. At the same time others might argue that merely to change the test will not necessarily increase the number of special verdicts. Accordingly, the experience of the United States prior to the *Hinckley* verdict has recently led to the conclusion that 'although the impact of insanity defence reforms in the Liberal era has been poorly charted, it is likely that a small increase occurred in the actual number of people excused from their crimes because of insanity. This outcome may have been due either to changes in the insanity test or to other factors that occurred during this time'.[323] Post-*Hinckley* reforms reveal a similarly unclear picture as to whether a return to M'Naghten and the introduction of other measures designed to curtail the successful use of the insanity defence have achieved this objective.[324]

However, while the effect any change in the test for insanity might have on the number of special verdicts must remain a matter of conjecture, one is forced to return to the undeniable fact that as a defence, insanity is virtually non-existent under English law. It is a clearly documented fact that defendants like *Sullivan* and *Hennessy* have preferred to plead guilty than be declared legally insane. It is impossible to know how many cases like this arise each year, but even one such case is too many; for to 'force' such irresponsible defendants to plead guilty is surely quite untenable. If this is correct, then there is a strong argument that the insanity defence ought to be used more widely than at present. It is possible that the 1991 Act may help to achieve this effect but, until the M'Naghten rules are replaced by a wider test which no longer stigmatizes those who use it, one is forced to accept that the defence of insanity in England will continue to remain a rarely used but legally discredited mechanism of last resort.

[323] La Fond and Durham, *Back to the Asylum*, 137.
[324] Ibid. 137–40. Steadman et al. *Before and After Hinckley*, 151 conclude 'the result from our work that is probably most clear is that legislative reforms are likely to have subtle and often unintended consequences'.

3

Self-induced Incapacity, Mental Disorder, and the Doctrine of Fault

The purpose of this Chapter is to discuss the relevance of intoxication to mental disorder and the attitude of the law towards defendants who seek to use some form of self-induced incapacity as a defence to a criminal charge. This in turn calls for consideration of the doctrine of 'fault liability' which the courts have developed in order to ensure that not all such incapacitated defendants necessarily escape penal sanctions.

Although the major legal developments within this area have naturally enough concerned alcohol and other forms of drugs taken for the purposes of intoxication, the courts have also had to deal with cases where incapacity can be traced to other factors, which in turn have required a different policy analysis. Further, the judiciary have been willing to permit their attitude towards self-induced intoxication to affect their reasoning towards the availability of other defences, a point which tends to have been neglected in legal analysis within this area. It is now proposed to address each of these topics within the broad context of fault liability. Before doing so however, it may be useful to say something about the effect which consumption of alcohol and/or drugs may have on individuals.

THE EFFECTS OF INTOXICANTS[1]

Although alcohol is a drug, in common parlance it tends not to be regarded as such mainly because it is imbibed on such a wide scale by a large section of the population. Accordingly, the consumption of alcohol tends not to be equated with other forms of drug abuse. However, there is no doubt that dependence on alcohol is a continuing source of grave concern.[2]

---

[1] See generally J. Gunn and P.J. Taylor, *Forensic Psychiatry—Clinical, Legal and Ethical Aspects* (Butterworth Heinemann, London, 1993), ch. 11.
[2] See S. Caruana (ed.), *Notes on Alcohol and Alcoholism* (Medical Council on Alcoholism, London, 1975).

Once consumed, alcohol is absorbed from the stomach and upper intestine into the body fluids where it is distributed according to tissue water content. The effect of alcohol on the brain has been described as follows: 'alcohol is a cortical depressant. Since it is the higher and the most recently evolved brain functions that are first effected by depressants, the immediate effect of a dose of alcohol is to inhibit those cerebral functions that are associated with orderly community behaviour and with fine critical judgments; an illusion of cerebral stimulation is thus precipitated.'[3] This removal of inhibitions and impairment of perception has, as will be seen, shaped the law's attitude towards the drunken offender.

Further, a similar legal response has been developed to deal with other forms of self-induced intoxication through drugs.[4] In relation to their effects,[5] as opposed to their penal consequences, drugs that are misused are commonly classified into three main groups.[6]

Firstly, the stimulants consisting mainly of cocaine and amphetamine make individuals more self-assured, lively, and talkative, and help them to keep awake; however, irritability, restlessness, and impairment of judgment and reasoning supervene if they are taken in excess. Ideas of persecution, delusions, and hallucinations may also occur and lead to irrational behaviour.[7] In extreme cases large overdoses may produce psychosis, sometimes resulting in violent episodes.

Secondly, there are the depressants which include heroin, morphine, and the barbiturates. These narcotic analgesics may have a stimulating effect on some individuals but they primarily result in euphoria, drowsiness, and inability to concentrate caused by depression of the central nervous system. Excessive doses may cause aggression as a result of psychosis.

Finally, there are the hallucinogens which include LSD and cannabis. The primary effect of LSD is one of distorted perceptions which are frequently extreme. The effects of cannabis are much milder and there is still considerable controversy as to its harmful effects particularly in relation to the possible existence of 'cannabis psychosis' caused by its long term use.[8] An interesting example of an hallucinogen not expressly controlled by the Misuse of Drugs Act 1971 is the so-called 'magic' mushroom such as the liberty cap, which contains psilocin and psilocybin. If eaten raw, this can cause hallucination and distortion of perception. Prosecution for their

---

[3] J.K. Mason, *Forensic Medicine for Lawyers* (2nd edn. Butterworth, London 1983), 263. See also D. Farrier, *Drugs and Intoxication* (Sweet and Maxwell, London, 1980), 27–31.

[4] See *R. v. Lipman* [1969] 3 All ER 410.

[5] See Gunn and Taylor, *Forensic Psychiatry*, 456–75.

[6] For a useful summary, see P. Bucknell, 'Notes on Some Controlled Drugs' [1985] Crim LR 260. For a detailed analysis, see E.H. Benton et al. 'Special Project: Drugs and Criminal Responsibility' (1980) 33 *Vanderbilt Law Review* 1145. See also *Tackling Drugs Together— A Consultative Document on a Strategy for England 1995–98*, Cmnd 2678 (1994), 20.

[7] Mason, *Forensic Medicine*, 253.   [8] Ibid. 256.

possession has been attempted in the Magistrates' Courts on several occasions without success. However, in *Hodder* v. *DPP*[9] the Divisional Court ruled that once picked, packaged and frozen the mushrooms constituted a 'product' within Schedule 2 of the Misuse of Drugs Act, which in turn meant that their possession in that state was unlawful.

Persistent excessive drinking can of course lead to major medical complications and in particular to the condition often referred to as alcoholism. The World Health Organisation defines alcoholics as: 'those excessive drinkers whose dependence on alcohol has attained such a degree that it shows a noticeable mental disturbance or an interference with their bodily and mental health, their interpersonal relationships and their smooth social and economic functioning; or who show prodromal signs of such developments'.[10] This definition led to the inclusion of alcoholism as a mental illness in the International Classification of Diseases,[11] and was heavily influenced by the work of Jellinek, who regarded alcoholism as a disease process.[12] Although the disease model of alcoholism has been influential, it has recently been seriously questioned by Fingarette who has described it as a 'great myth' that is unsupported by the scientific evidence.[13]

Few now subscribe to the disease concept as originally described by Jellinek. Indeed the concept of alcoholism now tends to be regarded as a pejorative term,[14] and has been widely replaced by the notion of Dependence Syndrome which may arise from the abuse of a wide variety of drugs including alcohol and is defined in the International Classification of diseases as: 'a cluster of behavioural, cognitive, and physiological phenomena that develop after repeated substance abuse and that typically include a strong desire to take the drug, difficulties in controlling its use, persisting in its use depite harmful consequences, a higher priority given to drug use than to other activities and obligations, increased tolerance, and sometimes a physical withdrawal state'.[15]

In simple terms these are persons whose drinking has got out of control and professionals working in this difficult area now tend to think in terms of the 'problem drinker',[16] acknowledging that drinking patterns, both

[9] *The Times*, 14 December 1989.
[10] J. Moser, 'WHO and Alcoholism' in S. Caruana (ed.), *Notes on Alcohol and Alcoholism*, 165.   [11] Ibid.
[12] E.M. Jellinek, *The Disease Concept of Alcoholism* (Millhouse Press, New Haven, Connecticut, 1960).
[13] H. Fingarette, *Heavy Drinking—The Myth of Alcoholism as a Disease* (University of California Press, Berkeley, California, 1988).
[14] See Trent Regional Health Authority *Health Gain Investment Programme for Alcohol* (1994), 15.
[15] *International Statistical Classification of Diseases and Health Related Problems*, Tenth Revision, (World Health Organisation, Geneva, 1992), 321 para FO9.2.
[16] *Health Gain Investment Programme*, 15.

normal and abnormal, are examples of learned behaviour. The problem of assessing the number of people with problems associated with alcohol consumption was recently described as 'potentially controversial because of the difficulties in defining alcohol related problems'.[17] Despite this the Health Survey for England for 1991 concluded that '7% of men and 5% of women who drank were classified as problem drinkers'.[18] The scale of the problem is such that alcohol consumption continues to be a Health of the Nation priority.[19]

Problem drinking is associated with a number of other recognised conditions, some of which deserve particular mention. Firstly, 'pathological intoxication' is a term used to refer to uncharacteristic behaviour during a spell of drinking. Some observers have claimed that such behaviour often follows the ingestion of relatively small quantities of alcohol and implies the presence of some inherent predisposition in the form of latent epilepsy which has been activated by the alcohol. It has been suggested that in such cases, the ingestion of small amounts of alcohol would evoke EEG patterns similar to those seen in cases of psychomotor epilepsy. If this were so, such claims could have important implications in relation to the issue of criminal responsibility where such behaviour resulted in criminal proceedings. However, this condition is the subject of considerable medico-legal dispute and will be discussed further below.

Secondly, alcoholic amnesia is frequently caused by heavy drinking.[20] There may be total inability to recall events, commonly referred to as an alcoholic black-out, whilst in less acute cases there may be patchy recollection. An alternative explanation is that memory retrieval in some of these cases is actually dependent upon the existence of the intoxicated state itself. The suggestion here is that of 'state dependent memory' in which recall is dependent upon the individual being in 'a similar subjective state to that prevailing when the memory trace was originally laid down'.[21] In their study entitled 'Amnesia for Criminal Offences',[22] Taylor and Kopelman found that, out of a total of 19 men claiming amnesia for offences of which they had been convicted, 18 were serious alcohol abusers. They concluded that whilst 'there was a tendency for the alcohol abusers to be over-represented in the amnesia group' neither these amnesias, caused by the pharmacological effects of alcohol, nor any of the others they encountered had any special legal implications owing to the absence of any organic disorder, other than the effects of intoxication, at the time of the

---

[17] *Health Survey of England 1991* (HMSO 1993), 111.   [18] Ibid. 107.
[19] *On the State of Public Health, Annual Report of the Chief Medical Officer for the year 1993* (HMSO 1994), 95–7.
[20] See *International Classification of Diseases*, 322 para FO9.6, describing alcohol-induced amnesic syndrome.
[21] P.J. Taylor and M.D. Kopleman, 'Amnesia for Criminal Offences' (1984) 14 *Psychological Medicine* 581.   [22] Ibid, 581.

offence. In short, this study reflects the legal position which refuses to accept amnesia *per se* as a defence in criminal proceedings.

Drug abuse is also of considerable concern in that 'the picture which emerges does suggest that drug misuse is a major and growing problem in England'.[23] The *International Classification of Diseases* uses the term 'psychoactive substances' to embrace an extremely wide spectrum of substances,[24] including alcohol, which can effect a comparable range of biological functions. This Chapter, however, is naturally only concerned with those drugs which affect mental functioning and behaviour, and thus may be the subject of abuse. For the most part, these drugs fall within the statutory framework of the Misuse of Drugs Act 1971 which creates the concept of 'controlled' drugs. The categorisation of controlled drugs into classes A, B, and C is related to the punishment of the offences of production, supply, and possession, with the heaviest penalties being available for class A and the least heavy for class C.[25]

Psychiatric complications ranging from problems caused by an individual's emotional reaction to drugs to severe drug-induced psychosis are commonplace.[26] Indeed, medical complications generally are on the increase owing to the changing pattern of drug abuse in the United Kingdom.[27]

VOLUNTARY INTOXICATION AND CRIMINAL RESPONSIBILITY

Voluntary intoxication and the manner in which it affects criminal responsibility has continued to be the subject of extensive criticism.[28] The reasons for this criticism stem from the fact that the courts have felt it necessary to develop special rules to deal with this particular problem—rules which run counter to the basic principles underlying criminal liability—in particular the need for proof of *mens rea*. In order to justify this departure from principle, the courts have relied heavily on factors relating to policy and social control with the result that the law has developed in a haphazard and unsatisfactory manner as described below.[29]

Firstly, it is important to emphasise that drunkenness by itself has never been regarded as a defence in criminal law. The reason for this is quite straightforward. As already mentioned, the consumption of alcohol lessens inhibitions and self-control, frequently causing ill-considered and stupid behaviour. No one would seriously consider that such behaviour, if it

---

[23] *Tackling Drugs Together*, 15.
[24] *International Classification of Diseases*, 320.
[25] Gunn and Taylor, *Forensic Psychiatry*, 461–5.   [26] Ibid.
[27] *Tackling Drugs Together*, 17–18.
[28] See The Law Commission, *Intoxication and Criminal Liability* (1993), Part III.
[29] See The Law Commission, *Legislating the Criminal Code: Intoxication and Criminal Liability* (1995), Part III.

breaches the criminal law, should result in an acquittal. For, as the Court of Appeal pointed out in *R. v. Sheehan* 'the mere fact that the defendant's mind was affected by drink so that he acted in a way in which he would not have done had he been sober does not assist him at all, provided that the necessary intention was there. A drunken intent is nevertheless an intent.'[30] There seems little doubt that the vast majority of drunken offenders fall within this category,[31] and do in fact have the required *mens rea* at the time of the commission of the offence. The same is also true of those who commit offences whilst under the influence of drugs.

However, in extreme cases, there is equally no doubt that drink or drugs or a combination of the two may produce an effect which is incompatible with the formation of *mens rea*. But can this lack of *mens rea* lead to the accused's acquittal? One cannot safely answer this question yes or no! The answer depends on a number of variables which stem from recent judicial pronouncements in the House of Lords.

THE RULE IN *MAJEWSKI*

Firstly, in *DPP* v. *Majewski*[32], the accused, in answer to a charge of assault occasioning actual bodily harm and assaulting the police, claimed that he was unaware of what he was doing owing to intoxication through drink and drugs. In unanimously dismissing the accused's appeal, the House of Lords made it clear that because the offences in question merely required proof of a 'basic' intent, the intoxication in question, no matter how severe, could not act as a defence. The position was summarised by Lord Elwyn Jones LC as follows:

If a man of his own volition takes a substance which causes him to cast off the restraints of reason and conscience, no wrong is done to him by holding him answerable criminally for any injury he may do in that condition. His course of conduct in reducing himself by drugs and drink to that condition . . . supplies the evidence of mens rea, of guilty mind certainly sufficient for crimes of basic intent. It is a reckless course of conduct and recklessness is enough to constitute the necessary mens rea in assault cases. . . . The drunkenness is itself an intrinsic, an integral part of the crime, the other part being the unlawful use of force against the victim.[33]

This statement admirably demonstrates the policy approach of the court towards cases of self-induced intoxication. However, at the same time, the decision in *Majewski* is far from problem-free. A major difficulty is the fact

---

[30] [1975] 2 All ER 960, 963. Quoted with approval by the House of Lords in *R.* v. *Kingston* [1994] 3 All ER 353, 364.

[31] For general discussion, see Law Commission, *Intoxication and Criminal Liability*, paras 1.10–16.   [32] [1976] 2 All ER 142.

[33] Ibid. 150.

that their Lordships made it clear that self-induced intoxication could act as a defence in two types of case. The first was where the intoxication gave rise to legal insanity. This merits separate consideration and will be dealt with later in this Chapter; the second was where the offence required proof of a 'specific' as opposed to a 'basic' intent. If this was the case, then evidence of self-induced intoxication could be used in support of a defence of lack of *mens rea*. But how, it may be asked, is one to distinguish between 'basic' and 'specific' intent? Unfortunately, the answer is far from clear as none of the judgments in *Majewski* contains a convincing definition of 'specific' intent. Indeed, it is probable that no such definition is to be found, in view of the fact that the distinction in question is clearly not based upon logic but is instead founded on public policy. This has led Smith and Hogan to conclude that 'in order to know how a crime should be classified for this purpose we can look only to the decisions of the courts.'[34]

So what then are the policy reasons for this illogical distinction? The answer is founded on compromise. The courts are markedly reluctant to allow the intoxicated offender an outright acquittal, but at the same time recognise that severe cases of intoxication may result in a lack of *mens rea*. In order to allow both of these principles to operate, the judiciary have been prepared to label some, often more serious, offences as requiring proof of a 'specific' intent and the rest as offences of 'basic' intent. A good example of the way in which the distinction operates is to be found in the division between murder and manslaughter. Thus, whilst murder is a crime of 'specific' intent to which voluntary intoxication can act as a defence,[35] an intoxicated accused will inevitably be convicted of manslaughter as this is a crime of 'basic' intent.[36]

The 'specific/basic' intent dichotomy is far from satisfactory if, as has been suggested, we have to wait for a judicial pronouncement before we can safely categorise a particular offence.[37] However, the dichotomy has become less important as a result of a second House of Lords' decision, namely *R. v. Caldwell*[38], where Lord Diplock interpreted the Lord Chancellor's remarks in *Majewski* as meaning that self-induced intoxication is not a defence to *any* crime in which recklessness is enough to constitute the necessary *mens rea*. The offence in question was aggravated criminal damage contrary to section 1(2) of the Criminal Damage Act 1971, which

[34] J.C. Smith and B. Hogan, *Criminal Law* (7th edn., Butterworths, London, 1992), 221. See also Law Commission, *Legislating the Criminal Code* (1995), which states at para 3.27: 'It is apparent . . . that there is no general agreement on the test which should be applied in order to distinguish offences of basic and of specific intent'.

[35] *R. v. Sheehan* [1975] 2 All ER 960.   [36] *R. v. Lipman* [1969] 3 All ER 410.

[37] For a recent example, see *DPP v. Kellet* [1994] Crim LR 916 which decided that the offence under s 1(7) of the Dangerous Dogs Act 1991 is one of 'basic' intent.

[38] [1981] 1 All ER 961.

requires intention or recklessness both as to damaging property and also as to endangering another's life. This meant that, as long as the prosecution relied on recklessness in the charge in question, then the fact that the accused was unaware of the risk of endangering life 'owing to his self-induced intoxication would be no defence if that risk would have been obvious to him had he been sober'.[39]

The effect of this ruling seems to be that any offence, in so far as it can be committed recklessly, may now be classed as virtually equivalent to an offence of 'basic' intent. Thus, for intoxication to be able to act as a defence under section 1(2) of the 1971 Act, the charge would have to refer merely to intention and to exclude any reference to recklessness, now a most unlikely occurrence. On the other hand, if the only mental element specified in an offence is one of intention, as, for example, 'intention permanently to deprive' in theft, then the offence must remain one of 'specific' intent.

The practical significance of *Caldwell*, rather than to reduce the number of 'specific' intent offences, has been to reduce the number of occasions on which evidence, medical or otherwise, of self-induced intoxication will be admissible in order to demonstrate a lack of *mens rea*. Indeed, if the accused is charged with a 'basic' intent or 'recklessness' offence, any attempt by him to use this type of evidence will usually be fatal to his case as the effect of it will be to relieve the prosecution from their normal burden of having to prove *mens rea*. Even if the evidence points to the fact that the risk in question would not have been obvious to the accused had he been sober, there are now strong indications that the courts will refuse to apply this 'conditionally subjective' test and will instead use an entirely objective test based upon what the reasonable, and hence sober, man would have appreciated in such circumstances.[40]

EXCEPTIONS TO THE RULE IN *MAJEWSKI*

The legal position relating to the use of intoxication as a defence has been further complicated by the emergence of two exceptions to the rule in *Majewski*. In the first, the courts have confirmed that self-induced intoxication may yet be successfully used if a statute expressly provides that the accused's knowledge or belief shall be a defence to the charge. Thus in *Jaggard* v. *Dickson*[41] the accused was convicted of simple criminal damage having drunkenly damaged a neighbour's house in an attempt to enter it, believing that the house in question belonged to her friend who had given her permission to force an entry. The accused relied on section 5(2) of the

[39] [1981] 1 All ER 961, 967.   [40] See Smith and Hogan, *Criminal Law*, 224.
[41] [1980] 1 All ER 716.

Criminal Damage Act 1971, which provides that a person has a defence if he believes that the owner would have consented to the damage in these circumstances. In quashing the accused's conviction, the Divisional Court decided that although the offence in question was one of 'basic' intent, the accused's drunkenness was not being used to negate intention or recklessness but instead was merely being relied upon to explain and substantiate her belief. The result has been described as 'anomalous',[42] and has been the subject of considerable criticism. Clearly, subtleties of this nature do the law a disservice and only serve to add complexity to a body of legal principles which is already unsatisfactory and in urgent need of reform.

The second exception concerns involuntary intoxication where the House of Lords recently made it clear in *R.* v. *Kingston*[43] that, unless the intoxication negatived *mens rea*, it could not act as a defence despite its involuntary nature. Accordingly, if drink or drugs, surreptitiously administered, caused a person to lose his self-control and for that reason to form an intent which he would not otherwise have formed, the law should not exculpate him as the absence of moral fault on his part could not act as a defence. In his robust rejection of any such novel defence, Lord Mustill considered a major difficulty was that: 'in point of theory, it would be neccessary to reconcile a defence of irresistible impulse derived from a combination of innate drives and external disinhibition with the rule that irresistible impulse of a solely internal origin (not necessarily any more the fault of the offender) does not in itself excuse although it may be a symptom of a disease of the mind'.[44] Clearly his Lordship was worried about the dangers of permitting such a lack of control defence when it has been consistently rejected as a form of legal insanity within the M'Naghten Rules.[45] A further inconsistency which would arise from the recognition of such a defence would be that, while it would lead to an outright acquittal in a murder charge, by way of contrast a defendant who suffered from an uncontrollable urge to kill through a combination of mental disorder and drink or drugs voluntarily consumed would be likely to fail in any diminished responsibility plea and would be convicted of murder. Although the prospect of convicting the former of murder led Lord Mustill to hesitate in rejecting the creation of such a novel defence, he felt that this 'was not a sufficient reason to force on the theory and practice of the criminal law an exception which would otherwise be unjustified'.[46] This seems plainly correct,[47] and the problem created by murder is yet another reason why the mandatory penalty should be abolished.

[42] Smith and Hogan, *Criminal Law* 225. See now Law Commission, *Legislating the Criminal Code*, para 7.18, which recommends 'that the same rules should apply to statutory defences as to defences in general'.   [43] [1994] 3 All ER 353.
[44] Ibid. 370.   [45] See Chapter 2.   [46] [1994] 3 All ER 353, 371.
[47] But for a contrary view, see G.R. Sullivan, 'Involuntary Intoxication and Beyond' [1994] Crim LR 272.

OTHER FORMS OF SELF-INDUCED INCAPACITY

The rule relating to self-induced intoxication is undeniably strict and is the result of policy factors. Thus in *Majewski* it was made clear that an intoxicated person could be convicted of a basic intent offence even if his condition was akin to automatism. Originally there had been some suggestion that the rule in *Majewski* might apply to other forms of self-induced incapacity and that an automatism plea would be unavailable to anyone who was at 'fault' in allowing himself to become incapacitated. For example in *R. v. Quick*, Lawton LJ commented: 'a self-induced incapacity will not excuse (see *Lipman*) nor will one which could have been reasonably foreseen as a result of either doing, or omitting to do something as, for example, taking alcohol against medical advice after using certain prescribed drugs, or failing to have regular meals whilst taking insulin'.[48] It has been pointed out that this dictum needs qualification as it seems clear that if the accused's incapacitated condition is self-induced but without any 'fault' on his part, then he will not be convicted of any offence.[49] Further, as Quick was prosecuted for a crime of 'basic' intent, the dictum took no account of what might occur in similar cases where proof of a 'specific' intent was required.

These points have now been addressed by the Court of Appeal, which on two occasions has decided not to follow this approach and in consequence has restricted the rule in *Majewski* to cases of voluntary intoxication. Firstly, in *R. v. Bailey*[50], a case very like *Quick*, the accused was a diabetic who seriously assaulted his girlfriend during what was alleged to be a hypoglycaemic episode, caused by his failure to eat food after drinking a mixture of sugar and water. The trial judge directed the jury that the defence of automatism was unavailable because the accused's incapacity was self-induced. In deciding that this was a misdirection, the Court of Appeal held that self-induced automatism of this nature could provide a defence even to a crime of 'basic' intent on the ground that a distinction ought to be made between intoxicants and other substances which might give rise to incapacity. In the words of Griffiths LJ:

It is common knowledge that those who take alcohol to excess or certain sorts of drugs may become aggressive or do dangerous or unpredictable things . . . But the same cannot be said, without more, of a man who fails to take food after an insulin injection. If he does appreciate that such a failure may lead to aggressive, unpredictable and uncontrolled conduct and he nevertheless deliberately runs the risk or otherwise disregards it, this will amount to recklessness. But we certainly do not think that it is common knowledge, even among diabetics, that such is a consequence of a failure to take food.[51]

---

[48] [1973] 3 All ER 347, 356.
[49] R.D. Mackay, 'Intoxication as a Factor in Automatism' [1982] Crim LR 146, 148.
[50] [1983] 2 All ER 503.   [51] Ibid. 507.

Similarly, in R. v. *Hardie*[52], the accused set fire to his common law wife's flat after he had taken about five Valium tablets, being ignorant of their effect. The trial judge ruled that as the accused had voluntarily self-administered the drug, its effect on him could not act as a defence to reckless arson contrary to section 1(2) of the Criminal Damage Act 1971. In allowing the accused's appeal against his conviction, the Court of Appeal endorsed the distinction made in *Bailey* saying:

> There was no evidence that it was known to the appellant or even generally known that the taking of Valium in the quantity taken would be liable to render a person aggressive or incapable of appreciating risks to others or have other side effects such that its self-administration would itself have an element of recklessness. It is true that Valium is a drug and it is true that it was taken deliberately and not taken on medical prescription, but the drug is, in our view, wholly different in kind from drugs which are liable to cause unpredictability or aggressiveness . . . if the effect of a drug is merely soporific or sedative, the taking of it, even in some excessive quantity, cannot in the ordinary way raise a 'conclusive' presumption against the admission of proof of intoxication for the purpose of disproving mens rea in ordinary crimes, such as would be the case with alcoholic intoxication or incapacity or automatism resulting from the self-administration of dangerous drugs.[53]

The combined effect of *Bailey* and *Hardie* is both to confirm the effect of and to restrict the scope of the rule in *Majewski*. These decisions make it clear, firstly, that because of the 'conclusive presumption' relating to intoxicants, a person takes alcohol and/or drugs (including solvents etc) of an intoxicating nature at his own risk. Thus, provided the substance is one which is generally known to have an intoxicating effect, the fact that the accused may be unaware of the effect which such a substance may have upon him will do nothing to prevent a conviction for a crime of recklessness or basic intent. All that is needed to secure such a conviction in this type of case is proof that the accused voluntarily took such a substance.[54]

In marked contrast to this, the approach to be adopted in all other cases of self-induced incapacity, is to enquire whether the accused was 'reckless', in the sense of his being aware that his action or inaction is likely to make him aggressive and unpredictable and involve a risk of injury to others or a risk of damage to property. The effect of this approach will be to make the task of the prosecution much more difficult in this type of case; for unless there is proof that the accused has reacted in this manner on at least one previous occasion, there is little likelihood of the prosecution being able to prove 'recklessness' in the required sense. Clearly, however, it has been felt that the policy reasons giving rise to the rule in *Majewski* should not be allowed to extend beyond clear-cut cases of self-induced intoxication.

---

[52] [1984] 3 All ER 848.   [53] Ibid. 853.
[54] Cf. R. v. *Allen* [1988] Crim LR 698 discussed below.

Insofar as the *Majewski* rule is itself illogical and difficult to apply, this is a commendable restriction. Any limitation of the application of the 'specific/basic' intent dichotomy seems desirable and it can only be hoped that any statutory reform within this area will ensure its abolition.[55]

However, until this happens the criminal law will continue to be bedevilled by the following difficult issues.

The Nature of the 'Recklessness' Involved

The distinction between *Majewski* recklessness and *Bailey* recklessness involves the assumption that, while the antisocial effects of excess alcohol and 'certain sorts of drugs' are well known, the same is not true of drugs such as insulin taken for medicinal purposes nor of drugs taken for soporific or sedative purposes. In the latter types of case, therefore, an added burden is placed on the prosecution to prove a generalised form of 'recklessness' relating to knowledge not only of the incapacity but also how the accused might react during this time. An important point here is that the cases of *Bailey* and *Hardie* involve a number of significant distinctions. In the first place, *Bailey* was a case of automatism while *Hardie* deals with the negation of *mens rea*. Secondly, while Bailey was concerned with an offence of 'subjective' recklessness (see *Cunningham*)[56], *Hardie* faced a charge which clearly consisted of 'objective' recklessness (see *Caldwell*). These points seem to have been ignored by the court in *Hardie* and yet they could have an important bearing on the development of the law within this area, as there is clear authority for the proposition that once the accused's incapacity reaches the stage of automatism, then *Caldwell* recklessness is irrelevant. This was made clear in R. v. *Bell*[57], a decision reached shortly before *Hardie*. Accordingly, it seems clear that, even if *Bailey* had been charged with criminal damage he would still have been acquitted, provided the prosecution was unable to prove 'recklessness' in the sense of an awareness of the risk of becoming unpredictable etc. By way of contrast, however, the defence of *Hardie* was that he lacked *mens rea*, and yet the court applied *Bailey*. This has led the Law Commission to conclude that the principle developed in the latter case 'applies, it would seem, even to offences to which *Caldwell* recklessness applies'[58] while at the same time pointing out that this view 'seems inconsistent with the reasoning in *Elliot* v. *C:* [as] it is difficult to discern, for the purpose of explaining why the defendant did not give thought to an obvious and serious risk, a principled

[55] See now Law Commission, *Legislating the Criminal Code*, which states at para 1.36 'our recommendations would dispense with the need to classify the offence charged as one of "specific" or "basic" intent in order to determine which régime applies to it'.
[56] [1957] 2 QB 396.   [57] [1984] 3 All ER 842, 847.
[58] Law Commission, *Intoxication and Criminal Liability*, para 2.29.

distinction between reliance upon an innate incapacity and reliance on incapacity caused by taking (even a non-dangerous) drug'.[59] There is much force in this type of criticism which makes it all the more regrettable that the court in *Hardie* did not explore the precise nature of the recklessness required. In this context, however, it can be pointed out that the court does refer at one stage to the fact that, if the jury considered that the effect of the Valium had resulted in a lack of *mens rea*, 'they should then consider whether the taking of the Valium was itself reckless'.[60] This strongly suggests that the fault element is similar to that in *Majewski*, in the sense that, if it is not commonly known that the taking of a non-dangerous drug would lead to incapacity, then the further question the jury must decide is simply '*Majewski* recklessness [in the sense of] *Caldwell* recklessness as to becoming intoxicated.' The rationale behind this is that 'it is recklessness as to becoming intoxicated and not recklessness as to the actus reus occurring; the fault element lying in D allowing himself to become dangerous or destructive'.[61] Whether this is the correct interpretation of the rule in *Majewski* must be open to question.[62] However, there is no doubt that as the law stands at present it is difficult to fully reconcile *Hardie* and *Bailey*. Despite this difficulty it is equally clear that these cases demonstrate a reluctance on the part of the courts to extend the strictures of *Majewski* beyond alcohol and dangerous drugs. This in turn leads to the problem of deciding precisely what conduct will result in the accused being caught by the *Majewski* rule. There are two related points which now merit consideration.

First, how is one to decide whether the substance which leads to the accused's incapacity should attract the *Majewski* rule? The answer seems to revolve around the notion that, while the effect of intoxicants such as alcohol and 'dangerous' drugs is common knowledge, the same is not true of certain other substances such as insulin and Valium. However, the court seems to have reached its conclusion in *Bailey* without any investigation into what levels of awareness there are amongst diabetics about the onset of hypoglycaemia.[63] For while this may not be common knowledge amongst the population in general, the conclusion that the effects of insulin are unknown 'even among diabetics'[64] is at least deserving of further scrutiny by the court.

By way of contrast, however, the fact that the accused is unaware of the

---

[59] Law Commission, *Intoxication and Criminal Liability*, 22 n 65, referring to *Elliot* v. *C* [1983] 2 All ER 1005.
[60] [1984] 3 All ER 842, 853.
[61] E. Macdonald, 'Reckless Language and *Majewski*' (1986) 6 *Legal Studies* 239, 247.
[62] See Law Commission, *Intoxication and Criminal Liability*, paras. 2.4–2.21.
[63] See G. Maher et al., 'Diabetes Mellitus and Criminal Responsibility' (1984) 24 *Medicine, Science and the Law* 95.
[64] [1983] 2 All ER 503, 507. There is also some evidence to suggest that 'valium can cause aggression': see Law Commission, *Legislating the Criminal Code*, para 5.42 n 9.

alcoholic strength of the beverage he is voluntarily consuming will not permit evasion of *Majewski*. This was made clear in *R. v. Allen*[65] where the Court of Appeal stated: 'where an accused knows that he is drinking alcohol, such drinking does not become involuntary for the reason alone that he may not know the precise nature or strength of the alcohol that he is consuming. It is nonetheless the voluntary imbibing of alcohol.' Similarly the rule in *Majewski* would presumably include the accused whose first drinking spree leads him to commit a basic intent offence whilst in an incapacitated condition. The fact that he might legitimately claim to be unaware what effect the excessive consumption of alcohol might have upon him would not seem to prevent the 'common knowledge' approach in *Majewski* from applying. However, what is noticeable in these latter examples is that the accused's condition can be traced to the excessive consumption of alcohol. Where, however, there is a combination of alcohol with other factors the position is more complex and will now be considered separately.

ALCOHOL COMBINED WITH OTHER FACTORS

It seems likely from the facts of *Quick*[66] that the effects of the alcohol contributed to the accused's state of automatism. Despite this the additional factor of the insulin injection seems to have been enough to remove the accused from the province of voluntary intoxication, although it must be conceded that this matter was not under express consideration by the court in that case. However, in *R. v. Stripp*[67] where the accused was drunk but later sustained a blow to the head causing concussion, the Court of Appeal ruled that if the drunkenness was only one of two or more 'causes operating', the combined effect of which might have resulted in automatism, then it was not proper to withdraw automatism from the jury merely because intoxication was present. In the opinion of the Law Commission commenting on *Stripp*: 'the case suggests, obiter, the possibility that where there is a cause of automatism clearly separable in time or effect from the intoxication, and supported by a foundation of evidence, then a defence of automatism may be available; but where the causal factors are less easily separable, it would seem that the presence of the intoxication will, on the policy grounds adopted in *Majewski*, exclude reliance on automatism'.[68]

---

[65] [1988] Crim LR 698.
[66] [1973] 3 All ER 347, 356 where Lawton LJ refers to 'taking alcohol against medical advice after using certain prescribed drugs.'
[67] (1978) 65 Cr App R 318.
[68] Law Commission, *Intoxication and Criminal Liability*, para 2.33. In its final report, *Legislating the Criminal Code* (1995), the Law Commission adopts this approach by recommending (at para 6.44) that there should be no defence 'where the automatism is caused partly by voluntary intoxication and partly by some other factor'. However, it is made clear

No specific authority is given in support of this last point concerning the problem of incapacity which results from a combination of intoxication with other causal factors. But, if the opinion expressed by the Commission is correct, then it seems likely that the dictum in *Quick* would need to be reconsidered,[69] since the drink and the insulin could not be separated in that case in the manner which occurred in *Stripp*. They might be regarded as separate causal factors where the effect of the alcohol led to confusion over the quantity of insulin to be injected, rather than the alcohol reacting directly with the insulin prior to the onset of hypoglycaemia. However, this hardly seems an acceptable distinction. Indeed there is authority in *R. v. Burns*[70] to suggest that in either case the accused should be acquitted, although that decision was further complicated by considerations of the insanity defence.

, In *Burns* the accused was convicted of indecent assault. At his trial medical evidence was given to show that, although the accused was suffering from a 'disease of the mind', namely alcoholism, his state of automatism was triggered off by the consumption of pills containing morphia or morphine, which he had been 'given' for a stomach upset,[71] coupled with a small amount of alcohol. In addition, the medical evidence suggested that the brain impairment by itself would not have produced such a condition and that it was necessary that there should be drink or drugs before the state of automatism supervened.[72]

The decision in *Burns* has been criticised by Smith and Hogan on the ground that 'It is difficult to see how [it] can be right, since neither of the concurrent causes entitled D to be absolutely acquitted.'[73] Such an approach however overlooks the nature of the external factors which were operating in *Burns*; for it was not only alcohol which reacted upon the accused's alcoholism but also the Mandrax pills. Indeed, the Court of Appeal made this clear in the following remark: 'there was evidence that the appellant's unawareness resulted not simply from his disease of alcoholism and the brain damage caused by it nor from alcohol added to that disease, but from alcohol and the drug Mandrax added to that disease'.[74] While it may be true, therefore, that where the defendant does not know what he is doing 'partly because of voluntary intoxication and partly through disease of the mind ... he must be found either guilty or "not

that this rule is to apply only in those cases where 'the intoxication was a *cause* of the automatism' (para 6.45).

[69] For discussion of this point, see Chapter 2.   [70] (1973) 58 Cr App R 364.
[71] Ibid. 366. The use of the word 'given' suggests that the pills were not prescribed. However, they were taken for 'therapeutic' purposes and thus surely fall within the type of 'non-dangerous' drug envisaged by the Court of Appeal in *Hardie* [1984] 3 All ER 848, 853.
[72] (1973) 58 Cr App R 364, 370.
[73] Smith and Hogan, *Criminal Law* (6th edn., 1988), 191.
[74] (1973) 58 Cr App R 364, 370.

guilty by reason of insanity"',[75] this reasoning should surely *only* apply where drinking and/or dangerous drugs alone produce insanity. In a case such as *Burns*, where a non-dangerous drug is involved, it can be argued that the reasoning in *Bailey* ought fairly to apply, in which case the accused should in principle receive an acquittal unless the prosecution can prove 'recklessness'.

A result such as that in *Bailey* was, however, criticised by Williams who went on to suggest that in *Burns* 'a verdict of insanity should be the correct one even if the outburst was triggered by taking drugs for medicinal purposes, if there is sufficient likelihood of repetition'.[76] On that view, *Burns* should have been adjudged insane even if his unconscious outburst was triggered by drugs prescribed by his doctor.[77] The problem with this approach is that, as soon as the accused's condition is regarded as having resulted primarily from a 'disease of the mind', any investigation into prior fault automatically becomes irrelevant. This means that, while a diabetic in a case like *Bailey* may, if fault free, receive sympathy in respect of his insulin-induced hypoglycaemia, his hyperglycaemic counterpart will be found 'not guilty by reason of insanity', even if he is in no way to blame for the onset of his condition. This much seems to have been accepted by the Court of Appeal in *Hennessy*[78] where, after ruling that the accused's hyperglycaemia was due to a disease of the mind, namely diabetes, Lord Lane CJ concluded: 'it is not in those circumstances necessary for us to consider the further arguments . . . based on the decision in *R. v. Bailey*'.[79] Clearly, therefore, any consideration of fault on the defendant's part in respect of the onset of his incapacitated condition was automatically foreclosed as soon as the court ruled that his condition was automatism of the insane variety. In short, the doctrine of fault liability appears to take second place to the overriding notion that legal insanity must preclude criminal responsibility, irrespective of the fact that the primary cause of the accused's diseased mind might be traced to, for example, a reckless disregard of his doctor's instructions.

There seem to be three interrelated reasons for this overall approach. The first concerns the fundamental notion that it is wrong to punish those who are adjudged legally insane.[80] The result has been a failure on the part of English law to make any attempt to distinguish between mental diseases, the onset of which the accused might bear some responsibility for, and those over which he had no control. This leads to the second reason,

---

[75] Law Commission, *Intoxication and Criminal Liability*, para 2.31.

[76] G. Williams, *Textbook of Criminal Law* (2nd edn., Stevens, London, 1983), 681.

[77] Law Commission, *Legislating the Criminal Code*, supports such a result: see clause 2(4) Draft Criminal Law (Intoxication) Bill at p 102 and see also paras 6.46–49.

[78] [1989] 2 All ER 9; see also *R. v. Bingham* [1991] Crim LR 433.

[79] [1989] 2 All ER 9, 15.   [80] For discussion of this point, see Chapter 2.

which stems from the fact that 'the law now assumes that genuine mental illness is always inadvertent.'[81] Thus, as long ago as 1920, the House of Lords stated that 'the law takes no notice of the cause of insanity'.[82] This in turn leads to the third reason, which is that, because a successful insanity defence previously led to automatic and indeterminate hospitalization,[83] the courts had no reason to be concerned by social defence worries upon returning a special verdict.

However, the reasons given in support of this approach are open to objection. With regard to the last point concerning disposal, it has already been made clear in Chapter 2 that flexibility of disposal has now been introduced under the Criminal Procedure (Insanity and Unfitness to Plead) Act 1991 for all special verdicts excepting those which result from a murder charge. While this has been broadly welcomed, it seems to bring with it some worrying implications. For example, in one of the first cases disposed of under the 1991 Act the defendant was given an absolute discharge having been found not guilty by reason of insanity to a charge of attempted rape. The medical evidence pointed to the fact that the defendant was suffering from brain damage which could induce violent action after the consumption of a small quantity of alcohol.[84] On the assumption that the defendant was aware of this fact, it must now surely be open to question as to why he should receive an absolute discharge when his intoxicated, or *Bailey* reckless, counterpart would be convicted of a basic intent offence. Of course, it can be responded that the judge could send such an insane defendant to hospital under the provisions of the 1991 Act.[85] However, returning to the first and second reasons, this fails to answer the point that in a case such as this the defendant is declared criminally irresponsible, while in similar cases such as *Burns*[86] and *Bailey* the courts have created a fault test which can result in a conviction. Not only that, while the fault mechanism prevents a defendant such as *Bailey* from being convicted of a specific intent offence, no similar mechanism operates to protect those who choose to plead guilty despite the provisions of the 1991 Act in order to prevent a finding of legal insanity, unless the

---

[81] C.N. Mitchell, 'Culpable Mental Disorder and Criminal Liability' (1986) 8 *International Journal of Law and Psychiatry*, 273.   [82] *DPP* v. *Beard* [1920] AC 479, 500.

[83] This was the position before the Criminal Procedure (Insanity) Act 1964 was amended by the Criminal Procedure (Insanity and Unfitness to Plead) Act 1991.

[84] *R.* v. *Bromley*, Winchester Crown Court, 15 January 1992, referred to by the Law Commission, *Intoxication and Criminal Liability*, 22 n 70. The accused's condition seems likely to have been the result of 'pathological intoxication', which will be discussed later in this Chapter.

[85] See S. White, 'The Criminal Procedure (Insanity and Unfitness to Plead) Act' [1992] Crim LR 5, 10 who suggests that 'a court may make an admission order even though it does not think such an order to be the most suitable disposition [as for example where] outright release might provoke public outrage'.

[86] On the assumption that the court's reasoning in that case is correct.

judge is prepared to accept a guilty plea to a lesser charge as occurred in the case of *Sullivan*.[87] However, there is no obligation on the judge to accept such a compromise. These various problems stem from the first two points mentioned above, namely the fact that a finding of insanity automatically results in a special verdict of acquittal which in turn precludes any investigation into fault.

But should the law continue to adopt this approach? Certainly, in some cases it is difficult to see how such an approach can be justified. This has led one commentator to conclude that 'if mental illness results in truly uncontrollable behaviour the rules of culpable automatism should apply. Any diseased person is under a duty to avoid harming others and, if necessary, to seek treatment. Certain persons, for example, may be required to follow special diets, avoid alcohol, take specific medication, or failing that, to face liability'.[88] There seems little doubt that such a view has prevailed in relation to driving offences where the courts have conveniently ignored the issue of insanity in favour of fault liability.[89] As a result, there have been a host of road traffic cases where the problems surrounding the 'sane/insane automatism' dichotomy and the 'external factor doctrine' seem to have been sidestepped. Thus conditions such as 'blackouts', diabetic comas, and somnambulism have all resulted in convictions for careless or dangerous driving based on prior fault. While in some of these cases the defendant could not be regarded as having triggered off his own disability,[90] this is certainly not true of all these cases. Thus in *Moses* v. *Winder*,[91] where the defendant drove after realising that he was going into a diabetic coma, a conviction for careless driving was upheld on the ground that insufficient precautions had been taken to prevent the onset of the coma. However, as has already been pointed out, the defendant in *Hennessy* had his case heard in the Crown Court where the issue of insanity could be raised. As a result, since he already suffered from the internal condition of diabetes, which directly caused his disability i.e. hyperglycaemia, it was possible, once his condition was classed as legal insanity, for the fact that he may have failed to take steps to avoid the onset of this disability to be completely ignored.

It might be pointed out that these road traffic cases are distinguishable from other insanity cases on the ground that they primarily concern an enquiry into prior fault of the accused occurring at a time when the accused was not incapacitated. In short, the issue of whether to convict the

---

[87] [1983] 2 All ER 673, 675.
[88] Mitchell, *Culpable Mental Disorder and Criminal Liability*, 298.
[89] See generally Williams, *Textbook of Criminal Law* (2nd edn.), 676–9.
[90] See e.g. *Watmore* v. *Jenkins* [1962] 2 QB 572; *Broome* v. *Perkins* [1987] Crim LR 271. Neither defendant seems to have been at fault in respect of the onset of hypoglycaemia.
[91] [1980] Crim LR 232.

accused concerns an earlier time during the driving episode, the time before he fell asleep or suffered from a blackout etc. This much was made
clear in the early case of *Hill* v. *Baxter*[92] where Pearson J said:

Then suppose that the man in the driving seat falls asleep. After he is asleep he is
no longer driving, but there is an earlier time at which he was falling asleep and
therefore failing to perform the driver's elementary and essential duty of keeping
himself awake and therefore he was driving dangerously. Similarly, in the case of
a man who knows that he is liable to have an epileptic fit but, nevertheless, drives
a vehicle on the road, there is a question of fact whether driving in these circumstances can properly be considered reckless or dangerous. The answer might depend on the degree and frequency of the epilepsy and the degree of probability that
an epileptic fit might come upon him.[93]

However, the readiness of courts to convict drivers on this basis was
criticised by the High Court of Australia in *Jiminez* v. *R.*[94] where it was
stated: 'No doubt it may be proper in many cases to draw an inference
that a driver who falls asleep must have had warning that he might do so
if he continued to drive or that otherwise he knew or ought to have known
that he was running a real risk of falling asleep at the wheel. But it does
not necessarily follow that because a driver falls asleep he has had a
sufficient warning to enable him to stop'.[95]

Although the majority of the High Court of Australia made it clear that
driving while asleep was neither conscious nor voluntary, one judge considered that it had been incorrect for the Crown to concede that 'a driver
who is asleep is not then driving in a manner dangerous to the public'.[96]
According to McHugh J:

It is a matter of degree whether a person who has 'dozed off' has functioned at
such a low cognitive level for such a length of time that it can fairly be said that
the vehicle was no longer 'being driven' by that person. In some cases the loss of
consciousness of the 'driver' may be such that it cannot be said that that person
was driving the vehicle; but in other cases, the loss of consciousness may be so
transient that it can be said that the vehicle was 'being driven' by that person.[97]

The fundamental difference here lies in the fact that while the majority
decision based the conviction on the notion of 'ante-dating', McHugh J
was prepared to accept that the driver who fell asleep could be convicted
after he dozed off. This distinction is not without importance; for the
approach of McHugh J avoids many of the problems caused by the notion
of 'ante-dating'.[98] An obvious problem is that, if the accused is charged

---

[92] [1958] 1 QB 277.   [93] Ibid. 286–7.
[94] (1992) 173 CLR 572. For discussion, see D. Lanham, 'Involuntary Acts and the Actus
Reus' (1993) 17 *Criminal Law Journal* 97.   [95] (1992) 173 CLR 572, 581.
[96] Ibid. 585.   [97] Ibid. 586.
[98] See Williams, *Textbook of Criminal Law* (2nd edn.), 678.

with a more specific type of road traffic offence such as failing to obey a traffic sign, retrospective enquiry will no longer assist the prosecution; as Hart succinctly put it, 'You cannot shoot your lights before you come to them'.[99]

However, McHugh J's approach seems to resemble that taken by the English Divisional Court in *Broome* v. *Perkins*[100] where it was held that the accused's driving remained voluntary despite evidence to the contrary.[101] A similar approach was recently adopted by the Court of Appeal in *Attorney-General's Reference (No 2 of 1992)*[102], where the Lord Chief Justice was able to avoid the issues of fault and insanity.[103] He concluded that a trance-like state caused by 'repetitive visual stimuli experienced on long journeys on straight, flat, featureless motorways'[104] did not involve 'total destruction of voluntary control'[105] and was therefore insufficient evidence to lay a proper foundation for a defence of automatism.

While the process of 'ante-dating' may be problematical, its use could be regarded as removing the defendant from the scope of insanity on the ground that at the earlier time he was not suffering from an operating disability. In addition, since the *actus reus* of many driving offences can be regarded as continuing, those offences lend themselves to this approach. Thus, while the vehicle may be regarded as not 'being driven' while the accused is in a state of automatism, he may still be convicted on the ground that before the onset of the disability he should have stopped. At that earlier stage, there would be no real difficulty in making a finding that the accused was 'driving'.

While it is certainly true, by contrast, that the *actus reus* of crimes of violence is such that they do not lend themselves to this approach, it is undeniable that, for example in self-induced intoxication cases relating to crimes of violence, the courts have not been averse to coupling a *mens rea* formed at some earlier stage with an *actus reus* committed during incapacity. Further, in all these various automatism cases, whether road traffic or otherwise, it is the incapacitated condition which gives rise to the enquiry into fault. This means that, if the prosecution fails to prove fault, then the accused will be acquitted. But again it may be asked: why should the epileptic driver who is not at fault be found not guilty when an epileptic

---

[99] H.L.A. Hart, *Punishment and Responsibility* (Clarendon Press, Oxford, 1968), 111.
[100] (1987) Cr App R 321.
[101] This case was regarded as harsh by the Law Commission in its Commentary on the Draft Criminal Code, *A Criminal Code for England and Wales* (1989), Vol 2, para 11.4.
[102] [1993] 4 All ER 683.
[103] See the commentary by J.C. Smith [1994] Crim LR 693, who argues that if the driver had been in a state of automatism it would have been of the insane variety as 'a person who is exceptionally susceptible to "ordinary motorway conditions" and causes damage cannot expect simply to walk away free to do it again'. For discussion of external factors and susceptibility, see Chapter 1.
[104] [1993] 4 All ER 683, 686.   [105] Ibid. 689.

defendant such as *Sullivan* is in danger of being labelled as legally insane unless he changes his plea to guilty?

Of course, it can legitimately be pointed out that the vast majority of the relevant road traffic cases are decided in the Magistrates' Courts where the insanity defence and the M'Naghten Rules are not live issues.[106] However, to permit the development of the law within this area to rest upon such a procedural distinction is at best unprincipled,[107] and at worst unjust. For to return to the case of *Hennessy*, it seems clear that, had his case fallen for decision in the Magistrates' Court, the issue of fault liability would have been a live one. Instead, however, the case was disposed of in the Crown Court where the accused 'chose' to plead guilty, which meant that the prosecution was never required to test the evidence of fault against the accused. This seems manifestly unfair; for there is no guarantee that the prosecution could have proved that the defendant was at fault in failing to take insulin, since stress, anxiety, and depression played a role in the failure. In short, the prosecution's burden of proving fault was suddenly negated as soon as the defendant's condition was classed as legal insanity. This in turn could be used by the prosecution as part of its strategy, in the sense that it could be advantageous for the Crown to argue in favour of insanity rather than guilt in circumstances where evidence of prior fault was thin.

Unless the criminal law makes special provision for fault liability in road traffic cases, even where the defendant's condition would otherwise be classed as legal insanity, it is difficult to support the present legal position which denies an accused such as Hennessy an opportunity to have this issue tested merely because he is prosecuted for an indictable offence in the Crown Court. Further, while in *Hennessy* it was to the defendant's advantage to avoid the draconian disposal consequences of an insanity defence by pleading guilty, the point has already been made that, with the passing of the Criminal Procedure (Insanity and Unfitness to Plead) Act 1991, it may be in the defendant's interests to proceed with this defence in the hope of an absolute discharge. In which case, why should the prosecution not be able to bring forward evidence of fault in the expectation of securing a conviction? If this cannot be done, then the law is once more hidebound by the absurdity that while the hypoglycaemic motorist can be convicted, his hyperglycaemic counterpart cannot. As the law stands at present, in cases other than road traffic cases, it is only where insanity is conveniently ignored, that the prosecution can introduce evidence of fault. Two manslaughter cases can be used to illustrate the point. First, in the Australian case of *R.* v. *Egan*[108] a mother who overlaid her child while

---

[106] See S. White, 'Insanity Defences and Magistrates' Courts' [1991] Crim LR 501.

[107] The point is recognised in *Hill* v. *Baxter* [1958] 1 QB 277, 286 by Devlin J where he remarks: 'So it would be very surprising to find this defence raised in answer to charges under the Road Traffic Act, 1930. Whatever the theory of the law may be, mental disease is in practice not available as an excuse for the commission of any of the lesser crimes.'

[108] (1897) 23 VLR 159.

in a drunken stupor was acquitted of manslaughter on the basis of accident. If such a case arose today, then there seems little doubt that a court would be reluctant to consider insanity,[109] but would instead wish to investigate the issue of fault. Similarly, in the case of *R. v. Beale*,[110] the accused was convicted of the manslaughter of one of his young daughters and inflicting grievous bodily harm on the other when they rolled off a 40 foot cliff after he had allegedly suffered an epileptic fit while sitting with the children on his lap at the cliff edge. In his summing up Sheldon J referred to *R. v. Caldwell*[111] and directed the jury to consider two questions. First, in all the circumstances did the accused subject the children to a serious and inexcusable risk of injury which would have been recognised by any ordinary prudent person? Secondly, was the accused at the time of the events in question aware of that risk? Although the issue of insanity does not seem to have been raised, it is difficult to avoid the conclusion that, had it been a live issue, the accused would have been the subject of a special verdict irrespective of the level of fault involved. Clearly, the jury must have been sure that the accused was at fault in order to return the guilty verdicts. However, the issue of fault would not have been left to the jury had the judge ruled that the accused's epilepsy was a disease of the mind.[112]

This then leads to the wider question of whether the issue of fault liability should become part of the overall equation when a court comes to consider whether a defendant should be exculpated on the basis of legal insanity. In order to explore this issue further, it is proposed to discuss the problem of 'pathological intoxication' where the boundaries between fault liability and insanity are unclear.

'PATHOLOGICAL INTOXICATION'

'Pathological intoxication', known also as 'pathological reaction to alcohol', has been described as 'a temporary psychotic reaction, often manifested by violence, which is triggered by consumption of alcohol by a

---

[109] Presumably *Burgess* [1991] 2 All ER 769 could be distinguished on the ground that in *Egan* the accused's sleep was 'normal' sleep as opposed to sleepwalking, despite the fact that in both cases the automatism is entirely dependent on sleep.

[110] [1983] *Current Law Yearbook* 716.

[111] [1981] 1 All ER 961. If a case similar to *Beale* arose today, the trial judge would be required to direct the jury differently by referrring to *R. v. Adomako* [1994] 3 All ER 79 and *R. v. Parmenter and Savage* [1991] 4 All ER 698 which relate respectively to manslaughter and grievous bodily harm charges.

[112] In the light of *Sullivan* [1983] 2 All ER 673, there is a strong argument that any epileptic seizure which results in what would otherwise be criminal conduct should fall within the M'Naghten Rules unless the distinction referred to in Chapter 1 between convulsions and outwardly purposeful conduct can be applied. Certainly, on the facts of *Beale* the accused seems to have suffered a convulsion as opposed to 'assaulting' his children. If this distinction was to be applied, then this would leave the jury free to consider whether the accused was fault free.

person with a predisposing mental or physical condition. The underlying condition may be temporal lobe epilepsy, traumatic brain damage, metabolic disturbances, or a variety of other factors ... Automatic behaviour results ... There is an absence of motor coordination, slurred speech and diplopia (blurred vision) that characterize ordinary alcohol intoxication ... The amount of alcohol ingested is irrelevant ... The factor of critical significance is the absence of the ordinary signs of intoxication'.[113] Although the very existence of pathological intoxication as a condition in its own right has been questioned,[114] it has been powerfully argued[115] not only that it does exist but also that the criminal law's over-reliance on self-induced intoxication has led to a refusal to recognise the defence potential attached to such a condition.

The single exception to this failure has been the US Model Penal Code which in section 2.08(4) states:

Intoxication which (a) is not self-induced or (b) is pathological is an affirmative defense if by reason of such intoxication the actor at the time of his conduct lacks substantial capacity either to appreciate its criminality [wrongfulness] or to conform his conduct to the requirements of law.

Subsection 5(c) then provides:

'pathological intoxication' means intoxication grossly excessive in degree, given the amount of the intoxicant, to which the actor does not know he is susceptible.

The combined effect of these provisions and subsection (3), which excludes intoxication from the definition of 'mental disease' in respect of the insanity defence, has been interpreted as introducing the notion of 'surprise intoxication' into the Code's defence structure.[116] It is not involuntary intoxication, as the accused knows that he is consuming alcohol; instead he is 'surprised' by the resulting degree of intoxication. In short, 'the actor's intoxication is pathological if the actor does not know his susceptibility to the intoxicant'.[117] The difficulty with this approach is that it proceeds on the basis that pathological intoxication would not be recognised as a 'mental disease' within the scope of legal insanity; this, it has been suggested, ignores the fact that 'historically, mental disease cases were

---

[113] L.P. Tiffany and M. Tiffany, 'Nosologic Objections to the Criminal Defense of Pathological Intoxication: What do the Doubters Doubt?' (1990) 13 *International Journal of Law and Psychiatry* 49–50. See also L.P. Tiffany and M. Tiffany, *The Legal Defense of Pathological Intoxication—with Related Issues of Temporary and Self-inflicted Insanity* (Quorum Books, New York, 1990), 1.

[114] J. Coid, 'Mania a Potu: A Critical Review of Pathological Intoxication' (1970) 9 *Psychological Medicine* 709.

[115] Tiffany and Tiffany, *The Legal Defense of Pathological Intoxication*.

[116] Tiffany and Tiffany, ibid. 345. For further comment, see P. Robinson, 'Causing the Condition of One's Own Defense: A Study of the Limits of Theory in Criminal Law Doctrine' (1985) 71 *Virginia Law Review* 45.   [117] Robinson, ibid. 46.

at the core of the concept of pathological intoxication'.[118] A major reason why the Model Penal Code adopted this approach seems likely to have been the desire to build a fault limitation into the pathological intoxication defence in order to restrict its use, while at the same time not wishing to 'place a similarly explicit fault limiter on the insanity defense'.[119] The crucial question is whether it is acceptable to single out pathological intoxication in this way and the reluctance of States to adopt this approach may well be indicative of a negative answer. Certainly, as far as English law is concerned, there has never been any suggestion that pathological intoxication is deserving of special legal status. However, d'Orban suggests that the distinction between sane and insane automatism would apply to cases of pathological intoxication,[120] with the result that while fault-free alcohol-induced hypoglycaemia would be regarded as sane automatism, an alcohol-induced epileptic seizure would be classed as insanity. While it has been suggested that both of these examples would 'fall within virtually everyone's definition of pathological intoxication if alcohol triggers the reaction of the actor',[121] the distinction drawn by d'Orban, although resting on the well-established legal distinction between sane and insane automatism, would at first glance seem to be open to question. The problem stems from the notion that the criminal law might classify some types of pathological intoxication as sane and other types as insane automatism. Of course, it can be argued that this might be justified by reference to the underlying causes, which are different, in much the same way as the courts have drawn a distinction between hypoglcaemia and hyperglycaemia irrespective of the fact that an underlying condition, namely diabetes, is present in both cases; yet, if pathological intoxication exists as a psychiatric diagnosis in its own right, then it might at first sight seem odd that it should be capable of being used in different cases to support both forms of automatism. However, once it is recalled that automatism is a legal concept rather than a psychiatric one, there is no reason why a particular diagnosis should not be used to support both sane and insane automatism in appropriate cases.[122]

It is strongly argued by Tiffany and Tiffany that pathological intoxication in fact consists of the following three paradigms:

The abnormal reaction is triggered by consumption of alcohol or other drug by a person with (1) a mental disease or defect, (2) a physical disability or recent trauma

---

[118] Tiffany and Tiffany, *The Legal Defense of Pathological Intoxication*, 343.

[119] Ibid. 342.

[120] P.T. d'Orban, 'Drugs and Alcohol: The Psychiatrist as Expert Witness in Court' (1986) 81 *British Journal of Addiction* 631, 634.

[121] Tiffany and Tiffany, *The Legal Defense of Pathological Intoxication*, 208.

[122] See e.g. *R. v. Rabey* (1977) 79 DLR (3d) 414 which supports the view that a psychological blow leading to dissociation could be used to support either sane or insane automatism depending on the accused's susceptibility to such stress and the severity of the blow in question.

involving the brain or (3) who is alcohol sensitive, temporarily or permanently. Depending upon which is involved . . . these three types of pathological intoxication respectively fit most logically within the defenses of insanity, automatism and intoxication [and] whether the defense succeeds or fails should turn on the actor's culpability in contributing to the abnormal mental state.[123]

It may be, therefore, that pathological intoxication is something of an umbrella term which brings with it considerable difficulties not only in terms of what defence should apply to any particular case but also whether the issue of fault liability is always relevant to such cases. Both of these points deserve comment. The first stems from the fact that although it might seem legitimate to class pathological intoxication as a form of voluntary intoxication, it is clear that this is not the case. Rather 'alcohol is only the catalyst' for a condition which 'is a qualitatively different event. It does not result in drunkenness at all; it results in a temporary psychosis.'[124] Further, as already demonstrated it is not clear whether pathological intoxication should be treated as sane or insane automatism. On the one hand, it can be argued that as the condition is triggered off by an 'external factor', namely a small amount of alcohol, it should qualify as sane;[125] while, on the other hand, if the result is a temporary psychosis, then this in turn 'is a symptomatic manifestation of a disease or defect of the brain (or mind)',[126] which ought to result in automatism of the insane variety.

The second point follows from the fact that, pathological intoxication is difficult to place within existing defences, but nonetheless it is clear that while voluntary intoxication and sane automatism are subject to the notion of fault liability, the defence of insanity is not. And yet the degree of fault may be identical in some cases of pathological intoxication irrespective of which defence the condition is regarded as supporting. Although this absurdity has already been discussed within the broad context of automatism, it is manifest in relation to pathological intoxication. If two defendants know they are alcohol-sensitive and subject to pathological reaction to alcohol, then it seems insupportable that if the condition is induced by hypoglycaemia, fault is relevant but that it is irrelevant if induced by epilepsy. Surely it is time, therefore, to reconsider the blanket exclusion of fault once the insanity defence is raised. This is not an easy task for it has been pointed out that 'fault as a limitation on defenses in general is not developed and is even more obscure in pathological intoxication cases'.[127]

Despite this difficulty it would seem not unreasonable to suggest that

---

[123] Tiffany and Tiffany, *The Legal Defense of Pathological Intoxication*, 2.
[124] Ibid. 3–4.   [125] Cf. *Burns* (1974) 58 Cr App R 364.
[126] Tiffany and Tiffany, *The Legal Defense of Pathological Intoxication*, 12.
[127] Ibid. 372.

any future development of fault liability should encompass the insanity defence. Indeed, in their extensive discussion of the meaning of fault as a limitation on the defence of pathological intoxication, Tiffany and Tiffany point to a tendency on the part of US courts 'to want to simplify and then dichotomize the issues into 'voluntary intoxication' and 'involuntary intoxication', much of this fed by a lack of an explicitly recognised fault limitation on the insanity defense'.[128] Further, even those few US jurisdictions which provide for fault in the context of insanity do so on the basis of the cause of the condition and do not require any further enquiry into actual awareness of risk.[129] It may be, therefore, that there is a need for a closer alignment between the required fault and the offence with which the accused is charged.

FINDING FAULT LEVELS

One of the most trenchant criticisms of the common law relating to self-induced intoxication concerns the fact that the fault upon which the accused's conviction is built 'consists in becoming intoxicated, and not, as in the normal case, of acting when aware that he might cause the harm prohibited by the particular [basic intent] offence. However, he is actually convicted of that very offence, and thus has to be punished for that very offence.'[130] In effect, therefore, when voluntary drunkenness is in issue the courts have shown no inclination to 'distinguish between the act of drinking, awareness of the intoxicating nature of what is being ingested, awareness of the incapacitating results of that conduct, and the question of the probability of engaging in harmful conduct as a result of self-incapacitation'.[131] By way of contrast, however, the earlier discussion of *Bailey* and *Hardie* shows that the courts have now considered it necessary to embark on the process of making just such a distinction.

Although this is a step in the right direction, these decisions are not without their difficulties. In particular, it was pointed out earlier that there are considerable problems over the precise form of 'recklessness' which is being used in *Hardie* to support the accused's conviction. Certainly, the reference by Parker LJ to the question of 'whether the taking of the Valium was itself reckless'[132] strongly suggests that the 'reckless' accused is to be

---

[128] Ibid. 485.

[129] Robinson, 'Causing the Conition of One's Own Defence', 24 n 85 cites two examples. They are Puerto Rico Laws Annotated tit 33 s 3154 (1983) ('transitory mental unsoundness caused purposely does not excuse criminal liability'); and Revised Code of Washington Annotated s 10.77.010(7) (Supp 1984–1985) ('No condition of mind proximately induced by the voluntary act of a person shall constitute "insanity."').

[130] Law Commission, 'Intoxication and Criminal Liability', para 3.21.

[131] Tiffany and Tiffany, *The Legal Defense of Pathological Intoxication*, 372.

[132] [1984] 3 All ER 848, 853.

punished in much the same way as his drunken counterpart; in which case, the above criticism extends to the 'reckless' Valium taker.

In order to deal with this problem Robinson suggests that liability ought to be imposed for culpable conduct which causes the conditions relevant to the defence, with liability being based on this initial conduct. He puts it as follows:

An actor may be culpable as to causing the ultimate offence when he causes the disability . . . or fails to terminate or at least to make allowance for a pre-existing disability. Assume that an epileptic fails to take his anti-seizure medicine, and during a seizure in an elevator he strikes and injures two people. His liability is properly determined by asking whether, at the time he failed to take his anti-seizure medicine, he was aware that his failure might subsequently cause physical injury to others. If so, he should be liable for reckless assault. If he intended to injure these people he should be liable for intentional assault.[133]

This approach is noticeably similar to that adopted by the Court of Appeal in *Bailey* where reckless assault was held to require proof that the accused 'knows that his actions or inaction are likely to make him aggressive, unpredictable or uncontrolled with the result that he may cause some injury to others and he persists in the action or takes no remedial action when he knows it is required'.[134] Clearly, the reference to the need for the knowledge that onset of the disability might eventually result in a risk of injury to others is a crucial element in the fault equation in that it ensures that the required level of culpability for the offence must be present if a conviction is to be possible.

A further point of note in respect of Robinson's proposal is that it ensures the conviction of the culpable epileptic by ignoring the issue of insanity. However, as already indicated, the refusal of English law to permit fault liability to be considered in relation to insanity, coupled with the decision in *Sullivan*, seems to make such a result difficult to achieve in this country. But why should the culpable epileptic not be capable of being adjudged 'reckless' in much the same way as the diabetic in *Bailey*? If there is no satisfactory answer to this question, then the approach suggested by Robinson deserves careful consideration. However, it must be conceded that to convict defendants on the basis of *Bailey* recklessness perpetuates the position whereby a conviction may be secured which does not truly satisfy the fault elements of the offence. In short, the accused is in reality being convicted of culpably reducing himself into an incapacitated condition which later leads him to commit the offence. Although the nature of the culpability enquiry is more closely tied to the elements of the offence in question than in the self-induced intoxication rule, to some it is still too

---

[133] Robinson, 'Causing the Conition of One's Own Defence' 33.
[134] [1983] 2 All ER 503, 507.

'unspecific' to be fully satisfactory.[135] Accordingly, it is now time to consider the merit of recent reform proposals in order to ascertain whether an attempt is being made to satisfactorily resolve this problem.

RECENT REFORM SUGGESTIONS

In its recent consultation paper *Intoxication and Criminal Liability* the Law Commission subjected the existing law to detailed criticism having concluded 'that a thorough review of the law of intoxication is now required in an attempt to provide rational and understandable provisions, suitable for immediate use'.[136] This conclusion was based on the Commission's opinion that:

The present law is . . . objectionable on three levels. It is very complicated and difficult to explain, to the extent that it is difficult to think that it operates in practice other than by its detailed rules being substantially ignored; it purports to apply a clear social policy, of ensuring that intoxicated people who commit criminal acts do not escape criminal sanctions, but only does so in an erratic and unprincipled way; and if taken seriously it creates many difficulties of practical application.

The result was that the Commission considered that the law was in need of change and provisionally recommended that one of two options should be adopted. The first option was to abolish the *Majewski* approach in favour of the approach contained in the High Court of Australia's decision in *R. v. O'Connor*,[137] which would permit the accused's intoxication to be taken into account together with other relevant evidence in deciding whether he had the necessary *mens rea* for the offence. This approach would have the merit of simplicity but might be regarded as failing to fulfil the policy requirements which have led to the *Majewski* rule. The second option also favoured abolishing the *Majewski* approach but recommended the creation of a new offence of 'criminal intoxication' the basis of which was summarised by the Commission as follows: 'the offence would be committed by a person who, when deliberately intoxicated to a substantial extent, caused the harm proscribed by a "listed" offence; it would be immaterial that he lacked the mens rea of the offence in question or even that at the material time he was in a state of automatism'.[138] With regard to the notion of a 'listed' offence, the Commission decided that 'the new offence should . . . be limited to substantial harms to the person, to the physical safety of property, or to public order. That would include conduct of the kind most

---

[135] Ashworth, *Principles of Criminal Law*, 191. See also Smith and Hogan, *Criminal Law* (6th edn.), 227.
[136] Law Commission, *Intoxication and Criminal Liability*, para 1.18.
[137] (1980) 54 ALJR 349.
[138] Law Commission, *Intoxication and Criminal Liability*, para 6.31.

likely to be committed by intoxicated persons'.[139] One advantage of this approach was 'that it does not depend on any vague or general characterisation of the intoxicated defendant's conduct as "dangerous", but rather requires the identification of specific conduct on his part that falls within the definition of an identified crime'.[140] A further advantage concerned the fact that the culpability of the intoxicated defendant could be tied to the harm contained in the listed offence, with the Commission provisionally proposing a 'maximum penalty of, say, two-thirds of that for the underlying listed offence'.[141]

Despite these advantages, the new offence proposed by the Commission contained a number of difficulties. First, despite being undeniably complex, the culpability required related only to the risk of becoming substantially intoxicated since in the Commission's opinion 'to go further and require awareness of the risk of causing the damage or harm that he caused when in that intoxicated state would in effect render the offence nugatory'.[142]

Once again therefore the notion of tying the defendant's culpability more closely to the 'offence' was sacrificed to expediency. Further, although the new offence was not to apply in cases where the 'intoxication was caused by an intoxicant taken solely for medicinal, sedative or soporific purposes',[143] thus leaving the rule in *Bailey* and *Hardie* intact, the Commission considered it appropriate that the new offence should extend to loss of control brought about by unusual susceptibility to otherwise innocuous substances. To illustrate the point, the Commission referred to the case of *Toner*[144], where the accused's incapacity was brought about 'by the ingestion of a small amount of carbohydrate after a long period of fasting'.[145] Although liability under the new offence would clearly require proof that in such a case the accused 'knew he was running a risk of loss of control in acting as he did',[146] it nonetheless seems incongruous that, while proof of a previous similar experience on the part of a defendant such as *Toner* would secure a conviction for dangerous intoxication, similar evidence if adduced by the prosecution in a case like *Bailey* would not only put the accused outside the scope of the new offence but would not of itself be sufficient to convict him of the assault with which he was charged. Such different approaches to what are broadly similar fault liability problems seem both illogical and capable of working injustice. Further, if *Toner*, knowing that his fasting had previously resulted in a loss of

---

[139] Law Commission, *Intoxication and Criminal Liability*, para 6.41.

[140] Ibid. para 6.35. The relevant 'listed' offences are to be found at ibid. para 6.41. It is noteworthy that neither attempts at nor offences of dishonesty are included.

[141] Ibid. para 6.47.   [142] Ibid. para 6.73.   [143] Ibid. para 7.5 (f).

[144] (1991) 93 Cr App R 382.   [145] Law Commission, ibid. para 6.57.

[146] Ibid.

control, took Valium for soporific purposes, then the chances are that he would escape the new offence.

Not surprisingly the Commission's proposals 'are not intended to affect the law of insanity',[147] which means that the problems referred to earlier would remain unresolved, including the perplexing problem of why fault liability should apply to sane but not insane automatism cases. However, in its discussion the Commission raised the interesting issue of 'whether the new offence should require that the defendant's act that caused the proscribed harm must itself arise *by reason of* his intoxication',[148] but concluded that to require such an additional causal connection 'would be impractical'.[149] The reasons given were first that to permit such a causal enquiry would 'concern uncharted territory, that of the highly problematic issue of whether a person's *mental state* was the cause of an event. In many cases it would involve formidable problems of proof.'[150] Secondly, because the proposed offence required the defendant to be substantially intoxicated, the Commission considered that 'it is highly unlikely that in practice, if someone in that condition caused harm of the seriousness to which the offence would be limited, his conduct could be said in any realistic way to be wholly unconnected with his intoxication.'[151]

The comparison that can be drawn here is with the Draft Criminal Code's provisions relating to the defence of insanity.[152] It may be recalled that clause 35(1) of the Draft Code would permit a mental disorder verdict to be returned on proof of severe mental illness or severe mental handicap, which is what the Butler Report originally recommended.[153] If the proposal had stopped there, then there would have been an analogy between intoxication and severe mental disorder in that in both circumstances there would be, in effect, an irrebutable presumption of a connection between the offence and the substantial intoxication or severe disorder. However, the Commission was clearly unhappy about the operation of such a presumption in relation to severe disorders and provided in sub-clause 35(2) that the prosecution should be given the chance to persuade the jury 'that the offence was not attributable to the disorder'.[154] It follows from this that the Commission was quite prepared to enter into the 'uncharted territory' of deciding whether the accused's mental state was the cause of an event when severe disorder is in issue, but not when the problem is one of 'substantial intoxication'. And yet the latter is likely to be much more readily understood by a jury. Also, if the prosecution is to be given the opportunity to show that the severely disordered defendant's offence was uninfluenced by his condition, then why should the substantially intoxicated

[147] Law Commission, para 6.78.　　[148] Ibid. para 6.67 (emphasis in original).
[149] Ibid.　　[150] Ibid. para 6.68 (emphasis in original).　　[151] Ibid. para 6.69.
[152] Fully discussed in Chapters 1 and 2.　　[153] Cmnd 6244 (1975).
[154] Law Commission, *A Criminal Code for England and Wales* (1989) Vol 2, para 11.16.

defendant not be given a similar opportunity? For example, it seems somewhat unfair to a substantially and deliberately intoxicated schizophrenic that the prosecution, in answer to a plea of 'not guilty by reason of mental disorder', should be permitted to show that the offence was attributable to substantial intoxication rather than severe mental illness, when that opportunity is not available to the same defendant who claims that the offence was an accident. It may be that such cases will be rare, but, if the defendant has evidence which might satisfy a jury that the offence was not attributable to his intoxication, then fairness would dictate that he should be given this opportunity.

There is no doubt that the simplest way to reform the law within this area would be to adopt the Commission's first option namely:

Abolish the *Majewski* approach without replacement, so that the defendant's intoxication is taken into account with all other relevant evidence in determining whether he had the prescribed mental element of the offence.[155]

As the Commission pointed out, the Australian experience of the approach in *O'Connor* has not opened the floodgates to a host of intoxicated offender acquittals.[156] Rather the defence of voluntary intoxication seems to be rarely used and even more rarely results in an acquittal. Similar empirical studies do not exist in England. Thus, while the Commission considered that the potential role of the voluntary intoxication rule is 'vast',[157] there are no reliable statistics dealing with the question of how often the intoxication defence is raised in this country. Indeed, it has been argued in support of the Australian approach that the scientific evidence does not support the notion of intoxication leading to a lack of *mens rea* but rather 'what alcohol and other sedatives can seriously obstruct is memory'.[158] It could be, therefore, that the problem is not as considerable as one might think. In that case the approach in *O'Connor* certainly seems attractive in its return to basic principles. For not only would this approach rid the law of the *Majewski* approach but also it would rid it of the complexities of the rule in *Bailey* and *Hardie*. There is much to be said for such a straightforward approach.[159] However, as the Commission pointed out, the adoption of such an approach would raise concerns about public safety and respect for the law might suffer if voluntarily intoxicated defendants could be acquitted in this way. It was these considerations which led the Commission to consider the option of a new offence.

However, there is one further point which can be used in support of the

---

[155] Law Commission, *Intoxication and Criminal Liability*, para 7.4.
[156] Ibid. paras 5.15–17.   [157] Ibid. para 1.19.
[158] C. Mitchell, 'The Intoxicated Offender—Refuting the Legal and Medical Myths' (1988) 11 *International Journal of Law and Psychiatry* 77, 91.
[159] See G. Orchard, 'Surviving without *Majewski*—A View from Down Under' [1993] Crim LR 426.

Australian approach which is not fully discussed by the Commission. This concerns the effect of voluntary intoxication upon other defences. As the law stands at present in England, the judiciary have used intoxication to control the availability of other quite separate defences with the result that they have allowed the notion of self-induced incapacity to restrict alternative methods of exculpation which might be otherwise open to the accused. In the past I have referred to this as 'the taint of intoxication',[160] a prime example of which was given by the Commission in its discussion of intoxicated mistake. At present the law permits the accused's voluntary intoxication to be taken into account in assessing whether he formed the *mens rea* required for a specific intent offence but does not permit that same evidence to be taken into account where the defence is one of drunken mistake.[161] However, the problem does not stop there. For example, in both the defence of duress[162] and the newly developing excuse of necessity or duress of circumstances,[163] the courts have made it clear that the accused's reaction to threats of death or serious bodily harm must be judged in the light of how 'a sober person of reasonable firmness' would have reacted. In this connection it is emphasised not only that there must be a reasonable belief in the threat but also that 'the fact that a defendant's will to resist has been eroded by the voluntary consumption of drink or drugs or both is not relevant to this test'.[164] The clear implication here, therefore, is that once again the nature of the offence charged is irrelevant where there is voluntary intoxication, in this case affecting how a defendant reacted to threats. In short, the 'taint of intoxication' secures a conviction for a specific intent crime in much the same way as was achieved in the intoxicated mistake cases referred to above. Yet here the intoxication may have no causal connection with the operation of the duress, as for example in a case where an accused goes out for an evening's heavy drinking with friends but on his way home is faced with a threat of what he considers to be serious bodily harm unless he drives some burglars from the scene of their crime. Because of his drunken condition the accused is both more easily intimidated and more willing to accept the severity of the threats. Such a person hardly fits into the rationale behind the rule in *Majewski*. But apparently his chances of running a successful duress defence are now much reduced because of his intoxicated condition. Further, in the context of both provocation and diminished responsibility, the taint of intoxication has had a major role to play in ensuring that neither plea will be

[160] For full discussion, see R.D. Mackay, 'The Taint of Intoxication' (1990) 13 *International Journal of Law and Psychiatry* 37.

[161] Law Commission, *Intoxication and Criminal Liability*, paras 2.24–5. See *R. v. O'Grady* [1987] 3 All ER 420; *R. v. O'Connor* [1991] Crim LR 135.

[162] *R. v. Howe* [1987] 1 All ER 771.

[163] *R. v. Conway* [1988] 3 All ER 1029; *R. v. Martin* [1989] 1 All ER 652; and *DPP. v. Harris*, *The Times*, 16 March 1994.   [164] *Howe* [1987] 1 All ER 771, 800.

available to defendants whose loss of self-control or substantial impairment of mental responsibility was influenced by voluntary intoxication. The effect of this has been to ensure the return of murder convictions in numerous cases where the defendant was provoked or mentally abnormal but was also found to be drunk or drugged at the time of the killing.[165] This is despite the fact that the mentally normal non-provoked intoxicated counterpart will be given the opportunity to use his self-induced condition to argue that he lacked the specific intent required for murder. With particular reference to diminished responsibility, one might have expected the law to have been more sympathetic towards those suffering from mental abnormalities; however, the taint of intoxication renders this virtually impossible.

Although the Commission dealt with the question of intoxicated mistake, it is regrettable that it did not address this question of the effect of intoxication upon other defences. For if the new offence of criminal intoxication was to be implemented, the problems relating to the 'taint' would remain. However, if the option in favour of the Australian case of *O'Connor* were to be preferred, then there would be an argument that with such a shift in policy the 'tainting devices' would themselves have to be reconsidered or indeed removed. For if voluntary intoxication was to be admitted as evidence in relation to *mens rea*, then it should follow that it ought to remain relevant when raised as a factor in other defences, particularly provocation and diminished responsibility, where in any event the success of such a plea does not result in an acquittal but a reduction of murder to manslaughter.[166]

CONCLUDING REMARKS

Reform of the type provisionally proposed by the Law Commission would have gone a long way to improving the law relating to self-induced intoxication. However, in its final report, the Commission felt unable to adopt either of its two preferred options described above. Predictably the first, which would have abolished the rule in *Majewski* without replacement, was viewed by many consultees as unacceptable on public safety and policy grounds,[167] while consultation about the second, which would have replaced *Majewski* with a new offence, persuaded the Commission 'that the new offence would, in practice, be likely to lead to more contested cases and to longer and more difficult trials.'[168] While this is likely to have

---

[165] See Mackay, 'The Taint of Intoxication', 40–8.

[166] The issue of 'abnormality of mind' and intoxication will be fully explored in Chapter 4.   [167] Law Commission, *Legislating the Criminal Code* paras 5.19–5.29.

[168] Ibid. para 5.18.

been true during the period immediately following the enactment of such a novel offence, it must surely be open to doubt whether such fears are well grounded in relation to the longer term. In any event with the abandonment of its two preferred options the Commission was left in the unenviable position of either doing nothing, an option which was clearly inappropriate,[169] or recommending that the present law of intoxication should be codified. In deciding to opt for the latter approach the Commission has prepared a draft Criminal Law (Intoxication) Bill which contains some significant amendments to the present law.[170] The primary purpose of the draft Bill is to rid the law of the uncertainties and anomalies which have been a product of the rule in *Majewski*.

Accordingly, it is proposed that:

Where the prosecution alleges any intention ... evidence of intoxication should be taken into account in determining whether that allegation has been proved.

For the purpose of any allegation of any other mental element of an offence (in particular, allegations of recklessness ...), a voluntarily intoxicated defendant should be treated as having been aware of anything of which he would have been aware but for his intoxication.[171]

This would have the effect of getting rid of the difficult and artificial distinction between 'specific' and 'basic' intent. In addition, the Commission has decided to remove the distinction created by the decision in *Hardie*[172] between 'dangerous' and 'non-dangerous' drugs 'and instead require the courts to look at the defendant's *purpose* in taking the drug, how drastic he expected its effect on him to be, and whether he obtained—and followed—medical advice'.[173] While there is little doubt that these measures would help to make the law more sensible, the conservative nature of these changes overall will doubtless come as something of a disappointment to those who might legitimately have expected more radical reform measures in the light of the Commission's provisional recommendations. However, even if the Criminal Law (Intoxication) Bill is implemented, these measures would leave the current law relating to insanity and road traffic offences intact. Although there is no simple resolution to the problem of fault in relation to insanity, it is surely time to give some consideration to the anomalies raised in this Chapter.

A radical approach to the problem would be to permit the prosecution to lead evidence of fault in response to a defence of insanity. If the Crown

---

[169] Law Commission, *Legislating the Criminal Code* paras 5.33–5.46.
[170] Ibid., Appendix A.   [171] Ibid. para 1.34.   [172] [1984] 3 All ER 842.
[173] Law Commission, *Legislating the Criminal Code*, para 1.38 (emphasis in original). This is achieved by a complex series of provisions relating to involuntary intoxication, see paras 8.9–8.36.

could show 'culpability in the context of origin',[174] then the accused could be convicted of an offence of recklessness or negligence despite evidence which would otherwise support an insanity defence.[175] Clearly, this would be less problematical for some conditions than for others. As already indicated, there seems no good reason why the hyperglycaemic defendant should not be encompassed by the fault doctrine in the same way as his hypoglycaemic counterpart. Similarly, a sleepwalker could easily fall within this doctrine. As Robinson has pointed out:

the defendant in *Fain v. Commonwealth*[176], who had a disorder that made him violent when aroused from sleep, could have been punished for his 'breach of social duty in going to sleep in the public room of a hotel with a deadly weapon on his person'. Because he 'no doubt [knew] his propensity to do acts of violence when roused from sleep', he could properly have been held liable for reckless homicide based on his earlier conduct of going to sleep in a public place with a gun in his lap.[177]

By way of contrast, in cases of serious mental illness such as schizophrenia, where the accused may have failed to follow his doctor's instructions in respect of his medication, it is questionable whether the prosecution would wish to adopt a similar strategy. For, although such a failure might be shown to contribute to a schizophrenic episode during which the accused committed the offence, it is doubtful whether the prosecution would be able,[178] or wish, to prove the appropriate level of fault in such a case.[179]

[174] See H. Fingarette and A. Hasse, *Mental Disabilities and Criminal Responsibility* (University of California Press, Berkeley, California, 1979), 211–16. Discussed further by N. Finkel, *Insanity on Trial: Perspectives on Law and Psychology* (Plenum Press, New York, 1988), 285–92.

[175] See D.B. Wexler, 'Inducing Therapeutic Compliance through the Criminal Law', ch. 7 of D.B. Wexler and B.J. Winick, *Essays in Therapeutic Jurisprudence* (Carolina Academic Press, Durham, North Carolina, 1991), 195 who refers to 'evidence in the literature suggesting that psychiatric patients often have the capacity to recognize their psychotic or prepsychotic behavior by methods such as self-monitoring and self-evaluation, and that clinicians may help patients to sharpen those capacities. If so, a previously violent mentally disordered patient who has been advised of appropriate steps to take if confronted by emerging symptoms ... might be a successful candidate for a reckless endangerment prosecution if he or she fails to take appropriate action when such symptoms begin to recur.' See also ibid. 197–8.

[176] 78 Ky 183 (1879).

[177] Robinson, 'Causing the Conition of One's Defence', 33.

[178] But cf. the following example given by Finkel, *Insanity on Trial*, 286 'where an allegedly paranoid schizophrenic defendant, who was being treated as an outpatient and who was told by her therapist that she needed treatment, nevertheless stops treatment and refuses to continue. Instead of asking experts and jurors to locate the origin of her schizophrenia, we can ask the jury to weigh her treatment refusal as to whether this constitutes a failure to take reasonable precautions to prevent what subsequently happened. Her treatment refusal occurred at a defined point in time, whereas the point of origin of her schizophrenia is far from clear and subject to disparate opinions'.

[179] Wexler, *Essays in Therapeutic Jurisprudence*, 195 remarks: 'a schizophrenic patient who fails to take antipsychotic medication may not be *culpable* with regard to ... treatment refusal. Instead of one's failure to take medication leading to decompensation, perhaps the

Rather, it is cases of insane automatism where the problem is most serious and there seems no good reason to deny the prosecution the opportunity to counter an insanity defence with proof of fault. Should the prosecution fail to satisfy the jury on this matter, then of course an insanity verdict will be returned. However, with the flexibility of disposal introduced by the Criminal Procedure (Insanity and Unfitness to Plead) Act 1991 the accused can expect a non-custodial disposal unless, despite the lack of fault, he has been shown to be a danger to others or has been charged with murder.[180]

person's *mental detorioration* led to the treatment refusal. That of course may be possible, and therefore an insanity defence might occasionally be successful . . . in prosecutions of such persons' (emphasis in original).

[180] The Criminal Procedure (Insanity and Unfitness to Plead) Act 1991 mandates indeterminate hospitalization when a special verdict results from a charge of murder: see s 5(3) of the Criminal Procedure (Insanity) Act 1964 substituted by s 3 of the 1991 Act.

4

Diminished Responsibility and Infanticide

In cases of murder the mandatory penalty obviously poses problems when dealing with the mentally disordered offender. Rather than follow the recommendation of the Royal Commission on Capital Punishment for extending the insanity defence,[1] the Government eventually decided to borrow the notion of 'diminished responsibility' from Scotland,[2] in order to give trial judges discretion over the sentencing of such offenders. The source of this discretion is contained in section 2(1) of the Homicide Act 1957 which states:

Where a person kills or is a party to the killing of another, he shall not be convicted of murder if he was suffering from such abnormality of mind (whether arising from a condition of arrested or retarded development of mind or any inherent causes or induced by disease or injury) as substantially impaired his mental responsibility for his acts and omissions in doing or being a party to the killing.

Subsection (2) makes it clear that, as with insanity, the burden of proving this defence on a balance of probabilities rests upon the accused,[3] and, if the plea is successful, subsection (3) ensures a conviction for manslaughter, thus enabling the judge to exercise his discretion as to sentence.

Although, as will be noted below, diminished responsibility has been widely used since its introduction, at the same time the plea has been the subject of continual criticism. The aim of this Chapter is to consider these criticisms in the light of the overall impact of the defence. In addition, the relationship between diminished responsibility and provocation will be discussed, together with current reform proposals.

---

[1] Royal Commission on Capital Punishment, Cmd 8932 (1953), para 333. See also para 413 where the Commission decided not to recommend the introduction of diminished responsibility.

[2] In Scotland the diminished responsibility plea has developed from judge-made law. For a full discussion, see G. Gordon, *Criminal Law of Scotland* (2nd edn., W. Green & Son Ltd, Edinburgh) ch. 11. See also N. Walker, *Crime and Insanity in England, Vol 1* (Edinburgh University Press, Edinburgh, 1968) ch. 9.

[3] See *R. v. Dunbar* [1958] 1 QB 36.

THE OPERATION OF THE DIMINISHED RESPONSIBILITY DEFENCE

The introduction of the plea of diminished responsibility has been comple-
mented by the decline of both unfitness to plead and the insanity defence.[4]
The reasons for this are not clear; one would have expected the number
of unfitness and insanity findings to remain constant, but with the diminished responsibility plea operating in a wider range of cases. Instead, the
reduction in both unfitness and insanity findings 'has been compensated by
verdicts of "diminished responsibility", *but no more*'.[5] It seems likely that
the explanation lies 'not only in the tactical attractions of diminished
responsibility for defending counsel, but also in the preferences of medical
witnesses'.[6] The result is that the diminished responsibility plea has continued to be fairly popular. Not only has it been a way to avoid the
inflexible disposal consequences of the insanity plea but also its scope
has encompassed a much wider range of mental disorders than could be
accommodated by the M'Naghten Rules.

The *Criminal Statistics* reveal that currently there are between 70 and 85
successful diminished responsibility pleas each year. For example, in the
period 1980–6 there was a total of 563 findings of diminished responsibility. These figures seem to account for the vast majority of such pleas,
since research has shown that the diminished responsibility defence enjoys
around a 90% success rate. In addition, the same research has demonstrated that in 1976–7 only about 20% of diminished responsibility cases
went to trial, the rest being cases where 'the prosecution's doctors did not
dispute that [the defence] was appropriate' so that a guilty to manslaughter
plea was accepted.[7] Indeed, the percentage of cases going to trial seems to
have diminished even further in recent years. Thus, in the period 1986–8,
while 178 of diminished pleas were accepted by the prosecution, a mere
18 (9.2%) were the subject of jury verdicts.[8]

A further point of interest is that 'when the prosecution does challenge
the defence, the defence is quite likely to fail'.[9] For example, Dell found
that during 1976–7 the prosecution achieved a 64% success rate.[10] However more recently the Crown Prosecution Service reported that during
1986–8 this rate had dropped to 42%.[11] It is clear therefore that the

---

[4] For current numbers, see Chapters 2 and 5.
[5] See Walker, *Crime and Insanity in England Vol 1*, 158 (emphasis in original). See also
R.F. Sparks, '"Diminished Responsibility" in Theory and Practice' (1964) 27 MLR 9, 32.
[6] Walker, *Crime and Insanity in England Vol 1*, 160.
[7] S. Dell, *Murder into Manslaughter—The Diminished Responsibility Defence in Practice*
(Oxford University Press, Oxford, 1984) 26.
[8] See House of Lords, *Report of the Select Committee on Murder and Life Imprisonment,
Vol. II—Oral Evidence*, Part 1 (1988–89), 115.   [9] Dell, *Murder into Manslaughter*, 28.
[10] 'Of 28 cases where this happened, 18 (64 per cent) resulted in murder convictions': ibid. 28.
[11] Supra note 8 at p 115. In this period, out of 31 contested cases the jury returned murder
convictions in 13.

diminished responsibility plea continues to be a frequent means of avoiding the mandatory penalty for murder. Presumably many homicide offenders who plead section 2 are hoping for some form of medical disposal which will be more acceptable to them than the indefinite detention offered by the insanity plea.[12] However, research by Dell has demonstrated a marked change in the sentencing pattern in diminished responsibility homicides over the period 1966–77. This change had manifested itself in a significant drop in the use of hospital orders for those convicted of section 2 manslaughter, with a corresponding increase in the use of imprisonment in such cases.[13] The effect of this was that while only 31% of diminished findings resulted in imprisonment in the period 1966–9, this had risen to over 50% by 1974–7. (During the period 1974–7, probation orders and conditional discharge accounted for the additional 8% of total disposals.) The corresponding reduction in the use of hospital orders from 68% to 40% of cases has been traced primarily to a change in the pattern of treatment recommendations made by examining doctors in their reports. In short, 'if doctors stop making recommendations, judges have to stop making orders'.[14] The reasons for this change are complex. However, it seems to have stemmed initially from a refusal by the Department of Health to admit to special hospitals any mentally ill offenders who were not in urgent need of special security. This in turn seems to have led to a reluctance on the part of psychiatrists to recommend that a section 2 offender should be sent to a special hospital; perhaps psychiatrists realised that such hospitals would be unprepared to accept such an offender/patient. However, this pattern of decline in the use of hospital orders as a means of dealing with diminished responsibility homicides seems to be changing again, since in the period 1980–6 although just over 39% of such offenders received terms of imprisonment, the percentage of hospital orders rose to 43%.[15] However, it must be emphasised that the current use of hospital orders in diminished responsibility cases still lags well behind the 1960s, when it reached a peak of around 70%.

This relative reduction in hospital orders was not accompanied by anything more than a marginal increase in the use of non-custodial sentences.[16] Instead there has been a marked increase in the use of imprisonment, which

[12] The Criminal Procedure (Insanity and Unfitness to Plead) Act 1991 retains this inflexibility in respect of murder charges.

[13] S. Dell and A. Smith, 'Changes in the Sentencing of Diminished Responsibility Homicides' (1983) 142 *British Journal of Psychiatry* 20.

[14] Ibid. 33.

[15] See House of Lords, *Report of the Select Committee on Murder and Life Imprisonment*, Vol II, 4.

[16] This pattern also seems to have changed: for while Dell's research reveals a mere 7% use of probation during 1974–7 (see Dell and Smith, 'Changes in the Sentencing' 30), this had risen to 16% for the period 1980–6 (see House of Lords *Report of the Select Committee on Murder and Life Imprisonment*, Vol II ibid.).

in part seems to have resulted from a 'judicial preference for retributive sentencing',[17] and in part from an increase in the number of defendants who had recovered by the time of the trial and no longer needed treatment. The result was that an accused who used diminished responsibility successfully had an almost even chance of being sent to prison. In addition, if he was dangerous and likely to re-offend, the likelihood was that he would be imprisoned for life as this was the only way that the judge could ensure his indefinite detention, provided, that is, no special hospital would take him. Glanville Williams sums up this position as follows: 'the absurdity of reconciling this practice with the notion of substantially diminished responsibility needs no emphasis, though the indeterminate sentence is necessary if the judge is unable to assess the danger that will be presented by the offender in future'.[18] Further, during her research, Dell discovered that those diminished responsibility offenders who receive an indeterminate prison sentence are likely to be detained a good deal longer than their special hospital counterparts who are the subject of restriction orders. The question of release for such section 2 offenders was found to be assessed in fundamentally different ways as between the penal and special hospital systems; and yet the two populations were found to be markedly similar, so much so that 'it was hardly possible to find any lifer in respect of whom a [restriction] order could not have been made, had the doctors concerned applied standards used in other cases in the sample'.[19] Thus, although, as already mentioned, the basis for giving a diminished responsibility offender a life sentence is dangerousness rather than culpability,[20] the eventual release of such offenders 'is heavily dominated by tariff (i.e. culpability) considerations'.[21] So, not only may the section 2 offender's dangerousness ensure an indeterminate sentence of imprisonment, but also having achieved the status of a 'lifer' this now operates to prejudice him in relation to the date of his release, as the question of whether he has been punished enough is automatically considered in tandem with the question of whether it is safe to release him. By way of contrast, only the second question of public safety is considered in relation to the release of the diminished responsibility offender who is the subject of a restriction order.

THE NATURE OF SECTION 2 HOMICIDE ACT 1957

From the time of its enactment, the wording contained in section 2 has been the subject of fierce criticism. The major charge levelled at the section

---

[17] Dell and Smith, 'Changes in the Sentencing', 33.

[18] Williams, *Textbook of Criminal Law* (2nd edn., Stevens, London, 1983), 688.

[19] S. Dell, 'The Detention of Diminished Responsibility Homicide Offenders' (1983) *British Journal of Criminology* 50, 57.   [20] See R. v. *Chambers* [1983] Crim LR 688.

[21] Dell, 'The Detention of Diminished Responsibility Homicide Offenders', 59.

is that it is full of conceptual confusion. Indeed, Griew has gone as far as to describe 'the wording [as] altogether a disgrace' and 'as being quite shockingly elliptical'.[22] Ignoring for a moment the aetiological problems raised by the phrase 'abnormality of mind' which will be considered in the next Section, the crux of any diminished responsibility plea is the need for a finding that such abnormality 'substantially impaired his mental responsibility for his acts . . . in doing . . . the killing' (section 2 (1)). The fundamental difficulty here is that as it stands this wording makes little or no sense. In his penetrating criticism, Griew concludes that: 'Parliament has clumsily packed two ideas together. They are respectively signalled by the words "impaired . . . mental" on one side of the word "responsibility" and the words "for his acts" on the other side. The result is that the word "responsibility" does double duty; so, perhaps, does "substantially" '.[23] By compacting these two ideas of 'reduced (impaired) capacity and of reduced (diminished) liability' we seem to reach an equation where 'the former presumably justifies the latter by virtue of a third idea—that of reduced culpability'.[24] In answer to this criticism, it has been pointed out that in its use of the word 'responsibility' it could be that Parliament did not intend this type of ethico-legal evaluation but instead was referring to 'a state or fact of being capable of rational conduct'.[25] However, such an interpretation is not only difficult to reconcile with the wording of section 2 but also would substitute the need for an enquiry into the accused's responsibility for his particular act with one akin to an enquiry as to status, namely 'that capacity for rational conduct [which] is a general state [or] status giving general exemption from criminal responsibility'.[26] Although the use of the word 'exemption' here is misplaced, it seems clear that it is most unlikely that this status approach can have been intended by Parliament.[27] In this connection it is noticeable that the courts have shown no willingness to delve into the meaning of section 2, perhaps being reluctant to reveal the 'irresoluble difficulty in proceeding from impairment of capacity to diminution of liability'.[28] Rather, the judiciary have

---

[22] E. Griew, 'Reducing Murder to Manslaughter: Whose Job?' (1986) 12 *Journal of Medical Ethics* 18.   [23] Ibid. 19–20.

[24] E. Griew, 'The Future of Diminished Responsibility' [1988] Crim LR 75, 81–2.

[25] 'Murder, Manslaughter and Responsibility', Editorial in (1986) 12 *Journal of Medical Ethics* 4.

[26] A. Kenny, 'Can Responsibility be Diminished' ch. 1 of R. Frey and C. Morris (eds.), *Freedom and Responsibility* (Cambridge University Press, Cambridge, 1991), 30. Cf. N. Walker, 'McNaughtan's Innings: a Century and a Half Not Out' (1993) 4 *Journal of Forensic Psychiatry* 207, 211–12 who seems to support the view that diminished responsibility is akin to a status excuse.

[27] But cf. G.R. Sullivan, 'Intoxicants and Diminished Responsibility' [1994] Crim LR 156, 160 who suggests that, where borderline subnormality is used in support of a diminished plea, it 'may not be necessary to establish any causal link between the condition of "arrested or retarded development" and the killing' as the accused's condition is 'closely analogous to the defence of infancy' which is a status excuse.

[28] Griew, 'Reducing Murder to Manslaghter: Whose Job?', 22.

instead been content to permit the diminished plea to operate in a largely pragmatic manner.

THE SCOPE OF THE DEFENCE

It is important now to assess what different forms of mental condition may be used to support a plea under section 2 and to ascertain what diminution of responsibility is needed before such a plea can be successful.

So far as the accused's mental condition is concerned, the crucial concept contained in section 2 is that of 'abnormality of mind', which has been interpreted in a wider manner than its 'disease of the mind' counterpart under the M'Naghten rules.[29] This wide interpretation stems from the leading case of *R. v. Byrne*[30] where Lord Parker CJ stated:

'Abnormality of mind', which has to be contrasted with the time honoured expression in the M'Naghten Rules, 'defect of reason', means a state of mind so different from that of ordinary human beings that the reasonable man would term it abnormal. It appears to us to be wide enough to cover the mind's activities in all its aspects, not only the perception of physical acts and matters and the ability to form a rational judgment whether an act is right or wrong, but also the ability to exercise will-power to control physical acts in accordance with that rational judgment.[31]

This judgment was to have a dramatic effect on the development of the diminished responsibility plea. First, with regard to the defendant in *Byrne*, it decided that a sexual psychopath who had strangled a young woman whilst under the influence of an impulse which he found very difficult, if not impossible, to control was entitled to be regarded as having been suffering from an abnormality of mind. In this way, the idea of irresistible impulse, a notion consistently excluded from M'Naghten insanity, became part of English law through the medium of the diminished responsibility plea. At the other end of the scale, the courts have been prepared to include a whole host of different types of less serious forms of mental condition within the scope of abnormality of mind in order that a lenient sentence or disposal may be achieved.[32] For example, killings which have been motivated by morbid jealousy, a form of psychosis, have resulted in section 2 pleas where probation or a suspended sentence was felt to be

---

[29] Great care must be taken in using the word 'insanity' in the context of diminished responsibility as it is apt to mislead a jury. See *Rose* v. *R.* [1961] AC 496 and *R.* v. *Seers* (1984) 79 Cr App R 261.

[30] [1960] 2 QB 396.   [31] Ibid. 403.

[32] This is well documented by Dell, *Murder into Manslaughter*, 33 and 35, who found in the non-psychotic population a very wide range of conditions including 'at the mildest end of the spectrum of personality disorders . . . those cases which would hardly have attracted the label had it not been for the offence' and milder forms of mental illness where the doctors faced an equally difficult task in trying 'to determine where stress and strain ended and illness began.'

appropriate because the accused was clearly not dangerous.[33] Similarly, pre-menstrual tension, although not regarded in law as a form of automatism, has been held to constitute an abnormality of mind.[34] However, the cases which seem to have stretched the idea of abnormality of mind the farthest have been those dealing with mercy-killing.[35] Here there may be little or no real medical evidence upon which to base a section 2 plea and yet expert psychiatric evidence is an essential prerequisite of a successful diminished responsibility defence.[36] In this type of case, as for example where a parent kills a severely handicapped child or where a terminally ill person is relieved of further suffering by a loved one,[37] a common diagnosis is reactive depression. Unlike endogenous depression which is due to inherent causes, it is difficult to see how the reactive variety fits into the bracketed words in section 2(1). The truth seems to be that 'the defence of diminished responsibility is interpreted in accordance with the morality of the case rather than as an application of psychiatric concepts'.[38] However, as Bluglass has pointed out,[39] in order to achieve the desired outcome for the accused, namely the avoidance of the mandatory penalty for murder, there must be something of a benevolent conspiracy between the psychiatrist and the trial judge. Thus psychiatric evidence must be 'stretched'[40] in order to achieve an acceptable result which in the case of some mercy killings may be no more than a psychiatric probation order.

Although 'abnormality of mind' was defined in *Byrne*, the court had little to say about the bracketed words which immediately follow that phrase other than to confirm two things. First, that the mental abnormality must arise from one of the causes mentioned in the bracketed words and, second, that 'the aetiology of the abnormality of mind (namely, whether it arose from a condition of arrested or retarded development of mind or any inherent causes or was induced by disease or injury) does . . . seem to be a matter to be determined on expert evidence'.[41] Accordingly it is now time to examine the causes mentioned in the bracketed words of section 2(1).

The Aetiology of Abnormality of Mind

The words in brackets referred to in section 2(1) restrict the defence to mental abnormality 'arising from a condition of arrested or retarded

---

[33] See the cases listed by Williams, *Textbook of Criminal Law* (2nd edn.), 692–3.

[34] *R.* v. *Craddock* [1981] Current Law Yearbook 476, c.f. *R.* v. *Smith (Sandie)* [1982] Crim LR 531.

[35] See the cases discussed by Dell, *Murder into Manslaughter*, 35–6.

[36] In *R.* v. *Dix* (1981) 74 Cr App R 306, 311 the Court of Appeal made it clear that medical testimony is 'a practical necessity if the defence is to begin to run at all'.

[37] See the cases cited by Williams, *Textbook of Criminal Law* (2nd edn.), 693–4.

[38] Ibid. 693.

[39] R. Bluglass, *'Psychiatry, the Law and the Offender'* (Institute for the Study and Treatment of Delinquency, London, 1980), 10–11.

[40] Butler Report, Cmnd 6244 (1975), para 19.5.   [41] [1960] 2 QB 396, 403.

development of mind or any inherent causes or induced by disease or injury'. This phrase, which qualifies the notion of 'abnormality of mind', is clearly modelled on the definition of 'mental defectiveness' in the Mental Deficiency Act 1927.[42] These words have been held to exclude ordinary emotions such as anger or jealousy.[43] In addition, states of self-induced intoxication through drink, drugs or glue sniffing have been held not to constitute an abnormality of mind within section 2.[44] However, beyond this, the English courts have once again shown a marked reluctance to discuss the causes specified in parenthesis other than to confirm that medical evidence is 'a practical necessity if the defence is to begin to run at all' and that an abnormality arising from a cause other than one so specified will not satisfy the requirements of section 2.[45] This reluctance most likely stems from the point already referred to in *Byrne*, namely that these brack-eted causes are regarded as a matter upon which experts should pronounce and that therefore there is no need to subject them to judicial scrutiny. However, in her research, Dell found 'a great deal of variation in how the same conditions were classified by different doctors' and concluded:

It is perhaps not surprising that doctors should vary among themselves in how they used the four specified aetiologies, for they have no defined or agreed psychiatric meaning, and the phrase 'inherent causes' in particular is obviously capable of being interpreted in many different ways. More surprising was the fact that the reports frequently omitted any reference at all to the cause of the abnormality, thereby leaving the court without any written evidence as to the applicability of section 2(1).[46]

With regard to this latter point it may be that some courts are prepared to accept medical reports which fail to specify any cause, although this technically seems to run counter to the requirements of the section. Certainly such omissions can cause problems, since some members of the judiciary require psychiatrists to reconsider and amend their reports in the light of the need to include specifically one or more of the specified causes.[47] However, this is not merely a practical problem for, if it is accepted that these specified causes have no 'agreed psychiatric meaning', then it is only right and proper that psychiatrists should be able to look to the courts for

[42] See Walker, *Crime and Insanity in England*, Vol 1, 151. The definition in the 1927 Act read 'a condition of arrested or incomplete development of mind existing before the age of eighteen years whether arising from inherent causes or induced by disease or injury.' As Walker points out, 'In the 1957 version "retarded" has been substituted for "incomplete", and the requirement that the condition should have existed before the age of eighteen has been omitted, since it would have excluded conditions which were not classified by psychiatrists as "mental defectiveness".'   [43] *R. v. Fenton* (1975) Cr App R 261.
[44] See e.g. *R. v. Waite* (1981) 145 Justice of the Peace 677.
[45] *R. v. Dix* (1981) 74 Cr App R 306, 311.
[46] Dell, *Murder into Manslaughter*, 39.
[47] See the transcript referred to by Dell, ibid. 39–40 and the case study referred to by R.D. Mackay, 'Diminished Responsibility—Some Observations Arising from Three Case Studies' (1986) 26 *Medicine, Science and the Law* 60, 60–1.

some guidance as to their meaning. In short, surely the words in parenthesis in section 2(1) involve legal rather than psychiatric concepts; yet while the English courts have shown considerable willingness to discuss 'disease of the mind' and 'defect of reason' within the M'Naghten Rules, the same is certainly not true in respect of the aetiology of abnormality of mind. By way of contrast, however, this reticence is not true of the Australian courts, where there has been some relevant judicial comment on the aetiological components of the diminished plea.

There are two Australian states which recognise a defence of diminished responsibility, New South Wales and Queensland. Although there are some significant differences between the drafting of the Australian measures and their English counterpart, the concept of 'abnormality of mind' is used in each and is followed immediately by the identical words in parenthesis.[48] A particular difficulty which has arisen over aetiology in Australia has been whether conditions of a temporary nature are capable of causing an 'abnormality of mind'. Initially there was some objection to this view when the New South Wales Court of Appeal concluded that, while 'inherent cause' was not the same as 'inherited cause', if there was an interaction of two sets of factors based on 'nature' on the one hand and 'nurture' on the other, then a resulting abnormality of mind 'must be one which has some continuance'.[49] However, this narrow interpretation was criticised in two subsequent cases.

In the first, *R. v. Whitworth*[50], the Queensland Court of Criminal Appeal gave detailed consideration to the aetiology of 'abnormality of mind'. In that case the medical evidence consisted of brain damage and a psychosocial history which included being the victim of a sexual assault at the age of seven. In considering this evidence the trial judge took the view that because there was no suggestion of this psychosocial history amounting to a psychiatric illness it could not be regarded as an abnormality of mind. The accused's appeal was based on the contention that it was a combination of all these factors which together had produced an abnormality of mind. In his detailed judgment Derrington J considered that the aetiological factors could be split as follows:

Although . . . the causes are defined in terms related to the mind, there is also the dichotomy referring in the first part to features naturally occurring, that is by the passage 'arising from a condition of arrested or retarded development of mind or inherent causes', and in the other part to that which is induced in the mind by external factors, that is by the passage, 'induced by disease or injury' . . . This logical framework manifests an intention to specify the various causes within their appropriate divisions.[51]

[48] D. O'Connor and P.A. Fairall, *Criminal Defences* (Butterworth, Sydney, 1984), 218–19.
[49] *R. v. McGarvie* (1986) 5 NSWLR 270, 272.   [50] (1987) 31 A Crim R 453.
[51] Ibid. 470.

In considering the notion of 'inherent causes' Derrington J was critical of *McGarvie* on two grounds. First, he considered that this term could not be applied 'to a cause which itself has been produced by an external cause'. Second, he considered that the decision in *McGarvie* had failed to draw a distinction between a purely ephemeral mental condition and 'a permanent condition of the mind which may not manifest any abnormality in ordinary circumstances, but which may have an ephemeral appearance under certain stress. In such circumstances the defence may be available.' In order to illustrate the scope of this approach, the problem of vulnerability to stress was referred to as follows:

One further condition of the mind that may be an inherent cause to an abnormal state of mind is the inherent limitation of the mind to withstand stress. It is not unreasonable to say that most if not all ordinary minds are vulnerable to abnormality if the stress applied is sufficiently severe and protracted, and in an appropriate case it is this limitation of such tolerance to stress which may constitute, in the context of such stress, an inherent cause for the abnormality of mind. Thus the defence would be available even if it could not be demonstrated that the person were pathologically injured so as to come within the reference to 'injury' . . . in the catalogue of causes.[52]

Accordingly, if stress was sufficiently severe and durable then an inherent limitation of the mind's capacity to withstand it might 'constitute, in the context of such stress, an inherent cause for the abnormality of mind [as] it is immaterial that the condition of abnormality of mind, as distinct from the underlying cause, may be ephemeral'.[53]

His Lordship also considered that the psychosocial factors which had affected the accused could only be considered in the context of the phrase 'disease or injury' as only those causes could be produced by external factors. This phrase, however, could apply as a result of physical or psychological disease and, although there was no evidence of any disease in *Whitworth*, nevertheless an injury could be inflicted by 'slow, merciless factors, little by little, and with hopelessness' as opposed to 'violent or dramatic psychological stress'.[54] However, in each case it was a question of degree whether the stress caused a true injury which is recognised as a pathological state as distinct from an ephemeral condition.

Having considered the aetiological factors, Derrington J ordered a new trial, concluding that the jury should answer the question of whether the accused suffered from an abnormality of mind which arose 'from the operation of psychosocial pressures in taking him beyond his inherent limits . . . but not the limit imposed, for example, by his religious views; or was it induced by a psychological injury . . . in respect of his childhood experience, or the physical injuries to his brain as manifested in

---

[52] (1987) 31 A Crim R 453, 472.   [53] Ibid. 472–3.   [54] Ibid. 474.

its dysfunction; or was it a result of a combination of all or any of these?'[55]

In the more recent case of *R.* v. *Tumanako*,[56] the accused fatally stabbed his victim during what was claimed to be a dissociative state of rage. In support of a diminished responsibility plea, two psychiatrists diagnosed a dependency personality disorder while a third disagreed. The trial judge informed the jury that the 'abnormality must be more than a temporary situation'. In dismissing the accused's appeal against a murder conviction, the New South Wales Court of Criminal Appeal drew a distinction between, on the one hand, an abnormality of mind due to a personality disorder which manifested itself at the time of the killing in a dissociative state and, on the other hand, an abnormality of mind comprising the dissociative state stemming from the personality disorder. The court ruled that while the former had to be permanent owing to the fact that it was an inherent abnormality of mind, the latter could be temporary, provided the inherent cause was permanent. This seems a rather clumsy way of emphasising that, if the abnormality of mind can be traced to an inherent cause, then such a cause must be permanent although the abnormality of mind itself, such as a transient dissociative state, may be 'fleeting'.[57]

What these Australian decisions show is an increasing awareness by the courts of the scope of the causative factors surrounding abnormality of mind. Thus, for example, if Derrington J's view of 'inherent causes' is correct, then the reactive depression mercy-killing cases described by Williams as 'hard to characterise as due predominantly to "inherent causes"'[58] may nonetheless be so classified 'if the stress applied is sufficiently severe and protracted . . . even if it could not be demonstrated that the person were pathologically injured so as to come within the reference to "injury"'.[59]

The aetiological complexities of section 2 have at last been given some consideration by the Court of Appeal in *R.* v. *Sanderson*[60] where the disputed condition was paranoid psychosis described by Dr. Coid, a psychiatrist for the defence, as a mental illness which 'arose from inherent causes, namely the appellant's upbringing . . . and amounted to an abnormality of mind'.[61] However, the trial judge was held to have misled the jury by informing them at one stage in his direction that the 'abnormality of mind was the paranoid psychosis',[62] which in turn led to confusion about whether the abnormality of mind in the form of an inability to control himself had arisen from inherent causes or was 'induced by disease'.

---

[55] (1987) 31 A Crim R 453, 476.   [56] (1992) 64 A Crim R 149.
[57] Ibid. 161. See the commentary on the case by Stanley Yeo, (1993) *Criminal Law Journal*, 112.   [58] Williams, *Textbook of Criminal Law* (2nd edn.), 693.
[59] *R.* v. *Whitworth* (1987) 31 A Crim R 453, 472.   [60] (1994) 98 Cr App R 325.
[61] Ibid. 328.   [62] Ibid. 335.

However, in the opinion of the court, 'if the real difficulty was whether the mental illness or paranoid psychosis was a disease within the meaning of the subsection, he should have directed them that the medical evidence they had was that this abnormality of mind was the mental illness of paranoid psychosis . . . and if Dr. Coid was correct as to the aetiology of that mental illness, then it came within the words 'arising from any inherent cause' and was therefore within the subsection'.[63] In short, the court made it clear that if the abnormality of mind was to be equated with the psychosis then, if the defence psychiatrist was right, it was not to be regarded as having been 'induced by a disease' but instead fell within the subsection on the basis that 'it came within the words "arising from any inherent cause".'[64] As the jury were left in some confusion as a result of the trial judge's direction over aetiology, the Court of Appeal allowed the accused's appeal and substituted a manslaughter conviction. In arriving at its decision the court made two other important points. The first was designed to assist future juries in dealing with such complex cases and concerned the fact it will 'rarely be helpful to the jury to read to them section 2(1) in its entirety.' Rather, if there is no evidence, as in the present case, of arrested or retarded development or injury, then it would be of greater assistance to read from the words in brackets only the words 'arising from any inherent cause or induced by disease'.[65] This ruling should at least enable juries to be more focussed in their approach towards the application of these bracketed terms. The second point concerned the meaning of the word 'disease' in the phrase 'disease or injury' which counsel for the defence submitted meant ' "disease of the mind" and was apt to cover mental illnesses which were functional as well as organic'.[66] Although the court considered that it did not have to answer this difficult question, it did express the view that although 'induced by disease or injury' referred to 'organic or physical injury or disease of the body including the brain . . . "any inherent cause" . . . would cover functional mental illness'.[67] Accordingly, a paranoid psychosis of the type suffered by *Sanderson*, as described by Dr. Coid, could properly be said to have arisen from an inherent cause. Prior to the decision in *Sanderson* one might have assumed that all diseases of the mind within the M'Naghten Rules would automatically be regarded as diseases within section 2(1). However, such a simplistic view is clearly incorrect. Provided, however, the accused's condition is properly described, a functional mental illness should be able to qualify at one and the same time as a 'disease of the mind' and an 'abnormality of mind'.

Of course an abnormality of mind is not by itself sufficient for a successful section 2 plea unless it has given rise to a 'substantial' impairment

---

[63] (1994) 93 Cr App R 325, 335   [64] Ibid.
[65] Ibid. 334.   [66] Ibid. 336.   [67] Ibid.

of 'mental responsibility' at the time of the killing. As was indicated earlier, the phrase 'mental responsibility' has been subjected to considerable
criticism on the ground that it is almost meaningless and thus creates
difficulty for both doctors and jurors. The Butler Report said of the phrase:
'it is either a concept of law or a concept of morality; it is not a clinical
fact relating to the defendant'.[68] To regard the issue as one of legal responsibility would, it has been strongly suggested, be begging the question.[69]
The reality therefore seems to be that psychiatrists are required to testify
as to the accused's moral responsibility, yet the expert medical witness is
in no better position to judge such moral questions than anyone else.

The problem is exacerbated by the use of the word 'substantial', which
again is not an issue of medical science but of personal opinion. Despite
this, psychiatrists are commonly prepared to testify as to whether the
accused's mental responsibility was substantially impaired and judges, for
the jury's sake, are prepared to allow them to do so.[70] That this is the true
position can be seen from the Court of Appeal's decision in *Byrne* where
Lord Parker CJ, in dealing with the difficulties of proof in relation to
irresistible impulse, said: ' "could not resist his impulse" . . . is incapable of
scientific proof. A fortiori there is no scientific measurement of the degree
of difficulty which an abnormal person finds in controlling his impulses.
These problems which in the present state of medical knowledge are sci-
entifically insoluble, the jury can only approach in a broad common-sense
way'.[71] Clearly, for a finding that the accused's responsibility was diminished, it is not necessary for the jury to have concluded that the impulse
was truly irresistible. Instead, it is necessary to decide, having regard to all
the relevant evidence (not only the medical testimony), that the accused
experienced 'substantial' difficulty in controlling his conduct, as opposed
to trivial or minimal difficulty.

That the issue of 'substantial impairment of mental responsibility' is, at
the end of the day, one for the jury is starkly demonstrated by the case of
Peter Sutcliffe, the notorious 'Yorkshire Ripper'. In that case all the psychiatrists, including those for the prosecution, agreed that Sutcliffe was
suffering from paranoid schizophrenia and ought to be convicted of manslaughter under section 2 rather than murder. Accordingly, the Attorney-
General was prepared to accept Sutcliffe's plea of guilty to manslaughter
by reason of diminished responsibility which would have prevented an
expensive and emotive trial. However, the trial judge, Boreham J, refused

[68] Butler Report, para 19.5.
[69] Williams, *Textbook of Criminal Law* (2nd edn.), 686.
[70] See Dell, *Murder into Manslaughter*, 29. See also Griew, 'The Future of Diminished
Responsibility', 83–4.   [71] [1960] 2 QB 396, 404.

to accept the plea and Sutcliffe was tried for murder.[72] After severe cross-examination of the psychiatrists, the jury eventually convicted Sutcliffe of murder, presumably because they had doubts about whether he was suffering from an 'abnormality of mind' at the time of the killings and/or because they considered that Sutcliffe's mental responsibility for the killings had not been 'substantially' impaired. Sutcliffe's leave to appeal was eventually refused by the Court of Appeal and he was eventually transferred from prison to Broadmoor in March 1984.

The Sutcliffe case attracted a great deal of publicity and caused consternation amongst psychiatrists,[73] partly because of the adverse criticism to which the expert witnesses were subjected after the case and partly because it had hitherto been accepted practice that the trial judge would accept a guilty to manslaughter plea if all the medical reports agreed that the accused's mental condition clearly fell within section 2. However, it must be remembered that the Sutcliffe case was very special, in view of its notoriety, and should not therefore be taken as altering the practice of prosecutors in their acceptance of diminished responsibility pleas.

Indeed, the Sutcliffe case can be compared with that of Dennis Nilsen who confessed to the killing of fifteen or sixteen young men.[74] In Nilsen's case, the psychiatrists were clearly in disagreement as to whether the accused's condition fell within section 2. Such disagreement can only be resolved by the jury, who eventually convicted the accused of murder having heard the psychiatrist for the defence testify in relation to Nilsen's mental condition that 'all of the features together amount to clear evidence of severe personality disorder... of an unspecified type'.[75]

Clearly, men like Sutcliffe and Nilsen will be detained indefinitely, irrespective of how their mental conditions are classified. A sentence of life imprisonment is the one definite way to ensure this and is therefore inevitable in cases such as these.[76] The jury's verdict not only endorses this but also confirms, that in their opinion, the requirements of section 2 were not met. Once notorious cases such as these go to trial, a murder conviction seems almost inevitable and, some would argue, is justified as being in the public interest.

[72] See H. Prins, 'Diminished Responsibility and the Sutcliffe Case: Legal, Psychiatric and Social aspects' (1983) 23 *Medicine, Science and the Law* 17; N. Boulas, *The Yorkshire Ripper: A Case Study of the Sutcliffe Papers*, (University of Manchester Occasional Paper No 11), (1983). [73] Prins, 'Diminished Responsibility and the Sutcliffe Case', 20.
[74] For an account of the Nilsen case, see B. Masters, *Killing for Company* (London, Coronet, 1985). [75] *Daily Telegraph*, 27 October 1983.
[76] A hospital order with restrictions under s 41 of the Mental Health Act 1983 would ensure indeterminate hospitalization. However, in cases such as these, even if a diminished responsibility plea had been successful, it seems more than likely that life imprisonment would have been the sentence owing to the dangerousness of the accused.

DRINK, DRUGS, AND DIMINISHED RESPONSIBILITY

There is no doubt that, if an accused's intoxicated state is found to have given rise to a disease of the mind within the M'Naghten Rules, then the defence of insanity may be open to him. In *R. v. Davis* the jury were directed in the following manner: 'drunkenness is one thing and the diseases to which drunkenness leads are different things; and if a man by drunkenness brings on a state of disease which causes such a degree of madness, even for a time, which would have relieved him from responsibility if it had been caused in any other way, then he would not be criminally responsible'.[77] Clearly, therefore, if the accused's intoxicated condition is in itself a distinct disease of the mind which rendered him incapable of knowing what he was doing or that it was legally wrong, then the insanity defence could be successfully used. By way of contrast, however, the courts have adopted a much harsher approach when dealing with the important question of whether self-induced intoxication can ever give rise to an 'abnormality of mind' within the meaning of section 2 of the Homicide Act 1957. One of the first cases to consider this question was *R. v. Di Duca*[78] where the court considered that it was 'very doubtful' if the transient effect of drink, even if it did produce a toxic effect on the brain, could cause an 'injury' within the meaning of the section.[79]

However, the problems surrounding the relationship in diminished responsibility between abnormality of mind and voluntary intoxication become more complex when there is evidence of some interaction between a pre-existing mental disorder and the effects of self-induced intoxication. Here the approach of the courts has been consistently to use a tainting device described more fully in Chapter 3 to ensure effective removal of the possibility of diminished responsibility pleas from mentally disordered but intoxicated defendants.

One of the first cases to achieve this result was *R. v. Fenton*[80] where the Court of Appeal had to deal with a case where the accused killed four people due to the combination of psychopathy, reactive depression, and a large quantity of alcohol. In upholding the trial judge's direction that the jury should ignore the effects of the alcohol, the court stated: 'we recognise that cases may arise hereafter where the accused proves such a craving for drink as to produce in itself an abnormality of mind; but that is not proved in this case . . . we do not see how self-induced intoxication can of itself produce an abnormality of mind due to inherent causes'.[81] The fallacy of this line of argument of course is that the accused did not seek to show

---

[77] (1881) 14 Cox CC 563, 564.   [78] (1959) 43 Cr App R 167.

[79] There is a marked similarity here with the way in which the courts have refused to permit the 'transitory' effects of drink to be considered under the reasonable man test in provocation, see e.g. *R. v. Newell* (1980) 71 Cr App R 331.

[80] (1975) 61 Cr App R 261.   [81] Ibid. 263.

that intoxication alone had caused in him an abnormality of mind, but instead had argued that it was a combination of factors which was responsible for his condition at the time of the killing. Despite this the courts have followed the approach in *Fenton* on a number of subsequent occasions. Thus in *R. v. Gittens*[82] the Court of Appeal made it clear that the jury should be expressly told to ignore the effect of alcohol or drugs on the defendant and should then go on to 'consider whether the combined effect of the other matters which do fall within the section amounted to such abnormality of mind as substantially impaired the defendant's mental responsibility'.[83]

This approach was further approved by the Court of Appeal in *R. v. Atkinson*[84] when it was stated that the proper questions for the jury are: 'have the defence satisfied you on the balance of probabilities that, if the defendant had not taken drink (i) he would not have killed as he in fact did? And (ii) he would have been under diminished responsibility when he did so?'[85] These questions may at first sight look straightforward but in reality they are not only hypothetical but also impossible to answer. How, it may be asked, is a jury to perform the task of answering them? If the effect of drink or drugs is the only factor involved, then it may properly be ignored, but, if it is inextricably intertwined with other factors such as personality disorder and depression, then it becomes impossible to tease out the independent effect of the drink or drugs. To attempt to compartmentalize the accused's mental condition like this is truly absurd and once again reflects the use of the 'taint', representing a policy which, while it will allow evidence of voluntary intoxication to act as a defence to murder where the defence is based on lack of specific intent, ignores any evidence of the accused's drunken state when he uses diminished responsibility as a defence to the same crime. The irony of this approach is that in this latter case the accused will be suffering from a pre-existing abnormality of mind while in the former case he is mentally normal. One might have expected the law to have been more sympathetic towards those suffering from mental abnormalities; however, the 'taint of intoxication' renders this almost impossible.

Indeed, it has been suggested that the recent Court of Appeal decision in *R. v. Egan*[86] goes even further 'by negating a defence that might otherwise have succeeded on the basis of internal factors alone'.[87] The important point here concerns the fact that although, like Atkinson, Egan was suffering from mental impairment and had consumed alcohol, it was strongly argued that the accused's 'responsibility was impaired because of his constitutive immaturity' which in turn meant that it was unnecessary 'to

---

[82] [1984] 3 All ER 252.   [83] Ibid. 256.   [84] [1985] Crim LR 314.
[85] Ibid. 315.   [86] [1992] 4 All ER 470.
[87] Sullivan, 'Intoxicants and Diminished Responsibility', 159.

establish any causal link between the condition of "arrested or retarded development" and the killing'.[88] The Court of Appeal was clearly unsympathetic towards this argument and concluded that the vital question must be 'was the appellant's abnormality of mind such that he would have been under diminished responsibility, drink or no drink?'[89] However, by focussing on the need for a causal connection between the impairment and the killing, the court effectively foreclosed any diminished defence where alcohol has been consumed even though the subnormality in its own right might otherwise be sufficient to ground a successful plea had the accused remained sober. If, as seems likely, there is no need for a causal connection between 'arrested or retarded development' and the actual killing, then, once again, the court in *Egan* can be seen to be using the 'tainting' device in a manner highly prejudicial to subnormal defendants.[90]

A final relevant issue which the Court of Appeal has been called upon to deal with concerns the problem of alcoholism. Thus in *R. v. Tandy*[91] the accused, who was an alcoholic, strangled her daughter after consuming almost a whole bottle of vodka. In concluding that the accused had been properly convicted of murder the court conceded that:

> If the alcoholism had reached the level at which her brain had been injured by the repeated insult from intoxicants so that there was gross impairment of her judgment and emotional responses, then the defence of diminished responsibility was available to her . . . Further, if the appellant were able to establish that the alcoholism had reached the level where although the brain had not been damaged to the extent just stated, the appellant's drinking had become involuntary, that is to say she was no longer able to resist the impulse to drink, then the defence of diminished responsibility would be available to her . . . because, if her drinking was involuntary, then her abnormality of mind at the time of the act of strangulation was induced by her condition of alcoholism.[92]

In this latter respect the court made it clear that the trial judge was correct 'in telling the jury that, if the taking of the first drink was not involuntary, then the whole of the drinking' leading up to the killing 'was not involuntary'.[93]

While the first part of this judgment is unobjectionable, namely that

---

[88] Sullivan, 'Intoxicants and Diminished Responsibility', 160.

[89] [1992] 4 All ER 470, 479.

[90] Further, as far as is known, the courts have not yet had to deal with the question of the effect of non-dangerous drugs in relation to diminished responsibility. It is therefore unclear how they would react in a case such as *Bailey* [1983] 2 All ER 503 or *Hardie* [1984] 3 All ER 848 were the accused unfortunate enough to kill and in turn claim that an 'abnormality of mind' had been triggered off by the voluntary consumption of non-dangerous drugs. Cf. D. Willamson and M. Humphreys, 'Might Anabolic Steriod Abuse Provide a Defence in Cases of Violent Crime?' (1993) 4 *Journal of Forensic Psychiatry* 481. It is, however, by no means clear whether the courts would classify steroids as 'non-dangerous'.

[91] [1989] 1 All ER 267.   [92] Ibid. 272.   [93] Ibid. 273.

alcoholism can amount to a 'disease or injury' within section 2(1) of the Homicide Act 1957, the second part is difficult to accept. What the court has done is to develop the 'craving for drink' dictum contained in *Fenton*[94] in such a way that it is almost impossible to satisfy. It is one thing to say that the accused may be suffering from an abnormal craving for drink, but quite another to require that before such a craving can be established, the first drink in the relevant series must be shown to have been consumed 'involuntarily'.[95] In addition, how can the fact that the first drink was involuntarily consumed make any practical difference as to the proper classification of the accused's condition?[96] Surely the accused's mental condition remains the same irrespective of whether the first, second or third drink is involuntarily consumed? The crucial time to examine the accused's mental state is at the time of the killing rather than at the time when he began to drink. In effect, therefore, the court is once more using the taint of intoxication effectively to remove the possibility of the diminished responsibility plea from what it perceives to be undeserving intoxicated offenders. The use of the notion of 'involuntariness' in relation to the drinking is a mere smokescreen behind which the taint can effectively operate.[97]

It seems clear, therefore, that the courts have used the issue of voluntary intoxication as means to cut down the scope of the diminished responsibility plea. However, such an approach not only seems harsh but also sits uncomfortably with the other common 'loss of self-control' plea, namely provocation. Thus, it has been pointed out that there has never been any suggestion that it would be appropriate for a trial judge to ask a jury in a case of a bad-tempered subnormal defendant who had killed his victim as a result of an alleged loss of self-control: ' "are you satisfied that [the accused] would have killed P irrespective of whether P had caused her to lose her temper?" '[98] And yet, had D been drunk at the time of the killing, the jury would be required to answer the analogous question as posed in *Egan*; namely would D have killed without the effects of the drink. It is possible then that the courts are more sympathetic towards the provoked mentally abnormal killer than his drunken counterpart.[99] Accordingly, it is now time to explore the interrelationship between diminished responsibility and provocation.

---

[94] (1975) 61 Cr App R 261, 263.
[95] The court's use of the word 'involuntary' is far from clear. For criticism, see the case note by Edward Griew (1991) 2 *Journal of Forensic Psychiatry* 79, 82.
[96] See Sullivan, 'Intoxicants and Diminished Responsibility', 158.
[97] See also *R. v. Inseal* [1992] Crim LR 36.
[98] Sullivan, 'Intoxicents and Diminished Responsibility', 162.
[99] Although it must be conceded that the courts are equally robust in denying provocation to those who lose their self-control while drunk, on the basis that the reasonable man is always sober. See *R. v. Newell* (1980) 71 Cr App R 331.

COMBINING THE PLEAS OF PROVOCATION AND DIMINISHED RESPONSIBILITY[100]

While provocation and diminished responsibility tend to have been treated as separate and distinct methods of reducing murder to manslaughter, the point that this is not always so is well made by the Criminal Law Revision Committee in the following remark:

It is now possible for a defendant to set up a combined defence of provocation and diminished responsibility, the practical effect being that the jury may return a verdict of manslaughter if they take the view that the defendant suffered from an abnormality of mind *and* was provoked. In practice this may mean that a conviction of murder will be ruled out although the provocation was not such as would have moved a person of normal mentality to kill.[101]

Although it has been argued that a verdict of manslaughter on the grounds of both provocation and diminished responsibility is illogical 'since the defence of provocation presupposes a reasonable man driven to the act of killing, whereas unreasonableness is endemic in the defence of diminished responsibility',[102] it is clear from case studies that neither juries nor trial judges have been unduly perturbed by any such illogicality.[103] Thus in *R. v. Thornton*, Beldam LJ said: 'there is no doubt that the two defences are not incompatible where the evidence which is given enables them to be combined'.[104] However, when this occurs, the combination brings with it a number of difficult issues. In particular, although the House of Lords' decision in *DPP v. Camplin*[105] permits the jury in provocation cases to endow the reasonable man with 'such of the accused's characteristics as they think would effect the gravity of the provocation to him',[106] this must be read subject to the Court of Appeal's decision in *Newell*[107] which restricts the legal scope of characteristics by laying down a dual test, namely that: 'a characteristic had to have a sufficient degree of permanence to be regarded as part of the individual's character or personality, not something transitory, to modify the concept of the reasonable man, and there had to be some real connection between the nature of the provocation and the

---

[100] R.D. Mackay, 'Pleading Provocation and Diminished Responsibility Together' [1988] Crim LR 411.

[101] Criminal Law Revision Committee, *Working Paper on Offences Against the Person*, (1976), para 53 (emphasis in original).

[102] See T. Morris and L. Blom-Cooper, *A Calendar of Murder* (Michael Joseph, London, 1964), 298 n 4.

[103] See R.D. Mackay 'Pleading Provocation and Diminished Responsibility Together', 411–16.   [104] [1992] 1 All ER 306, 315.

[105] [1978] 2 All ER 168.   [106] Ibid. 175.

[107] (1980) 71 Cr App R 331. This was followed by the Court of Appeal in *R. v. Morhall* [1993] 4 All ER 888 which decided that characteristics which were inconsistent with the concept of the reasonable man, in this case addiction to glue-sniffing, should not be left to the jury.

peculiar characteristic of the offender'.[108] There seems little doubt that if this test were to be strictly adhered to, few, if any, of the 'abnormalities of mind' which might support a diminished plea would fall within it; the reason being that the provocation cannot generally be regarded as being 'directed to a particular phobia from which the offender suffers'.[109] Instead, the accused's condition renders him much more susceptible to a loss of self-control. This difficulty doubtless led the New Zealand Court of Appeal in *R. v. McGregor*[110] to remark: 'special difficulties, however, arise when it becomes necessary to consider what purely mental peculiarities may be allowed as characteristics'.[111] Indeed, this very problem has now led the New Zealand Court of Appeal to abandon its earlier strict approach towards characteristics in favour of a more liberal test,[112] and there is now some reason to believe that the same process may have occurred in England as a result of the Court of Appeal's decision in *R. v. Ahluwalia*.[113] In that case, although Lord Taylor CJ purported to follow *Newell* by stating that 'characteristics relating to the mental state or personality of an individual can also be taken into account by the jury, providing they have the necessary degree of permanence',[114] the Lord Chief Justice cited as examples of such characteristics the New Zealand cases of *R. v. Taaka*[115] and *R. v. Leilua*[116] where conditions of 'obsessively compulsive personality' and post-traumatic stress disorder respectively were so regarded. He then made it clear that, had medical evidence of 'battered woman syndrome' been led, then this could well have been sufficient to bring the accused's condition with the ambit of such characteristics.

Two points can be made about this aspect of the decision in *Ahluwalia*. The first is that, although Lord Taylor CJ purports to follow *Newell* by relying on the need for the condition to possess a 'necessary degree of permanence', no mention is made of the connection requirement referred to above. Clearly it is difficult to envisage how that requirement could be satisfied in many cases of so-called mental peculiarities as it is unlikely that the provocation will be directed towards the accused's abnormal personality or the fact that she suffers from 'battered woman syndrome'.[117] Rather, it is the mental condition itself which renders the accused more susceptible to insult or abuse. It would appear therefore that the so-called connection

---

[108] *Newell*, (1980) 71 Cr App R 331.

[109] *R. v. McGregor* [1962] NZLR 1069, 1082 per North J, cited with approval in *Newell* (1980) 71 Cr App R 331, 340.

[110] [1962] NZLR 1069.   [111] Ibid. 1082.

[112] See *R. v. McArthy* [1992] 2 NZLR 550. Discussed by B.J. Brown, 'Provocation Reconstructed: the McArthyisation of *McGregor*' [1993] *New Zealand Recent Law Review* 329.

[113] [1992] 4 All ER 889.   [114] Ibid. 898.   [115] [1982] 2 NZLR 198.

[116] [1986] *New Zealand Recent Law Review* 188.

[117] Cf. A. McColgan, 'In Defence of Battered Women Who Kill' (1993) *Oxford Journal of Legal Studies* 508; C. Wells, 'Battered Women Syndrome and Defences to Homicide: Where Now?' (1994) 14 *Legal Studies* 266.

limb of the two-pronged test used in *Newell* may now have been dis-regarded,[118] thus allowing a jury more readily to consider the mental char-acteristics of allegedly provoked defendants.

The second point which arises from the decision in *Ahluwalia* concerns the issue of the admissibility of expert evidence. It seems clear that, had expert evidence of 'battered woman syndrome' been put before the court, then such testimony would have been permitted despite the decision of the Court of Appeal in *R. v. Turner*[119] which decided that 'jurors do not need psychiatrists to tell them how ordinary folk who are not suffering from any mental illness are likely to react to the stresses and strains of life'.[120] The reasoning behind the approach in *Turner* is that the loss of self-control essential to a successful provocation plea is something which the law regards as falling 'within the realm of the ordinary juryman's experi-ence'.[121] In short, it is a question of fact for the jury to be decided by them unaided by expert evidence. However, in *Turner* the accused was not suffering from any mental disorder and it is this fact which proved fatal to the admissibility of psychiatric evidence. By way of contrast, the defend-ant in *Ahluwalia* was not only later found to have been suffering from 'a major depressive disorder',[122] which led to a successful diminished respon-sibility plea, but she also might have used evidence of 'battered woman syndrome' to bolster her provocation plea. It seems clear therefore that expert evidence concerning this latter condition would have been admis-sible to explain the accused's loss of self-control. However, it is apparent, even in the light of *Camplin*, that such testimony would be inadmissible to assist the jury in its consideration of the question of whether the 'or-dinary person' would have been provoked. This certainly seems to have been the opinion of Lord Simon in *Camplin* when he remarked: 'whether the defendant exercised reasonable self-control in the totality of the circumstances ... would be entirely a matter for the jury without further evidence. The jury would, as ever, use their collective common sense to determine whether the provocation was sufficient to make a person of reasonable self-control in the totality of the circumstances (including per-sonal characteristics) act as the defendant did'.[123] In this respect English law seems to part company with New Zealand law where cases such as *Taaka* and *Leilua* seem prepared to accept as admissible expert medical evidence which related loss of self-control to the mental condition from which the accused had been suffering at the time of the offence, as well

---

[118] Cf. *McArthy* [1992] 2 NZLR, 558 where Cooke P refers to the difficulties caused 'by the suggestion that provocation must be "directed at" a particular characteristic'.
[119] [1975] 1 QB 834. For critical comment, see R.D. Mackay and A. Colman, 'Excluding Expert Evidence: A Tale of Ordinary Folk and Common Experience' [1991] Crim LR 800.
[120] Ibid. 842.   [121] *R. v. Smith (Stanley)* [1979] 3 All ER 605, 611.
[122] [1992] 4 All ER 889, 900.   [123] [1978] 2 All ER 168, 182–3.

as permitting this evidence, through the doctrine of 'characteristics', to assist the jury in deciding whether 'the provocation was sufficient to make a person of reasonable self-control act . . . as the defendant did'.[124]

However, it is apparent that the rule in *Turner* is being breached with increasing regularity, and in this context it is interesting to note that in the recent case of *R. v. Emery*,[125] dealing with post-traumatic stress disorder in relation to the defence of duress, the Lord Chief Justice, in concluding that expert testimony on the nature of this condition was properly admitted, said: 'the issue the jury had to decide . . . was, whether or not the prosecution had negatived duress, and therefore the question for the doctors was whether a woman of reasonable firmness with the characteristics of Miss Emery, if abused in the manner which she said, would have had her will crushed so that she could not have protected her child'.[126] This dictum seemed to suggest that expert testimony could be admissible in respect of the 'reasonable firmness' test in duress. However, that this is not the case has recently been confirmed by the Court of Appeal in *R. v. Hegarty*[127] and in *R. v. Horne*.[128]

It follows that, because expert testimony is so much more readily admitted when the plea is one of diminished responsibility, it would seem clear that there are considerable advantages in running the defences of provocation and diminished responsibility together as there is every chance that the jury will be unable to keep the issues separate. In this connection, it is illuminating to note the following remark of Beldam LJ in *R. v. Thornton*:[129]

having regard to the passages from the summing up both on provocation and on diminished responsibility . . . we would find it surprising if the jury approached the issues keeping them entirely separate. We think that, as in all such cases, the concepts of loss of self-control, abnormality of mind and substantial impairment of responsibility would have been regarded by the jury as interrelated, blending into one another, but distinguished by the essential feature that provocation produces a sudden and impulsive reaction leading to loss of control whereas impairment of mental responsibility is due to the effect of the long period of stress upon a disordered personality.

This need for 'a sudden and impulsive reaction' for provocation, which was confirmed in *Thornton* and proved fatal to her case, was endorsed by the Court of Appeal in *Ahluwalia*. It was made clear in that case, however, that, provided there was 'a sudden and temporary loss of self-control' at the time of the killing, 'provocation would not as a matter of law be negatived simply because of the delayed reaction',[130] although the longer

---

[124] *R. v. Camplin* [1978] 2 All ER 168, 183.
[125] (1992) 14 Cr App R (S) 394, 398.   [126] Ibid.   [127] [1994] Crim LR 352.
[128] [1994] Crim LR 584.   [129] [1992] 1 All ER 306, 316.
[130] [1992] 4 All ER 889, 896.

the delay the less likely the jury would be to accept provocation. This still makes it very difficult for abused women who kill, such as Thornton and Ahluwalia, to succeed in having a murder charge reduced to manslaughter using only the vehicle of provocation. Indeed, in the latter case, the court looked directly to diminished responsibility by admitting fresh psychiatric evidence in order to ensure a retrial, which in turn resulted in a manslaughter verdict and the accused's immediate release from prison. There seems little doubt that the failure of the defence to raise diminished responsibility at the original trial was a grave error especially as no medical evidence whatsoever was presented to the trial court. Had this been done, then in all likelihood a murder conviction would have been avoided. For, although one can never be sure how any particular jury will view combined pleas of provocation and diminished responsibility, there seems every chance that the jury will be unable to keep the issues separate. Indeed, the recognition by the judiciary that juries may return manslaughter verdicts based on both pleas implicitly accepts that this is so.[131] If this is the case, then juries may well be lenient and indulgent towards the requirements contained in each of the relevant formulae, allowing 'loss of self-control', 'abnormality of mind', and 'substantial impairment of mental responsibility' to inter-relate and blend into one another. In short, each in turn may contribute towards the satisfaction of the other and allow the jury more flexibility in their decision-making towards both pleas. It follows, therefore, that, if there is some psychiatric evidence which suggests that a provoked accused may have been mentally disordered at the time of the killing, then very serious consideration should be given to running both pleas concurrently as part of a defence strategy.

Reform Proposals

As a result of constant dissatisfaction expressed about the wording of section 2 of the Homicide Act, a number of reform measures have been suggested. In 1975 the Butler Report proposed that a person should not be convicted of murder if the mental disorder from which he suffered 'was such as to be an extenuating circumstance which ought to reduce the offence to manslaughter'.[132] The Criminal Law Revision Committee, while in broad agreement with the Butler Report proposals, preferred a formula which required that 'that the mental disorder was such as to be a substantial enough reason to reduce the offence to manslaughter'.[133]

It is this latter version which has found its way into the Draft Criminal Code.[134] Its authors, however, had a technical preference for the term

---

[131] For discussion of such verdicts, see Mackay, 'Pleading Provocation and Diminished Responsibility Together', 417.   [132] Butler Report, para 19.17.
[133] Criminal Law Revision Committee, Fourteenth Report, *Offences Against the Person* (1980) Cmnd 7844, para 93.   [134] See clause 56(1) of the Draft Code.

'mental abnormality' rather than 'mental disorder' although both are defined according to section 1(2) of the Mental Health Act 1983 as requiring 'mental illness, arrested or incomplete development of mind, psychopathic disorder, and any other disorder or disability of mind'. There seems no doubt that the abolition of the term 'abnormality of mind' together with the words in parenthesis in section 2(1) of the Homicide Act would go some way to improving the diminished plea insofar as it would enable psychiatrists to concentrate upon an issue which is clearly within their professional competence. At the same time, however, the phrase 'any other disorder or disability of mind' must surely have the potential of widening the types of conditions which may be capable of supporting a diminished plea.[135] By way of contrast it seems equally clear that psychiatric opinion will not be permitted on the issue of whether the accused's mental disorder 'was a substantial enough reason to reduce the offence to manslaughter' as this must be a matter for the court. This then makes the reformulation very different from the current section 2(1), since at present psychiatrists are positively encouraged to give testimony on the issue of 'substantial impairment of mental responsibility' thus encouraging 'role confusion' between fact finder and expert witness.[136] Accordingly, it has been powerfully argued that a result of the cessation of this practice of testimony would be a danger that diminished responsibility might cease to be as effective a means of avoiding a murder conviction; for the fact finder would no longer be able to rely on the assistance of experts on the ultimate issue, namely should 'liability be "diminished" to the level of manslaughter'.[137] With this assistance removed, the jury would have to make a finding of murder or manslaughter without the reassuring cushion of having had experts inform them that a diminished responsibility finding is appropriate. It is the uncertainty of how juries might respond to this new-found freedom which is perplexing enough to make some question the wisdom of the Draft Criminal Code's reformulation.[138]

A much more radical approach to reform would be to abolish the diminished responsibility plea. Indeed, this was the first choice solution of the Butler Report, but only on condition that the mandatory life sentence for murder be likewise abolished.[139] More recently, the Select Committee of the House of Lords on Murder and Life Imprisonment likewise recommended abolition of the mandatory penalty.[140] However, the Select Committee endorsed the view of the Criminal Law Revision

---

[135] See Griew, 'The Future of Diminished Responsibility', 79, 80. This is the reason why the phrase 'except intoxication' was needed at the end of the definition of 'mental abnormality' in clause 56(1) of the Draft Code in order to ensure that the transitory effects of drink or drugs should not be regarded as 'any other disorder of mind'.   [136] Griew, ibid. 85.
[137] Ibid. 86.   [138] Ibid.   [139] Butler Report, paras 19.14–19.16.
[140] See House of Lords, *Report of the Select Committee on Murder and Life Imprisonment, Vol I*, 36, para 118. See also House of Lords, *Report of the Select Committee on Medical Ethics, Vol 1*, para 261 which strongly endorses this recommendation.

Committee,[141] that both diminished responsibility and provocation 'should be retained whether or not the sentence for murder were to become discretionary'.[142] There seems every chance that the status quo will remain in respect of both the mandatory penalty and the diminished responsibility plea. However, what reform bodies have failed to address is whether it is desirable to retain a diminished responsibility plea in any form irrespective of whether the mandatory penalty for murder is retained or abolished. In this context, it is noteworthy that, while different jurisdictions rarely dispute the need for some form of insanity defence within the structure of criminal law excuses, there is not the same degree of consensus in relation to diminished responsibility: some jurisdictions such as New Zealand and the states of Victoria and Western Australia do not permit it.[143] Others such as Canada,[144] and the United States of America,[145] have considered a *mens rea* variant commonly termed 'diminished capacity', which permits mental abnormality short of insanity to go to the issue of whether or not the accused formed the *mens rea* for the offence charged.

This lack of consensus stems from a variety of criticisms,[146] including the argument that the partial responsibility plea contained in section 2 of the Homicide Act is unacceptably arbitrary and unfair in the sense that 'on very similar facts some will be convicted of murder and be sentenced to life imprisonment; others will be convicted of manslaughter and receive a much lighter sentence'.[147] Certainly, there seems little doubt that section 2 operates in a very pragmatic manner which as already mentioned could be regarded as one of its strengths. However, it is also clear that the development of the diminished responsibility plea has contributed to the demise of the insanity defence.[148] This point is fully supported by Dell, who reported finding 15 cases where, despite evidence of legal insanity, section 2

[141] Criminal Law Revision Committee, Fourteenth Report, *Offences Against the Person*, para 76.
[142] House of Lords, *Reports of the Select Committee on Murder and Life Imprisonment*, para 83.
[143] See I.G. Campbell, *Mental Disorder and Criminal Law in Australia and New Zealand* (Butterworth, Wellington, New Zealand, 1988).
[144] See J.C. Jordan, 'Diminished Capacity' (1982–83) 25 Criminal Law Quarterly 480.
[145] See S.J. Morse, 'Diminished Capacity' in S. Shute, S. Gardiner, and J. Horder (eds.), *Action and Value in the Criminal Law* (Clarendon Press, Oxford, 1993), 239.
[146] See in particular Morse ibid., and id., 'Undiminished Confusion in Diminished Capacity' (1984) 75 *Journal of Criminal Law and Criminology* 1 who argues at ibid. 35 against adoption of partial responsibility on the ground that 'responsible actors who commit crimes retain sufficient rationality and self-control to deserve whatever punishment the law decrees for the crime committed'. However, Morse does readily concede that some defendants, such as mercy-killers, may deserve lesser punishment but argues that those who suggest that such cases support the need for partial responsibility have confused culpability and responsibility: ibid. 35.
[147] A. Kenny, 'Can Responsibility be Diminished?' in R. Frey and C. Morris (eds.), *Liability and Responsibility* (Cambridge University Press, Cambridge, 1991), 21.
[148] See Walker, *Crime and Insanity in England, Vol I*, 158–9.

manslaughter convictions were recorded.[149] With the retention of mandatory indefinite hospitalization for those found not guilty by reason of insanity in relation to murder charges, the spectacle of lawyers advising potentially irresponsible defendants to plead guilty to manslaughter is bound to continue. However, there is something manifestly unpalatable about such a state of affairs, so much so that it is perhaps legitimate to question the nature of the overlap between insanity and diminished responsibility. Certainly, such an overlap is something which is rarely encountered in practice; for, although the prosecution are at liberty to adduce evidence of insanity in answer to a diminished responsibility plea,[150] there appear to be virtually no instances where advantage has been taken of this procedure.[151] This may be the reason why the courts seem to have had little to say about the potential overlap between 'disease of the mind' within the M'Naghten Rules and the 'disease' criterion within section 2,[152] with the result that one is left wondering whether all 'diseases of the mind' are at one and the same time 'diseases' for the purposes of diminished responsibility. If this is so then it seems clear that all those charged with murder who might otherwise rely upon an insanity defence will be able to plead diminished responsibility successfully. Surely it is arguable that a clear line should be drawn between the two pleas, so that 'it should not be possible to rely on diminished responsibility where the evidence discloses that the defendant' was legally insane.[153] The difficulty with this approach lies with the inflexible disposal consequences retained in the Criminal Procedure (Insanity and Unfitness to Plead) Act 1991. However, if this was swept away, then there might be some merit in such an approach. The danger would be where the jury rejected the insanity defence not because of any doubt about 'disease of the mind' but rather because of a finding that the accused knew the 'nature and quality of the act' and that it was 'legally wrong'. If such were the case, then there would still be a good chance that, had the accused run a diminished responsibility plea, he might well have succeeded. In this case, it would seem only fair to give the defence the opportunity to advance such a plea but only after the jury's initial rejection of legal insanity. This would have the merit of keeping the defences separate as well as ensuring that the insanity defence retains its primary status in cases where there is considered to be good evidence that the elements of the M'Naghten Rules (or whatever other test it might be replaced with),[154] have been satisfied.

---

[149] Dell, *Murder into Manslanghter*, 30.

[150] S 6 Criminal Procedure (Insanity) Act 1964.

[151] See Dell, *Murder into Manslaughter*, 31 and the letter by R.D. Mackay at [1992] Crim LR 751.   [152] But cf *Sanderson* (1994) 98 Cr App R 325.

[153] F. McAuley, *Insanity, Psychiatry and Criminal Responsibility* (Round Hall Press, Dublin, 1993), 176.

[154] See Dell, *Murder into Manslaughter*, 42 who argues that if the Butler proposals on the insanity defence were implemented then 'about a third of the men who are nowadays convicted under section 2 would . . . come within the scope of the special verdict'.

A final point concerning reform which may be raised is whether diminished responsibility should be extended to other offences.[155] It has been convincingly argued that there are no principles of desert and fairness which can deny the 'partially responsible armed robber, rapist or thief',[156] the same excuse as the equally partially responsible murderer. Accordingly, Nigel Walker has suggested that 'the extension of the defence of diminished responsibility to offences other than murder' could be done '[by]' providing simply that diminished responsibility should limit the choice or severity of the sentence'.[157] Of course this does not answer the point that, unlike murder, the majority of crimes cannot simply be reduced to a lesser charge. However, Walker dismisses this point as a technicality, claiming that there is no need for a lesser charge as 'it would be possible to convict a defendant of, say, robbery but add the rider "under diminished responsibility" '.[158] This would certainly have the merit of ensuring that a defendant's mental abnormality which had some bearing on his criminal responsibility could be used as a partial responsibility defence, rather than merely permitting his mental state to be considered as a plea in mitigation at the sentencing phase of the trial. An analogous approach suggested by Horder would be to 'create an intermediate "diminished responsibility" verdict . . . as a general defence', a finding of which would 'be a verdict in itself, distinct from finding the defendant guilty or not guilty [and] would have the effect of giving the trial judge the power to make an order in lieu of punishment or outright acquittal'.[159] Some might argue that to permit this type of approach would merely prolong and complicate the trial process in non-homicide cases without achieving any real advantage for the accused. However, in principle, there seems no just reason why a mentally abnormal defendant should be denied the opportunity to show that he was less responsible for, say, a shoplifting offence than his mentally normal counterpart would have been, and no good reason why such a finding should not appear on the trial record.

---

[155] In his *History of the Criminal Law of England, Vol II* (Burt Franklin, New York, 1883), 175, J.F. Stephen proposed an intermediate verdict of 'guilty, but his power of self control was diminished by insanity'. However, as Nigel Walker notes (*Crime and Insanity in England, Vol I*, 147), 'no notice was taken of the suggestion'.

[156] Morse, 'Diminished Capacity', 267.

[157] N. Walker, *'Butler* v. *The CLRC and Others'* [1981] Crim LR 596, 597. As a way of doing this, Walker suggests either that the permissible prison sentence be reduced by half or 'that no determinate sentence should exceed, say, three years for an indictable offence and three months for a non-indictable one'.

[158] N. Walker, 'McNaughtan's Innings: a Century and a Half Not Out' (1993) 4 *Journal of Forensic Psychiatry* 207, 209.

[159] J. Horder, 'Pleading Involuntary Lack of Capacity' (1993) 62 CLJ 289, 316. Horder suggests that these powers should be analogous to those contained in the Criminal Procedure (Insanity and Unfitness to Plead) Act 1991.

INFANTICIDE

An offence which is somewhat analogous to diminished responsibility, but was introduced earlier, is that of infanticide. The Infanticide Act 1938[160] permits murder to be reduced to infanticide in cases where the mother by any wilful act or omission causes the death of her child under the age of twelve months 'but at the time of the act or omission the balance of her mind was disturbed by reason of her not having fully recovered from the effect of giving birth to the child or by reason of the effect of lactation consequent upon the birth of the child'.[161] This statutory provision has been the subject of considerable criticism, a recent example of which was referred to by the Select Committee of the House of Lords on Murder and Life Imprisonment when it noted: 'the suggestion that the offence of infanticide is no longer necessary, and that the defence of diminished responsibility could be used instead'.[162] This particular suggestion, originating in 1975 in the Butler Report,[163] worried the Criminal Law Revision Committee, which recommended altering the present law in such a way as to extend infanticide to cover 'environmental or other stresses'.[164] This suggestion has since found its way into the Draft Criminal Code which provides in clause 64(1):

A woman who, but for this action, would be guilty of murder or manslaughter of her child is not guilty of murder or manslaughter, but is guilty of infanticide, if her act is done when the child is under the age of twelve months and when the balance of her mind is disturbed by reason of the effect of giving birth or of circumstances consequent upon the birth.[165]

The Select Committee was clearly ambivalent about what should be done in respect of reforming the Infanticide Act, stating: 'the Committee makes no recommendation on whether the law should be changed in England and Wales, but suggests that the matter should be further considered'.[166] Since

---

[160] This replaced the Infanticide Act 1922 which had restricted the offence to cases where the woman caused 'the death of her newly born child', a phrase which was held to be inapplicable to a 35 day-old child in *R. v. O'Donoghue* (1927) 20 Cr App R 132. For discussion of the historical development of infanticide, see Walker, *Crime and Insanity in England, Vol 1* (Edinburgh University Press, Edinburgh, 1968) ch. 7.

[161] Infanticide Act 1938, s 1(1).

[162] House of Lords, *Report of the Select Committee on Murder and Life Imprisonment* 1988 (H.L. Paper 78), Vol 1, para 84, referring to the memorandum given in written evidence by Feminists Against Eugenics at ibid. Vol 3, 551. For further criticism, see K. O'Donovan, 'The Medicalisation of Infanticide' [1984] Crim LR 259.

[163] Butler Report, para 19.27.

[164] Criminal Law Revision Committee, Fourteenth Report, *Offences Against the Person*, Cmnd 7844 (1980), para 103.

[165] Law Commission, *A Criminal Code for England and Wales*, Law Com No 177 (1989) Vol 1, Report and Draft Criminal Code Bill at clause 64 (1).

[166] House of Lords, *Select Committee on Murder and Life Imprisonment*, op. cit., para 84.

these words were written, new research findings have cast more light on the workings of the Infanticide Act. Accordingly, it is proposed to discuss these and other findings before considering the implications for reform.

THE OPERATION OF THE INFANTICIDE ACT

In his comprehensive study of 'Women who kill their Children',[167] d'Orban examined 89 such women during a six-year period from 1970–5. There were 109 relevant victims of which 48 (44%) were aged under one year. These cases resulted in 23 infanticide verdicts which included 10 guilty verdicts out of 11 cases of neonaticide,[168] and 10 guilty verdicts out of 15 battering cases where the women had killed suddenly owing to loss of temper. It is interesting to note that the final three cases included the only *two* mothers who were regarded as mentally ill. With regard to disposal, d'Orban found that:

> Of the 23 subjects convicted of Infanticide 18 were put on probation (7 with a condition of treatment . . .). Two (both battering mothers) were sentenced to imprisonment (for 18 months and two and a half years). Of the remaining three subjects one was given a nominal 1 day sentence, another was conditionally discharged and the third (suffering from a peurperal depressive illness) was admitted to hospital . . .[169]

In a more recent study,[170] Home Office statistics revealed that from 1982–8, 214 children under one year of age were the victims of homicide. Of those, 45 (21%) were neonaticides and in each case the mother was the chief suspect. The majority of these mothers (29) were not indicted while the others, with the exception of one acquittal and one finding of diminished responsibility, were all convicted of infanticide and received probation. When compared to the fathers, it was interesting to find not only that the fathers were convicted of more serious offences, infanticide being unavailable to men, but also that the fathers received stiffer penalties.[171] The authors conclude that their data 'suggest that parenthood places mothers and fathers at risk of becoming homicidal and that for mothers, but not fathers, this has been recognised and responded to by society with some compassion'.[172] This difference in treatment between mothers and fathers is confirmed by Wilcynski and Morris,[173] who conclude after an analysis

---

[167] P.T. d'Orban, 'Women who Kill their Children' (1974) 134 *British Journal of Psychiatry* 560.
[168] Ibid. 561. Defined in the study as women who killed or attempted to kill their children within 24 hours of birth. In the eleventh case there was no infanticide verdict as the child survived.   [169] Ibid. 567.
[170] M.N. Marks and R. Kumar, 'Infanticide in England and Wales' (1993) 33 *Medicine, Science and the Law* 329.
[171] Ibid. 336–7.   [172] Ibid. 339.
[173] A. Wilczynski and A. Morris, 'Parents who Kill their Children' [1993] Crim LR 31.

of criminal statistics from 1982–9, including 493 homicides where the principal suspect was a parent, that 'mothers were less likely than fathers to be convicted of murder or to be sentenced to imprisonment and were more likely to be given probation and psychiatric dispositions'.[174] However, as the authors concede, it is unclear what the reason are for these discrepancies.[175]

In a final study which attempts to shed light on the operation of the Infanticide Act, permission was obtained from the Crown Prosecution Service to examine the files of 36 females who had killed one of their children under the age of twelve months during the years 1982 to 1985.[176] In addition, the files in a further eleven cases were made available. These cases consisted of three females who had killed one of their children over the age of twelve months, one female who had killed another person's child, and seven males who had each killed very young children, two of whom were other people's children. It was hoped that an examination of these additional files might give some wider information on the consequences of killing very young children.

The results reveal a broadly similar picture as that painted by the other studies.[177] Once again the women were charged and convicted of less serious offences, with 14 infanticide convictions being recorded, 12 of which led to probation. However, by comparison, although all seven males avoided a murder conviction,[178] it is noticeable that, of the six convictions in these cases for manslaughter resulting in sentences of imprisonment, all except two were males; these men received on average 4.75 years imprisonment, with the other male receiving a hospital order with restrictions. There were in addition 13 cases which were not proceeded with; in all of them the accused was female.

In its discussion of infanticide, the Butler Report noted that a charge under the 1938 Act offered the woman two advantages over a plea of diminished responsibility.[179] The first was that it permitted the prosecution to charge infanticide rather than to proceed with murder and the second was that by so doing the prosecution conceded the mental disturbance which the woman would not have to prove. With regard to this first advantage, it is clear from my sample of cases that this was the way in which the vast majority of infanticide convictions were obtained, with 13 being the result of initial charges under the 1938 Act and only two being cases where murder was initially charged and the woman was later allowed to plead guilty to infanticide. In none of these cases was a jury

---

[174] Wilczynski and Morris, 'Parents who Kill their Children', 35.

[175] See also Marks and Kumar, 'Infanticide in England and Wales', 339.

[176] See R.D. Mackay, 'The Consequences of Killing Very Young Children' [1993] Crim LR 21.   [177] For detail, see ibid. 22–8.

[178] Two were acquitted.   [179] Butler Report, para 19.26.

required to consider the medical evidence, which was indeed conceded by the prosecution.

However, it is clear that there were a number of additional cases of potential infanticide, manslaughter, and concealment of birth which were never prosecuted and it is more than likely that this remains an important method of dealing with such cases.[180] This of course comes as no surprise, as cases which may lead to an infanticide or related charge tend to be of the type where prosecutorial discretion is likely to be exercised in the female defendant's favour.

In his earlier study, d'Orban concluded that for infanticide 'the degree of abnormality is much less than that required to substantiate 'abnormality of mind' amounting to substantially diminished responsibility under section 2 of the Homicide Act 1957',[181] a conclusion echoed by the Criminal Law Revision Committee.[182] While there was a small number of cases within my sample where psychiatrists considered that the defendant satisfied both statutes, there were others where this was clearly not the case. Indeed the overall impression gained from an examination of the psychiatric reports used in support of infanticide was that there was little room to doubt that the criteria within the 1938 Act were being used primarily as a legal device for avoiding the mandatory penalty and thus ensuring that leniency could be meted out in appropriate cases.[183]

Further, it is inaccurate to refer to the use of 'criteria' within the 1938 Act at all, since the only criterion within the 1938 Act referred to in the reports was the one relating to the effects of giving birth, no mention being made by any psychiatrist of 'lactation'. However, even this former criterion in a number of cases received little analysis or discussion by psychiatrists and in some cases, after prompting by the DPP, was quoted verbatim as a triggering device for an infanticide charge.

With regard to the other cases, it is interesting to note that, of the six females who were convicted of manslaughter, only one was convicted by reason of diminished responsibility. As far as the others were concerned, two convictions were based on gross negligence through neglect and three on the unlawful act doctrine within constructive manslaughter. These last cases account for the only two prison sentences given to the female defendants. In the first, the defendant, who had children of her own, was looking after another's nine-week old child, and struck it several times to stop it crying. She was convicted of manslaughter and sentenced to five years'

---

[180] This point is confirmed by Wilczynski and Morris, 'Parents who Kill their Children', 35. However, by way of contrast, Marks and Kumar, 'Infanticide in England and Wales', 335 found 'that there were no differences between mothers and fathers in their likelihood of being indicted or not'. However, they do not reveal the nature of the charges which were not proceeded with.   [181] d'Orban, 'Women Who Kill Their Children', 570.

[182] Criminal Law Revision Committee, *Offences Against the Person*, para 103.

[183] See R.D. Mackay, 'The Consequences of Killing Very Young Children', 29.

imprisonment. In the other, the defendant was alleged to have killed her twenty-two month old child by kicking her in the stomach. However, there were causation problems and she received a suspended sentence of two years with supervision by a probation officer.

It was clear from this sample that, as far as the females were concerned, these were viewed overwhelmingly as tragic cases which the prosecution was prepared to deal with leniently,[184] while the males, although avoiding murder convictions, were considered much more culpable. This of course leads on to the major criticism of infanticide and the way in which the law labels females who kill their children. For not only has it long been recognised that the 1938 Act criteria are psychiatrically unsound,[185] but also it has been consistently argued that 'the assumptions within the [1938] statute, i.e. of pathology related to female biology, are completely unacceptable'.[186] In this connection it is important to note the unique feature of infanticide: that it requires no causal relationship between the mother's mental imbalance and the killing. Rather, the 1938 Act merely requires that the imbalance coincides with the offence and then proceeds on the basis that once this is shown, then it can be presumed that the woman was not fully responsible. This 'medicalisation of the crime',[187] has come under increasing attack as failing to recognise that it is stress and environmental factors which are more often than not in issue in such cases.

With this in mind it is clear that an analysis of my sample lends no support to the fact that diminished responsibility is either being widely used in cases which might otherwise be infanticide, or that as it stands the 1957 Act would safely cover all cases which presently fall within the 1938 Act.[188] In conclusion, therefore, if the lenient consequences which women receive when convicted under the 1938 Act are to be ensured,[189] then there appears to be a continued need for a separate offence of infanticide. The question which then arises is whether clause 64 of the Draft Criminal Code is an appropriate vehicle to secure this.

---

[184] See Wilczynski and Morris, 'Parents who Kill their Children'. But compare Wilczynski, 'Images of Woman who Kill their Infants: The Mad and the Bad' (1991) 2 *Women and Criminal Justice* 71 who discusses 22 prosecuted cases of maternal infant-killing of which eight received prison sentences ranging between 18 months and seven years.

[185] R. Bluglass, 'Infanticide' (1978) *Bulletin of the Royal College of Psychiatrists*, 149.

[186] See e.g. the memorandum by Feminists Against Eugenics, set out in House of Lords, *Report of the Select Committee on Murder and Life Imprisonment*, Vol 3, 551.

[187] O'Donovan, 'The Medicalisation of Infanticide', 262.

[188] See also D. Maier-Katkin and R. Ogle, 'A Rationale for Infanticide Laws' [1993] Crim LR 903, 909–11.

[189] This lenient approach has been endorsed by the Court of Appeal in *R. v. Sainsbury* [1990] Crim LR 348 where the Court was informed that of the 59 infanticide convictions between 1979 and 1988, none had received custodial sentences. In the opinion of the court this established pattern of sentencing should not be departed from. For a similar approach to analogous cases dealt with as diminished responsibility, see *R. v. Lewis* [1990] Crim LR 348.

The vital change which clause 64 would make is to implement the Criminal Law Revision Committee's proposal that a reference to 'circumstances consequent upon the birth' be included. Although this has received broad support, it is not without its critics. For example, in its evidence to the Select Committee on Murder and Life Imprisonment, Justice considered that these words were too broad and concluded that 'in order to maintain the present protection given by the law to babies, we think that the offence of infanticide should remain as properly defined in the 1938 Act'.[190] Further, the link between mental imbalance and childbirth has recently been defended by Maier-Katkin and Ogle, who consider that 'even if most of the women who kill their own children do not suffer from psychoses or other extreme mental illnesses, many do; and others probably suffer from the types of emotional disturbances contemplated by the statute'.[191] In this context it is interesting to note that in New Zealand infanticide extends to cases where the balance of the accused's mind was disturbed 'by reason of any disorder consequent upon childbirth'.[192]

A second issue of importance relating to clause 64 of the Draft Criminal Code is why, if infanticide is to be extended to include stress and social factors, it should be restricted to mothers. Thus, the question has been posed: 'is it fair, for example, that fathers who might also experience a disturbance of the balance of the mind in response to changes in social circumstances (perhaps intensified sleep deprivation) cannot claim protection under the Act?'[193] This is a difficult point as it can certainly be argued that fathers ought to be so included. However, it seems most unlikely that any such proposal would be favourably received. And, in defence of the continued exclusion of fathers from infanticide, it has been pointed out that current practice continues to reflect the fact 'that childbearing women may . . . be peculiarly vulnerable to social and environmental adversity.'[194]

Finally, clause 64 retains the twelve month time-limit for infanticide. Again the question arises as to whether this is justified. Certainly, the Royal College of Psychiatrists thought not and recommended that the Act be changed to include children up to five years of age, provided the youngest victim was under twelve months.[195] This suggestion was designed to cover cases where the mother killed all her children at once and accords with d'Orban's finding that multiple victims were not uncommon.[196]

---

[190] House of Lords, *Report of the Select Committee on Murder and Life Imprisonment*, Vol II, 175.   [191] Maier-Katkin and Ogle, 'A Rationale for Infanticide Laws', 909.
[192] S 178 of the New Zealand Crimes Act 1961.
[193] Maier-Katkin and Ogle 'A Rationale for Infanticide Laws', 913.
[194] R. Kumar and M. Marks, 'Infanticide and the Law in England and Wales', ch. 20, J.A. Hamilton and P.N. Harberger (eds.), *Postpartum Psychiatric Illness: A Picture Puzzle* (University of Pennsylvania Press, Philadelphia, 1992).
[195] R. Bluglass, 'Infanticide', (1978) *Bulletin of the Royal College of Psychiatrists* 139, 141.
[196] d'Orban, 'Women Who Kill Their Children', 564.

However, what is not clear from this study is how many of these multiple victims were under twelve months of age at the time of the killings. In short, it seems difficult to justify the retention of the twelve-month limit while at the same time recommending the extension of infanticide to children up to five years of age. Here again, it is interesting to note that in New Zealand the offence of infanticide applies where the mother kills any of her children under the age of ten.[197] Further, the New Zealand courts have been generous in their interpretation of the offence by applying it to a child of whom the accused had been appointed guardian.[198] However, it has to be remembered that New Zealand has no diminished responsibility plea, which may go some way to explaining the willingness of that jurisdiction to extend the offence of infanticide to cover older children. It is worth noting here that in his study d'Orban found that diminished responsibility rather than infanticide was the most frequent verdict and also that 18% (16 subjects) 'offered no "psychiatric" defence and were convicted of ordinary manslaughter on the grounds of lack of intent to kill'.[199] Further, only 11% (12 victims) of d'Orban's sample were over five years of age; 48 (44%) were aged under one and 49 (45%) were aged from one year to under five years, which would tend to support the notion that the age of five years might be a realistic solution for any newly formulated infanticide offence.

CONCLUDING REMARKS

Both diminished responsibility and infanticide represent a pragmatic approach towards the use of mental conditions as a vehicle for considering the partial or reduced criminal responsibility of the accused. Neither section 2 of the Homicide Act nor the provisions of the Infanticide Act can be described as satisfactory. Both contain glaring anomalies and are clearly out of step with current psychiatric thinking. However, from a purely practical point of view, it has been strongly argued that diminished responsibility and infanticide work well and are worthy of retention.[200] Whether they should be retained in their current forms, however, must be open to doubt, especially having regard to the fact that the Draft Criminal Code readily endorses the Criminal Law Revision Committee's reform proposals.

---

[197] S 178 of the New Zealand Crimes Act 1961.

[198] See *R. v. P* [1991] NZLR 116. At the time of the killing the accused was also caring for her eighteen month old daughter and was breastfeeding her youngest child who was aged six months. However, she only killed the five year old child to whom she was not related.

[199] d'Orban, 'Women Who Kill Their Children', 566.

[200] For support of the defences of diminished responsibility and infanticide, see Griew, 'The Future of Diminished Responsibility' and Maier-Katkin and Ogle, 'A Rationale for Infanticide Laws' respectively.

While these changes might secure some improvement over the existing legal frameworks,[201] they do nothing to extend diminished responsibility beyond murder and continue to restrict infanticide to mothers who kill their own children under the age of twelve months. In principle it is difficult to accept such restrictions and it has been argued above that serious consideration should be given, firstly to extending diminished responsibility to other offences in order to ensure that there is a formal mechanism for the court to take account of the accused's reduced responsibility; and, secondly, to permitting an infanticide conviction to be returned where the mother kills one or more of her children who are under five years of age.

As the law stands, the issue of partial responsibility in non-fatal cases tends to be a matter which is relegated to the sentencing phase of the trial. For example, there can be little doubt that in many cases where the court gives a hospital order, the accused's mental disorder may well have been active at the time of the offence. Why then should the court not be permitted to consider the issue of partial responsibility during a trial for non-fatal or sexual offences in much the same way as occurs when a defendant pleads guilty to manslaughter by reason of diminished responsibility? At present, English law offers no practical mental disorder defence in non-fatal cases and, unless and until the Criminal Procedure (Insanity and Unfitness to Plead) Act 1991 begins to affect practice,[202] it is surely wrong that the courts should continue to record full convictions in these cases even if a medical disposal is chosen.[203]

---

[201] But see the warning by Griew ibid.

[202] For discussion of the operation of the 1991 Act in respect of the insanity defence, see Chapter 2.

[203] Even if the insanity defence becomes more widely used as a result of the flexibility of disposal introduced by the 1991 Act, the above argument remains compelling.

5

Unfitness to Plead

The law on disability in relation to the trial, or 'unfitness to plead' as it is more commonly known, has received scant attention in recent years.[1] The last major review of this complex and neglected area of criminal law was in 1975 when the Committee on Mentally Abnormal Offenders,[2] (known as the Butler Report) recommended sweeping reforms. However, as was recently pointed out by the Law Commission in its commentary on the Draft Criminal Code:

some of the Committee's procedural proposals were controversial. A consultative document issued by the Home Office in 1978 referred in particular to serious doubts as to the practicability of a recommendation that if the defendant is found to be under disability there should nevertheless be a 'trial of the facts'—at once if there is no prospect of the defendant's recovering, or as soon (during periods of adjournment not exceeding six months in total) as he may prove unresponsive to treatment.[3]

As is well known, no further action has been taken on any of the Butler Report's recommendations relating to fitness to plead or the insanity defence. In addition it is interesting to note that, although the Law Commission expressed the 'hope that the important matter of disability will be further considered as soon as possible with a view to reform',[4] the Commission itself effectively side-stepped any such immediate consideration of this area of the law by deciding to place disability in the projected Part III of the Code, rather than in Part I as was favoured by the Code team. However, the Commission's hope of reform has now become a reality with the enactment of the Criminal Procedure (Insanity and Unfitness to Plead) Act 1991.

It is proposed in this Chapter to consider the legal position governing unfitness to plead in the light of theoretical debate and recent empirical research. This will be followed by a discussion of the 1991 Act including the results of the first year of its operation.

[1] For an historical discussion, see N. Walker, *Crime and Insanity in England*, Vol 1 (Edinburgh University Press, Edinburgh, 1968), ch. 14.
[2] Report of the Committee on Mentally Abnormal Offenders, Cmnd 6244 (1975).
[3] The Law Commission, *A Criminal Code for England and Wales* (1989), Vol 2, para 11.7.   [4] Ibid. para 11.8.

The Rationale of Unfitness to Plead

It is a fundamental principle of the criminal law that an accused person is entitled to an impartial and fair trial, an important feature of which is the right to instruct or even conduct his own defence. It has long been recognised that, if the accused is clearly incapable of understanding or answering the allegations against him, then an ordinary trial should not take place. For example, in his *Commentaries* Blackstone stated: 'if a man in his sound memory commits a capital offence, and, before arraignment for it, he becomes mad, he ought not to be arraigned for it, because he is not able to plead to it with that advice and caution that he ought'.[5] Although there has been some recent criticism about the way in which the current common law test of unfitness seems exclusively concerned with intellectual ability rather than the broader notion on 'insanity',[6] there is no doubt that the authoritative definition continues to be that given by Baron Alderson in *R. v. Pritchard* when he stated that the accused must be 'of sufficient intellect to comprehend the course of proceedings in the trial so as to make a proper defence, to challenge a juror to whom he might wish to object and to comprehend the details of the evidence'.[7] Although this test was developed in a case dealing with a deaf mute, it has been applied to a wide variety of conditions including numerous forms of mental disorder, but excluding those who suffer from amnesia as to the events surrounding the offence but are otherwise capable of satisfying the *Pritchard* criteria.[8] However, before the application of the test is discussed it seems appropriate to consider why the law adopts such a paternalistic stance in relation to those who are adjudged to be unfit to plead.

The Theory Behind the Practice

Clearly to deny an accused person his opportunity to a full trial of all the issues in respect of the charges he is facing is a very serious infringement of his rights. So much so that it has led some commentators to advocate the abolition of the unfitness doctrine. Thus Norval Morris has suggested replacing unfitness with rules of court which would enable trial continuances,[9] adding: 'just as in exceptional cases we take the amnesiac to criminal trial, and those whose memory fails them because of the long time

[5] William Blackstone, *Commentaries* (9th edn., 1783), Vol 4, 24.
[6] See D. Grubin, 'What Constitutes Fitness to Plead?' [1993] Crim LR 748.
[7] (1836) 7 C & P 303.
[8] See *R. v. Podola* [1960] IQB 325. The Butler Committee at paras 10.4–10.11 gave full consideration to including amnesia within the scope of unfitness to plead but the majority considered that the objections to including it outweighed the arguments in favour.
[9] N. Morris, *Madness and the Criminal Law* (1969), 33–53. See also B. Winick, 'Restructuring Competency to Stand Trial' (1985) 32 UCLA Law Review 921.

between the events at issue and the trial, just as we take to trial one whose disruptive behavior precludes his physical presence . . . or as we pursue a criminal trial though important witnesses are dead or unavailable, so in exceptional circumstance we should take some unrestorable incompetents to trial'.[10]

Although such calls for abolition seem to have gone unheeded, it is important to assess what in the nature of the unfitness doctrine is regarded as so vital to the criminal process. When one turns to consider the literature which deals with the theoretical aspects of the unfitness doctrine, it soon becomes apparent that, so far as England is concerned, this topic has attracted very little discussion. Even in the United States of America similar comments have been made about 'the sparse theoretical literature on the competence of criminal defendants',[11] and the fact that although 'unfitness to stand trial is a frequent plea as compared to the insanity plea . . . yet it has received scant scholarly attention compared to the prodigious academic wrestling with the criminal responsibility of the mentally ill'.[12] One notable exception so far as England is concerned has been the contribution of Antony Duff who has sought to explore the nature of unfitness. In his analysis Duff concludes that 'the reason why such a person should not be tried is not merely that this might lead to an inaccurate verdict, or to distressing scenes in court . . . , but that his "trial" would be a travesty: we would be attempting to treat as a rational agent, answerable for his actions, someone who *cannot* answer for them'.[13] As part of the rational agent's required capacity Duff would include the ability 'to understand the moral dimensions of the law and of his own actions'.[14] However, this may be to go too far, for there are many defendants who have warped standards of morality but who are clearly fit to plead. However, Duff continues by making a distinction between one 'who understands the claims which the law makes on him, but refuses to accept those claims or to ascribe any legitimate authority to the law' and one who '*cannot* see the law as . . . anything more than a set of orders backed by threats which give him prudential reasons for obedience'.[15] The former is clearly fit to plead while

[10] Morris, *Madness and the Criminal Law*, 48.
[11] R.J. Bonnie, 'The Competence of Criminal Defendants: Beyond *Dusky* and *Drope*' (1993) 47 *University of Miami Law Review* 539, 541.
[12] Morris, *Madness and the Criminal Law*, 37, where it is also remarked that the American Bar Association Commission on the Mentally Disabled has estimated that 'more than a hundred times as many defendants are found incompetent to stand trial . . . [as] are acquitted on the grounds of insanity'. See also H.J. Steadman, *Beating a Rap?* (University of Chicago Press, Chicago, 1979) who considers (ibid. 4) that the 'best estimate of the number of people diverted as incompetent each year is around 9,000. This group represents about one-quarter of the approximately 36,000 for whom the issue is raised.'
[13] R.A. Duff, *Trials and Punishments* (Cambridge University Press, Cambridge, 1986), 119 (emphasis in original).
[14] Ibid. 120.   [15] Ibid. (emphasis in original).

the latter is not as 'he cannot understand the trial for what it purports to be'.[16] Clearly this goes well beyond the cognitive test of unfitness formulated in *Pritchard* as it would allow for the consideration of the moral and emotional capacities of the defendant. As such, it is more akin to the test adopted by the United States Supreme Court in *Dusky* v. US, which requires that the defendant have 'sufficient present ability to consult his lawyer with a reasonable degree of rational understanding—and whether he has a rational as well as a factual understanding of the proceedings against him'.[17]

It follows that mere factual understanding about the charges and the legal process, together with ability to consult with one's lawyer are not sufficient within the *Dusky* framework. Rather the rational understanding component adds the need for 'capacity to appreciate one's situation as a defendant in a criminal prosecution'.[18]

Many commentators seem to agree that there are three separate reasons for not permitting the trial of those who are unfit to plead. Bonnie has recently labelled these as 'dignity, reliability, and autonomy'.[19] The first concerns the need to maintain the moral dignity of the legal process by ensuring that those who are the subject of criminal proceedings understand their nature and purpose so as to be accountable rather than mere 'objects of the state's effort to carry out its promises'.[20] The second reason is aimed at the danger of convicting those who might be innocent, since those who are unfit to plead have no opportunity to rebut the charges against them or to otherwise defend themselves. In formulating the third and final reason, Bonnie has drawn 'a key conceptual distinction between a foundational concept of "competence to assist counsel" and a contextualised concept of "decisional competence" ',[21] the latter being 'an inherent, though derivative, feature of any legal doctrine that prescribes a norm of client *autonomy*'.[22] The notion here is that 'a defendant who is provisionally competent to assist counsel may not be competent to make specific decisions that are encountered as the process unfolds. Decision-making involves cognitive tasks in addition to those required for assisting in one's defense . . . including abilities to understand and choose among alternative courses of action'.[23] According to Bonnie, decisional incompetence should not necessarily mean a finding of unfitness to plead as 'in no other legal context does a finding of decisional incompetence have such paralysing consequences'.[24] Instead a more flexible approach should be adopted to deal with such problems, including recourse to surrogate decision-makers. Such an approach has the merit of promoting the autonomy of the defendant and might help, as well as protect, those who are mildly mentally handicapped or deaf and dumb.

---

[16] Duff, *Trials and Punishments*, 120.   [17] 362 US 402 (1960).
[18] Bonnie, 'The Competence of Criminal Defendants', 554.   [19] Ibid. 551.
[20] Ibid.   [21] Ibid. 554.   [22] Ibid. 553.   [23] Ibid. 556.   [24] Ibid. 557.

Certainly, as far as English law is concerned, no real effort has been made to consider decisional incapacity in relation to unfitness to plead, although the Law Commission has recently been giving this matter serious consideration within the broad context of the civil law and has arrived at the following provisional definition of incapacity:

A person should be considered unable to take a decision in question (or decisions of the type in question) if he or she is unable to understand an explanation in broad terms and simple language of the basic information relevant to taking it, including information about the reasonably foreseeable consequences of taking or failing to take it, or to retain the information for long enough to take an effective decision.[25]

It need hardly be pointed out that deciding whether to plead guilty, or whether to retain one's lawyer or defend oneself, may be some of the most important decisions which a person is ever likely to make. It may therefore be that the exclusive focus of English law on the intellectual abilities of the accused in respect of the trial process is misplaced, and that greater efforts should be made to consider whether those who have such capacity also possess capacity to make the decisions that may be required of them. Whether such an approach might be practical will be considered during the discussion of reform proposals, but first it is time to consider how the original law on unfitness to plead had previously been operating in England and the reasons for the enactment of the Criminal Procedure (Insanity and Unfitness to Plead) Act 1991.

CRITICISMS LEADING TO THE 1991 ACT

Prior to the 1991 Act, the law of disability in relation to the trial was governed by the Criminal Procedure (Insanity) Act 1964, which mandated indeterminate hospitalization for all those found to be unfit to plead in the Crown Court. The issue of unfitness could be raised by the prosecution, the defence or the judge who, in his discretion, might delay the trial of unfitness until the close of the prosecution case thus enabling the defence to submit that there was no case to answer. These provisions had been the subject of considerable criticism.[26] In relation to the first provision on mandatory hospitalization, it was argued that the inflexibility of disposal was unjustified. In this respect the Butler Report commented: 'as things stand at present it is not in the interests of the defendant to seek the

---

[25] The Law Commission, Consultation Paper No 128 *Mentally Incapacitated Adults and Decision-Making—A New Jurisdiction* (HMSO 1993), para 3.24. See now the Law Commission's Final Report, *Mental Incapacity* (1995), paras 3.16–3.18.

[26] See e.g. C. Emmins, 'Unfitness to Plead: Thoughts Prompted by Glenn Pearson's Case' [1986] Crim LR 604.

protection of a disability plea unless the charge is very serious. If the trial went ahead he might be acquitted altogether, but even if convicted he could hope to receive from the court a more acceptable sentence than committal to hospital for an indeterminate period'.[27] The second provision concerning postponement was also regarded by the Butler Report as inadequate owing to the fact that it gave the defence no opportunity to present evidence and that in general there was no provision for the facts of the case to be investigated by the court. Further criticisms surrounded not only the lack of any statutory criteria for fitness to plead, the existing law continuing to rely on the test laid down by Baron Alderson as long ago as 1836 in *Pritchard*,[28] but also the fact that these legal criteria 'do not fit neatly into any diagnostic categories'.[29]

A final source of criticism concerned the powers of the Home Secretary under the 1964 Act.[30] Apart from specifying the hospital to which the person found under disability must be admitted, the Home Secretary alone had power to remit for trial any patient whose condition had improved, provided he was satisfied, 'after consultation with the responsible medical officer . . . that the said person can properly be tried'.[31] The Butler Report noted that this power was 'sparingly' used,[32] which prompted the Report to comment in relation to those found under disability: 'a person so committed to hospital must remain there, untried, until the Home Secretary decides otherwise, and this may mean a very long period of detention, even detention for life'.[32a]

A crucial question was whether these criticisms were fully justified. Until recently, little research had been conducted into the operation of the law on disability in relation to the trial, which led one commentator to conclude that 'there are no published studies from England and Wales of cohorts of unfit defendants'.[33]

However, this gap has now been filled by a study of all cases of unfitness to plead for a period of fourteen years between 1976 and 1989.[34]

---

[27] Butler Report, para 10.18.   [28] (1836) 7 C & P 303.
[29] D. Chiswick, 'Fitness to Stand Trial and Plead, Mutism and Deafness', in R. Bluglass and P. Bowden (eds.) *Principles and Practice of Forensic Psychiatry* (Churchill Livingstone, London, 1990), ch. 5 of section 3.
[30] Although the 1991 Act retains these powers, on which see below, they will be much less frequently used as they are now only applicable in cases where the disposal is equivalent to a restriction order.   [31] S 5(4) Criminal Procedure (Insanity) Act 1964.
[32] Butler Report, para 10.17.
[32a] Ibid. para 10.18. For the truth behind this remark, see R.D. Mackay and T. Ward, 'The Long-Term Detention of Those Found Unfit to Plead and Legally Insane' (1994), 34 *British Journal of Criminology* 30.   [33] Chiswick, 'Fitness to Stand Trial and Plead', 174.
[34] R.D. Mackay *The Operation of the Criminal Procedure (Insanity) Act 1964—An Empirical Study of Unfitness to Plead and the Insanity Defence* (De Montfort University Law School Monograph, 1991). For a shorter version, see R.D. Mackay, 'The Decline of Disability in Relation to the Trial' [1991] Crim LR 87. For a contemporary study, see D.H. Grubin, 'Unfit to Plead in England and Wales 1976–1988: A Survey' (1991) 158 *British Journal of Psychiatry* 540.

The only exception to the prior lack of data was the recent study by Larkin and Collins who examined seventy-seven pre-trial psychiatric reports prepared on thirty-one patients who had been found unfit to plead and admitted to the special hospital at Rampton. As a result of their findings the authors concluded that: 'it was quite common for the issue of fitness to plead to be ignored altogether in cases where it would seem reasonable for the matter to have been commented upon. In addition, in a significant number of cases where an opinion about the issue was given, the criteria used were either unclear or incorrect'.[35] Although this study is interesting insofar as it reveals that psychiatrists may 'have a poor understanding of the issues surrounding unfitness to plead',[36] it does not attempt to give an overall picture of the current operation of the law in relation to unfitness to plead.

Accordingly, permission was given by the Home Office to examine the documentation in all cases of unfitness to plead for a period of fourteen years between 1976 and 1989.[37] What follows is an analysis of the findings of that research followed by a discussion of the changes to the existing legal position implemented by the 1991 Act.

RESEARCH RESULTS

INTRODUCTION

During the fourteen-year period researched from 1976 to 1989, there was a total of 302 findings of disability in relation to trial. While the greatest number of findings of unfitness to plead in any single year was 39 in 1980, what is immediately noticeable from Table 5.1 is the reduction in the number of annual findings of disability to a mere 11 in 1989. As far as sex and age distribution was concerned, there were 269 males compared to 33 females, with a majority of 192 males and 19 females falling within the age group 20 to 39. With regard to criminal records, 203 (67.2%) of the sample had previous convictions while 252 (83.4%) had some form of psychiatric history.

A breakdown of the criminal charges which resulted in a finding of disability is give in Table 5.2. As might be expected, there is a high number of offences against the person; including rape and robbery, they account for almost a half of the charges (48.9%), in addition to which there were 23 (7.6%) offences of indecent assault and 34 (11.3%) offences of arson. However, what is perhaps surprising is the number of Theft Act offences,

[35] E.P. Larkin and P.J. Collins, 'Fitness to Plead and Psychiatric Reports' (1989) 29 *Medicine, Science and the Law* 26, 31.   [36] Ibid. 26.
[37] Sincere thanks are owed to C3 division of the Home Office for permitting me access to relevant documentation and for their consistent co-operation throughout this research.

TABLE 5.1 *Disability Findings 1976–89*

	Frequency	As % of Sample
1976	38	12.6
1977	20	6.6
1978	14	4.6
1979	24	7.9
1980	39	12.9
1981	28	9.3
1982	34	11.3
1983	18	6.0
1984	18	6.0
1985	17	5.6
1986	12	4.0
1987	16	5.3
1988	13	4.3
1989	11	3.6
TOTAL	302	100.0

TABLE 5.2 *Disability Findings 1976–89—Types of Charge*

	Frequency	As % of Sample
Murder	27	8.9
Attempted murder	6	2.0
Manslaughter	1	0.3
S. 18 assault	32	10.6
Other assault	68	22.5
Rape	8	2.6
Indecent assault	23	7.6
Other sexual offence	3	1.0
Burglary	29	9.6
Robbery	6	2.0
Theft	21	7.0
Deception	16	5.3
Other dishonesty offence	5	1.7
Arson	34	11.3
Criminal damage	8	2.6
Other	15	5.0
TOTAL	302	100.0

TABLE 5.3   *Disability Findings 1976–89—Diagnostic Groups*

	Frequency	As % of Sample
Schizophrenia	169	56.0
Mental impairment	64	21.2
Brain damage	6	2.0
Dementia	11	3.6
Personality disorder	2	0.7
Psychosis	32	10.6
Deaf	5	1.7
Amnesia	3	1.0
Other	6	2.0
None	4	1.3
TOTAL	302	100.0

together with their relatively trivial nature. Prior to this research, it was supposed that unfitness was only used in cases of serious offences.[38] However, in practice this was clearly not the case, for in many instances of disability finding, Theft Act offences were committed by destitute and mentally ill defendants unable to pay for meals or services. In addition many of the offences in the 'other assault' category were minor inflictions of bodily harm resulting from bizarre behaviour and leading to unprovoked attacks some of which were on parents or close relatives. On a number of other occasions, the defendant assaulted the police after they had been called in response to minor breaches of the peace or other strange behaviour.

With regard to diagnostic groups, schizophrenia dominated, with over 50% of the sample falling within this diagnosis. The other diagnostic groups are given in Table 5.3 and it is interesting to note that in three cases there was amnesia which led to a finding of disability. In view of the Court of Appeal's decision in *R. v. Podola*[39] this might seem an unexpected result.

As far as *multiple findings* of disability were concerned, these arose in 16 cases. The majority of these were cases where an earlier finding of unfitness was followed by a subsequent finding of unfitness but for a separate offence. This occurred in 13 of these cases but in only eight of the 13 did both unfitness findings take place within the research period, the other five being cases where the first finding took place before 1979. In the other three cases of the 16, one was remitted for trial for a minor assault and found unfit to plead on a second occasion for the same offence.

[38] See the remark in the Butler Report, para. 10 18.   [39] [1960] 1 QB 325.

In view of the triviality of the offence, the Home Office terminated restrictions and the patient was discharged after having spent a year in hospital. In the second case, the patient had been found under disability on four occasions between 1971 and 1981. In the final case, the patient had been found unfit to plead in 1981 and 1974 for deception offences. The 1974 finding was followed by remission for trial in 1975 which resulted in a verdict of not guilty by reason of insanity. It is interesting to note that this was the only case within the research sample where remission for trial resulted in a special verdict. The effect of these multiple findings is of course to reduce the number of *individuals* involved in the sample to 293. However, in view of the fact that these multiple findings predominantly concerned separate offences, it was decided that it would be appropriate to analyse the data on the basis of the total of 302 unfitness findings rather than on the basis of the 293 individuals involved.

THE CRITERIA FOR A FINDING OF UNFITNESS

As indicated earlier, the legal test relating to unfitness to plead was laid down in 1836 in the leading case of *Pritchard*[40] where it was stated by Baron Alderson that the accused should be able to 'plead to the indictment' and be 'of sufficient intellect to comprehend the course of the proceedings in the trial so as to make a proper defence, to challenge a juror to whom he might wish to object and comprehend the details of the evidence'. In essence, therefore, there appear to be five basic criteria to be satisfied where fitness to plead is in issue. These include the ability to plead to the indictment, to understand the course of the proceedings, to instruct a lawyer, to challenge a juror, and to understand the evidence.

An examination of the psychiatric reports within the research sample revealed that in only nine cases was mention made in any single report of all five criteria having been satisfied. Nor is this surprising in view of the fact that it seemed to be accepted by all concerned that the criteria in question are individually necessary and individually sufficient conditions for a finding of disability.[41] With regard to the individual criteria already mentioned, the order in which they were referred to most frequently by

---

[40] (1836) 7 C & P 303.
[41] F. McAuley, *Insanity, Psychiatry and Criminal Responsibility* (Round Hall Press, Dublin, 1993), 139–40 criticises this approach on the ground that its selectivity 'is apt to subvert the fundamental principle they [the criteria] are designed to secure: namely that no one should be tried on a criminal charge unless he is capable of rational participation at *all* levels of the trial process'. Accordingly, he would prefer the *Pritchard* criteria to be 'seen as a cumulative indicia of the defendant's fitness for trial'. However, while it would be preferable if psychiatrists in fitness assessments took account of all five criteria, it is difficult to accept that their failure to do so may act to the detriment of an accused since failure to satisfy even one of the five should result in an unfitness finding.

psychiatrists was as follows. Instructing a lawyer predominated, followed closely by understanding the proceedings. There was then a marked drop in the use of the other criteria, with challenging a juror appearing in third place, followed by the ability to plead and, finally, understanding the evidence. In many of these reports, as was also found by Larkin and Collins, 'various combinations of the criteria ... were used'.[42] Equally, in 84 of the cases within the sample 'there was no explicit mention of these standard criteria' although there were indications that the issue had been considered. Such cases fell into two broad categories. In the first, a conclusion about unfitness was reached without the mention of any criteria, as, for example, in one typical case where the report merely opined that 'because of psychosis the patient is unfit to plead'. In the second, the reports made mention of some other criteria beyond those referred to in *Pritchard*. A fairly common example of this was to the effect that the patient is unable to understand the nature of the charges or their implications, while another referred to the patient being unable to comprehend the imposition of the sentence of the court.

Further, in 58 of the cases in question no mention of fitness to plead could be found in any of the available psychiatric reports. However, six of these cases can be accounted for by lack of information. As far as the other cases are concerned, the explanation is more than likely to lie within the availability of relevant psychiatric testimony at the time of relevant court proceedings which led to the finding of disability.

Although it is difficult to draw any definite conclusions from the manner in which the unfitness criteria were used within the research sample, there did seem to be some ignorance and confusion in many of the cases about the criteria, which echoes the conclusions reached by Larkin and Collins.

THE CONSEQUENCES OF BEING FOUND UNFIT

Before the 1991 Act, the Criminal Procedure (Insanity) Act 1964 mandated hospitalization following a finding of disability, with the Home Secretary being required to specify a particular hospital and ensure admission to that hospital within two months of the court order. Although this occurred in the vast majority of cases, there were four instances where hospitalization did not occur. In two of these cases the defendants were remitted for trial around two months after being found unfit to plead, during which time they remained in prison. In the third and fourth cases the court neglected to inform the Home Office of its finding of disability within the two month period with the result that the power to detain the patient lapsed.

---

[42] Larkin and Collins, 'Fitness to Plead and Psychiatric Reports', 29.

In the other cases, while 92 (30.5%) were sent to Special Hospitals, an overwhelming majority of 206 (68.2%) were sent to local hospitals, including Regional Secure Units.

Of course an extremely important question in the handling of all these cases concerns the issue of remission for trial which will be considered in the next Section.

REMISSION FOR TRIAL

The decision whether or not to remit for trial a formerly unfit patient was, and continues to be, one which is vested solely in the Home Secretary under section 5(4) of the 1964 Act.[43] However such a decision is dependent on the opinion of the patient's responsible medical officer whom the Home Secretary is obliged to consult before he can be 'satisfied that the said person can properly be tried'.[44] If the Home Secretary decided that a trial should take place, he could then remit the person in question to prison and on his arrival at the prison,[45] the original order relating to hospitalization would cease to have effect.

The significance of the issue of remission for trial can hardly be overestimated. But little was known about the practice. As already mentioned the Butler Committee received evidence from the Home Office in 1975 to the effect that in practice the power was 'sparingly' used and not surprisingly this was still regarded by commentators as correct.[46] In the course of its evidence to the Butler Committee the Home Office gave several reasons which might weigh against a decision to remit for trial. They included: 'practical difficulties in proceeding with the prosecution of a person who has been detained in hospital for a long time, and if he were returned to hospital after trial either in consequence of a finding of not guilty by reason of insanity, or in pursuance of a hospital order with restrictions made on conviction, his status in the hospital would be effectively unchanged'.[47] Since prior to the 1991 Act there had been no change in the law relating to remission for trial, one might have expected Home Office practice to have remain unchanged. It is interesting to note therefore that this was not the case. Instead a marked increase had occurred in cases where the Home Secretary had decided to remit for trial. Overall during the research period there was a total of 77 cases (25.5%) where remission for trial occurred. However, three additional cases were discovered where trials took place without any warrant for remission having been issued by

---

[43] Under the 1991 Act remission for trial is now dealt with under Schedule 1 para 4.
[44] S 5(4) Criminal Procedure (Insanity) Act 1964.
[45] Under the 1991 Act remission may now be direct to court rather than to prison.
[46] See e.g. Chiswick, 'Fitness to Stand Trial and Plead', 174.
[47] Butler Report, para 10.17.

TABLE 5.4   *Disability Findings 1976–89—Subsequent Trials*

	Number of disability findings		Number of resulting trials		As % of annual disability findings
1976	38		6		15.8
1977	20		2		10.0
1978	14		2		14.3
1979	24		3		12.5
1980	39		4		10.3
1981	28		5		17.9
1982	34		16		47.1
1983	18		7		38.9
1984	18		5		27.8
1985	17		5		29.4
1986	12		6		50.0
1987	16		10		62.5
1988	13		6		46.2
1989	11		3		27.3
Total Findings	302	Total Trials	80	Overall Average	26.5

the Home Office. In effect therefore there was a total of 80 (26.5%) cases where a trial subsequently followed a finding of disability. However, it can be seen from Table 5.4 how the number of trials increased during recent years from a minimum of two in each of 1977 and 1978 to a maximum of sixteen in 1982. Table 5.4 also gives the percentage of annual disability findings which subsequently resulted in trials where once again it can be seen how the rate of such trials increased from 15.8% in 1976 to a maximum of 62.5% in 1987. It need hardly be pointed out that the low number of trials for 1989 reflects the fact that this was the most recent year in the research sample and that a number of negotiations concerning trials in respect of unfitness findings during that year were still underway. In addition, the average waiting time before remission for trial took place was around 13.5 months, a figure which is inevitably distorted by the fact that in a small number of cases remission did not take place for very long periods of time, as for example in a case decided in 1978 where the trial was not held until 1986.

Further, as far as indicators of remission for trial are concerned, it is noteworthy that a much larger percentage of those detained in Special Hospitals were remitted, namely 35 out of a total of 92 (38%) compared to only 45 out of the 206 (21.8%) detained in ordinary hospitals. Of course, this is hardly surprising in view of the fact that the Special Hospitals inevitably deal more regularly with such patients and their psychiatrists, who have a forensic background, can be expected to be more familiar with remission procedures. In addition, the vast majority of those remitted were mentally ill, with 59 having been diagnosed as schizophrenic and ten psychotic. Again, however, this is not surprising as mental illness leading to unfitness is more likely to result in effective treatment, which in turn may lead to a more rapid return to fitness.

The reason for the increase in the number of subsequent trials can be traced to the change of government and in particular to a change of ministerial policy over a number of issues, including the desirability of remitting for trial those patients who, in the opinion of their responsible medical officers, were fit to be tried.

Although there has never been any formal procedure contained in the 1964 Act before or after the amendments made by the 1991 Act for reviewing a patient's fitness to plead at any particular time after a finding of disability, the Home Office has instituted its own procedure to ensure that such a review takes place, which it describes as follows:

as a matter of policy the Home Office will review the case of a patient who has been found unfit to plead at six monthly intervals during the first two years after admission to hospital to establish whether he has become fit to stand trial. It is consequently important that responsible medical officers recognise that the first consideration is the patient's fitness for trial rather than his full recovery from mental disorder. Wherever possible, a court should have the opportunity of considering the evidence against a defendant. If he is convicted and remains sufficiently mentally ill to warrant detention in hospital for treatment, it will be open to the courts to make a hospital order.[48]

It can be seen from this that Home Office policy has altered significantly since the time of the Butler Report in 1975. In particular the fact that a trial may mean a return to hospital is no longer viewed as a valid reason for deciding not to remit for trial. Nor should it be, as it is surely not the task of the Home Office to 'second-guess' the decision of the court in such cases.

Indeed, with regard to such decisions it is instructive to note the results of the 80 cases where trials took place. Table 5.5 shows that whilst thirty-eight were the subject of hospital orders, eight secured acquittals, and ten were the subject of probation orders. In addition it should be pointed out that the overall majority of those remitted were not returned to hospital but were dealt with in some other manner. Indeed only twenty-five of the hospital orders were coupled with restrictions, meaning that under a third

---

[48] *Mentally Disordered Offenders, Restricted Patients Detained in Special Hospitals—Information for the Special Hospitals Service Authority* (1989) distributed by the Home Office, para 5.9.

TABLE 5.5 *Disability Findings 1976–89—Subsequent Trial Results*

	Frequency	As % of total trials
Not guilty	8	10.0
Left on file	3	3.7
Prison	10	12.5
Hospital order	13	16.3
Restriction order	25	31.3
Probation	10	12.5
Other	7	8.7
Unknown	4	5.0
TOTAL	80	100.0

of those remitted found their status in hospital to be unchanged; a result which surely argues for remission for trial whenever possible.[49]

THE ACQUITTAL CASES

There were six cases where defendants were subsequently acquitted by a jury on the merits and two cases which could legitimately be classed as technical acquittals in the sense that there seems to have been insufficient evidence offered by the prosecution to support a conviction.

Of the six jury acquittals, two were for burglary where the defendants were remitted after four and nine months respectively. In a third case, one of indecent assault, the defendant was remitted after six months and was acquitted owing to doubts over the evidence. The fourth case concerned a robbery charge where the defendant remained in custody for seven months before being remitted because the Home Office was not informed about the unfitness finding until shortly before the date of remission. As a result this case was dealt with without the defendant ever having been admitted to hospital. In the fifth case the accused hit his father with a candlestick in an unprovoked attack and was charged with wounding under section 18 of the Offences Against the Person Act 1861. The trial, which resulted in an acquittal, was delayed because of the ill health of prosecution witnesses with the result that remission took place after about a year. In the sixth and final case the accused was charged with arson after it was alleged that she had set fire to her flat whilst drunk. She was remitted after five months and at her trial there was evidence given that her two year-old son had stuffed paper between the bars of an electric fire and that this had caused the blaze.

[49] Whether this point has been adequately answered by the 1991 Act is at best questionable: see below.

As to the two cases referred to as technical acquittals, one was a case where the accused was prosecuted for a minor burglary in a farm building. She was remitted after ten months but lack of evidence led to the charges being dismissed. In the other case the accused was prosecuted for obtaining services by deception after he had refused to pay for a taxi. He was remitted after two months and the case against him was dismissed, the prosecution having appeared to offer no evidence against him.

In all these acquittal cases the defendants had been diagnosed as suffering from schizophrenia or psychosis.

THE OTHER TRIALS

As regards those seven cases classed in Table 5.5 as 'other', they covered the following situations. In one case an Asian male, who was alleged to have assaulted a passenger on the underground railway, was remitted, found unfit to plead, and remitted again on the same charge only to be found unfit to plead once again. Some four months later the Home Office terminated restrictions as the offence was considered to be relatively minor and the patient had already been detained in hospital for over a year. In a second case a defendant who had been found unfit to plead on an assault charge was remitted some eighteen months later, only to be found unfit to plead again. He was then remitted again after a further four months, and was convicted and sentenced to a term of four and a half years' imprisonment. The third and fourth cases relate to the same individual, who on separate occasions was charged with theft and going equipped and each time was remitted convicted, and conditionally discharged for six months. In the fifth case a female who assaulted a prison officer was remitted and, on conviction, received an absolute discharge. In the sixth case a defendant was remitted on an arson charge having set fire to a bed in the hospital where he was residing. On remission he was convicted and was bound over on condition that he continued treatment and resided with his parents. In the seventh and final case the defendant was alleged to have set fire to a haystack. He was remitted some nine months later and on conviction was given a guardianship order under section 37 of the Mental Health Act 1983.

THE CASES WHERE NO REMISSION TOOK PLACE

In addition to the 80 cases which resulted in trials, the research revealed another 44 cases where, although responsible medical officers assessed their patients as fit to stand trial, no remission took place. Of course some of these cases can be accounted for by patients whose mental conditions did not improve rapidly, which is a serious problem for a number of reasons. The difficulties of securing remission in such cases are alluded to by the Home Office in the following comment: 'if a patient who has been found unfit to plead remains in this condition after a period of about two years in hospital the Home Secretary will review the continuing need for the restriction order and will terminate it in cases where he is satisfied it is unnecessary for the protection of the public from serious harm'.[50] However, it is clearly not impossible to bring to trial those who recover fitness late. Indeed, in two cases of unfitness findings made in 1986, successful trials took place around 78 and 94 months after the finding of disability and, in another finding made in 1978, the trial did not take place until 1986, some 102 months after the accused had been found unfit to plead. Naturally, this type of case was found to be somewhat rare which is hardly surprising in view of the practical problems of mounting prosecutions after the patient has been in hospital for a long period of time. Clearly such a lapse of time will often result in a loss of interest in the case by the police and the prosecution. Exhibits and files may have gone missing, and key witnesses may no longer be available. Indeed, this type of difficulty has recently led the Home Office to issue a Circular advising the police that it is essential, where a person is found unfit to plead, that all the relevant evidence should be preserved, either until the accused is remitted for trial or until formal notification is received from the Crown Prosecution Service or Home Office that a trial will not be held.[51] This should go some way to alleviating the above difficulties.

However, it is inevitable that cases will remain where remission for trial continues to be impossible or is felt to be impractical. An important question, therefore, is what befalls this other group of patients.

THE OTHER PATIENTS

There was a total of 222 cases where at the end of the research period no trial had taken place, although it should be pointed out that in several of the more recent cases active negotiations were still taking place concerning the possibility of future trials.

Of these 222 cases, 80 were still in hospital as restricted patients, 72 had had their restrictions lifted by the Home Office, 37 and 14 had received conditional and absolute discharges respectively, 14 had died, 3 had been transferred to other countries and in the 2 final cases the Home Office's power over the patient had lapsed owing to lack of notification within the two month period from the date of the court's decision.

As already mentioned the majority of those found unfit to plead were

---

[50] Home Office, *Mentally Disordered Offenders*, para 5.10. This was indeed a major consideration which led to the termination of restrictions in a considerable number of the cases in the research sample.　　　　[51] See Home Office Circular No 66/90, para 5.

sent to local hospitals rather than to Special Hospitals. As might be expected therefore, a distinction was found between these two groups of patients. For example 36 (39.1%) of the 92 sent to Special Hospital were still in hospital compared to 44 (21.4%) of the 206 sent to local hospitals. In addition, when it came to release decisions, only nine Special Hospital patients, compared to 63 in local hospitals, had restrictions lifted and a mere 10 and 2 sent to Special Hospitals had received conditional and absolute discharges respectively, compared with 27 and 12 respectively from those sent to local hospitals.[52]

DISCUSSION

Despite the increase in remission for trial, there can be no doubt about the overall decline in the number of disability findings in England and Wales.[53] Indeed, if this decline continues at a similar rate, unfitness to plead will become almost as rare an occurrence as the defence of insanity.[54] It is difficult to trace this decline to any particular factor. A possible reason which has been canvassed is the introduction of section 36 of the Mental Health Act 1983. This section resulted from a recommendation of the Butler Report; it permits the Crown Court to remand certain mentally disordered defendants for treatment in hospital rather than remanding them in custody. The Butler Report made it clear that this power should be available where a 'defendant is found under disability in relation to the trial'.[55] Accordingly, Bluglass considers that this provision may now be being used as an alternative to the use of unfitness.[56] However, it should be pointed out that section 36 was not implemented until the end of October 1984; its implementation thus fails to explain the fall during the years 1983 and 1984, although it could be a cause of the continuing downward trend thereafter. Another reason is likely to have been the continuing dissatisfaction with the state of the law under the 1964 Act which had led one psychiatrist to comment: 'for some unfit defendants a hospital order with restrictions on discharge is clearly inappropriate. It is therefore not surprising that psychiatrists have exercised increasing caution before recommending that defendants are unfit to plead'.[57]

---

[52] For details of long-term detention cases, see R.D. Mackay and T. Ward 'The Long-Term Detention of Those Found Unfit to Plead and Legally Insane' (1994) 34 *British Journal of Criminology* 30.

[53] In comparison, unfitness to plead is used much more frequently in Scotland. For discussion, see A.C. Normand, 'Unfitness for Trial in Scotland' (1985) 7 *International Journal of Law and Psychiatry* 415.

[54] For discussion of a similar experience in Eire, see F. McAuley, *Insanity, Psychiatry and Criminal Responsibility*, 206–18.   [55] Butler Report, para 12.7.

[56] R. Bluglass, 'The Mental Health Act 1983' in Bluglass and Bowden (eds.), *Principles and Practice of Forensic Psychiatry*, 1179.

[57] Chiswick, 'Fitness to Stand Trial and Plead', 175.

The above research could be interpreted as supporting two of the major criticisms aimed at the 1964 Act as originally enacted. The first concerned the lack of any automatic trial of the facts in cases where fitness to plead was in issue. In this context it was disquieting to find eight cases where subsequent trials resulted in acquittals. In addition, in one well known case in 1985, a mentally handicapped woman confessed to the murder of her father and was found to be under disability. Some twelve months later it was discovered that the patient's nephew had committed the offence which prompted her release and a subsequent compensation claim against the Home Office. The fact that in the majority of disability cases within the research sample the accusation continued to remain unresolved was a clear cause for concern.

The second criticism related to the inflexibility of disposal under the 1964 Act. Many of the cases within the research sample did not warrant a restriction order,[58] and could have been more appropriately dealt with in other ways. Further, even the flexible approach, once practised by the Home Office, of terminating restrictions on admission in appropriate cases was no longer available owing to a change in policy.

There was little doubt that the original position under the 1964 Act was unsatisfactory and that reform was essential if the law on disability in relation to the trial was to operate in a fair and sensible manner. It was encouraging, therefore, to find the Home Office not only recognising and accepting the above criticisms but also successfully backing calls for reform, which in turn gave rise to the 1991 Act to which the next Section is devoted.

THE CRIMINAL PROCEDURE (INSANITY AND UNFITNESS TO PLEAD) ACT 1991[59]

This statute received the Royal Assent on 27 June 1991 and came into force on 1 January 1992. As already mentioned, it was the direct result of major dissatisfaction with the way in which those found mentally unfit to stand trial, or not guilty by reason of insanity, were dealt with under the Criminal Procedure (Insanity) Act 1964. This dissatisfaction was originally voiced in 1975 when the Butler Report recommended *inter alia* the introduction of wide discretion of disposal in all such cases together with a trial

---

[58] Cf. *R.* v. *Birch* (1989) 90 Cr App R 78 where the Court of Appeal clarified the law governing the making of restriction orders by establishing *inter alia* that such an order is unlikely to be appropriate in cases of where there is merely a high possibility of recurrence of minor offences.

[59] See S. White, 'The Criminal Procedure (Insanity and Unfitness to Plead) Act' [1992] Crim LR 4.

of the facts in unfitness to plead cases. However, these recommendations proved to be controversial and were never acted upon.

Early in 1991 the Law Society sponsored a Private Member's Bill to reform this area of the law.[60] The proposals contained in the Bill were based on the recommendations of the Butler Report, albeit in a modified form, and were in due course fully supported by the Government. As a result the 1991 Act was passed without dissent.

Although it must be emphasised that the 1991 Act leaves the legal tests for both unfitness to plead and the defence of insanity unchanged, it nonetheless enacts procedural reforms of fundamental importance.[61]

The major changes introduced by the 1991 Act are as follows.

1. TRIAL OF THE FACTS[62]

A completely new procedure has been introduced in all cases where the jury has decided that the accused is unfit to plead. In essence this procedure requires the jury to examine any evidence already given, together with any further evidence adduced by the prosecution and the defence, in order that it may be satisfied that the accused 'did the act or made the omission charged against him as the offence'. If the jury is so satisfied, then they will make a finding to that effect. However, this 'finding' is not the equivalent of a conviction. On the other hand, if the jury is not so satisfied, then a verdict of acquittal will be returned.

This procedure, referred to as 'a trial of the facts' in the long title to the 1991 Act, is clearly designed to remedy the criticism that under the 1964 Act there was no automatic requirement which ensured that the case against an accused found unfit to plead was tested, with the result that it was possible for innocent but mentally unfit persons to be detained in hospital indefinitely. The provision is an important safeguard for mentally unfit defendants, but the enquiry to be undertaken by the jury is a limited one insofar as the 1991 Act does not permit consideration of *mens rea*. The reasons for this limitation seem to have been; first, a desire for simplicity and; second, the alleged incongruity of attempting to assess *mens rea* in cases where defendants had already been found unfit to plead. However, this latter point misses the mark since unfitness to plead is concerned with the accused's current mental condition rather than his state of mind at the time of the alleged offence. It is therefore perfectly possible for a mentally unfit defendant to have been mentally sound at the time of the offence but

---

[60] Law Society (Mental Health Sub-Committee), *Criminal Procedure (Insanity and Unfitness to Plead) Bill: Briefing on the Private Member's Bill* (1991).

[61] Full details of these can be found in Home Office Circular No 93/91 (hereafter referred to as the 1991 Circular) dated 20 November 1991. See also S. White, 'The Criminal Procedure (Insanity and Unfitness to Plead) Act'.

[62] See s 2 of the 1991 Act substituting new provisions for s 4 of the 1964 Act.

to have lacked *mens rea* in some ordinary way. However, as the law stands, such an issue cannot be tested within the 'trial of the facts'.[63]

Two further points concerning this novel procedure deserve comment. First, the quest for simplicity may not have been fully achieved in the sense that there are a number of offences the *actus reus* of which require some consideration of the accused's state of mind. An obvious example is possession of a controlled drug where the 'possession' element depends to some extent on the accused's state of mind.[64] What is the prosecution to do in a case where the accused has been found unfit to plead to a charge of possession of a controlled drug? Further, what is to happen where the defendant pleads automatism in answer to an allegation that 'he did the act'? If, as many would argue, a defence of automatism negatives *actus reus* rather than *mens rea*, then there seems to be nothing in principle to prevent the accused using such a defence during the trial of the facts. A possible solution to these problems could be the retention in the 1991 Act of the power, originally given to the court under the 1964 Act, of postponing consideration of the question of fitness until any time before the opening of the case for the defence,[65] thus providing some opportunity for the jury to consider the accused's state of mind.

The second point worthy of comment concerns the burden of proof in relation to the trial of the facts. The 1991 Act is silent on this matter,[66] merely stating that the jury must be 'satisfied' that the accused 'did the act or made the omission charged'.[67] However the 1991 Circular clearly states at paragraph 9 that 'the test in regard to burden of proof should be consistent with other criminal proceedings (beyond reasonable doubt)', which seems right in principle.

2. FLEXIBILITY OF DISPOSAL[68]

The 1991 Act introduces a much more flexible range of disposals for both unfitness to plead and the defence of insanity. In addition to the restriction

---

[63] By way of contrast the Criminal Justice (Scotland) Bill 1994 seeks to introduce for cases of insanity in bar of trial 'an examination of facts' which is analogous to a 'trial of the facts' but requires the court to be satisfied 'on the balance of probabilities, that there are no grounds for acquitting him' (see s 174ZA (1)(b)) which would also permit acquittal on the ground of insanity (see s 174ZA (1)(4)). Further s 174ZA (5) provides that 'the rules of evidence and procedure and the powers of the court shall, in respect of an examination of the facts, be as nearly as possible those applicable in respect of a trial'. It seems clear, therefore, that this proposed Scottish procedure is more akin to what was recommended by the Butler Report.

[64] See *Warner v. Metropolitan Police Commissioner* [1969] 2 AC 256.

[65] S 4(2) of the 1964 Act.

[66] Again by way of contrast, the Criminal Justice (Scotland) Bill is explicit, stating at s 174ZA (1)(a) that the court must be satisfied 'beyond reasonable doubt . . . that he did the act or made the omission constituting the offence'.

[67] S 2 of the 1991 Act substituting a new section 4A of the 1964 Act.

[68] S 3 of the 1991 Act substituting a new section 5 of the 1964 Act.

order which inevitably resulted from a finding of unfitness or legal insanity under the 1964 Act, the court has been given the discretion to order admission to hospital without restrictions or to make a guardianship order under the Mental Health Act 1983, or a supervision and treatment order, or an order for the absolute discharge of the accused. However, with regard to a finding of unfitness to plead, none of these powers will be available unless the jury has found that the accused did the act or made the omission charged.

Each of these orders deserves a brief comment.

(a) Admission Orders

The provisions relating to admission orders are set out in Schedule 1 of the 1991 Act which makes it clear that a hospital order with or without restriction will now be available for all offences charged with the exception of murder where the court will continue to be required to impose a restriction order without limitation of time (see (e) below).

(b) Guardianship Orders

Section 37 of the Mental Health Act 1983 has been adopted by the 1991 Act for the purpose of enabling those found unfit to plead and legally insane to receive care and protection rather than medical treatment. The information set out in *Provision for Mentally Disordered Offenders* (Home Office Circular 66/69) at paragraph 8(1)(c)(v) is equally applicable to the making of such orders under the 1991 Act.

(c) Supervision and Treatment Orders

Schedule 2 of the 1991 Act contains detailed provisions relating to the operation of this new form of order which is modelled on psychiatric probation orders under the Powers of Criminal Court Act 1973 as amended by the Criminal Justice Act 1991. The order, which is not a punitive measure, will allow for the supervision to be carried out by a social worker or a probation officer for a period of not more than two years. However an order cannot be made unless the court considers that this is the most suitable means of dealing with the accused and is in possession of the necessary evidence of at least two doctors, one of whom must be duly approved.

The order also requires the supervised person to 'submit' to medical treatment with a view to the improvement of his mental condition. In this context it is interesting to note that although paragraph 4(1) of Schedule 2 of the 1991 Act uses the word 'submit', the 1991 Circular prefers the word 'undergo' (see paragraph 17(c)(vii)) in order to emphasise that 'in the final analysis the order should not be conditional on the willingness of the accused to comply [as] the court will have no power to enforce the order or otherwise intervene in cases of non-compliance'. Accordingly, if the supervisor considers that compulsory medical treatment has become necessary, then the provision of Part II of the Mental Health Act 1983 will have to be used.

Finally, Part III of Schedule 2 of the 1991 Act contains detailed provisions relating to the revocation and amendment of such orders, which can be done upon application to the magistrates' court.

(d) Absolute Discharge

Section 5(2)(b)(iii) of the 1991 Act gives the court the option to make an order for the absolute discharge of the accused, while section 5(4) of the 1991 Act expressly applies section 1(A)(1) of the Powers of Criminal Courts Act 1973 to cases of unfitness to plead and insanity. The 1991 Circular's comment on this form of order is brief and is to the effect it might be used 'where the alleged offence was trivial and the accused clearly does not require treatment and supervision in the community'. But this surely understates the utility of the power to order a discharge. Even if the alleged offence is not trivial, no order involving treatment (whether in hospital or in the community) should be made if the defendant does not suffer from a condition requiring treatment.

(e) Murder Charges

It is important to note that the only restriction on these flexible disposal provisions is in relation to a charge of murder, where the trial judge will continue to be required to impose a restriction order. On this point the only comment made by the Minister of State, John Patten, during the debate was that this preservation of the mandatory hospital disposal was 'very important for public protection'.[69] It is abundantly clear, therefore, that this decision to retain restriction orders for murder charges is a pure policy decision. It is a cause for concern since there seems little doubt that its effect will be to continue to 'force' those mentally ill defendants charged with murder to avoid unfitness and insanity by pleading guilty to manslaughter by reason of diminished responsibility and thus to retain for this group of offenders the very difficulties which the Act seeks to remedy.

Another important and related point concerns the fact that, as far as unfitness is concerned, the trial of the facts will not examine the *mens rea* of the accused as this is felt to be inappropriate in relation to someone mentally unfit to stand trial. However, this very issue of *mens rea* can be a crucial factor in deciding whether the charge and/or conviction should be murder or manslaughter; indeed, what distinguishes murder from manslaughter will often be *mens rea*. And yet, this will form no part of a jury's

---

[69] Hansard, 1 March 1991, Volume 186 No 67 at Column 1275.

deliberations when dealing with the trial of the facts. In short, the facts may regularly be capable of establishing that D did the act or made the omission charged irrespective of whether the charge be murder or manslaughter. Similarly, in cases where D might wish to use the diminished responsibility plea, the crucial issue of substantial impairment of mental responsibility which could have resulted in a manslaughter verdict will be excluded from consideration by the jury on the trial of the facts, leaving the murder charge intact with the consequent inflexible position as to disposal. This much has now been decided in one of the first murder cases under the 1991 Act where there was strong psychiatric evidence supporting diminished responsibility. However, the trial judge decided that, as the new section 4A(2) substituted in the 1964 Act refers to 'the act . . . charged against him as the offence', this effectively tied his hands as it clearly related to the offence with which the accused had originally been charged, namely murder. Accordingly, the 1991 Act afforded the court no opportunity to consider the evidence of diminished responsibility with a view to the charge being reduced to one of manslaughter. Further, not only is it legally impossible for the prosecution to charge the accused with manslaughter by reason of diminished responsibility, as this is an optional defence which must be raised by the defence in answer to a murder charge, but also, even if the defendant uses an insanity defence in a murder case, while the medical evidence may be equally supportive of a diminished plea, such evidence cannot be used to reduce the charge as the defendant is seeking an acquittal, albeit by means of the special verdict. In short, the accused's position in such cases seems unenviable, and it seems more than likely that such defendants will, if at all possible, prefer to proceed to a trial for murder in the hope of a diminished manslaughter verdict that would untie the judge's hands as far as sentencing is concerned.

3. Miscellaneous Matters[70]

Section 1 of the 1991 Act provides that a jury is not to acquit on the ground of insanity except on the evidence of two or more doctors, one of whom must have special experience in the field of mental disorder, while section 2(6) introduces a similar provision in respect of unfitness to plead.

Schedule 1 of the 1991 Act retains the Home Secretary's power to remit for trial those found unfit to plead who are detained in hospital with restrictions, provided he is satisfied that the patient can properly be tried.[71]

---

[70] S 4 of the 1991 Act amends the Criminal Appeal Act 1968 thus making, with respect to appeals to the Court of Appeal, provision corresponding to that made in ss 1–3 of the 1991 Act. Also the new ss 4(5) and 4A substituted in the 1964 Act deal with the question of when it is appropriate for a fresh jury to be empanelled to decide the issue of fitness to plead, or to deal with the trial proper, or to decide the 'trial of the facts'.

[71] Schedule 1 para 4(1).

Further, Schedule 1 now gives the Home Secretary the option of remitting such persons direct to court rather than to prison. The 1991 Act makes it clear that remission for trial in respect of hospital orders without restrictions is now impossible,[72] but is silent in relation to other forms of disposal under the 1991 Act. However, as the 1991 Act does not expressly prevent proceedings being otherwise recommenced, one must assume that it will be legally permissible for the Crown Prosecution Service to revive proceedings against those who later regain fitness but who were not subject to a restriction order.[73] How often this is likely to happen is difficult to know but as there is no specific legal machinery contained in the 1991 Act to deal with such 'revivals' it seems likely that they may be rare. In any event, the chances of it being in the public interest to reprosecute those subject to guardianship orders or supervision and treatment orders seem remote, unless the defendant himself is insisting on his right to a full trial of the issue over and above the trial of the facts which in any event will already have led to a finding that 'he did the act or made the omission charged'.

The primary importance of the 1991 Act lies in the much needed flexibility of disposal which it introduces. There seems little doubt that the mandatory disposal measure contained in the 1964 Act was a major reason why both unfitness to plead and the insanity defence were rarely used. There was thus some reason to suppose that, once lawyers, psychiatrists, and other interested parties began to appreciate the full effect of the 1991 Act, this would lead to an increased use of these new provisions. However, ongoing research into the 1991 Act shows the following figures for 1992—the first year of the 1991 Act's operation—set out in Table 5.6.[74]

It can be seen from Table 5.6 that the number of unfitness findings in 1992 was 13.[75] However, two of the unfitness cases were disposed of

---

[72] Schedule 1 para 4(2).

[73] For the analogous procedure in Scotland, see D. Chiswick et al. 'Reprosecution of Patients Found Unfit to Plead: A Report of Anomalies in Procedure in Scotland' (1990) 14 *Psychiatric Bulletin* 208 where it is stated that 'authority to reprosecute rests exclusively with procurator fiscals and the Crown Office'. However, the status of the original restriction order in such cases is unclear.

[74] Funded by Economic and Social Research Council Grant No R000 23 3773 and conducted with the cooperation and assistance of C3 division of the Home Office, the Lord Chancellor's Department, and the Crown Prosecution Service.

[75] Coincidentally, the figures given above have become available at approximately the same time as the 1992 *Statistics of Mentally Disordered Offenders for England and Wales* (Home Office Statistical Bulletin—Issue 04/94), which for the first time (table 3) give a breakdown of the number of cases as between unfitness to plead and insanity. However, that table is limited to restricted patients; therefore, although it covers 1992, the number of cases it records does not of course reflect the true number of cases disposed of during the first year of the operation of the 1991 Act. This discrepancy is further exacerbated by the fact that, in the notes to the statistics at page 20, not only is there no mention of the existence of the 1991 Act but also it is stated that in cases of unfitness and insanity 'restrictions are automatic'. This is most unfortunate because it is clearly wrong. Further, it gives the impression that the number of restricted patients in table 3, namely three who were unfit to plead and

TABLE 5.6   *Unfitness Disposals in 1992 under the Criminal Procedure*
            (Insanity and Unfitness to Plead) Act 1991

Criminal Charge	Age	Diagnosis	Sex	Disposal
Affray	39	Autism/Epilepsy	F	Restriction Order
Indecent Assault	26	Schizophrenia	M	Restriction Order
Attempted Rape	26	Mental Impairment and Schizophrenia	M	Restriction Order
Robbery	20	Mental Impairment	M	Hospital Order
Attempted Robbery	37	Schizophrenia	M	Hospital Order
S. 18 Assault	27	Mental Impairment	M	Hospital Order
Indecent Assault	40	Mental Impairment	M	Supervision and Treatment Order
Buggery (4 charges)	72	Alzheimer's	M	Guardianship Order
Importing 'Class A' Drug	61	Depression/Anxiety	F	Absolute Discharge
Attempted Rape	35	Mental Impairment	M	Acquittal
Robbery (6 charges)	26	Schizophrenia	M	Acquittal
Arson	17	Schizophrenia	M	1964 Act—Restriction Order
Rape	38	Mental Impairment	M	1964 Act—Restriction Order

under the old law; they were adjourned in the hope that advantage could be taken of the new disposal flexibility, but in neither of these cases was the trial judge willing to accept these delay tactics. This meant that a mere eleven unfitness cases were dealt with under the new law, which in turn means that the annual number of unfitness cases remains similar to the low numbers recently experienced under the previous law.[76] This is perplexing, for, although it seems that barristers and solicitors have not brought many cases forward during the first year of the 1991 Act, it has become clear that when this is done the courts have been quick to take full advantage of the new disposal powers under the 1991 Act. Thus, in the 11 cases dealt with during the first year of the new law, only three resulted in restriction orders and indefinite hospitalization, with the other cases being dealt with as follows: one supervision and treatment order; three ordinary hospital orders without restrictions; two acquittals after the trial of the facts; one

three who were NGRI (all these NGRI cases were disposed of under the old law and are classed by the Home Office as 1992 cases because the warrant was issued during that year), accounts for the total number of such cases during the first year of the 1991 Act. But this is manifestly not the case. It is to be hoped that in future the Home Office statistics will no longer overlook the very existence of the 1991 Act.

[76] See above Table 5.1.

absolute discharge and one guardianship order. To date, therefore, although the 1991 Act has not yet had an effect so far as any increase in the number of cases is concerned, it is clear that the courts are happy with the new flexible disposal powers. It is also interesting to note that while the offences dealt with under the first year of the 1991 Act covered non-fatal offences, sexual offences, and robbery, none of the cases included a murder charge; this might indicate a reluctance on the part of defendants and their legal advisers to risk the automatic restriction order which continues to flow from such a charge in both unfitness and insanity cases. However, early assessment of unfitness to plead cases for 1993 indicates that this is not the case in that 4 out of a total of 11 unfitness findings have resulted from murder charges.

It appears from these figures that barristers and solicitors have failed to realise that the courts are already making full use of their new flexible disposal powers. Once this message is communicated, it is to be hoped that the apparent reluctance so far displayed by practitioners in using the 1991 Act will be replaced by a greater willingness to take full advantage of these new measures. In theory this should lead to an increase in the number of cases of unfitness to plead, which in turn would ensure that the 1991 Act achieves its full purpose.

THE QUESTION OF REFORM

It is clear that the 1991 Act was a compromise measure which for many does not go far enough. Although the introduction of flexibility of disposal is to be welcomed, this has been marred by the refusal to extend this discretion to those charged with murder. Further, confining the trial of the facts to an investigation into *actus reus* alone seems unduly narrow, and it is here that the 1991 Act begins to part company with the Butler Report's recommendations which supported a trial where the prosecution would be required to establish the defendant's state of mind.[77] If the elements of the offence were proved against an unfit defendant, the jury would be directed to find 'that the defendant should be dealt with as a person under disability',[78] failing which the accused would be acquitted. It was also proposed that, if there was medical evidence indicating speedy recovery, the judge should be given the opportunity to adjourn the trial for a maximum of six months. If recovery took place within that period, a normal trial would take place, if not then the trial of the facts should be conducted.[79] This emphasis on trying to ensure that the accused is tried in the normal way in appropriate cases is something not expressly dealt with

---

[77] Butler Report, para 10.24.   [78] Ibid.   [79] Ibid. para 10.19.

in the 1991 Act where the emphasis is rather on disposal. Indeed, there is no mention in the 1991 Act of what length of time between an unfitness finding and a trial of the facts might be considered appropriate, and an analysis of the 1992 cases suggests that most trials of the facts take place immediately after the unfitness findings. It seems clear therefore that, with remission for trial confined to restriction order disposals, the opportunities for those who have recovered their fitness to be tried in the normal way will be rare indeed. Whether such an approach is correct is certainly open to question. For example, the law of Canada by way of contrast, which has recently undergone comprehensive reform in respect of mentally disordered offenders, makes it quite clear that the primary policy of the new Criminal Code provisions dealing with the unfit is to send the accused back for trial as soon as is practicable.[80] In this connection, section 672.48 ensures that the Review Board,[81] as part of its function, must decide whether the accused is fit to stand trial and if so he must be sent back to court so that the fitness issue may be retried, although he may be detained in hospital up to the time of trial if the Review Board 'has reasonable ground to believe that the accused would become unfit to stand trial if released'.[82] Further, section 672.33 requires a Canadian court to 'hold an enquiry, not later than two years after the verdict [of unfitness] is rendered and every two years thereafter . . . to decide whether sufficient evidence can be adduced at that time to put the accused on trial'. If the prosecution cannot satisfy the court on this matter, then according to section 672.33(6) the court must acquit the accused. This is an important provision as it ensures that the prosecution has a good case against the unfit accused, irrespective of time lapse. There is no similar provision in England, which means that unfit defendants who are not remitted for trial, or otherwise reprosecuted, cannot clear their names. However, what is noticeable here is that the philosophy behind the English provisions concerns the best method of disposing of the unfit defendant rather than attempting to ensure, as in Canada, that he is rendered fit and sent back for trial.[83] Nevertheless, it does seem somewhat anomalous that unfit English defendants should have lost any prospect of having their cases remitted for trial except where they have been subject to a hospital order with restrictions.

---

[80] See S. Davis, 'Fitness to Stand Trial in Canada in the Light of the Recent Criminal Code Amendments' (1994) 17 *International Journal of Law and Psychiatry* 319.

[81] The nearest Canadian equivalent to our Mental Health Review Tribunals.

[82] S 672.49(1).

[83] A point which is rarely considered concerns the treatment process for unfit to plead defendants. As Wexler has pointed out 'Treatment is probably rarely tailored to the specific abilities needed to be competent to stand trial. It probably has as a goal the treatment of the patient's psychopathology, rather than the short term goal of the restoration to trial competence, or more appropriately, to competency to perform the specific trial-related task the defendant has been found unable adequately to do': see D.B. Wexler and B.J. Winick, *Therapeutic Jurisprudence* (Carolina Academie Press, Durham, North Carolina, 1991), 314.

Another point of contrast between the 1991 Act and the new Canadian Criminal Code provisions is that, unlike the 1991 Act, the Code now defines the phrase 'unfit to stand trial' in section 2 in the following manner:

'Unfit to stand trial' means unable on account of mental disorder to conduct a defence at any stage of the proceedings before a verdict is rendered in respect of an offence charged against the accused or, the inability to instruct counsel to do so and, in particular, the inability of the accused to
  (a) understand the nature or object of the proceedings,
  (b) understand the possible consequences of the proceedings, or
  (c) communicate with counsel.

Further, section 2 defines 'Mental Disorder' as a 'disease of the mind'. This, together with the abolition of the 'natural imbecility' provision, might seem to indicate that the fitness provisions no longer apply to those who are mentally handicapped.[84] If this is so, then there would seem to be a major gap in the new Canadian law.

One of the first cases to examine the new Canadian test of fitness to stand trial was *R. v. Taylor*[85] where the accused, a paranoid schizophrenic, was able to understand the nature and object of the proceedings and its possible consequences and thus met the first two criteria in the new section 2. However, there was disagreement over his ability to communicate with counsel in the sense that it was argued for the Crown that the accused 'suffered from delusions so pervasive and irrational that he was "unable to perceive his own best interests and how those interests should be addressed in the course of a trial"'.[86] In essence this meant that the court was being invited to adopt an 'analytic capacity' test rather that a 'limited cognitive capacity' test. In rejecting the former, Lacourcière JA considered that it 'established too high a threshold ... by requiring that the accused be capable of making rational decisions beneficial to him'.[87] In the judge's opinion, to require this high threshold would interfere with the liberty of the accused to conduct his own defence 'even if this meant that the accused may act to his own detriment in doing so'.[88] It seems clear therefore that Canadian law has retained a test for fitness to stand trial which remains similar to that adopted by the common law of England in *R. v. Robertson*.[89]

In this respect it could be argued that little is to be gained by incorporating the *Pritchard* criteria into statute. However, this was not the view taken by the Butler Report, which recommended retaining the ability 'to understand the course of the proceedings at the trial, so as to make a proper defence, and to understand the substance of the evidence' but

---

[84] For discussion, see D. Hitchen, 'Fitness to Stand Trial and Mentally Challenged Defendants: A View from Canada' (1993) 4 *International Bulletin of Law and Mental Health* 5.
[85] (1993) 11 OR(3d) 323.   [86] Ibid. 338.   [87] Ibid. 339.
[88] Ibid. 338.   [89] [1968] 3 All ER 557.

omitting any reference to challenging a juror but at the same time adding two more criteria: 'namely, whether the defendant can give adequate instructions to his legal advisers, and plead with understanding to the indictment'.[90] Again it is doubtful if this adds anything of substance to the existing common law criteria. However, a more fundamental point concerns the question of whether the fitness criteria should be limited to cognitive defects or 'expanded to include other distortions caused by mental illness'.[91] The problem with which one is confronted here concerns the scope of any such expansion. As already pointed out, the Supreme Court of the United States seemed to adopt a wider approach by referring to the need for 'rational as well as factual understanding'.[92] But this still seems vague. Indeed, the difficulty of fashioning satisfactory criteria has led Grubin, a psychiatrist, to suggest abandoning specific criteria altogether and instead leave it to 'the trial judge to decide, in the light of the facts of the case, whether a mentally disordered defendant is fit to be tried',[93] with a view to deciding whether the defendant can 'in spite of a disordered mental state, still have a fair trial'.[94] However, it is clear that Grubin would be content to permit a trial to proceed for 'a minor offence in which the evidence is clear',[95] even though the accused's psychotic condition might otherwise render him unfit according to the *Pritchard* criteria. Apart from the odd notion of permitting the trial judge to make such a ruling based on his own preliminary assessment of the defendant's guilt, this narrow reading of what constitutes a fair trial has been roundly criticised by Duff as neglecting the essential requirement of a criminal trial, namely that the accused 'should be a *participant* in his trial. He is not merely someone *about* whom the court must reach a determination, but someone *with* whom the court must try to engage in a communicative process of accusation, argument and judgment'.[96]

In this context Duff draws a clear distinction between the 'trial of the facts' under the 1991 Act and a full criminal trial. For while the former is primarily concerned with the disposal of an unfit defendant, the latter treats him as 'a rational and responsible agent' whose conviction may result in punishment.[97] This fundamental distinction seems impossible to ignore and leads one back to the question of how best to improve the current unfitness criteria. It may be that a way forward would be to place more reliance on the question of 'decisional competence'. As suggested above, it does seems odd that although this notion is beginning to achieve

---

[90] Butler Report, para 10.3.
[91] D. Grubin, 'What Constitutes Fitness to Plead?' [1993] Crim LR 748, 754.
[92] 362 US 402 (1960).   [93] Grubin, 'What Constitutes Fitness to Plead', 757.
[94] Ibid.   [95] Ibid. 758.
[96] R.A. Duff, 'Fitness to Plead and Fair Trials: (1) A Challenge' [1994] Crim LR 419, 421 (emphasis in original).   [97] Ibid. 420.

prominence in the civil law in relation to decision-making, it continues to be ignored in the context of unfitness to plead. In this respect it is interesting to note the definition of decisional incapacity proposed by the Law Commission in its Final Report on 'Mental Incapacity': 'a person is without capacity if at the material time he or she is: (1) unable by reason of mental disability to make a decision on the matter in question . . .'[98] While the text contains 'a diagnostic threshhold of "mental disability"',[99] the Commission had recognised that some people might be suffering from an inability to communicate rather than an incapacity to make any decision.[100] Accordingly the Commission proposes in its final report 'that a person should not be regarded as unable to communicate his or her decision unless all practicable steps to enable him or her to do so have been taken without success'.[101] As such inability can be caused by physical disabilities, the requirement to establish 'mental disability' is rightly considered inappropriate in such cases.

There are many decisions to be made by a defendant who is facing a criminal trial. However, the current test of unfitness to plead merely requires that he or she has a rudimentary understanding of the trial process. Thereafter the accused is free to make decisions even though they are not in his best interests.[102] It is at this stage that one must question why the criminal law refuses to protect those who cannot make 'true choices' in relation to decisions about the trial process. If, for example, a defendant insists on pleading guilty against his lawyer's advice, then surely that choice should be investigated in order to ascertain whether it is to be relied upon. It may be that including decisional incapacity within a reworked test of unfitness to plead would increase the number of such findings. However, this would be no bad thing. At present, with such a minimal number of unfitness cases each year, the law is markedly unsuccessful in fulfilling what should be a protective function for the mentally disordered. Indeed, it does seem remarkable that in a country the size of England and Wales there are currently less that twenty unfitness findings annually. Now that the Criminal Procedure (Insanity and Unfitness to Plead) Act 1991 has achieved a much more favourable approach towards the disposal of such cases,[103] one would have expected to see an increase in this number. However, as was noted above, this has not yet occurred and one suspects that without a change in the unfitness criteria, such as to encompass decisional

---

[98] Law Commission, Mental Incapacity, para 3.14.
[99] 'Mental disability' is widely defined to 'mean any disability or disorder of the mind or brain, whether permanent or temporary, which results in an impairment or disturbance of mental functioning': ibid. para 3.12.
[100] Law Commission, *Mentally Incapacitated Adults and Decision-Making*, para 3.39
[101] Law Commission, *Mental Incapacity*, para 3.21.
[102] *R. v. Robertson* [1968] 3 All ER 557.
[103] With the notable exception of findings of unfitness in respect of murder charges.

incompetence, no meaningful increase in numbers will take place. This in turn will result in the doctrine of unfitness to plead, much like the insanity defence, continuing to be honoured in name only, thereby ensuring that very little protection is given to vulnerable mentally and physically disordered offenders who deserve to be better safeguarded.

Index